Metaphorical

World Politics

Rhetoric and Public Affairs Series

Metaphorical

World Politics

Edited by
Francis A. Beer and
Christ'l De Landtsheer

Michigan State University Press
East Lansing

g green press INITIATIVE Michigan State University Press is a member of the Green Press Initiative and is committed to developing and encouraging ecologically responsible publishing practices. For more information about the Green Press Initiative and the use of recycled paper in book publishing, please visit www.greenpressinitiative.org.

∞ The paper used in this publication meets the minimum requirements of ANSI/NISO Z39.48–1992 (R 1997) (Permanence of Paper).

Michigan State University Press
East Lansing, Michigan 48823-5245

Printed and bound in the United States of America.

10 09 08 07 06 05 04   1 2 3 4 5 6 7 8 9 10

Library of Congress Cataloging-in-Publication Data

  Metaphorical world politics / edited by Francis A. Beer and
Christ'l de Landtsheer.
    p. cm. — (Rhetoric and public affairs series)
    Includes bibliographical references.
    ISBN 0-87013-726-3 (pbk. : alk. paper)
    1. Communication in politics. 2. Metaphor—Political aspects. 3. World
politics—1989–   I. Beer, Francis A. II. Landtsheer, Christ'l de. III. Series.
    JA85.M45 2004
    320'.01'4—dc22
                                                    2004012349

Cover and book design by Sans Serif, Inc.

Visit Michigan State University Press on the World Wide Web at:
www.msupress.msu.edu

To Diana and Hans

The State (I learn too late) does not exist;
Man lives by love, and not by metaphor.

Donald Hall, "The Body Politic,"
Exiles and Marriages (New York: Viking, 1955), 79.

Contents

Figures

Tables

Foreword

This book explores the connection between metaphor and world politics. There are ample literatures for each of these discrete topics but very little work that joins them. By bringing the two areas together, we hope to provide a space that will enrich both fields, stimulating new questions and research.

Metaphors stand at the strategic intersection of language, ideas, and politics. They are critical components of the way we speak and hear, write and read about politics. They reflect and shape the way we think and feel about politics. They are an important element of political action. They help determine, in subtle and complex ways, who we are and how we act as political beings, domestically and on the world stage.

The introduction provides an overview of the relationship between metaphors, politics in general, and world politics in particular. It defines metaphor very broadly in terms of the linguistic-psychological interaction that occurs when names or terms previously associated with different domains combine with each other. In this context, it outlines a theory of metaphorical reasoning that relies on cognitive blending of multiple schemata. Metaphors function rhetorically by stimulating such reasoning dynamics and combining them with deeper appeals to authority and emotion. The chapter describes several groups of common metaphors for politics—for example, bodies, sports, disasters—and the way that such metaphors are used in different cultures. Political leaders use these metaphors strategically to prime audiences, frame issues, mobilize coalitions of supporters, and neutralize opponents. Metaphors reflect and construct meaning, and they are part of the political struggle for collective meaning, a crucial resource in the competition for political power by political leaders, elites, and ordinary citizens.

The contributors and empirical subject matter are primarily American, but consideration of other societies—the Netherlands and Russia—gives the book a multinational dimension. The authors also bring a multidisciplinary diversity to the subject, specializing in communication, rhetoric, political science, and international relations. Most of the studies use qualitative methods, but some are quantitative. The book connects this multinational, multidisciplinary, multimethod view of metaphors with an equally textured view of politics. It shows how metaphors are connected with specific dimensions of politics—identities of political communities, particularly democratic regimes, and the international activities of foreign policy, war, peace, and globalization. It focuses on the metaphors used by political elites and their meaning for ordinary citizens. It details the metaphors used by public leaders and by political professionals, the metaphors of press reports, of electoral and war propaganda.

The book provides new insights and information about how metaphor works in world politics. At the same time, it suggests how much further work remains to be done. An empirically based understanding of political language could use descriptive lists of the most politically relevant metaphors, taxonomic orderings, and metaphorical frequencies in different political contexts. Regular relationships of metaphors to various objective dimensions of political systems and processes, structures, and functions could be further identified and specified. These should relate language and rhetoric to the web of interrelated causes and consequences of other forms of political behavior and should advance the agenda of political explanation, prediction, and policymaking.

From a more interpretive perspective metaphors are important, as they reflect and construct political meaning and orient political action: more work is necessary to advance our understanding of the subjective wellsprings of politics. The chapters in this book pose questions that we hope will stimulate further thought, discussion, and research in these directions. They are early steps toward what we hope is a better understanding of the many complex dimensions of politics and international relations and more sophisticated interpretation of the many worlds of meaning of global politics.

The central argument of the book is clear. Metaphors matter. World politics are metaphorically imagined and articulated in issues of democratic leadership, in the relations of democracies to non-democracies, in issues of war and peace, and in the largest issues concerning global identities and issues, conflict and cooperation, processes and policies. Metaphors are significant condensation symbols of similarity and difference, inside-outside, self-other. Metaphors prime audiences and frame issues; they organize communities and cooperation; they stimulate division and conflict; they mobilize support and opposition. Domestic and international leadership and power are the subjects and the stakes in the struggle for meaning embedded in metaphorical world politics.

Metaphorical

World Politics

◆ Introduction

Metaphors, Politics, and World Politics

Metaphors, Politics, and World Politics

Francis A. Beer and Christ'l De Landtsheer

Metaphor is the subject of a mounting body of work. Its rate of growth is so strong that, according to one estimate, "by the year 2039 there will be more students of metaphor than people."[1]

Most writing on metaphor focuses on communication, language, literature, and rhetoric.[2] A smaller but growing body of work has also applied metaphorical analysis to areas such as anthropology, architecture, economics, education, geography, philosophy, psychology, religion, and sociology.[3] Metaphors in a political context have, however, received relatively little focused academic attention.[4] In spite of the sophisticated appreciation of language and metaphor in other fields, some political analysts believe that actions speak louder than words, political talk is cheap, and political language is "mere" rhetoric.[5] Such a narrow view of metaphors assumes that they are essentially ornaments that may enliven oral discourse and decorate written text without affecting its meaning. Metaphors are irrelevant, since they merely speed the information on its way, or harmful, if they get in the way of clear ideas and the plain truth.[6] For this reason, it is an easy step for students of world politics to devalue metaphors as a superficial stylistic accessory.

According to this naive perspective, style is not substance; language is form, not function. Ideas and ideologies, arguments and facts are supposedly independent of the way they are expressed; they are not affected by language. Language is implicitly–and metaphorically–seen to be a "conduit" to convey ideas, which are typically seen as "objects."[7] Some observers of politics, however—such as George Orwell—believe that language has political weight, that speech acts and verbal behavior matter. The eminent political theorist John Nelson suggests that "most political scientists can benefit immensely from better attention to their rhetoric and its roles in their inquiry." William Riker, a leading political scientist, in his final book focused on the importance of rhetoric in structuring preferences during the Federalist campaign for the ratification of the American Constitution. He concluded that "rhetorical manipulation . . . contributed to the simplification that eliminated voting cycles and produced a definitive and stable decision."[8]

The conduit metaphor of language and the ornamental view of metaphor are both too complex and too simple. They are too complex because they inappropriately divide the message and its content. They are too simple because they assume that the ideas and facts speak for themselves. In reality, as we learned long ago from major communication and rhetorical theorists such as Marshall McLuhan, Kenneth Burke, and I. A. Richards, the medium and the message go together. Language is an independent form of political action (speech acts) and political behavior (verbal behavior). Language also mediates other forms of political action and political behavior. In so doing, it joins the objective world of political fact and action with the subjective world of political ideas, knowledge, and information.[9]

As forms of language, metaphors are significant rhetorical tools that affect political behavior and cognition. They are part of political speech in all its forms, for example, politicians' rhetoric; political information mediated by television, radio, and the press; political texts written by popular and academic authors. Metaphors provide sound bites and food for thought.[10] Metaphors are crucial devices in framing discourse, in maintaining and shifting political ideas. Metaphors instantly create new contexts and establish new relationships. If politics is metaphorical game X, chess, for example, then every political coordinate is linked with a host of chess variables in a specific matrix. If politics is game Y, football, for example, then every political coordinate is linked with a host of football attributes in a completely different space. If political community is a family, then every element of political life is interpreted in terms of the categories and roles that family life provides. If political life is war, warlike patterns of thought, talk, and behavior prevail.

This book, we hope, represents a step toward a more sophisticated understanding of the way that metaphor interacts with international relations. It draws upon a rich tradition of international and multidisciplinary discourse. It presents examples of some current theorizing and research on metaphors in world politics, though the vast expanse of possible metaphorical combinations limits the reasonable ambition to compile a comprehensive inventory of international metaphors.

The nature of metaphor does not lend itself easily to rigorous demonstrations of causality. Metaphorical power may exist, but it is hard to nail down. Metaphorical power implies effects.[11] How can metaphors have consequences, and how can we know that they did? Just because a politician uses metaphors to communicate does not mean that they have immediate, direct results. Any particular metaphor is consistent with a wide range of political outcomes. Yet this is far from meaning that metaphors have no causal influence. Other political variables also have subtle and complex effects. For example, it appears that democratic regimes tend to be peaceful, but only when interacting with other democratic regimes. Similarly, talk does not exist in a vacuum. It has a genealogy of antecedents and consequents in thought and behavior. Different metaphors have variable persuasive effects in different contexts, changing with a host of factors that include the speaker, the audience, the issue, and other aspects of the situation in which they are used. Further, metaphorical cumulation and interaction can lead to intricate, complex cascades of consequences. The details are not always easy to unravel, but an increased appreciation of metaphorical process seems desirable as we strive to attain a more sophisticated understanding of language and politics.

Metaphors are part of the political struggle for collective meaning, the interpretation of the forms or patterns of human political life. Metaphorical politics are about the meaning of power, how power is interpreted. They are also about the power of meaning, the persuasive consequences of such interpretation.

Metaphorical Meanings and Models

Metaphor has multiple dimensions and meanings, which are largely determined by the context in which they are situated.[12] We shall here identify three different metaphorical models consistent with the major linguistic areas of semantics, syntax, and pragmatics.

In a semantic context, the first, canonical definition of metaphor relies on differences in meaning between words that come from different domains. This "paradigmatic view of words (words substituting for each other)"[13] is embedded in the metaphorical *substitution model.* The model emerged from classical philosophy and derives from the Greek *metapherein,* to transfer or carry beyond.[14] According to traditional Aristotelian theory, metaphors included the substitution of one name for another. "Metaphor," Aristotle said, "is the application of an alien name."[15] The *Oxford English Dictionary* seems to follow this path when it defines metaphor as "the figure of speech in which a name or descriptive term is transferred to some object of different form, but analogous to, that to which it is properly applicable."[16] In this conception, specific names or words have proper, literal meanings; they denote specific objects or forms. Metaphor involves the rupture of this meaning dyad, the detachment of words from their standard referential partners and the reattachment of other, less obviously suitable ones to create figural meanings. A more flexible and generalizable statement of this view would seem to be Kenneth Burke's assertion that "metaphor is a device for seeing something *in terms of* something else." Going further, he suggests that "it is by the approach through a variety of perspectives that we establish . . . reality."[17]

For example, a proper literal phrase, a standard referential pair, might be "Marie is a woman" or "a rose is a flower." "Marie" is a name; "woman" is a form. Each of these phrases implies a positive analytic truth condition. "Marie is a flower" is a possible example of metaphorical substitution. In this case, the name remains the same and an objective referent of different form, "flower," is substituted as the referent. In this view, each word has a literal meaning through which the proper name is attached to the proper form.[18] The metaphorical substitution transforms that meaning from a literal to a figural one. On the other hand, it is not always clear where the literal boundaries of different names and forms lie. "Marie" might be the proper name for a variety of rose. "Rose" is syntactically positioned as a name but might also be defined as a form. Are "woman," "rose," and "flower" pure forms or another set of names referring to forms? Is "form" a name or a form? If it is a form, is it a metaphorical "object" or a "container"?

The substitution model developed in a context of rhetorical invention, where speakers were concerned with proper encoding for maximum effect. Rhetors saw metaphor as one arrow among many in the quiver of rhetorical action. Metaphor, together with other rhetorical forms—for example, metonymy and synecdoche—would fly to the target audience and hit the bull's-eye of persuasive cognitive and behavioral effects. This practical context, in the phrase of Kenneth Burke, nurtured a " 'dramatistic' approach to language." An alternative " 'scientistic' approach," he believed, focused on "questions of naming and definition." The dramatistic tradition is concerned with the speaker's proper encoding of speech acts; both traditions are interested in proper decoding by audiences and observers and are reflected in the concerns of contemporary stylistics with very fine-grained distinctions among different figures and tropes.[19]

Two additional metaphorical models move away from these concerns toward a larger granularity. One of these is the *syntactical model* of metaphor that relies on grammatical structures to serve as clear metaphorical identifiers. For example, "target-is-a-source" offers a simple syntactical template for the substitution "Marie-is-a-rose." A syntactical strategy for identifying metaphors might thus search for the textual string "is-a" to identify a metaphor in a particular text. Paul Ricoeur, for example, says that "the place of metaphor is neither the name, nor the sentence, nor even discourse, but the copula of the verb *to be*. The metaphorical 'is,'" he says, "at once signifies both 'is not' and 'like.'" This appears close to the principle that has guided George Lakoff in his attempt to compile a "master list" of metaphors.[20] The syntactical model thus implies that we have moved from one meaning of metaphor to another, from metaphor-as-substitution to metaphor-as-copula. At the same time, it also suggests a possible semantic error. The semantically proper phrase "Marie-is-a-woman" might now be syntactically classified improperly as a metaphor.

A final *combination model* of metaphor shifts away from the semantic, substitutive view of words, and away from syntactical identifiers, toward a more fluid appreciation of "syntagmatic relationship (the contiguity of words to each other)."[21] In so doing, metaphor-as-combination moves from classical speech and philosophy and from traditional semantics toward contemporary cognitive science and pragmatic linguistics. It thus follows the direction of the earlier prophecy of Viennese language critic Fritz Mauthner that "once the full impact of metaphor is acknowledged, philosophy will become psychology."[22]

 Emerging metaphorical theory has created terminology to denominate elements of the metaphorical expression. In this lexicon, (A) is the target or tenor, which is the actual subject of discussion; (B) is the source or vehicle, which is associated with a different sphere of life, and which is literally used to describe the subject (A). We shall here use "source" and "target" for the (A) and (B) terms, though many of the authors of subsequent chapters will use the more traditional "tenor" and "vehicle." Between (A) and (B) exists a blended space in dialectical tension (C). The interaction between these two words and their associated ideas (A) and (B) generates a fresh blended meaning (C) and a new view upon a new subject. Older theories of metaphorical comparison and substitution neglect (C), the value added by the fusion of (A) and (B), which is at the core of the combination model.[23] The source does not simply transfer its meaning to the target. The interaction between the source and the target generates a new meaning. The new meaning is in the new interaction or relationship.[24]

The combination model has semantic, syntactic, and pragmatic implications. Semantically, it ignores "the myth of semantic correspondence between the sign and the referent"[25] and the distinction between the literal and the figural. It suggests that we need to consider not just the (A) and (B) terms of the metaphor individually, but rather the full combined phrase (C) holistically. Syntactically, it suggests that grammatical construction may provide useful cues, but that these are only a part of the entire configuration of the phrase.

In some circumstances, (A) and (B) terms might simply be juxtaposed and appear contiguously without additional syntactical markers such as "is-a." In this process, juxtaposition becomes itself a metaphor for substitution. The sense of each word is at least partly applied or transferred to another, and a metamorphosis occurs. Both words are incorporated and fused into the identity of a new interactive trope, the blended identity and meaning of a new linguistic, psychological, behavioral space. From this perspective, "Marie is a rose," "Marie is a woman," "Marie rose," "Marie woman," "rose Marie," and "woman Marie" are functionally comparable phrases that create new blended spaces, though each phrase may have a different meaning. The phrases can be considered metaphorical in certain contexts. Their meaning spaces are not identical, but the similarities and differences of items of the juxtaposed combinations between each other and other metaphorical sets are subject to empirical investigation. In this formulation, the identity of metaphor becomes more diffuse, and metaphors appear in a wider range of situations.

More broadly yet, some of the source or target referents might never be specifically mentioned. All of the metaphorical models we have so far been considering rely on the presence of explicit words internally in the text. Nevertheless, some metaphors may be implicit, with sources or targets that are extrinsic rather than intrinsic. With weaker cues in the text, interpretation in such cases must rely on more holistic pattern recognition. Public speech or literature in repressive political regimes, for example, may studiously avoid the political targets at which it is directed. Such discourse must be interpreted indirectly, perhaps in terms of allegory or parable. In such contexts, it has important metaphorical dimensions.

Pragmatically, the combination model shifts focus from linguistic structure to psychological function, from signs and referents to audience, from the text or speech to the reader or hearer. Metaphors in this model are much more than trivial elements of literary style, involving simple replacement of verbal elements. Different metaphors index alternative psychological and behavioral registers. They bring with them networks of assumptions and entailments. They imply alternative interpretations; they convey alternative meanings.

Modern cognitive science suggests that both the source and the target exist as prior ideas, images, or schemata in the mind.[26] The mind generates schemata, conceived here as virtual simulations, similar to computer software programs, which interpret the physical world. Basic terms used to discuss metaphor are themselves embedded in schemata—form, frame, idea, name, object, pragmatics, referent, semantics, syntax, word, and schemata. And the schemata are activated in terms of metaphors.[27] The schemata are in memory as the learned product of past experience. They rely on neural networks involved in linguistic, affective, and motor processing. Appropriate external stimuli activate these internal schemata, which help us understand and react.[28] Metaphors reflect and constitute these schemata. Metaphor is thus both a facet of language and a dimension of cognition. Metaphorical interaction produces something new—the tension and surprise of hybrid, or blended schemata. In metaphorical terms, metaphor involves "rearranging the furniture of the mind."[29]

The idea of metaphorical interaction draws strength from the fact that many metaphors may initially appear absurd or meaningless. Metaphor introduces a surprise; one has to accept its invitation to active interpretation.[30] A novel metaphorical source may initially appear incompatible with the target. Resolution of this tension results in completion of the metaphor to create a new interactive space. This resolution implies "the hermeneutics of metaphor" that "develops the heuristic power wielded by fiction"[31] Multiple agents may compete in this fictional redescription. From the perspective of Marie's Prince Charming, it might appear that Marie and the rose are both objects of the same form, a beautiful form, objects of admiration.

Alternatively, Marie's jealous stepsister might respond that the rose is infected with aphids. With this change in the value of the rose, the stepsister simultaneously extends the metaphor and transforms its meaning. In return, the Prince might again recombine meanings by answering the stepsister, "and you are one of the aphids."

Proponents of each metaphoric model can argue about which is the "true" metaphor, but, it seems to us, such an argument misses the point. Each model emerges from a different context, is embedded in a different culture, and serves different purposes. Just as the semantic model comes from philosophy, rhetoric, and literary criticism; the syntactic model from linguistics; the combination model is now situated in the space of cognitive psychology.[32] The substitution and syntactic models focus on attempts to specify philosophical and linguistic structures. The combination model concentrates on cognitive dynamics and tries to show how the substitution and syntactic models achieve psychological effects.

The combination model has implications for politics. For example, political topoi such as the environment and terrorism can be juxtaposed with terms from other domains. These phrases are not metaphors in the classic sense of the substitution or syntactic models. However, the juxtapositions represent the same kind of interaction that classic metaphors imply. If one were to unpack some of them grammatically, provide them with the proper form of the verb "to be," and transform them into full sentences, they would become more recognizably metaphorical in the earlier sense. For example, we can imagine phrases formed when an anterior meaning shifter[33] serves as a source and combines with the target, terrorism, to produce a specific, individual rhetorical effect. Examples of such phrases might be "academic terrorists" or "aesthetic terrorists." In more properly syntactic form these would become "academics are terrorists," "aesthetes are terrorists," "terrorists are academics," or "terrorists are aesthetes." In these cases the metaphorical phrases would meet the criteria of the substitution and syntactic models. More important than their structural characteristics is the fact that the phrases illustrate the more general functional dynamics of the metaphorical interaction model. They create new metaphorical combinations that index different families of meaning. In this context, we can think of terrorism traveling along different axes of meaning, depending on its combination with other words.[34] Alternatively we may think of meanings as continuous rather than discrete. The meaning of a term such as terrorist would then vary directly with its context. Each terrorist phrase morphs smoothly between forms as it moves through linguistic, psychological, and referential space. As this happens, each metaphorical phrase becomes a metaphor for another reality. Each activates, stimulates, mobilizes, motivates another world of meaning.

This theoretical discussion still leaves us with the practical problem of how we know a metaphor when we see one. To answer this question, we return to the Aristotelian doctrine of "alien names" and our earlier syntagmatic criterion. "The difference between the literal and the figurative" in this context "amounts merely to a distinction between the customary and the novel vehicles of discourse, a distinction based on 'frequency and rarity' instead of reality and fiction." Metaphor is defined by novelty, by the a-normality of verbal collocation.[35]

Generally used metaphors are those where the associated terms appear together relatively frequently. They are commonly combined phrases of habit that generate weak references to independent meanings of separate embedded terms. Sometimes the metaphors are elided or implicit, so that one of the independent terms may have disappeared and the genealogical origins of the other are lost in the mists of ancient history. An example of such a ghost metaphor is our use of the word "form," which may have had earlier, more concrete incarnations in the shapes of dance, pottery, sculpture, architecture, or geometry.[36] More relevant to this volume's concern with world politics may be the implicit metaphors embedded in current phrases such as "balance of power" or "Cold War," which are easy to swallow without chewing. Such old metaphors are well-worn pathways in our neural networks; they may be so accepted that they are no longer considered to be metaphors. Older metaphors are so sedimented through time and use that we employ them unawares, draw on their accumulated cultural capital for persuasive power. They are like enthymemes, relying on the audience's knowledge of the missing term of the argument.[37] They blindly and effortlessly move on an ocean of convention, conformity, majority usage, habit, and opinion until they are called out.[38]

Clifford Geertz suggests that such sedimented metaphors are part of "ideology as a cultural system, built up through the uses of images and other symbols taken from the culture itself." He notes the power of metaphor as a culturally derived symbolic formula: "The power of a metaphor derives precisely from the interplay between the discordant meanings it symbolically coerces into a unitary conceptual framework and from the degree to which that coercion is successful in overcoming the psychic resistance this semantic tension inevitably generates in anyone in a position to perceive it."[39]

As Geertz suggests, metaphors constitute powerful ideological arguments that legitimate some institutions and policies rather than others. In so doing, metaphors help to generate political power. Metaphors identify and constitute not only the identity of power but also related structures of hierarchy and authority. Conversely, political power includes control over authoritative communication, the ability to impose some metaphors and constrain the use of others.[40]

Metaphors can also be instruments of political change. In this book, Richard D. Anderson, Jr. demonstrates the way that metaphors have been used to transform Russian politics. In so doing, he contrasts metaphors employed by authoritarian rulers of the Soviet Union and electoral politicians in post-Soviet Russia. Earlier rulers and later politicians made very different use of metaphorical families, homes, and other tropes. At the same time, metaphors often constitute and support the status quo—the existing political regime with its norms and institutions, rules and practices. Metaphors justify political repression. A good example is the way that Prime Minister De Klerk and his party managed to give an international impression of a "new" South Africa while preserving their privileges.[41]

Robert Ivie, in his chapter for this volume, goes further, arguing that this metaphorical consolidation can have tragic consequences. "Commonsense and factual styles of representations," he says, "transform tenuous similarities of diverse terms into culturally reified and nearly incontestable categories. . . . The more literally a key metaphor is taken, the less subject it is to constructive, comic critique." Such "comic correctives, aimed at broadening overly narrow and simplistic representations of reality," draw out inconsistencies, complexities, and alternatives. Without them, metaphor "functions heuristically to develop perspectives or general frames of acceptance out of which tragic orientations toward perfectly evil Others emerge. Tragic orientations lead readily to deadly victimage rituals such as war."[42]

Newer metaphors are more easily recognizable, though they may be more difficult to understand. They combine strange elements in unexpected ways, producing surprise, perhaps even shock.[43] They can dissolve the aura of the old, the ethos of historical habit; they cannot, however, rely on the same easy acceptance as older metaphors. New metaphors are phrases where the combination of terms or context of use has been relatively infrequent, in which case the metaphor is said to be alive. Living metaphors are original inventions that create new meanings. Like a new pair of unmatched shoes, they catch our attention but may take some getting used to. Dead metaphors are like an old pair of matched shoes; they are so comfortable that one is no longer aware of wearing them.

The juxtaposition of two previously separate domains of knowledge can be an energizing force for creative thought.[44] For example, according to one account, a core image of Einstein's theory of relativity came from a trolley ride around the Ring in Vienna.[45] More mundanely, a bicycle metaphor has been used in connection with the political unification of Europe: one has to ride a bicycle in order to keep it moving. The mixing of the issue in question, the European Union, with an issue completely strange to the context, bicycle, generates new meaning. European integration should progress in order not to abolish former results. Alternatively, to picture Europe as the Titanic generates a completely different image.[46]

In spite of the canonical authority of Aristotle, there is no essential, rigid meaning of metaphor, no firm Archimedean point on which to rest. Theory and research in this area must, therefore, accept the fact that metaphor is elastic. There are multiple metaphorical traditions, discourses, and contexts. Each metaphorical model above is partial, reflecting a different dimension that is a part, but only a part, of the rich inventory of metaphorical meaning. We, therefore, in this book take a very broad approach to metaphors, including under a large tent the crisp textual typologies and distinctions favored by philosophy, rhetoric, and literature; the criteria of syntactic linguistics; the mental structures and processes specified by cognitive scientists; and the broad connotations found in sociology and political science. Different authors work in different traditions, using different methods, and this book represents a space where they come together. We follow Ricoeur in endorsing "a plurality of modes of discourse" and "the methodologies proper to each point of view."[47] Our common concern is with the general relation of the *tropos* of metaphor applied to the *topos* of politics and their interaction in specific contexts.

Metaphorical Political Sources

Current theory and research suggest that different metaphorical sources for political targets vary in importance. Some basic metaphorical categories are universal. According to one school of thought, there exists a deep metaphorical structure, a generative metaphorical grammar, resting on the common human experience of embodiment. In other words, our bodies provide a global root metaphor, a fundamental, archetypal "source" schema for much of our relation to the world and an important basis for shared intersubjective meaning.[48]

It is obvious that the metaphor of the body underlies a good deal of contemporary political discourse.[49] Historical political theorists constructed their metaphors of politics using bodily metaphors. Traditional political philosophy relied heavily on the implied metaphor of the "body politic," giving a corporeal form to an abstract, intangible entity, the state. Plato's ideal state, the Republic, was modeled on the ideal citizen. The frontispiece of Hobbes's *Leviathan* was a picture of a giant man, within whom were multitudes of smaller men. *The Federalist Papers* moved in the direction of a more mechanical metaphor, but again the political machine was composed of human beings. Without such mechanical transformation, the people remained, as Tocqueville would have it, a great uncivilized beast. In another context, Hitler used the "worker body" as a powerful persuasive trope.[50]

An extensive language of the body is available to do heavy lifting in various areas of political life. Terms such as "birth," "youth," "vigor," "decadence," "blood," and "death," for example, commonly refer to the origin, rise, and fall of political nations and empires, cultures and civilizations. Male and female, masculine and feminine are obviously important metaphorical sources for politics.[51]

Some work has sought to translate the language of the body into a more general, deep metaphorical structure of international relations theory. Words derived from the body translate into words of world politics: attraction (alliance), balance (balance of power), blockage (blockade), center (center-periphery), collection (coalition), compulsion (compellence), container (containment), contact (contacts). Horizontal and vertical orientation and movement are fundamental categories that reflect the orientation of the body in physical space. An example is provided by the words of Chinese chairman Mao exhorting his followers to greater efforts in the "long march" and the "great leap forward." Another is the longer-term metaphor of historical progress or cycles. Richard Anderson's chapter below, with its focus on vertical and horizontal metaphors, follows the same coded logic of embodiment.[52]

Bodies interact directly in sports, and sports metaphors can be found liberally scattered through the speeches of Western political leaders. The populist discourse by the right-wing Italian politician Silvio Berlusconi, for example, shows a preference for metaphors from the domains of soccer, war, and the Bible. Sports metaphors were used in a distinct way by former U.S. presidents Lyndon Johnson and Ronald Reagan. Johnson's rhetoric used the "starting line" metaphor to describe the need to establish equal competitive conditions. Reagan emphasized the "runners" idea in stressing that competitors need to rely on athletic character. Further, news media often cast political election campaigns as horse races. Team sports and team play are also important.[53] The chapter by Dale Herbeck, "Sports Metaphors and Public Policy: The Football Theme in Desert Storm Discourse," carries this theme forward.

Another political metaphor with bodily associations is the family. Different family types seem to affect underlying conservative (paternal, hierarchical, or disciplining) and liberal (maternal or nurturing) metaphorical models. Terms such as "fatherland" and "motherland"; "wedding," "marriage," and "honeymoon"; "founding fathers," "founding brothers," and "genealogy" are also part of the set of explicit or implicit metaphors in this cluster. Other common metaphors include those from daily life, for example, "house," "home," or "homeland." Such metaphors can be used to foster a feeling of connection.[54]

Metaphorical sources with direct bodily referents focusing on disease and medicine (germs, viruses) and other living organisms (microbes, rats) have also been popular. These images tend to appear frequently in crisis situations and to be frequently used in extreme ideology, for example, authoritarian, racist discourse. Such metaphors were central tropes, for example, in the Third Reich, where enemies were cast as harmful animals and organisms, and Hitler was the competent medical doctor for German society.[55] Chapters in this book by Gregg, Ivie, De Landtsheer and De Vrij, and Shimko explore the importance of the disease metaphor for democracy, war, and globalization.

Metaphors taken from drama also offer a significant way of understanding politics. Kenneth Burke, for example, believed that such dramatistic metaphors offered a key to understanding "the basic forms of thought which, in accordance with the nature of the world as all men necessarily experience it, are exemplified in the attributing of motives. These forms of thought," he believed, "are equally present in systematically elaborated metaphysical structures, in legal judgments, in poetry and fiction, in political and scientific works, in news, and in bits of gossip offered at random." "The five key terms taken of dramatism" are "Act, Scene, Agent, Agency, Purpose." He continues:

> In a rounded statement about motives, you must have some word that names the *act* (names what took place, in thought or deed,) and another that names the *scene* (the background of the act, the situation in which it

occurred); also, you must indicate what person or kind of person (*agent*) performed the act, what means or instruments he used (*agency*), and the *purpose*. Men may violently disagree about the purposes behind a given act, or about the character of the person who did it, or how he did it, or in what kind of situation he acted; or they may even insist upon totally different words to name the act itself. But be that as it may, any complete statement about motives will offer some kind of answers to these five questions: what was done (act), when or where it was done (scene), who did it (agent), how he did it (agency), and why (purpose).[56]

Metaphors from the natural environment, for example, landscape, have offered a powerful way of interpreting political and personal life.[57] Technological metaphors for politics are also important. In a seminal work late in his career, the distinguished political scientist Karl Deutsch suggested that machines had provided a powerful modern template for political life. The Newtonian formulation of celestial mechanics thus found its political counterpart in the checks and balances of the American Constitution. The smelting furnaces of the Industrial Revolution had suggested the metaphor of the melting pot. Deutsch imagined a new, emerging model for politics: the network. Modeled on the protoscience of cybernetics in vogue during the middle of the twentieth century, the network concept has considerable resonance in the communications revolution at century's end. It has also been important in political discourse, for example, in debates about immigration.[58]

The everyday physicality of metaphors having to do with the body, its functions or activities (disease, sports, violence), makes them easy to spot. Other more abstract metaphors (drama, models, networks, systems) stand out less.[59] Though we have focused here on metaphorical sources for political targets, it is also important to note that political sources may also be used for political and other targets. Empire, nation, and revolution are some common metaphorical sources.[60]

An outline of some metaphorical sources for politics, arranged in one possible order, is presented in table 1. The categories in this table represent sets of metaphorical clusters, lattices of loosely associated source terms for political targets. An earlier version of this categorization was used to rank metaphorical power in the chapter by De Landtsheer and De Vrij, where it is discussed more fully.[61] Many of the metaphorical sources listed here appear throughout the rest of the book.

It seems reasonable to suggest different clusters of metaphors inhabit different cultures in different degrees. Political leaders and civic cultures

Table 1. Some Metaphorical Sources for Political Targets

6.1 POLITICS-AS-BODY	6.2 POLITICS-AS-DISEASE	6.3 POLITICS-AS-DEATH
Politics-as-Abortion	Politics-as-Addiction	Politics-as-Corpses
Politics-as-Blood	Politics-as-Cancer	Politics-as-Death
Politics-as-Body	Politics-as-Deafness	Politics-as-Euthanasia
Politics-as-Diet	Politics-as-Decline	Politics-as-Funeral
Politics-as-Force	Politics-as-Dentistry	Politics-as-Horror
Politics-as-Health	Politics-as-Disease	
Politics-as-Organism	Politics-as-Doctors	
Politics-as-Pregnancy	Politics-as-Health	
Politics-as-Race	Politics-as-Illness	
Politics-as-Sex	Politics-as-Indigestion	
Politics-as-Strength	Politics-as-Infection	
	Politics-as-Medicine	
	Politics-as-Psychiatry	
	Politics-as-Surgery	
	Politics-as-Therapy	

5.1 POLITICS-AS-GAME	5.2 POLITICS-AS-SPECTACLE	5.3 POLITICS-AS-CULTIVATION
Politics-as-Baseball	Politics-as-Carnival	Politics-as-Antiquity
Politics-as-Boxing	Politics-as-Circus	Politics-as-Art
Politics-as-Chess	Politics-as-Detective	Politics-as-Ballet
Politics-as-Competition	Politics-as-Drama	Politics-as-Culture
Politics-as-Contest	Politics-as-Fairy Tale	Politics-as-Dance
Politics-as-Fishing	Politics-as-Folklore	Politics-as-Education
Politics-as-Football	Politics-as-Joke	Politics-as-History
Politics-as-Hunting	Politics-as-Movie	Politics-as-Music
Politics-as-Race	Politics-as-Opera	Politics-as-Myth
Politics-as-Sailing	Politics-as-Science-Fiction	Politics-as-Nobility
Politics-as-Team	Politics-as-Soap Opera	Politics-as-Opera
	Politics-as-Story	Politics-as-Orchestra
	Politics-as-Television	Politics-as-Poem
	Politics-as-Theater	Politics-as-Painting
	Politics-as-Wild West	Politics-as-Religion

4.1 POLITICS-AS-DISASTER	4.2 POLITICS-AS-VIOLENCE
Politics-as-Accident	Politics-as-Army
Politics-as-Hell	Politics-as-Battle
Politics-as-Nightmare	Politics-as-Crime
	Politics-as-Dominance
	Politics-as-Force
	Politics-as-Incest
	Politics-as-Murder
	Politics-as-Noise
	Politics-as-Pollution
	Politics-as-Poison
	Politics-as-Prison

(Continued)

Table 1. Continued.

4.1 POLITICS-AS-DISASTER	4.2 POLITICS-AS-VIOLENCE
	Politics-as-Rape
	Politics-as-Repression
	Politics-as-Slavery
	Politics-as-Suffering
	Politics-as-Submission
	Politics-as-Torture
	Politics-as-War

3.1 POLITICS-AS-SOCIETY	3.2 POLITICS-AS-TECHNOLOGY
Politics-as-Activism	Politics-as-Airplane
Politics-as-Bureaucracy	Politics-as-Architecture
Politics-as-Business	Politics-as-Balance
Politics-as-Class	Politics-as-Building
Politics-as-Coalitions	Politics-as-Calculation
Politics-as-Coercion	Politics-as-Complexity
Politics-as-Communication	Politics-as-Computing
Politics-as-Community	Politics-as-Construction
Politics-as-Competition	Politics-as-Engine
Politics-as-Contract	Politics-as-Geography
Politics-as-Conversation	Politics-as-Geometry
Politics-as-Cooperation	Politics-as-Library
Politics-as-Corporation	Politics-as-Machine
Politics-as-Discourse	Politics-as-Mechanics
Politics-as-Elections	Politics-as-Modernization
Politics-as-Market	Politics-as-Navigation
Politics-as-Neighborhood	Politics-as-Network
Politics-as-Party	Politics-as-Order
Politics-as-Peace	Politics-as-Pattern
Politics-as-Police	Politics-as-Process
Politics-as-Power	Politics-as-Progress
Politics-as-Village	Politics-as-Reason
	Politics-as-Resources
	Politics-as-Science
	Politics-as-Statistics
	Politics-as-Structure
	Politics-as-System
	Politics-as-Technique
	Politics-as-Traffic
	Politics-as-Train
	Politics-as-Transportation
	Politics-as-Tunnel
	Politics-as-Vehicle

Table 1. Continued.

2.1 POLITICS-AS-NATURE	1.1 POLITICS-AS-EVERYDAY LIFE	1.2 POLITICS-AS-FAMILY
Politics-as-Agriculture	Politics-as-Bakery	Politics-as-Child
Politics-as-Beast	Politics-as-Cleaning	Politics-as-Family
Politics-as-Commons	Politics-as-Colors	Politics-as-Father
Politics-as-Farming	Politics-as-Container	Politics-as-Mother
Politics-as-Fire	Politics-as-Cooking	Politics-as-Mistress
Politics-as-Jungle	Politics-as-Dinner	Politics-as-Partner
Politics-as-Land	Politics-as-Dream	Politics-as-Promiscuity
Politics-as-Landscape	Politics-as-Furniture	Politics-as-Prostitution
Politics-as-Gardening	Politics-as-Garbage	Politics-as-Wedding
Politics-as-Grapes	Politics-as-Fantasy	
Politics-as-Rainbow	Politics-as-Food	
Politics-as-Rose	Politics-as-Grocery	
Politics-as-Season	Politics-as-Home	
Politics-as-Water	Politics-as-House	
Politics-as-Weather	Politics-as-Housekeeping	
	Politics-as-Meal	
	Politics-as-Path	
	Politics-as-Proverb	
	Politics-as-Romance	
	Politics-as-School	
	Politics-as-Seduction	
	Politics-as-Singing	
	Politics-as-Smell	
	Politics-as-Song	
	Politics-as-Taste	
	Politics-as-Time	
	Politics-as-Travel	

determine which metaphors are acceptable or taboo, strong or weak. Those metaphors, in turn, help mold other aspects of the culture. Physical body orientation is obviously a prime metaphorical source. There are, however, plenty of other categories. Different cultures tend to use different metaphors, and these metaphors help configure their collective identities.

The metaphorical variation of political cultures has been partly explored. Gannon, for example, suggests that there are different types of cultures, characterized by master metaphors that include vertical, horizontal, and circular orientations. He suggests several types of political cultures that include distinct metaphorical sources: authority ranking cultures (the Thai kingdom, the Japanese garden, the Indian dance of Shiva, Bedouin jewelry and Saudi Arabia, the Turkish coffeehouse, the Brazilian samba, the Polish village church, kimchi and Korea); equality matching cultures (the German symphony; the Swedish *stuga;* Irish conversations); market pricing cultures (American football, the traditional British house); cleft national cultures (the Malaysian *balik kampung,* the Nigerian marketplace, the Israeli *kibbutzim* and *moshavim,* the Italian opera, Belgian lace); torn national cultures (the Mexican fiesta, the Russian ballet); same metaphor, different meanings (the Spanish bullfight, the Portuguese bullfight); beyond national borders (the Chinese family altar).[62] Cultural novices, first-time business visitors, and vacation travelers have found these metaphors useful as they enter strange cultures and start to learn about them. At the same time, one wonders if they are as amusing to the inhabitants as they are to the tourists: for experts, there are always more metaphors.

A complete cultural catalog of metaphors is not possible.[63] There is enormous variety in metaphors relating to politics. Metaphors suggest multiple shadings of meaning for politics, a blended, hybrid space where the metaphorical sources and political targets coexist in a dynamic relationship. The use of political metaphors depends not only on relatively stable cultural patterns, but also on shifting contextual factors such as the economy and political events. The analysis of metaphors therefore provides us with relevant information about both the characteristics of particular cultures and about the nature of political events and economic conditions of particular societies.[64] In their broadest reach, metaphors include multiple forms of figurative speech joined in "metaphor's linguistic web."[65] The variety of choice, the richness of the metaphorical menu provides political actors and observers with an infinite inventory of rhetorical combinations to apply in specific situations to particular targets.

Metaphorical Political Agents

Political leaders and followers are metaphorical agents. Within the exigency of political situations, political leaders rhetorically mobilize groups that support them and oppose their adversaries.[66] Figure 1 provides a visual image of the process.

The power to name is the power to identify and differentiate—to say what is the same and what is different—to define where boundaries begin and end, what is the form and texture. Metaphor plays an important role in delineating such political identities.[67] Metaphors characterize political actors. These metaphorical profiles are part of a larger political strategy. As

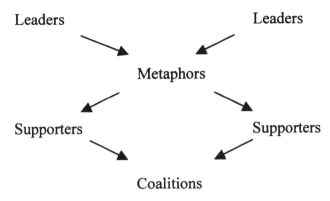

FIGURE 1. Metaphorical Mobilization

Herbert Barry says, a "metaphoric characterization evokes a vivid image that can have a powerful effect on the public attitude toward the national leader." He notes that "The metaphorical 'father' was applied to the first four presidents and to the Civil War president. Washington was 'the father of his country.' John Adams was 'the father of American independence.' Jefferson was 'the father of the Declaration of Independence.' Madison was 'the father of the Constitution.' Lincoln was 'Father Abraham.'" He goes on to observe that "nineteenth century presidents were frequently characterized by a metaphor for another person or status. . . . An object, animal, or place was a frequent metaphor for five nineteenth century presidents. . . . The twentieth century presidents instead have generally been characterized by slogans that describe purposes of their administrations. Examples are the New Deal of Franklin D. Roosevelt and the New World Order of the first President Bush."[68]

Such identifying metaphors can appear in public speeches and texts; they can also be in the form of photos, videos, or music. Good examples of the metaphorical use of visual images come from campaign advertising, for example, the photo of Massachusetts governor and presidential candidate Michael Dukakis wearing a helmet while riding in a tank. This photo, combined with another of pollution in Boston harbor, metaphorically depicted the candidate's ineptitude and impotence. On the other hand, President George W. Bush's cowboy costume, ranch, baseball cap, and flight jacket helped him create a metaphorical political character with which much of America could identify.[69]

Metaphorical naming is an example of the way that metaphors activate alternative schemata to persuade audiences. Political leaders use
these and other metaphors as tools of persuasive communication, to
bridge gaps and build identification between strangers; to frame issues; to
create, maintain, or dissolve political coalitions; to generate votes and
win elections.[70] To be effective, the metaphors must reflect and engage
the audiences to which they are directed. Audiences are not simply inert
receptacles waiting for metaphorical deposits. Rather, they actively participate in constructing political discourse. Metaphors draw on memories
of experiences shared by leaders and followers. They help to establish
and cement the connection of speaker and audience and to trigger desired audience responses. Political leaders search for the most appropriate
metaphors to support a position. A final selection is made on the basis of
estimated audience appeal. The same holds for the metaphorical style
that politicians choose (more or less formal, dialect or not, what kinds of
metaphors, etc.).[71] Political metaphors function within the context of the
needs and interests of the audience involved: the audience is incorporated into the chosen metaphors.

When we consider persuasive political appeals to audiences, we are
squarely in the land of rhetoric. The traditional dimensions of rhetoric, beginning again from Aristotle, are *logos*, or reason, *ethos*, or authority, and
pathos, or emotion. These are major ways in which rhetoricians characterize persuasive appeals to popular audiences. An effective speech should
have a reasonable argument. It should carry weight, coming from an authoritative, trustworthy source, and it should arouse sufficient emotion to
motivate the audience in the direction that the speech intends. Metaphors
are important in all three rhetorical phases.

Metaphorical Political Reason

Modern philosophy has rested on a belief in the perfectibility of human
reason, including reasoning and reasonable decision makers and citizens.
Logos in a rhetorical context refers to the appeal to reason. Logos should
not be confused with formal logic. Logos means simply that the speaker
should give a more or less coherent argument. Arguments can be of various origins: personal, historical, religious, cultural. These should, however,
meet the criterion that they are plausible, or seem to have a reasonable
correspondence with reality based on the audience's experience.[72]
Metaphor has often been separated from and opposed to reason. Yet, as we
have already suggested, metaphorical processes are unavoidably connected

with human reason, not only reasoning about the world but also reasoning about the way that we reason.[73] Post-classical philosophers as early as Vico viewed metaphor as a way of experiencing facts.[74] Metaphor, in this view, precedes, historically or logically, the concretized meanings of scientific discourse.[75]

Metaphors reflect, frame, and activate rational, scientific, logical schemata. One classical syllogism begins: "All men are mortal. Socrates is a man. Socrates is mortal." This syllogism aims to be literal, not figural or metaphorical. In it, Socrates is not a metaphorical man; he is a "real" man. Nevertheless, the phrase recalls the models of metaphor, particularly the syntactical one, as it uses the phrase "is a" to connect the target, Socrates (A), with the source, man (B), and creates the new blended space (C) of the syllogism. Other forms of reasoning follow similar dynamics.[76]

Indeed, as Kennedy says, "metaphor itself is a metaphor and literally means 'carrying something from one place to another, transference,'"[77] As we have already noted, there is no *degré zéro*, no metaphor-free zone. It is hard to avoid Derrida's conclusion that "the general taxonomy of metaphors . . . would presuppose the solution of important problems . . . which constitute the entirety of philosophy in its history." Further, "the constitution of the fundamental oppositions of metaphorology . . . has occurred by means of the history of a metaphorical language." There are no "properly philosophical" categories, no pure forms that are uncontaminated by metaphor. Such categories "are so many metaphors," whose origins are largely forgotten and form a "blind spot or central deafness." It is simply not possible to return to a nonmetaphorical "proper origin" that has "archaeological simplicity, the virginity of a history of beginnings." There is no such pure point of origin, no external point that could represent a firm foundation for "metaphilosophy," "meta-poetics," or "metametaphorics."[78] From this perspective, metaphors eventually merge with the infinite web of dynamic symbolic interaction.

The reflexive problem of infinite metaphorical regress is stubborn and irreducible. Contemporary research programs on reasoning have thus reasonably relied on inherited metaphorical formulations as they have tried to build their own computational models of decision making. Three of these models center on models, rules, and cases as metaphors in reasoning. Model-based reasoning uses mathematical models as core metaphors for interpreting social behavior. Rational choice models are one example of the application of such templates to various social phenomena. Such models have cognitive appeal because they make use of multiple metaphorical schemata. Their analysis includes the theoretical metaphors of formal methods and mathematical formulas. At the same time, they employ popular metaphors with memorable names—the game of chicken, prisoners' dilemma, the tragedy of the commons.[79]

Rule-based reasoning, as the name suggests, begins with rules and principles. In rule-based reasoning, bodies of rules or laws compose metaphors applied to current cases. Continental European jurisprudence, for example, tends to rely heavily on principles derived from central legal codes. Other examples of the metaphorical application of rule to political situations come from the customary distinction between the rulers and the ruled as well as the model of the separation of powers as rule making, rule application, and rule adjudication.[80]

Case-based reasoning, finally, is at the heart of the Anglo-American legal tradition. In case-based reasoning, a prior case is a metaphor for a current situation. An abortion case comes before the United States Supreme Court; it is understood, at least partly, in terms of the Court's earlier decision in *Roe* v. *Wade*.

There are many other variants of reason. A partial list of examples shows how anterior meaning shifters can become quasi-metaphorical sources for targets of reason. These include bureaucratic reason, celestial reason, commonsense reason, computational reason, constructive reason, contractual reason, critical reason, deconstructive reason, deductive reason, democratic reason, dialectical reason, diplomatic reason, discursive reason, divine reason, executive reason, formal reason, geometrical reason, hermeneutic reason, hierarchical reason, higher reason, inductive reason, instrumental reason, intrinsic reason, judicial reason, legal reason, legislative reason, logical reason, mathematical reason, military reason, moral reason, natural reason, nonmonotonic reason, pluralistic reason, political reason, practical reason, procedural reason, pure reason, ritual reason, scientific reason, structural reason, and sufficient reason.[81]

These variants of reasoning illuminate possible ways that leaders and followers in domestic and international politics may think about decision making in international relations. They also suggest ways that we may think metaphorically about political agents thinking about politics.[82] In this volume, Beer and Boynton's chapter develops a path metaphor as a model of the practical reasoning process of political actors deliberating about world politics.

Metaphorical Political Authority and Emotion

Beyond *logos* comes *ethos,* the appeal to authority. Ethos depends upon the status of the speaker; the higher the position, the better his or her reputation, the more authoritative the rhetoric is perceived to be. In political debate, leaders use the authority of high government positions to advance their agendas. President George W. Bush, for example, led the United States into the war on terrorism in a way that Texas governor or private citizen George W. Bush could never have done. In scholarly or scientific work, a good example is the use of references to appeal to the authority of well-respected individuals or groups. In these cases, the status of the speaker transfers metaphorically to the status of the argument, giving it a weight that it might not carry on its own.[83]

The third element of the Aristotelian rhetorical triad is *pathos,* commonly translated as emotion. Pathos is rhetorically effective precisely because of its explicitly metaphorical invocation of prior experiences from a wide spectrum of collective life. The speaker tunes his or her words to evoke high doses of emotion in order to persuade the audiences of his or her point of view. We may think of such audience receptivity in terms of "affective schemata."[84] Pathos suggests a dimension of politics that some analytic and scientific observers find disturbing. On many occasions, emotion dominates reason. The speaker's main objective is audience support, not logical consistency.

In spite of their common human foundations, reason and emotion have traditionally been viewed dualistically, as opposing forces. Because of rhetoric's emotional content, classical philosophy opposed it. Rhetoric became philosophy's evil twin, "the worst fear of idealized reason," in exile from the "cognitive kingdom."[85] Reason and emotion are, nevertheless, very compatible and have a delicate relationship with each other. We have already suggested the metaphorical dimension of reason itself, as abstract models of reason are applied in the world. It is also worth noting that reason itself involves emotion: the passion for reason can be as powerful and productive, misleading and counterproductive, as other emotions. As we have noted, metaphors activate conscious and subconscious, rational and emotional responses. These different kinds of appeals coexist in an uneasy relationship.

Metaphors have important rhetorical uses in communication with large audiences, particularly for issues in which the audience is emotionally invested. Political leaders use metaphors as keys to citizens' sentiments: the powerful suggestion mechanism activated by metaphors triggers underlying emotions and connects them with political individuals and policies. Most election campaigns are full of emotion-activating rhetoric, and metaphor plays an important role. Political leaders intentionally produce metaphors, because they feel that arousing emotions in the audience is a good way to persuade the audience. After the elections, the corpses fall out of the closet, Karel van Miert, the former European commissioner, used to say while he was an opposition party leader of the Belgian Social Democrats.[86] His metaphor argued that the governing parties did not keep the promises made during the election campaign. This refined metaphor was a powerful mixture of reason and emotion.

One example of a metaphor with strong emotional overtones is the combination of "mother" with "war"—as in Saddam Hussein's assertion that the Gulf War was the mother of all wars. This combination, in terms of a distinction that we introduced earlier, is a very "live" metaphor. Much of its impact comes from the normal separation of the two key words. "Mother" and "war" belong in different, conflicting spheres of life. "Mother" offers an embrace of love, comfort, protection, and warmth. "War" is death and killing. Another powerful emotional trigger is the "disease" and "prophylaxis" combination, to which several of the chapters in this book refer, which lays the emotional groundwork for violent domestic purges, ethnic cleansings, and demands for unconditional surrender. Alternatively, the metaphorical source and target may be reversed, as in the "war on drugs" metaphor used by the U.S. government, which directs emotional attention to punitive, restrictive measures and away from sympathetic treatment, prevention, and curing. There are also "wars of information," "wars of words," and "wars of metaphors."[87]

Metaphors may reflect and affect anxiety levels among leaders and followers. Political psychology suggests that the strong drive felt by politicians to establish a firm sense of self may positively affect their symbolic capacities. The compensation hypothesis suggests that some politicians may have poor self-integration. Poorly integrated individuals seem to lack adequate boundaries between self and other, between feeling and thought, and between fantasy and reality. Both the creative activity of producing metaphors and the interpretation of metaphors may reduce anxiety.[88]

The interpretation of metaphors may also make anxiety more painful. Psychiatry considers the handling of metaphor as one of the most striking aspects of schizophrenic language. Metaphors have tremendous effects upon subjects with nonintegrated personalities. The seriously disturbed seem to get emotionally upset by metaphors. Novel metaphorical utterances of others are responded to as if they are literal communications. In less-disturbed subjects, moderate anxiety levels may also heighten creativity, which is necessary for the production of metaphors.[89]

One of the major emotive functions of metaphors can be to reassure the audience.[90] Metaphors may suggest that political issues are simple: they simplify complex situations and thereby give the audience a sense of confidence. Everyday life and nature metaphors are particularly fitted for democracy, prosperity, and democratic politicians. Metaphors can change the subject. Thus, Italian politicians have used horticultural metaphors in order to forget about past scandals and to give a rosy description of current affairs.[91] Metaphors also allow people to escape from reality, sometimes referring to drama, music, film, games, and other forms of entertainment. Metaphors relax the audience, sometimes by reflecting repressed aggressive feelings. For example, the Belgian Christian-Democratic opposition used a "bikini-policy" metaphor to complain about the social economic policy of the purple-green government (with the Liberal Party, the Socialist Party, and the Green Party). The bathing suit would suggest a lot but at the same time it would hide the essential contents of policy measures.[92]

Metaphors can introduce ambiguity that reduces stress. De Landtsheer and De Vrij's chapter in this book discusses the way that political leaders use metaphors and low complexity in crisis situations. At the same time, they argue that higher complexity tends to moderate international violence. Irony and humor can also be elements of this dynamic.[93]

Metaphors are a form of indirect communication that has many advantages for politicians who know where, when, why, and how to use them. Sometimes they do so because they live in a totalitarian society, in which free expression is prohibited. Political and economic crises also affect the directness and explicitness of political rhetoric. Politicians in prosperous democratic society, however, may also see advantages in oblique linguistic strategies.[94] Commercialization of society, media, and politics reinforces this trend. Floating voters form an increasing segment of the electorate, and politicians want to attract these voters by means of indirect statements with limited political content.

Metaphors tell us not only about the political world as it is, but also as we should like it to be, the spaces between fear and desire. Timothy W. Luke explores this terrain with his chapter on "megametaphorics," discussing metaphors of globalization and virtualization in global political discourse.

Metaphorical Politics and World Politics

We have considered the importance of metaphors in thinking and acting in a variety of different political contexts. Metaphors, as we have seen, are deeply and inevitably embedded in our political reasoning processes. Metaphors reflect and construct political ideas and political cultures. Some of these metaphors are widely used; others have a more limited scope. Metaphors are intertwined with political identities and political cultures. Metaphors help constitute, maintain, and transform political power, decision, and discourse. Political leaders use metaphors self-consciously to create, maintain, and dissolve political coalitions. In so doing, they combine appeals to reason with others to authority and emotion.

The power of metaphor is the power to understand and impose forms of political order. Metaphors reflect, interpret, and construct politics. Metaphors lie at the heart of political analysis, communication, and decision. Understanding the metaphorical construction of politics reveals previously hidden dimensions of political communities and previously hidden meanings of political discourse. It suggests new solutions to long-standing political conflicts and new areas for political cooperation. In our globalized, multicultural society, metaphors tap primary human experiences and cross boundaries. They can encourage greater mutual understanding and advance the search for peace. Metaphorical rhetoric is often successfully used by national political elites during severe political, military, and economic crises. Metaphors, as these elites know, can reassure and comfort their citizen audiences. Metaphors may help people to face periods of misery. During more prosperous times, political elites are aware that metaphors widen their voter audiences. Metaphorical sound bites have considerable persuasive and mnemonic effects. Bright metaphors bring politics closer to the citizen. Metaphors increase political participation and further democracy. New elites may use new metaphors to define new situations and to stimulate political change. Metaphors, however, may also carry stereotypes, deceit, and manipulation, in the various forms in which they are distributed, from traditional storytelling to Web pages. They may tranquilize people, and they may promote war, crime, and civil disturbance; they may euphemize torture and state terrorism.[95] Metaphors can be instruments of propaganda. The master of metaphor dominates his or her environment, regardless of its scale. And he or she always can deny what metaphors imply.

The main focus of the book is the way in which metaphor interacts with world politics. The rhetorical turn in international relations has involved a new focus on the language through which world politics is reflected and constructed.[96] International rhetoric persuades in multiple ways. Metaphor is an important dimension of that rhetoric, though certainly not the only one. Argument, image, style, symbolic interaction, discourse formations, and many other topics at the intersection of language and politics are also significant. At the same time, a concern with metaphor allows us to focus on the interaction of previously separate worlds. This seems particularly relevant to the interactions of world politics, a field that has been characterized as "the clash of civilizations."[97]

The metaphors of world political leaders modulate multiple meanings of world politics, and these different meanings of world politics, in turn, flow metaphorically into different foreign policies and international coalitions. In the chapters that follow, different authors discuss the way that metaphors interact with world politics in three major sections on democracy, war and peace, and globalization. All three are major concerns of the politics and foreign policy of major contemporary nation-states. Democracy focuses on the internal structures and processes of national regimes. War and peace includes conflictual and cooperative interactions between them. Globalization begins with the territorially fragmented past of states and empires and looks toward a more aggregative postnational political future.[98]

Notes

We should like to express our thanks to colleagues for their contributions to this project. These include G. Robert Boynton, Joan Cleveland, Ofer Feldman, Amy Grim, Robert Hariman, Gerard Hauser, Robert Ivie, Robert L. King, James McDaniel, John Nelson, Rolf Norgaard, Laszlo Pook, Eric White, David Winter, and the late Scott Zakon. We are particularly grateful to Britt Cartrite for his extensive work on the references.

1. Peter Stockwell, review of *Researching and Applying Metaphor,* ed. Lynne Cameron and Graham Low, *Metaphor and Symbol* 15, no. 4: (2000) 275–77. The quip is attributed to Wayne Booth.
2. A comprehensive review of work in the field of communication is provided by David Douglass, "Research and Metaphor in Communication Studies" (paper presented at the annual meeting of the Western States Communication Association, Sacramento, Calif., February

2000). See also Richard Nate, "Metaphor," in *Encyclopedia of Rhetoric*, ed. Thomas O. Sloane (Oxford: Oxford University Press, 2001), 493–96; Lynne Cameron and Graham Low, eds., *Researching and Applying Metaphor* (Cambridge: Cambridge University Press, 1999); Patti Nogales, *Metaphorically Speaking* (Stanford, Calif.: Center for the Study of Language and Information, 1999); Andrew Goatly, *The Language of Metaphors* (London: Routledge, 1997); Jeffrey S. Mio and Albert N. Katz, eds., *Metaphor: Implications and Applications* (Mahwah, N.J.: Lawrence Erlbaum Associates, 1996); Betty Rogers Youngkin, *The Contributions of Walter J. Ong to the Study of Rhetoric: History and Metaphor* (Lewiston, N.Y.: Mellen University Press, 1995); Gerard Steen, *Understanding Metaphor in Literature* (Harlow, U.K.: Longman, 1994); Andrew Ortony, ed., *Metaphor and Thought* (Cambridge: Cambridge University Press, 1993); Lawrence Marks, Robin J. Hammeal, Marc H. Bornstein, and Linda B. Smith, eds., *Perceiving Similarity and Comprehending Metaphor* (Chicago: University of Chicago, 1987); Wolf Paprotté and René Dirven, eds., *The Ubiquity of Metaphor: Metaphor in Language and Thought*, History of Linguistic Science, series 4, vol. 29 (Amsterdam: J. Benjamins, 1985).

3. Lynne Cameron, *Metaphor in Educational Discourse (Advances in Applied Linguistics)* (New York: Continuum, 2002); Juan Antonio Ramírez, *The Beehive Metaphor: From Gaudi to Le Corbusier*, trans. Alexander R. Tulloch (London: Reaktion, 2001); Michael P. Brown, *Closet Space: Geographies of Metaphor from the Body to the Globe* (New York: Routledge, 2000); Sabine Maasen and Peter Weingart, *Metaphors and the Dynamics of Knowledge* (London: Routledge, 2000); Raymond Gozzi, Jr., *The Power of Metaphor in the Age of Electronic Media*, Hampton Press Communication Series (Cresskill, N.J.: Hampton Press, 1999); Gwyneth Jones, "The Neuroscience of Cyberspace: New Metaphors for the Self and Its Boundaries," in *The Governance of Cyberspace: Politics, Technology and Global Restructuring*, ed. Brian D. Loader (London: Routledge, 1997), 46–63; Trevor J. Barnes, *Logics of Dislocation: Models, Metaphors, and Meanings of Economic Space* (London: Taylor and Francis, 1996); Dennis Bartels, "Metaphor, Morality, and Marxism," *Journal of Communication Inquiry* 2 (1995): 118–31; David E. Leary, ed., *Metaphors in the History of Psychology*, Cambridge Studies in the History of Psychology (Cambridge: Cambridge University Press, 1990); Sharon L. Pugh, ed., *Bridging: A Teacher's Guide to Metaphorical Thinking* (Urbana, Ill.: National Council of Teachers of English; Bloomington, Ind.: ERIC Clearinghouse on Reading and Communication Skills, 1992); James

W. Fernandez, ed., *Beyond Metaphor: The Theory of Tropes in Anthropology* (Stanford Calif.: Stanford University Press, 1991); Robert J. Sternberg, *Metaphors of Mind: Conceptions of the Nature of Intelligence* (New York: Cambridge University Press, 1990); Jean-Pierre Van Noppen and Edith Hols, *Metaphor II: A Classified Bibliography of Publications 1985 to 1990* (Amsterdam: J. Benjamins, 1990); Trevor Whittock, *Metaphor and Film* (Cambridge Studies in Film) (New York: Cambridge University Press, 1990); Janet Soskice, *Metaphor and Religious Language* (Oxford: Clarendon, 1985); Jean-Pierre Van Noppen, Sabine de Knop, and René Jongen, *Metaphor: A Bibliography of Post-1970 Publications* (Amsterdam: J. Benjamins, 1985); Mary Gerhart and Allan Russell, *Metaphoric Process: The Creation of Scientific and Religious Understanding* (Fort Worth: Texas Christian University Press, 1984); J. David Sapir and J. Christopher Crocker, *The Social Use of Metaphor: Essays on the Anthropology of Rhetoric* (Philadelphia: University of Pennsylvania Press, 1977); Warren Shibles, *Metaphor: An Annotated History and Bibliography* (Whitewater, Wis.: Language Press, 1971).

4. Work cited in this book is an exception. See inter alia Mark Schlesinger and Richard Lau, "The Meaning and Measure of Policy Metaphors," *American Political Science Review* 94, no. 3 (September 2000): 611–26; Francis A. Beer and Christ'l De Landtsheer, "Metaphorical Politics: Mobilization or Tranquilization," in *Proceedings of the Fourth International Conference of the International Society for the Study of Argumentation,* ed. Frans H. van Eemeren, Rob Grootendorst, J. Anthony Blair, and Charles A. Willard (Amsterdam: SIC STAT, 1999), 42–48; Martin J. Medhurst, Robert L. Ivie, Philip Wander, and Robert L. Scott, *Cold War Rhetoric: Strategy, Metaphor, and Ideology* (East Lansing: Michigan State University Press, 1997); George Lakoff, *Moral Politics: What Conservatives Know That Liberals Don't* (Chicago: University of Chicago Press, 1995); Francesca Rogotti, *Metafore della Politica* (Bologna: Il Mulino, 1989); Elliot Zashin and Phillip C. Chapman, "The Uses of Metaphor and Analogy: Towards a Renewal of Political Language," *Journal of Politics* 36 (1974): 290–326. Examples of studies of specific metaphors in particular contexts include Emma Coleman Jordan, *Lynching: The Dark Metaphor* (New York: Basic Books, 1999); Peter T. Markman and Roberta H. Markman, *Masks of the Spirit: Image and Metaphor in Mesoamerica* (Berkeley and Los Angeles: University of California Press, 1994); William B. Stanford, *Greek Metaphor: Studies in Theory and Practice* (New York: Johnson Reprint Corp., 1972).

5. Cf. Thomas B. Farrell, *Norms of Rhetorical Culture* (New Haven and London: Yale University Press, 1993), 9.
6. For a broader view, set in the appropriate historical context, see George A. Kennedy, "Classical Rhetoric," in *Encyclopedia of Rhetoric*, ed. Thomas O. Sloane (Oxford: Oxford University Press, 2001), 112. Kennedy says:

> Ornamentation of style, a priority in declamation and important in literary prose as well, involved the use of tropes, figures, rhythms, and periods. Quintilian defines a *tropus* in 8.6.1 as the change of a word or phrase from its proper meaning to another. Metaphor, Latin *translatio*, is the most important trope, but Quintilian identifies six others that affect the meaning of a passage: synecdoche, metonymy, *autonomasia*, poeia, *catachrēsis*, and metalēpsis; in addition, there are tropes that he regards as useful only as ornaments: epithet, allegory, *periphrasis*, *hyperbaton* and hyperbolē. A trope was usually thought of as substitution of one word or phrase for another or a change in the placement of a word or phrase. A figure (Gk. *schēma*, Lat. *figura*), in contrast, was a change in the configuration of a passage involving several words, and was divided into figures of word (*figurae verborum*), later often referred to as 'grammatical figures,' and figures of thought (*figurae sententiarum*). The earliest account is found in *Rhetoric to Herennius* (4.19–69), giving Latin names and defining forty verbal figures and nineteen figures of thought. In the more detailed account by Quintilian (Book 9, chapters 1–3), both Greek and Latin names are used, though the Greek terminology seems to have become standard in the schools. The classification of an artistic usage as a trope, a verbal figure, or a figure of thought was often arbitrary and differs in different handbooks.

7. George Lakoff, *Women, Fire and Dangerous Things* (Chicago: Chicago University Press, 1987), 114; Michael Reddy, "The Conduit Metaphor: A Case of Frame Conflict in Our Language about Language," in *Metaphor and Thought*, 2d ed., ed. Andrew Ortony (Cambridge: Cambridge University Press, 1993), 164–201.
8. John S. Nelson, *Tropes of Politics: Science, Theory, Rhetoric Action* (Madison: University of Wisconsin Press, 1998), 3; William H. Riker, *The Strategy of Rhetoric: Campaigning for the American Constitution* (New Haven: Yale University Press, 1996), 263. See also John S. Nelson and G. R. Boynton, *Video Rhetorics* (Urbana: University of Illinois Press,

1997); Frank Fischer and John Forester, eds., *The Argumentative Turn in Policy Analysis and Planning* (Durham, N.C.: Duke University Press, 1993); Donald N. McCloskey, *The Rhetoric of Economics* (Wisconsin: University of Wisconsin Press, 1985); Murray Edelman, *Constructing the Political Spectacle* (Chicago: University of Chicago Press, 1988); Murray Edelman, *The Symbolic Uses of Politics* (Urbana: University of Illinois Press, 1974); Fred R. Dallmayr, *Language and Politics: Why Does Language Matter to Political Philosophy?* (Notre Dame, Ind.: University of Notre Dame Press, 1984); Michael Shapiro, ed., *Language and Politics* (New York: New York University Press, 1984); Doris Graber, *Verbal Behavior and Politics* (Chicago: University of Illinois Press, 1976); Harold D. Lasswell, Daniel Lerner, and Ithiel De Sola Pool, *The Comparative Study of Symbols: An Introduction* (Stanford, Calif.: Stanford University Press, 1952); Harold D. Lasswell, Nathan Leites and associates, *The Language of Politics: Studies of Quantitative Semantics* (Cambridge Mass.: MIT Press, 1949).

9. Marshall McLuhan, *Understanding Media* (London: Routledge and Kegan Paul, 1964); Kenneth Burke, *Language as Symbolic Action* (Berkeley and Los Angeles: University of California Press, 1966); I. A. Richards, *A Philosophy of Rhetoric* (Oxford: Oxford University Press, 1936). For recent approaches from communications and rhetoric that represent this idea, see Christ'l De Landtsheer, "Introduction to the Study of Political Discourse," in *Politically Speaking: A Worldwide Examination of Language Used in the Public Sphere,* ed. Ofer Feldman and Christ'l De Landtsheer (Westport, Conn.: Praeger, 1998), 1–16; Christ'l De Landtsheer and Lise van Oortmerssen, "A Psycholinguistic Analysis of the European Union's Political Discourse regarding the Israeli-Palestinian Conflict," in *Beyond Public Speech and Symbols: Explorations in the Rhetoric of Politicians and the Media,* ed. Christ'l De Landtsheer and Ofer Feldman (Westport, Conn.: Praeger, 2000), 158–82.

10. Jeffrey Scheuer, *The Sound Bite Society: Television and the American Mind* (London: Routledge, 2001); Victor Kennedy, "Metaphors in the News—Introduction," *Metaphor and Symbol* 15, no. 4 (2000): 209–11; Pierre Bourdieu, *On Television,* trans. Priscilla Parkhurst (New York: New Press, 1996); Joseph Opfer and Peter Anderson, "Explaining the Sound Bite: A Test of a Theory of Metaphor and Assonance" (paper presented at the Western Speech Communication Association Convention, Boise, Idaho, 1992).

11. For discussions of metaphorical power in other contexts, see Michael Berman and David Brown, *The Power of Metaphor* (Carmarthen, U.K.: Crown House Publishing, 2000). See also Kenneth L Hacker, "Political Linguistic Discourse Analysis: Analyzing the Relationships of Power and Language," in *The Theory and Practice of Political Communication Research*, ed. Mary E. Stuckey (Albany: SUNY Press, 1996), 28–55; Robin Tolmach Lakoff, *Talking Power: The Politics of Language* (New York: Basic Books, 1989); Steven Mailloux, *Rhetorical Power* (Ithaca, N.Y.: Cornell University Press, 1989).

12. For a fuller discussion of contextual influences on meaning, see Francis A. Beer, *Meanings of War and Peace* (College Station: Texas A&M University Press, 2001). See also Josef Stern, *Metaphor in Context* (Cambridge, Mass.: MIT Press, 2000); Celeste M. Condit et al., "Recipes of Blueprints for Our Genes? How Contexts Selectively Activate the Multiple Meaning of Metaphors," *Quarterly Journal of Speech* 88, no. 3 (August 2002): 303–25.

13. Paul De Man, *Allegories of Reading: Figural Language in Rousseau, Nietzsche, Rilke, and Proust* (New Haven: Yale University Press, 1979), 6.

14. See Eric Partridge, *Origins: A Short Etymological Dictionary of Modern English* (London: Routledge and Kegan Paul, 1982), 399–400. The characteristics and functions attributed here to metaphors are not exclusive. They overlap significantly with those of other figures and tropes. Metaphor is certainly not the only figure of speech to include various modalities of transformation. This principle is obvious in the many words with common "meta" roots and lexemes, for example, "metonymy." It is also an important aspect of allegory, analogy, parable simile, and synecdoche. A proper discussion of similarities and differences would require a separate book comparing metaphor with each separate figure or trope. See, for example, René Dirven, *Metaphor and Metonymy in Comparison and Contrast* (New York: Mouton de Gruyter, 2002); Antonio Barcelona, *Metaphor and Metonymy at the Crossroads: A Cognitive Perspective* (New York: Mouton de Gruyter, 2000); n. 6, above.

15. See Samuel H. Butcher, *Aristotle's Theory of Poetry and Fine Art*, 4th ed. (New York: Dover Publications, 1951), 77; George A. Kennedy, *Aristotle on Rhetoric: A Theory of Civic Discourse* (Oxford: Oxford University Press, 1991), 295. See also Max Black, "More about Metaphor," in *Metaphor and Thought*, 2d ed., ed. Andrew Ortony (Cambridge: Cambridge University Press, 1993), 19–41.

16. *Oxford English Dictionary II,* 2d ed., CD-ROM, version 3.0 (Oxford: Oxford University Press).

17. Kenneth Burke, *A Grammar of Motives,* (Berkeley and Los Angeles: University of California Press, 1969), 503–4.

18. Discussion of "Kripke's doctrine that theoretical identity sentences involving rigid natural kind terms are necessary if true can be salvaged" is found in Scott Soames, *Beyond Rigidity: The Unfinished Semantic Agenda of Naming and Necessity* (Oxford: Oxford University Press, 2002), 307. For a skeptical perspective on rigidity, see Elizabeth Bredeck, *Metaphors of Knowledge: Language and Thought in Mauthner's Critique* (Detroit: Wayne State University Press, 1992).

19. Burke, *Language as Symbolic Action,* 44. See n. 14, above.

20. Paul Ricoeur, *The Rule of Metaphor: Multidisciplinary Studies of the Creation of Meaning in Language,* trans. Robert Czerny, Kathleen McLaughlin, and John Costello (Toronto: University of Toronto Press, 1975), 7; George Lakoff, "Master Metaphor List" (http://cogsci.berkeley.edu/) (accessed February 21, 2004). For further discussion of the associational implications of the noun-is-a-noun model of metaphor, see Walter Kintsch and Anita R. Bowles, "Metaphor Comprehension: What Makes a Metaphor Difficult to Understand?" *Metaphor and Symbol* 17, no. 4 (2002): 249–63.

21. De Man, *Allegories of Reading,* 6.

22. Bredeck, *Metaphors of Knowledge,* 97.

23. See Vimala Herman, ed. *Cognitive Linguistics and the Verbal Arts: From Metaphor to Blending* (Cambridge: Cambridge University Press, 2004); Gilles Fauconnier and Mark Turner, *The Way We Think: Conceptual Blending and the Mind's Hidden Complexities* (New York: Basic Books, 2003); Mark Turner and Gilles Fauconnier, "Conceptual Integration and Formal Expression," *Metaphor and Symbolic Activity* 10, no. 3 (1995): 183–205; Black, "More about Metaphor"; I. A. Richards, *Richards on Rhetoric: I. A. Richards, Selected Essays (1929–1974),* ed. Ann E. Berthoff (New York: Oxford University Press, 1991), 282–83; C. K. Ogden and I. A. Richards, *The Meaning of Meaning* (New York: Harcourt, Brace, Jovanovich, 1989); Burke, *A Grammar of Motives,* 503–5; See also Christ'l De Landtsheer and Ilse De Vrij's chapter in this book for a fuller discussion of these and related terms.

24. See inter alia Marie-Dominique Gineste, Bipin Indurkhya, and Veronique Scart, "Emergence of Features in Metaphor Comprehension," *Metaphor and Symbol* 15 (2000): 117–36; Raymond, W. Gibbs and Gerard J. Steen, eds., *Metaphor in Cognitive Linguistics* (Amsterdam:

J. Benjamins, 1999); Zdravko Radman, *Metaphors: Figures of the Mind* (Boston: Kluwer Academic, 1997); Zdravko Radman, *From a Metaphorical Point of View: A Multidisciplinary Approach to the Cognitive Content of Metaphor* (New York: W. de Gruyter, 1995); Marie-Laure Ryan, *Possible Worlds, Artificial Intelligence, and Narrative Theory* (Bloomington: Indiana University Press, 1991), 82–83; Eva F. Kittay, *Metaphor: Its Cognitive Force and Linguistic Structure* (Oxford: Clarendon Press, 1987), chap. 3; Robert E. Haskell, ed., *Cognition and Symbolic Structures: The Psychology of Metaphoric Transformation* (Norwood, N.J.: Ablex Publishing Corporation, 1987).

25. De Man, *Allegories of Reading* 6.
26. We may also think of schemata in terms of spreading activation and reinforcement across habituated pathways in the neural network. See John R. Anderson, *Learning and Memory: An Integrated Approach* (New York: Wiley, 2000). Cf. Walter Kintsch, *Comprehension: A Paradigm for Cognition* (Cambridge: Cambridge University Press, 1998); Earl R. MacCormac, *A Cognitive Theory of Metaphor* (Cambridge, Mass.: MIT/Bradford, 1985). Image is a concept related to both metaphor and schema, which has been used extensively in discussion of domestic and world politics. Discussions of images relevant to sections 2 and 3 below include Katherine Kinney, *Friendly Fire: American Images of the Vietnam War* (Oxford: Oxford University Press, 2000); David T. Lindgren, *Trust but Verify: Imagery Analysis in the Cold War* (Annapolis, Md.: U.S. Naval Institute Press, 2000); Catherine A. Luthur, *Press Images, National Identity and Foreign Policy* (New York: Routledge, 2002); Jianwei Wang, *Limited Adversaries: Post–Cold War Sino-American Mutual Images* (Oxford: Oxford University Press, 2000); Yahya Kamalipour, *Images of the U.S. around the World: A Multicultural Perspective* (Albany: SUNY Press, 1999); Steven F. Lobell, "Second Image Reversed Politics: Britain's Choice of Freer Trade or Imperial Preferences, 1903–1906, 1917–1923, 1930–1932," *International Studies Quarterly* 43, no. 4 (1999): 671–93; Shoon K. Murray and Jonathan A. Cowden, "The Role of 'Enemy Images' and Ideology in Elite Belief Systems," *International Studies Quarterly* 43, no. 3 (1999): 455–81; Cor van der Weele, *Images of Development: Environmental Causes in Ontogeny* (Albany: SUNY Press, 1999); Richard K. Herrmann et al., "Images in International Relations: An Experimental Test of Cognitive Schemata," *International Studies Quarterly* 41, no. 3 (1997): 403–35; Mark Schafer, "Images and Policy Preferences," *Political Psychology* 18, no. 4 (1997): 813–29; Shannon L. Blanton, "Images in Conflict: The Case of Ronald Reagan

and El Salvador," *International Studies Quarterly* 40, no. 1 (1996): 23–44; Daniel Heradstveit and G. Matt Bonham, "Attribution Theory and Arab Images of the Gulf War," *Political Psychology* 17, no. 2 (1996): 271–92; Renny Christopher, *The Vietnam War/the American War: Images and Representations in Euro-American and Vietnamese Exile Narratives* (Amherst: University of Massachusetts Press, 1995); Wade L. Huntley, "Kant's Third Image: Systemic Sources of the Liberal Peace," *International Studies Quarterly* 40, no. 1 (1996): 45–76; Robert Jervis, *The Logic of Images in International Relations* (New York: Columbia University Press, 1989).

27. See George Lakoff and Mark Johnson, *Philosophy in the Flesh: The Embodied Mind and Its Challenge to Western Thought* (New York: Basic Books, 1998).

28. Experimental psychological research supports this interpretation. See, for example, Francis A. Beer, Alice F. Healy, and Lyle E. Bourne, Jr., "Dynamic Decisions: Experimental Reactions to War, Peace, and Terrorism," in *Political Psychology as a Perspective on Politics: Advances in Political Psychology*, vol. 1, ed. Margaret G. Hermann (London: Elsevier, 2004).

29. David W. Allbritton, "When Metaphors Function as Schemas: Some Cognitive Effects of Conceptual Metaphors," *Metaphor and Symbolic Activity* 10 (1995): 33–46; Eva F. Kittay, "Metaphor as Rearranging the Furniture of the Mind: A Reply to Donald Davidson's 'What Metaphors Mean,'" in *From a Metaphorical Point of View: A Multidisciplinary Approach to the Cognitive Content of Metaphor*, ed. Zdravko Radman (New York: W. de Gruyter, 1995), 73–116; Stephen R. Chandler, "Metaphor Comprehension: A Connectionist Approach to Implications for the Mental Lexicon," *Metaphor and Symbolic Activity* 6 (1991): 227–58.

30. See, for example, Stern, *Metaphor in Context.*

31. Ricoeur, *The Rule of Metaphor*, 6.

32. There is, however, a strong interactionist tradition in philosophy and rhetoric. This includes not only figures such as Richards, Burke, and Black, to whom we have already referred, but also many others as well. See, for example, Kirsten Malmkjaer, ed., *The Linguistics Encyclopedia* (London: Routledge, 1991), 310–12; Chaim Perelman, *The Realm of Rhetoric*, trans. William Kluback (Notre Dame: University of Notre Dame Press, 1982), chap. 10; De Man, *Allegories of Reading*, 6; Jacques Derrida, *Margins of Philosophy*, trans. Alan Bass (Chicago: University of Chicago Press, 1982), 219–29; Michael Leff, "Topical Invention and

Metaphoric Interaction," *Southern States Communication Journal* 48 (1983): 214–29.

33. See Francis A. Beer, *Meanings of War and Peace,* (College Station TX: Texas A & M University Press, 2001) 33.

34. Lakoff, *Women, Fire, and Dangerous Things.*

35. Ivie, "Cold War Motives and the Rhetorical Metaphor: A Framework for Criticism," in *Cold War Rhetoric,* Medhurst et al., 72–73. See also Sam Glucksberg (with a contribution by Matthew S. McGlone), *Understanding Figurative Language: From Metaphors to Idioms* (New York: Oxford University Press, 2001); Kuang-ming Wu, "Novelty, the Emerging Norm in Metaphor," in *On Metaphoring: A Cultural Hermeneutic* (Leiden: Brill, 2001), 167–73; Malmkjaer, ed., *The Linguistics Encyclopedia,* 301–3; Paul Cantor, "Friedrich Nietzsche: The Use and Abuse of Metaphor," in *Metaphor: Problems and Perspectives,* ed. David S. Miall (Atlantic Highlands, N.J.: Humanities Press, 1982), 71.

36. An early associated Greek root of "form" may have been *morphē,* though the Latin one is *forma* (Partridge, *Origins,* 228–29). See also Margaret Alexiou, *After Antiquity: Greek Language, Myth, and Metaphor* (Ithaca, N.Y.: Cornell University Press, 2002); David Metzger, *The Lost Cause of Rhetoric: The Relation of Rhetoric and Geometry in Aristotle and Lacan* (Carbondale: Southern Illinois University Press, 1995); William L. Nothstine, " 'Topics' as Ontological Metaphor in Contemporary Rhetorical Theory and Criticism," *Quarterly Journal of Speech* 74 (1988): 151–63.

37. See John T. Gage, "The Reasoned Thesis: The E-word and Argumentative Writing as a Process of Inquiry," in *Argument Revisited; Argument Redefined: Negotiating Meaning in the Composition Classroom,* ed. Barbara Emmel, Paula Resch, and Deborah Tenney (Thousand Oaks, Calif.: Sage, 1996), 3–18.

38. Older, more commonly used metaphors may be more frequently used in times of prosperity, less in times of crisis and in discourse by extremist political groups. See Christ'l De Landtsheer, "The Language of Prosperity and Crisis: A Case Study in Political Semantics," *Politics and the Individual* 4, no. 2 (1994): 63–85; Sergiy Taran, "Mythical Thinking, Aristotelian Logic, and Metaphors in the Parliament of Ukraine," in *Beyond Public Speech and Symbols: Explorations in the Rhetoric of Politicians and the Media,* ed. Christ'l De Landtsheer and Ofer Feldman (Westport, Conn.: Praeger, 2000), 120–43; Christ'l De Landtsheer, "The Language of Unification: Specification of a Coding Process as a Basis for Observation," in *Sprache im Umbruch. Politischer Sprachwandel*

im zeichen von "Wende" und "Vereinigung" [Language in transition in the German unification process], ed. Armin Burkhardt and K. Peter Fritzsche (Berlin and New York: W. de Gruyter, 1992), 287–314; Christ'l De Landtsheer, "The Political Rhetoric of a Unified Europe," in *Politically Speaking: A Worldwide Examination of Language Use in the Public Sphere*, ed. Ofer Feldman and Christ'l De Landtsheer (Westport Conn.: Praeger, 1998), 129–46.

39. Clifford Geertz, *The Interpretation of Cultures*, quoted in David Green, *Language and Politics in America: Shaping Political Consciousness from McKinley to Reagan* (Ithaca, N.Y.: Cornell University, 1987), 9–10.

40. See Phillip Wander, "Critical and Classical Theory: An Introduction to Ideology Criticism" in *Cold War Rhetoric*, Medhurst et al., 131–52; Christopher Collins, *Authority Figures: Metaphors of Mastery from the Iliad to the Apocalypse* (Lanham, Md.: Rowman and Littlefield; University Press of America, 1996); Christ'l De Landtsheer, "Language and Ideology: A Representation of the Function of Ideology in the Political Use of Language," in *Political Psychology in the Netherlands: Proceedings of the First Conference on Political Psychology in the Netherlands* (Amsterdam: Mola Russa, 1986), 91–97.

41. Ngure wa Mwachofi, "Apprehending the Power and Ideological Import of Metaphor in President De Klerk's Rhetoric," *Howard Journal of Communications* 5, no. 4 (summer 1995): 331–52.

42. Ivie, pp. 76 below.

43. Walter Benjamin suggests that the "shock experience" may be a strong component of artistic creativity. See "On Some Motifs in Baudelaire," in *Illuminations: Essays and Reflections*, ed. Hannah Arendt, trans. Harry Zohn (New York: Schocken, 1969), 163. See also Elizabeth Closs Traugott, " 'Conventional' and 'Dead' Metaphors Revisited," in *The Ubiquity of Metaphor*, 17–56.

44. Keith J. Holyoak and Paul Thagard, *Mental Leaps: Analogy in Creative Thought* (Cambridge Mass.: MIT Press, 1995).

45. Lewis S. Feuer, *Einstein and the Generations of Science* (New York: Basic Books, 1974).

46. Michael Emerson, "1992 and after: The Bicycle Theory Rides Again," *Political Quarterly* 59, no. 3 (July–September 1988): 289–99. See also De Landtsheer, "The Political Rhetoric of a Unified Europe," 129–45; Jan J. Mooij, *A Study of Metaphor: On the Nature of Metaphorical Expressions, with Special Reference to Their Reference* (Amsterdam: North Holland, 1976).

47. Ricoeur, *The Rule of Metaphor*, 7.

48. Some common metaphors reflect philosophical or religious interpretations of the body's relation with the physical environment. Among these are the optical (light and dark) and the elemental (earth, air, fire, and water). For further discussion of these and other archetypal and root metaphors in specific contexts, see Dan F. Hahn, *Political Communication: Rhetoric, Government, and Citizens,* 2d ed. (State College, Penn.: Strata, 2003), 117–120; Lynn M. Stearney, "Feminism, Ecofeminism, and the Maternal Archetype: Motherhood as a Feminine Universal," *Communication Quarterly* 42 (1994): 145–59; Ruth C. Smith and Eric M. Eisenberg, "Conflict at Disneyland: A Root-Metaphor Analysis," *Communication Monographs* 54 (1987): 367–80; Sarah Russell Hankins, "Archetypal Alloy: Reagan's Rhetorical Image," *Central States Speech Journal* 34 (1983): 33–43; Thomas B. Farrell and G. Thomas Goodnight, "Accidental Rhetoric: The Root Metaphors of Three Mile Island," *Communication Monographs* 48 (1981): 271–300; Michael Osborn, "The Evolution of the Archetypal Sea in Rhetoric and Poetic," *Quarterly Journal of Speech* 63 (1977): 347–63; Michael Osborn, "Archetypal Metaphor in Rhetoric: The Light-Dark Family," *Quarterly Journal of Speech* 53 (April 1967): 115–26.

49. See Sarah F. Taub, *Language from the Body: Iconicity and Metaphor in American Sign Language* (New York: Cambridge University Press, 2001); Mary M. Lay, Laura J. Gurak, Clare Gravon, and Cynthia Myntti, eds., *Body Talk: Rhetoric, Technology, Reproduction* (Madison: University of Wisconsin Press, 2000); John Durham Peters, "Bowels of Mercy," *BYU Studies* 38 (1999): 27–41; Jack Selzer and Sharon Crowley, eds., *Rhetorical Bodies* (Madison: University of Wisconsin Press, 1999); José Gil, *Metamorphoses of the Body* (Minneapolis: University of Minnesota Press, 1998); Lakoff and Johnson, *Philosophy in the Flesh;* Carl A. Raschke, *Fire and Roses: Postmodernity and the Thought of the Body* (Albany: SUNY Press, 1996); Theodore Schatzki and Wolfgang Natter, eds., *The Social and Political Body* (New York: Guilford, 1996); George Lakoff, "Metaphors of War," *Propaganda Review* 8 (fall 1991): 18–21, 54–59; George Lakoff, "Metaphor and War: The Metaphor System Used to Justify War in the Gulf," *Peace Research* 23 (1991): 25–32 (http://lists.village.virginia.edu/sixties/HTML_docs /Texts/Scholarly/Lakoff_Gulf_Metaphor_1.html); (accessed February 21, 2004); Mark Johnson, *The Body in the Mind: The Bodily Basis of Meaning, Imagination and Reason* (Chicago: University of Chicago Press, 1990); Jonathan G. Harris, *Foreign Bodies and the Body Politic: Discourses*

of Social Pathology in Early Modern England (Cambridge: Cambridge University Press, 1988); Bryan S. Turner, *The Body and Society: Explorations in Social Theory* (Oxford: Basil Blackwell, 1984); George Lakoff and Mark Johnson, *Metaphors We Live By* (Chicago: University of Chicago Press, 1980). Tim Rohrer, "Understanding through the Body? Increased fMRI and ERP Activity in the Motor and Perceptual Cortices in Response to Relevant Semantic Stimuli" (Boulder: Institute of Cognitive Science, public speech), suggests that "at the neurophysiological level of analysis, the embodiment hypothesis implies that dynamic patters of activation in somatopic perceptual-motor neural maps are crucial to semantic comprehension."

50. Antoine De Baecque, *The Body Politic: Corporeal Metaphor in Revolutionary France, 1770–1800* (Stanford, Calif.: Stanford University Press, 1993); Zoltán Kövecses, "Tocqueville's Passionate 'Beast': A Linguistic Analysis of the Concept of American Democracy," *Metaphor and Symbolic Activity* 9 (1994): 133–33; Daisuke Tano, "The Birth of the *Arbeiter* Body and Politics in the Third Reich," *Soshioroji* 40, no. 2 (October 1995): 59–78.

51. Cf. Carolyn Marvin and David W. Ingle, *Blood Sacrifice and the Nation: Totem Rituals and the American Flag* (Cambridge: Cambridge University Press, 1999); Barbara Spackman, *Fascist Virilities: Rhetoric, Ideology, and Social Fantasy in Italy* (Minneapolis: University of Minnesota Press, 1996).

52. Francis A. Beer and Barry J. Balleck, "Body, Mind, and Soul in the Gulf War Debate," in *The Theory and Practice of Political Communication Research,* ed. Mary E. Stuckey (Albany: SUNY Press, 1996), 159–76; Jon Tolaas, "Notes on the Origin of Some Spatialization Metaphors," See also B. Dancygier, "How Polish Structures Space: Prepositions, Direction Nouns, Case, and Metaphor," *Amsterdam Studies in the Theory and History of Linguistic Science, Series IV, Current Issues in Linguistic Theory,* no. 178 (2000): 27–46. *Metaphor and Symbolic Activity* 6 (1991): 203–18. (Amsterdam: J. Benjamins, 1997).

53. Kathleen Hall Jamieson and Paul Waldman, *The Press Effect: Politicians, Journalists, and the Stories That Shape the Political World* (Oxford: Oxford University Press, 2003), 84; Elena Semino and Michela Masci, "Politics Is Football: Metaphor in the Discourse of Silvio Berlusconi in Italy," *Discourse and Society* 7, no. 2 (April 1996): 243–69; Stephan R. Walk, "The Footrace Metaphor in American Presidential Rhetoric," *Sociology of Sport Journal* 12, no. 1 (March 1995): 36–55; Paul E. Corcoran, "Presidential Concession Speeches: The Rhetoric of Defeat,"

Political Communication 11, no. 2 (April–June 1994): 107–64; Marvin K. Ching, "Games and Play: Pervasive Metaphors in American Life," *Metaphor and Symbolic Activity* 8 (1993): 43–65; Robert A. Palmatier, *Sports Talk: a Dictionary of Sports Metaphors*, (New York: Greenwood Press, 1989); Isaac Balbus, "Politics as Sports: The Political Ascendancy of the Sports Metaphor in America," *Monthly Review* 26, no. 10 (1975): 26–39.

54. See, for example, Dan F. Hahn, "The Marriage Metaphor in Politics," in *Political Communication: Rhetoric, Government, and Citizens,* 163–88; Francis A. Beer and Laura Brunell, "Women's Words: Gender and Rhetoric in the Gulf War Debate," in *Meanings of War and Peace,* Francis A. Beer (College Station: Texas A&M University Press, 2001), 106–14; Kenneth S. Zagacki, "Pope John Paul II and the Crusade against Communism," *Rhetoric and Public Affairs* 4 (2001): 698–700; Joseph J. Ellis, *Founding Brothers: The Revolutionary Generation* (New York: Alfred A. Knopf, 2000); Carl L. Kell and L. Raymond Camp, *In the Name of the Father: The Rhetoric of the New Southern Baptist Convention* (Carbondale: Southern Illinois University Press, 1999); Michael Osborn, "Patterns of Metaphor among Early Feminist Orators," in *Rhetoric and Community: Case Studies in Unity and Fragmentation,* ed. J. Michael Hogan (Columbia: University of South Carolina Press, 1998), 3–26; Paul A. Chilton, *Security Metaphors: Cold War Discourse from Containment to Common House* (New York: Peter Lang, 1996); George Lakoff, "Metaphor, Morality, and Politics, or Why Conservatives Have Left Liberals in the Dust," *Social Research* 62, no. 2 (summer 1995): 177–213; Stearney, "Feminism, Ecofeminism, and the Maternal Archetype"; Paul Chilton and Mikhail Ilyin, "Metaphor in Political Discourse: The Case of the 'Common European House,'" *Discourse and Society* 4, no. 1 (January 1993): 7–31; Kathleen Hall Jamieson, "The Metaphoric Cluster in the Rhetoric of Pope Paul VI and Edmund G. Brown, Jr.," *Quarterly Journal of Speech* 66 (1980): 51–72.

55. See, for example, Christine L. Harold, "The Green Virus: Purity and Contamination in Ralph Nader's 2000 Presidential Campaign," *Rhetoric & Public Affairs* 4, no. 4 (winter 2001): 581–603; De Landtsheer, "The Language of Prosperity and Crisis." See also Daniel Goldhagen, *Hitler's Willing Executioners: Ordinary Germans and the Holocaust* (New York: Knopf, 1996); Robert A. Palmatier, *Speaking of Animals : A Dictionary of Animal Metaphors,* (Westport, Conn: Greenwood Press, 1995); Stephen Perry, "Rhetorical Functions of the Infestation

Metaphor in Hitler's Rhetoric," *Central States Speech Journal* 34 (winter 1983): 229–35.

56. Burke, *A Grammar of Motives*, xv. The dramatistic metaphor, of course, drives the basic questions of the working journalist: who, what, where, when, why, and how. For an example of its application in world politics, see Stephen G. Walker, ed., *Role Theory and Foreign Policy Analysis* (Durham, N.C.: Duke University Press, 1987). See also Yaron Ezrahi, "The Theatrics and Mechanics of Action: The Theater and the Machine as Political Metaphors," *Social Research* 62, no. 2 (summer 1995): 299–322.

57. Martin Friedman et al., *Visions of America: Landscape as Metaphor in the Late Twentieth Century* (Denver: Denver Art Museum, 1994); Avril Horner, *Landscapes of Desire: Metaphors in Modern Women's Fiction* (New York: Harvester Wheatsheaf, 1990); Robert M. Young, *Darwin's Metaphor: Nature's Place in Victorian Culture* (New York: Cambridge University Press, 1985); Shay Docking, *The Landscape as Metaphor* (Frenchs Forest, N.S.W.: Reed, 1983).

58. Karl W. Deutsch, *The Nerves of Government: Models of Political Communication and Control* (New York: Basic Books, 1966); James Collins Ross, *Talking Immigration: A Rhetorical Analysis of U.S. Senate Debates, 1924–1965–1996* (Ph.D. diss., University of Colorado, Boulder, 2002).

59. See, for example, Linda E. Olds, *Metaphors of Interrelatedness: Toward a Systems Theory of Psychology*, SUNY series, Alternatives in Psychology (Albany: SUNY Press, 1992). Tolaas, "Notes on the Origin of Some Spatialization Metaphors."

60. Stephan Feuchtwang, *Popular Religion in China: The Imperial Metaphor* (Richmond: Curzon Press, 2001); Alon Confino, *The Nation as a Local Metaphor: Wurttemberg, Imperial Germany, and National Memory* (Chapel Hill: University of North Carolina Press, 1997); Melvin J. Lasky, *Utopia and Revolution: On the Origins of a Metaphor, or Some Illustrations of the Problem of Political Temperament and Intellectual Climate and How Ideas, Ideals, and Ideologies Have Been Historically Related* (Chicago: University of Chicago Press, 1985).

61. De Landtsheer and De Vrij in their chapter for this book use this order as a ranking of metaphor power. They take the highest ranked category 6 as referring to the more powerful sources for metaphors, the last ranked category 1 as pointing to the least powerful sources. See also De Landtsheer, "The Language of Prosperity and Crisis." Another taxonomic model for coding political metaphors appears in Roderick P. Hart et al., *Political Keywords: American Language at Work* (New York:

Oxford University Press, forthcoming). This model relies on such major categories as decline-strength, change-stability, utility-imagination, community-controversy, nature.

62. Martin J. Gannon, *Understanding Global Cultures: Metaphorical Journeys through 23 Nations* (abridged) (Thousand Oaks, Calif.: Sage, 2001). See also, for example, René Dirven, *Metaphor and Nation: Metaphors Afrikaners Live By* (New York: Peter Lang, 1994).

63. Partial compilations include Peter Wilkinson, *Thesaurus of Traditional English Metaphors*, 2d ed. (London: Routledge, 2002); Archibald Cary Coolidge, *Political Metaphors* (Mount Pleasant, S.C.: Maecenas Press, 2000); Elyse Sommer and Dorrie Weiss, eds., *Metaphors Dictionary* (New York: Gale Research, 1995); Robert Claiborne, *Loose Cannons and Red Herrings: A Book of Lost Metaphors* (New York: Ballantine Books, 1989).

64. See Shoji Azuma, "Linguistic Strategy of Involvement: An Emergence of New Political Speech in Japan," in *Beyond Public Speech and Symbols: Explorations in the Rhetoric of Politicians and the Media*, ed. Christ'l De Landtsheer and Ofer Feldman (Westport, Conn.: Praeger, 2000), 69–85; Christ'l De Landtsheer, "Function and the Language of Politics: A Linguistic Uses and Gratifications Approach," *Communication and Cognition* 3/4 (1991): 299–344.

65. Ivie, "Cold War Motives and the Rhetorical Metaphor," 72.

66. Early discussions of metaphor's rhetorical significance include Michael Osborn, "Rhetorical Depiction," in *Form, Genre, and the Study of Political Discourse*, ed. Herbert W. Simons and Aram A. Aghazarian (Columbia: University of South Carolina Press, 1986), 79–107; Michael Osborn and Douglas Ehninger, "The Metaphor in Public Address," *Speech Monographs* 29 (1962): 223–34. For a discussion of the rhetorical mobilization process in the context of an international alliance, see Francis A. Beer, *Integration and Disintegration in NATO* (Columbus: Ohio State University Press, 1969).

67. For a discussion of metaphor and identity, see Aaron D. Gresson, "Transitional Metaphors and the Political Psychology of Identity Maintenance," in *Cognition and Symbolic Structures: The Psychology of Metaphoric Transformation*, ed. Robert E. Haskell (Norwood, N.J.: Ablex Publishing Corporation, 1987), 184–85.

68. Herbert Barry III, "Popular Metaphors for Some Presidents of the United States" (paper presented at the International Society of Political Psychology, Amsterdam, 1999). See also Gillian Rhodes, "Super-

portraits: Caricatures and Recognition," *Metaphor and Symbol* 14, no. 2 (1999): 149–57.

69. See Robert Hariman and John Louis Lucaites, "Performing Civic Identity: The Iconic Photograph of the Flag Raising on Iwo Jima," *Quarterly Journal of Speech* 88, no. 4 (November 2002): 363–92; Kathi L. Groenendyk, "The Importance of Vision: Persuasion and the Picturesque," *Rhetoric Society Quarterly* 30, no. 1 (winter 2000): 9–28; Robert Hariman and John Louis Lucaites, "Dissent and Emotional Management in a Liberal-Democratic Society: The Kent State Iconic Photograph," *Rhetoric Society Quarterly* 31, no. 3 (summer 2001): 5–31; John Michael McGuire, "Pictorial Metaphors: A Reply to Sedivy," *Metaphor and Symbol* 14, no. 4 (1999): 293–302; Charles F. Forceville, *Pictorial Metaphor in Advertising* (London: Routledge and Kegan Paul, 1996); Victor Kennedy and John Kennedy, "Metaphor and Visual Rhetoric," special issue, *Metaphor and Symbolic Activity* 8 (1993): 149–255; Sonia Sedivy, "Metaphoric Pictures, Pulsars, Platypuses," *Metaphor and Symbol* 12, no. 2 (1997): 95–112; Nelson and Boynton, *Video Rhetorics.*

70. Donald Kinder and Adam Berinsky, "Making Sense of Political Issues through Frames," *The Political Psychologist* 4, no. 2 (1999): 3–8; William H. Riker, *The Strategy of Rhetoric: Campaigning for the American Constitution* (New Haven: Yale University Press, 1996); Jan Bosman and Louk Hagendoorn, "Effects of Literal and Metaphorical Persuasive Messages," *Metaphor and Symbolic Activity* 6 (1991): 271–92; Arthur C. Graesser, Jeffrey S. Mio, and Kevin Millis, "Metaphors in Persuasive Communication," in *Models of Literary Understanding,* ed. Dietrich Meutsch (Amsterdam: Elsevier, 1988), 13:131–54; Jan Bosman, "Persuasive Effects of Political Metaphors," *Metaphor and Symbolic Activity* 2 (1987): 97–113. See also Michael Warner, *Publics and Counterpublics* (New York: Zone Books; Cambridge, Mass.: MIT Press, 2002); John Peters, *Speaking into the Air* (Chicago: University of Chicago Press, 1999).

71. See particularly Robert Hariman, *Political Style* (Chicago: University of Chicago Press, 1995).

72. See Gerard Hauser, *Introduction to Rhetorical Theory,* 2d ed. (Prospect Heights, Ill.: Waveland, 2002), chaps. 7, 14.

73. See Donald F. Miller, *The Reason of Metaphor: A Study in Politics* (Newbury Park, N.J.: Sage, 1992); Bipin Indurkhya, "Modes of Metaphor," *Metaphor and Symbolic Activity* 6 (1991): 1–27; Bipin Indurkhya, "The Thesis That All Knowledge Is Metaphorical and Meanings of

Metaphor," *Metaphor and Symbolic Activity* 9 (1994): 61–73; Sternberg, *Metaphors of Mind.*

74. See A. J. Grant, "Vico and Bultmann on Myth: The Problem with De-mythologizing," *Rhetoric Society Quarterly* 30, no. 4 (fall 2000): 49–82; Marcel Danesi, *Vico, Metaphor, and the Origin of Language* (Bloomington: Indiana University Press, 1993); Samuel R. Levin, "Vico and the Language of the 'First Poets,'" in *Metaphoric Worlds: Conceptions of a Romantic Nature* (New Haven: Yale University Press, 1988), 106–30; Ferald J. Bryan, "Vico on Metaphor: Implications for Rhetorical Criticism," *Philosophy and Rhetoric* 19 (1986): 255–65; Hayward R. Alker, "Rescuing 'Reason' from the 'Rationalists': Reading Vico, Marx and Weber as Reflective Institutionalists," *Millennium* 19, no. 2 (1990): 161–84. See also Francis Bacon, *The New Organon,* ed. Lisa Jardine and Michael Silverthorne (New York: Cambridge University Press, 2000).

75. For body and optical metaphors in philosophy and science, see particularly George Lakoff and Rafael Nuñez, *Where Mathematics Comes From: How the Embodied Mind Brings Mathematics into Being* (New York: Basic Books, 2001); Lakoff and Johnson, *Philosophy in the Flesh;* Richard Rorty, *Philosophy and the Mirror of Nature* (Princeton: Princeton University Press, 1979); Jerold J. Abrams, "Philosophy *after* the Mirror of Nature: Rorty, Dewey, and Pierce on Pragmatism and Metaphor," *Metaphor and Symbol* 17, no. 3 (2002): 227–42. Discussions of scientific discourse and the role of metaphors include Thomas M. Lessl, "Gnostic Scientism and the Prohibition of Questions," *Rhetoric and Public Affairs* 5, no. 1 (2002): 133–57; Joseph Little, "Analogy in Science: Where Do We Go from Here?" *Rhetoric Society Quarterly* 30, no. 1 (winter 2000): 69–92; Sabine Massen, *Metaphors and the Dynamics of Knowledge,* Routledge Studies in Social and Political Thought (New York: Routledge, 2000); Jeanne Fahnestock, *Rhetorical Figures in Science* (New York: Oxford University Press, 1999); John T. Battalio, ed., *Essays in the Study of Scientific Discourse: Methods, Practice, and Pedagogy* (Stanford, Conn.: Ablex, 1998); Victor Kennedy, "The Computational Metaphor of Mind: More Bugs in the Program," *Metaphor and Symbol* 14, no. 4 (1999): 281–92; Bruno Latour, *Pandora's Hope: Essays on the Reality of Science Studies* (Cambridge: Harvard University Press, 1999); Derek Gatherer, "Why the 'Thought Contagion' Metaphor Is Retarding the Progress of Memetics," *Journal of Memetics: Evolutionary Models of Information Transmission* 2 (1998), http://www.cpm.mmu.ac.uk/jom-emit/1998/v012/gatherer_d.html; Robert L. Sproull, *A Scientist's Tools for Business: Metaphors and Modes of Thought* (Rochester, N.Y.:

University of Rochester Press, 1997); Pavel Büchler and Nikos Pa-
pastergiadis, eds., *Random Access: On Crisis and Its Metaphors* (London:
River Oram Press; Concord, Mass.: Paul and Company, 1995); Mary
C. Lacity et al., *Information Outsourcing: Myths, Metaphors, and Realities*
(New York: John Wiley and Sons, 1995); Eileen C. Way, *Knowledge,
Representation, and Metaphor* (Boston: Kluwer Academic Publishers,
1991); Philip Goldberg, *The Babinski Reflex: And 70 Other Useful and
Amusing Metaphors from Science, Psychology, Business, Sports, and Everyday
Life* (Los Angeles: J. P. Tarcher; New York: St. Martin's, 1990.
76. Francis A. Beer, "Validities: A Political Science Perspective," *Social
Epistemology* 7, no. 1 (1993): 85–105; Francis A. Beer, "Words of Rea-
son," *Political Communication* 11 (summer 1994): 185–201.
77. George A. Kennedy, *Aristotle on Rhetoric*, 222 n. 25.
78. Jacques Derrida, *Margins of Philosophy*, 228–29. See also Giuseppe Stel-
lardi, *Heidegger and Derrida on Philosophy and Metaphor: Imperfect
Thought* (Amherst, N.Y.: Humanity Books, 2000); Jerry H. Gill,
Wittgenstein and Metaphor (Atlantic Heights, N.J.: Humanities Press,
1996); Sarah Kofman, *Nietzsche and Metaphor*, trans. Duncan Large
(London: Athlone, 1993); Bredeck, *Metaphors of Knowledge;* Andráes
Mireille, *Lacan et la question du métalangage* (Paris: Point hors ligne,
1987); Roland Barthes, *Writing Degree Zero*, trans. Annette Lavers and
Colin Smith (New York: Hill and Wang, 1968).
79. Donald A. Sylvan and James F. Voss, eds., *Problem Representation in
Foreign Policy Decision-Making* (Cambridge: Cambridge University Press,
1998); James R. King, "Models as Metaphors," *Metaphor and Symbolic
Activity* 6 (1991): 103–18; Max Black, *Models and Metaphors* (Ithaca,
N.Y.: Cornell University Press, 1962); Francis A. Beer, "Games and
Metaphors," *Journal of Conflict Resolution* 30, no. 1 (March 1986):
171–91. See also Marijke Breuning, "The Role of Analogies and Ab-
stract Reasoning in Decision-Making: Evidence from the Debate over
Truman's Proposal for Development Assistance," *International Studies
Quarterly* 47(2003): 229–245; John A. Barnden and Mark G. Lee, eds.,
"Metaphor and Artificial Intelligence," special issue, *Metaphor and
Symbol* 16, nos. 1/2 (2001): 1–142; Kennedy, "The Computational
Metaphor of Mind."
80. Gabriel A. Almond and G. Bingham Powell, Jr., eds., *Comparative Poli-
tics Today: A World View*, 7th ed. (New York: Longman, 2003). See also
Nicholas Greenwood Onuf, *World of Our Making: Rules and Rule in So-
cial Theory and International Relations* (Columbia: University of South
Carolina Press, 1989).

81. Beer, "Words of Reason."

82. See also Mark Schlesinger and Richard Lau, "The Meaning and Measure of Policy Metaphors," 611–26; Ota Weinberger, "Argumentation in Law and Politics," *Communication and Cognition* 28, no. 1 (1995): 37–39, 52.

83. Bruno Latour, *Science in Action: How to Follow Scientists and Engineers through Society* (Cambridge: Harvard University Press, 1987).

84. See Zoltán Kövecses, *Metaphor and Emotion: Language, Culture, and Body in Human Feeling* (Cambridge: Cambridge University Press, 2000); Philip Lewin, "Affective Schemas in the Appropriation of Narrative Texts," *Metaphor and Symbolic Activity* 7 (1992): 11–34; Theodore Windt and Beth Ingold, *Essays in Presidential Rhetoric* (Dubuque, Iowa: Kendall/Hunt Publishing, 1987), xvii–xviii.

85. Farrell, *Norms of Rhetorical Culture*, 1, 107. Cf. George Lakoff and Mark Turner, *More Than Cool Reason: A Field Guide to Poetic Metaphor* (Chicago: University of Chicago Press, 1989).

86. Belgian National Television BRT I, "Confrontatie" [Confrontation], 25 February 1986.

87. See inter alia Philip Eubanks, *A War of Words in the Discourse of Trade: The Rhetorical Constitution of Metaphor* (Carbondale: Southern Illinois University Press, 2000); Klaus Müller-Richter, *"Kampf der Metapher!" Studien zum Widerstreit des eigentlichen und uneigentlichen Sprechens: Zur Reflexion des Metaphorischen im philosophischen und poetologischen Diskurs* (Vienna: Österreichische Akademie der Wissenschaften, 1996); William N. Elwood, "Declaring War on the Home Front: Metaphor, Presidents, and the War on Drugs," *Metaphor and Symbolic Activity* 10, no. 2 (1995): 93–114; Barry James Balleck, *Talking War and Peace: Realist and Idealist Rhetoric in the Persian Gulf Debate* (Ph.D. diss., University of Colorado, Boulder, 1994); Martin J. Medhurst, ed., *Eisenhower's War of Words* (East Lansing: Michigan State University Press, 1994); Dickinson McGaw, "Governing Metaphors: The War on Drugs," *American Journal of Semiotics* 8, no. 3 (1991): 57–74; Ann S. Pancake, "Taken by Storm: The Exploitation of Metaphor in the Persian Gulf War," *Metaphor and Symbolic Activity* 8 (1993): 281–95; James F. Voss et al., "Experts at Debate: The Use of Metaphor in the U.S. Senate Debate on the Gulf Crisis," *Metaphor and Symbolic Activity* 7 (1992): 197–214; Enrique González Manet, *The Hidden War of Information*, trans. Laurien Alexandre (Norwood, N.J.: Ablex, 1988); Francis A. Beer, *Peace against War* (San Francisco: W. H. Freeman, 1981). See also section 2 n. 2, below.

88. Ofer Feldman, "Personality and Politics in Japan," *Politics and the Individual* 4, no. 2 (1994): 27–46; Harold D. Lasswell, *World Politics and Personal Insecurity* (New York: Free Press, 1965). See also section 3 n. 2, below.

89. Claude M. Braun, "A Note on the Effect of Semantic Anomaly on the Intensity of Emotional Impact of Metaphors," *Metaphor and Symbolic Activity* 7 (1992): 1–10; Richard Billow et al., "Metaphoric Communication and Miscommunication in Schizophrenic and Borderline States," in *Cognition and Symbolic Structures: The Psychology of Metaphoric Transformation,* ed. Robert E. Haskell (Norwood, N.J.: Ablex Publishing, 1987), 151–56; Gresson, "Transitional Metaphors and the Political Psychology of Identity Maintenance"; Gregory Bateson, *Steps to an Ecology of Mind* (New York: Ballantine Books, 1972). Clinical experiences teach that different metaphorical forms, such as similarity metaphors, proportional metaphors, metonymy, and proverbs, may have variable psychological effects. In the case of more unusual metaphors, the schizophrenic individual will feel the need to disturb communication by inaccurate, autistic, and exaggerated responses. This is often not the case when other forms of figurative language are used. New and powerful metaphors may generate even more effects than dead metaphors. Reasons may lie in the fact that the interpretation of new metaphors relies upon the context, while other forms depend upon learned associations (Margaret S. Mahler and Manuel Furer, *On Human Symbiosis and the Vicissitudes of Individuation* [New York: International University Press, 1968]). It can be concluded that a main rhetorical effect of metaphorical communication is a broadening of the emotional dimension of cognition.

90. De Landtsheer, "Function and the Language of Politics."

91. De Landtsheer, "The Language of Prosperity and Crisis"; Franco Ferrarotti, "Le radici tagliate" [Cut roots], *Critica Sociologica* 116 (January–March 1996): iii–iv.

92. *De Standaard,* 22 November 2002.

93. Shelly Dews and Ellen Winner, "Muting the Meaning: A Social Function of Irony," *Metaphor and Symbolic Activity* 10 (1995): 3–19; Roger J. Kreuz, Debra L. Long, and Mary B. Church, "On Being Ironic: Pragmatic and Mnemonic Implications," *Metaphor and Symbolic Activity* 6 (1991): 149–62; Jeffrey S. Mio and Arthur C. Graesser, "Humor, Language, and Metaphor," *Metaphor and Symbolic Activity* 6 (1991): 87–102.

94. Christ'l De Landtsheer, "Political Communication," in "How to Make a Politician," special issue, *Politics, Groups and the Individual* 2 (1995): 1–20; Christ'l De Landtsheer, "Public Speech, Symbols, and Democratic Citizenship East West," in *Beyond Public Speech and Symbols: Explorations in the Rhetoric of Politicians and the Media,* ed. Christ'l De Landtsheer and Ofer Feldman (Westport, Conn.: Praeger, 2000), 401–44.

95. Ronald D. Crelinstein, "In Their Own Words: The World of the Torturers" (paper presented at the III Pioom Symposium, *Torturers and Their Masters: The Politics of Pain,* University of Leiden, the Netherlands, 1991); A. Ping-Lin Liu, *Adaptation of Traditional Storytelling to Political Propaganda in Communist China* (Cambridge, Mass.: Center for International Studies, MIT, 1965).

96. See, for example, Beer, *Meanings of War and Peace;* Francis A. Beer and Robert Hariman, *Post-realism: The Rhetorical Turn in International Relations* (East Lansing: Michigan State University Press, 1996); Medhurst et al., *Cold War Rhetoric;* Paul A. Chilton, *Security Metaphors.* A significant body of prior work has been done at the intersection of rhetoric and foreign policy. Such work has analyzed in detail the language of foreign policy decision, for example, Denise M. Bostdorff, *The Presidency and the Rhetoric of Foreign Crisis* (Columbia: University of South Carolina Press, 1994); Medhurst, *Eisenhower's War of Words;* Lynn B. Hinds and Theodore O. Windt, *The Cold War as Rhetoric: The Beginnings, 1945–1950* (New York: Praeger, 1991). It has examined how actors employ different rhetorical styles: Hariman, *Political Style.* It has shown how political actors deploy language strategically in many foreign policy issue areas, for example, imperialism, the environment: Karen Litfin, *Ozone Discourses: Science and Politics in Global Environmental Cooperation* (New York: Columbia University Press, 1994). In a related vein, there is also relevant work on the relationship between language, international culture, and political violence: Michael J. Shapiro, *Violent Cartographies: Mapping Cultures of War* (Minneapolis: University of Minnesota Press, 1997). Such current work, of course, is joined to a longer political science tradition that includes pioneering work by such eminent scholars as Harold Lasswell, Ithiel De Sola Pool, Karl Deutsch, Robert North, and Murray Edelman.

97. Samuel Huntington, *The Clash of Civilizations and the Remaking of World Order* (New York: Simon and Schuster, 1996).

98. For further discussion of the way these processes interact, see Beer, *Peace against War.*

◆ Section I

Metaphorical Democracy

Metaphorical Democracy

Francis A. Beer and Christ'l De Landtsheer

Metaphors are important in the way that we imagine and discuss democracy. Tocqueville saw the people collectively as a passionate beast. The Federalists built a complex republican political machine with second and third order representation. In their construction of checks and balances, the self-interested desires of each were supposedly harnessed to the good of all. The city on the hill; the open society; tensions between nature and artifice, individual and collective, middle-of-the-roader and extremist, frontiersman and cowboy have all been important metaphorical themes in the American context. Further, we often talk and think of democratic institutions and issues in metaphorical terms: the president as interpreter-in-chief; the press as storyteller, amateur psychologist, soothsayer, shaper of events, patriot, and custodian of fact; parties as red or black, the environment as green. Metaphors are also obviously important in the framing of public policy issues to generate popular attention and appeal: the phenomenon of "bowling alone" has become a widespread metaphor for the decline of civil society.[1]

The first two chapters of this section rely heavily on metaphors associated with the body as a metaphorical source for a democratic target. Richard Gregg's "Embodied Meaning in American Public Discourse during the Cold War" discusses the metaphorical formulation of the democratic

American body politic as a "fortress" under attack by the disease of communism, which must be contained. Robert Ivie's earlier work has also contained an extensive discussion of disease imagery and containment rhetoric.[2] His essay here, "Democracy, War, and Decivilizing Metaphors of American Insecurity," develops this theme further. Two enemies, the threatening other and the untrustworthy democratic self, interact dynamically. The external enemy other is metaphorically described through "savagery." The democratic self remains an "object of desire," but it is also associated with source metaphors of "disease . . . , death, destruction, and chaos." "Decivilizing metaphors" carry the message that the threatening nondemocratic enemy outside the walls and the dangerous democratic enemy within must both be contained—peacefully if possible, through violence if necessary.

Both of these chapters rely on rhetorical interpretation to argue the power of metaphors as constitutive forces in democratic politics. Gregg believes that metaphor is a "rhetorical cognitive process . . . that provides us with the schema and orderings that make sense of our experiences" and "initiates perception, conception, intention, and action." Ivie goes further, suggesting that "generative or guiding metaphors become progressively less figurative over time and are taken increasingly literally." As this reification occurs, the metaphorical representation of reality becomes both more widely accepted and increasingly narrow. Diversity goes unrecognized and dissent is ignored or repressed, with potentially tragic consequences.

Richard Anderson's chapter, "The Causal Power of Metaphor: Cueing Democratic Identities in Russia and beyond," pushes the causal argument for metaphorical power a step beyond its constitutive theme. Taking his evidence from the neodemocratic transformation of Russian politics at the birth of the post-Soviet era, Anderson analyzes political texts from authoritarian, transitional, and electoral time periods. He focuses on vertical and horizontal metaphors, which are, again, based on bodily sources. Anderson argues that the metaphors in political leaders' speeches present elite and mass audiences with cues about political identity and political change.[3] As Russian leaders shifted from "metaphors of personal superiority or subordination" to those of "community and of negotiation" and "sides," they signaled Russian citizens about the way they viewed the future and how citizens might appropriately participate. As the new metaphors were heard and acted upon, they helped move forward political change and the creation of the new political reality of a major democratic transformation.

Notes

1. Cf. Robert Hariman, "Allegory and Democratic Public Culture in the Postmodern Era," *Philosophy and Rhetoric* 35 (2002): 267–96; Christine L. Harold, "The Green Virus: Purity and Contamination in Ralph Nader's 2000 Presidential Campaign," *Rhetoric & Public Affairs* 4, no. 4 (winter 2001): 581–603; William D. Harpine, "Bryan's 'A Cross of Gold': The Rhetoric of Polarization at the 1896 Democratic Convention," *Quarterly Journal of Speech* 87, no. 3 (2001): 303–25; Paul Gilroy, *Against Race: Imagining Political Culture beyond the Color Line* (Cambridge, Mass.: Belknap Press, 2000); Robert D. Putnam, *Bowling Alone: The Collapse and Revival of American Community* (New York: Simon and Schuster, 2000); Craig Waddell, ed., *And No Birds Sing: Rhetorical Analyses of Rachel Carson's Silent Spring* (Carbondale: Southern Illinois University Press, 2000); Jacob S. Hacker, *The Road to Nowhere: The Genesis of President Clinton's Plan for Health Security* (Princeton: Princeton University Press, 1997); Zoltán Kövecses, "Tocqueville's Passionate 'Beast': A Linguistic Analysis of the Concept of American Democracy," *Metaphor and Symbolic Activity* 9 (1994): 113–33; Ronald H. Carpenter, "America's Tragic Metaphor: Our Twentieth-Century Combatants as Frontiersmen," *Quarterly Journal of Speech* 76 (1990): 1–22; Nicholas Howe, "Metaphor in Contemporary American Political Discourse," *Metaphor and Symbolic Activity* 3 (1988): 87–104; David W. Noble, *The End of American History: Democracy, Capitalism, and the Metaphor of Two Worlds in Anglo-American Historical Writing, 1880–1980* (Minneapolis: University of Minnesota Press, 1985); Phillip L. Gianos, *Political Behavior: Metaphors and Models of American Politics* (Pacific Palisades, Calif.: Palisades Publishers, 1982); Ann-Janine Morey-Gaines, *Apples and Ashes: Culture, Metaphor, and Morality in the American Dream*, American Academy of Religion Academy Series, no. 38 (Chico, Calif.: Scholars Press, 1981). For a discussion of other democratic metaphors (nature and artifice, individual and collective, middle-of-the-roaders and extremists) in the American context, see David Green, *Language and Politics in America: Shaping Political Consciousness from McKinley to Reagan* (Ithaca, N.Y.: Cornell University Press, 1987). See also Kathleen Hall Jamieson and Paul Waldman, *The Press Effect: Politicians, Journalists, and the Stories That Shape the Political World* (Oxford: Oxford University Press, 2003); Mary E. Stuckey, *The President as Interpreter-in-Chief* (Chatham, N.J.: Chatham House, 1991).

2. Robert L. Ivie, "Distempered Demos: Myth, Metaphor, and U.S. Political Culture," in *Myth: A New Symposium*, ed. Gregory A. Schrempp

and William F. Hansen (Bloomington: Indiana University Press, 2002), 165–79; Robert L. Ivie, "Realism Masking Fear: George Kennan's Political Rhetoric," in *Post-realism: The Rhetorical Turn in International Relations,* ed. Francis A. Beer and Robert Hariman (East Lansing: Michigan State University Press, 1996), 55–74.

3. See also Anthony D. Buckley and Mary Catherine Kenney, *Negotiating Identity: Rhetoric, Metaphor, and Social Drama in Northern Ireland,* Smithsonian Series in Ethnographic Inquiry (Washington, D.C.: Smithsonian Institution Press, 1995).

Embodied Meaning in American Public Discourse during the Cold War

Richard B. Gregg

Tracking and accounting for metaphors as they are found in public discourse is one of the ways rhetorical critics can unlock the kinds of symbolic inducements that underlie and drive human perception, feeling, and action. I propose to adopt this approach to examine one aspect of American public discourse that arose in the context of confrontation, crisis, and high tension during the Cold War. Specifically, I shall present some of the findings we are led to perceive if we examine American public discourse looking for metaphors that evoke "embodied meaning." As preface to my analysis, I must explain how I understand both embodied meaning and metaphorical processing. I begin with metaphor.

On the very first page of her book *AIDS and Its Metaphors,* Susan Sontag begins her discussion stating that by metaphor, she means nothing more or less than Aristotle did, who, in his *Poetics,* defined metaphor as giving something a name that belongs to something else. On its surface, this succinct definition seems overly simplistic, unable to account for the dynamic cognitive processing we attempt to capture when we apply the label "metaphor." In her next sentence, however, Sontag provides a more complex explanation when she notes that metaphoric thought "is a mental operation as old as philosophy and poetry, and the spawning ground of most kinds of understanding, including scientific understanding, and expressiveness." She further acknowledges that "one cannot think without metaphors."[1] In two sentences, Sontag has traveled a long historic road from metaphor as stylistic flourish to metaphor as a way of knowing, from linguistic extravagance to cognitive innovation, from metaphor as aesthetic emotionalism to metaphor as a process for structuring and organizing thought.

From the seventeenth century through much of the twentieth century, the mainstream of intellectual thought perceived metaphor to be a vehicle of ambiguity and emotion, irrelevant with regard to reason and indeed to be purged from reason and rationality whenever possible. But some years ago, rhetorical scholars came to understand that all linguistic meaning was partial, laced with perspective acting to induce feeling and action, and therefore rhetorical. What rhetorical scholars came to realize is that style argues. In his book *Metaphor and Thought*, Andrew Ortony describes the historic journey of metaphor as follows: "As the various disciplines of human enquiry gained their independence over the centuries, adopting their own domain, techniques, and metalanguages, the study of metaphor survived as a curiosity in some, disappeared as irrelevant in others, and became the hallmark of only one, rhetoric."[2]

Scholars of rhetoric understand that metaphor is a thoroughly rhetorical cognitive process. It is a process that culminates in a point of view; it encourages us to adopt some particular perspective and refrain from attending to others. It induces us to act in accord with one set of attitudes, feelings, values, and intentions while blinding us to other possibilities. Most fundamentally, metaphor is not merely a linguistic device. It is rather a cognitive process that shapes the scheme by which we come to structure and know ourselves and the environments in which we live. It provides us with the schema and orderings that make sense of our experiences. It initiates perception, conception, intention, and action. It is partial, and thus biased in the presentation of its structuring, calling forth feelings, intentions, and actions in accord with its meaning. Metaphor, then, can be a powerful analytical key to unlocking rhetorical meanings.

I now turn my attention briefly to what is meant by "embodied meaning." For several centuries the philosophies of Western intellectual thought have held that the most important aspects of human being—thought and reason—were separated from the rest of mankind's physiological makeup. The idea was, and still is in many quarters, that human cognition can be located in some immaterial substance, such as the soul, or some kind of detached or disembodied mind. This is a conceptualization rendered discursively by Descartes, seconded by the intellectual efforts of Kant, and sent to us down through history. But the findings of the cognitive sciences in recent years show this view to be a myth, and its explanatory implications to be counterfactual and specious. Rather, our meanings and our reasonings are thoroughly embodied. As Mark Johnson explains:

> The centrality of human embodiment directly influences what and how things can be meaningful for us, the ways in which these meanings can be developed and articulated, the ways we are able to comprehend and reason about our experience, and the actions we take. Our reality is shaped by the patterns of our bodily movement, the contours of our spatial and temporal orientation, and the forms of our interaction with objects. It is never merely a matter of abstract conceptualization and propositional judgments.[3]

In a recent book, Lakoff and Johnson point out that what we call reason arises from our brains, our bodies, and our bodily experience. For example, such concepts as space and time, fundamental to perception, thought, and reason, are formed on the basis of the relationship between our bodies and other phenomena. Our cognitive structuring of the motion of container, contain, and containment comes directly from our bodily functioning; our cognitive schema for such thinking as "life is a journey," "our policy is a risky path," or "love is often a rocky road" are based on the experience of our bodily movements. Examples such as these, say Lakoff and Johnson, demonstrate that when we say "reason is embodied" we are not making the obvious claim that we need our bodies to reason, but that the very structure of our reasons comes from the "details of our embodiment." They emphasize that our reason is not purely literal, but largely imaginative and metaphorical, and further that it is always emotionally engaged and not dispassionate. They summarize that "reason is not, in any way, a transcendent feature of the universe or of a disembodied mind. Instead it is shaped crucially by the peculiarities of our human bodies, by the remarkable details of the neural structure of our brains, and by the specifics of our everyday functioning in the world."[4] Following the lead presented by Lakoff and Johnson, the possibilities for metaphorical perception, conceptualization, and thought are multitudinous across the interfaces and cross-modal transfers of brain, body, and environment.

To sum up, our most fundamental meanings are those that grow out of our bodily experience as it interacts with our environment. All meaning is embodied. Our fundamental motives and feelings have to do with survival, control, and comfort. The more closely our emotions and feelings are related to issues of our bodies, the more salient and pervasive they become. Such meanings radiate outward, spreading the principles of their saliency through layers of meaning. Their force may dissipate a bit as they move away from core concerns, but their potential to emerge with intensity is always present. They are fundamental to our being, to the way we interpret events and actions around us, and to the general climate of opinion that coalesces from the aggregate of these personal, social, and cultural feelings.

Neurologist Antonio Damasio emphasizes the privileged status we need to accord to emotions and feelings when we analyze human meanings and actions:

> because of their inextricable ties to the body, they come first in development and retain a primacy that subtly pervades our mental life. Because the brain is the body's captive audience, feelings are winners among equals. And since what comes first constitutes a frame of reference for what comes after, feelings have a say on how the rest of the brain and cognition go about their business. Their influence is immense.[5]

Emotions and feelings are, therefore, the inevitable foundations for the ordering of values, thoughts, and actions that comprise the events we refer to as the Cold War. Embodied meanings have the potential to evoke visceral responses that can constrain perceptions, conceptions, and reflections of reality, and therefore metaphorical statements that embrace them beckon the attention of rhetorical analysts.

In the investigation that follows, my examples shall come from a variety of sources running the gamut from government documents on the one hand to Hollywood films on the other, to try to display the scope of the sources of embodied meanings and the meanings themselves.

The groundwork for the emotionalism of the Cold War period was established even prior to the turn of the century. Personal accounts of visits to Russia that included descriptions of some of the deplorable conditions in Russian society began to appear in books in the late 1800s. Most notable among these was *Siberia and the Exile System*, published first in serial form in *The Century* in 1888, then as a book in 1891 by George Kennan Sr. This account, and others like it, led to a highly successful cottage industry in the following years. Various articles with titles such as "House of Bondage," "In the Grip of the Tsar," and "Stolypin and the New Terror" appeared in magazines and journals of the time, promulgating negative images of Russia.

These literary accounts were aided and abetted by the personal tales of immigrants from Russia and Russian-controlled areas who were escaping religious and political persecution, protracted military service enforced by the Russian government, and poverty. Such immigrants felt no loyalty to the czarist regime and harbored memories of various kinds of oppression. In addition to all of this, Russian pogroms against Jews, especially the Kishinev massacre of 1903, were appalling to many Americans.[6]

The Communist Revolution in Russia did not result in the encouraging of more positive feelings among America's governmental leaders. When Vladimir Lenin pronounced the coming of a worldwide proletarian revolt shortly after he came to power, the ideological world of Lenin's communism faced off against American president Woodrow Wilson's democracy. Wilson implacably opposed the Communist regime and surreptitiously aided anti-Russian forces whenever and wherever he could. As the world war ground to an end and the prospects for peace became a reality, Wilson believed that his idea of a world run according to the principles of moderate liberal democracy must win out over a world prone to Communist domination. Wilson found his views supported by friends and advisers. For instance, just as Wilson arrived in Paris for the great peace conference, he received a cable from Joseph Tumulty that perfectly echoed Wilson's belief. The stage was set, cabled Tumulty, for the final issue between a world that emphasizes a balance of power and one that operates according to the League of Nations: if America fails now, socialism rules the world, and if international fair play under democracy cannot curb nationalistic ambitions, there is nothing left but socialism, upon which Russia and Germany have already embarked. If the statesmanship at Versailles cannot settle these things in the spirit of justice, Bolshevism will settle them in a spirit of injustice."[7] A bit earlier, Secretary Robert Lansing wrote that "there are two great evils at work in the world today: absolutism, the power of which is waning, and Bolshevism, the power of which is increasing. We have seen the hideous consequences of Bolshevik rule in Russia, and we know that the doctrine is spreading westward. The possibility of a proletariat despotism over Central Europe is terrible to contemplate." President Wilson, at sea on his way to Europe, spoke of the need to build a new world order, because the "poison of Bolshevism" was readily accepted by the world in protest to the way the world had worked.[8]

In the words of Lansing and Wilson, we see the elements of danger and destruction focused on mind and body: Lansing refers to the spreading doctrine of communism, the ever-expanding web of beliefs operating with a kind of inevitability to penetrate the thought worlds of Western civilizations; Wilson depicts supplicant people opening themselves, their bodies, to ingest a foreign substance, a lethal potion, to symbolize a defiant gesture of self-destruction in the face of a hostile world. Both images evoke visceral, physical aspects of meaning and employ embodied terminology to characterize the threat.

A combination of events and public discourse galvanized the attention of the American public to be on the alert against the pollution of America by radical Bolsheviks. Newspapers of the time were filled with rumors of such possibilities. Events interspersed among these warnings put flesh on the spectral bones. In 1919 radicals identified with communism set off bombs in eight cities. In 1920 a bomb blast in New York City at the corner of Broad and Wall Streets, America's financial center, killed thirty-three persons and injured hundreds of others. During those noisy times, President Wilson continued to call Bolshevism a "poison" and dispatched Attorney General Mitchell Palmer to apply an antidote. Palmer began to round up suspects and deport them, sometimes without benefit of trial. On New Year's Day in 1920, raids were staged in thirty-three cities, and four thousand suspects were arrested.

Visceral emotions calling up images of illness or penetration of the body by harmful substances often turned up in public discourse in the years between the two world wars. Republican Party attacks against Democratic candidate Upton Sinclair in the 1932 gubernatorial campaign in California provide one example. Sinclair was a known Communist sympathizer, a supporter of Franklin Roosevelt, and founder of the End of Poverty in California movement. He advocated the seizure of farm warehouses and idle factories to house surplus food for the poor and employ the unemployed, a scheme that sounded extreme to many Americans. The *Los Angeles Times,* an influential Republican mouthpiece, opened fire on Sinclair and his supporters: "What is eating at the heart of America are a maggot-like horde of Reds who have scuttled to Sinclair's support. . . . They are termites secretly and darkly eating into the foundations and roof beams of everything that the American heart has held dear and sacred. . . . To this end they rally uncleanly to every sore spot. They drop poison in every bruise."[9]

The physical aspects of meaning here emphasize both external and internal vulnerabilities—the external wounding of the body providing openings for the introduction and spread of noxious substances throughout the American body. The nature of the enemy was transformed from qualities associated with humans to those associated with burrowing insects, a horde of flesh-eating maggots; a swarm of termites operating in dark, secret places to eat at the foundation of the American heart; unclean insects to find sore spots and bruises on the American body to drop poison into.

The Red Scare of this period was intense and out of proportion to any real danger. The total number of radicals at the time was estimated to be 0.2 percent of the American population, an extremely underwhelming force. But the fear generated among the American public did not go away. Public polls conducted between 1937 and 1939 show that the majority opinion believed that communism was more threatening than fascism, that free speech ought to be curtailed in order to silence Communist sympathizers, that repressive measures ought to be employed against Communists, that Communists ought to be barred from governments, that the party ought to be outlawed, and that Christianity and communism were absolutely incompatible.[10]

Public opinion reversed to a large extent during World War II, as Americans adjusted to the idea that Russia was an ally, but then reverted back again as Soviet–U.S. relations became strained over postwar readjustments. With the reversal came the return of the embodied terminology reflecting the nature of the perceived threat. Initially, it came at the highest levels of American government. On 22 February 1946 U.S. Charge d'Affaires in Moscow, George Kennan, sent what came to be called the "Long Telegram," a landmark document that contained a persuasive analysis of Soviet history, outlook, intentions, and goals that established the intellectual undergirding for the policy of "containment" that influenced U.S. policy for years.[11]

In the telegram, Kennan stated that the Kremlin view of the world was neurotic, based on a sense of insecurity. Such a view, he said, perceives the outside world to be evil, hostile, and menacing, "but as bearing within itself germs of creeping disease and destined to be wracked with growing internal convulsions until it is given final coup de grace by rising power of socialism and yields to a new and better world." Perhaps with that claim in mind, toward the end of Kennan's cable, he writes, "Much depends on health and vigor of our own society. World communism is like a malignant parasite which feeds only on diseased tissue. This is point at which domestic and foreign policies meet."[12]

Kennan's terms such as "germs," "creeping disease," and "internal convulsion" invite one's focus to matters of sickness and wellness; the focus on matters of the body becomes pronounced. In a larger scope, the overall concept of containment that emerged from arguments in Kennan's telegram, and that became the master cognitive scheme for animating and organizing U.S. Cold War strategies, was a thoroughly embodied concept. As Johnson points out:

> Our encounter with containment and boundedness is one of the most pervasive features of our bodily experience. We are intimately aware of our bodies as three-dimensional containers into which we put certain things (food, water, air) and out of which other things emerge (food and water wastes, air, blood, etc.). From the beginning, we experience constant physical containment in our surroundings (those things that envelop us). We move in and out of rooms, clothes, vehicles, and numerous kinds of bounded spaces. We manipulate objects, placing them in containers (cups, boxes, cans, bags, etc.). In each of these cases there are repeatable spatial and temporal organizations. In other words, there are typical schemata for physical containment.[13]

Johnson further notes that the bodily origins of the schema "container" and the cognitive entailments that come with it suggest tactics and strategies for existence: "The experience of containment typically involves protection from, or resistance to, external forces."[14]

The "containment" metaphor works well with the terminology of Kennan's telegram. If the Soviet Union is driven by neuroses, then those neuroses must be contained. If the Soviet Union waits to move upon the diseased bodies of the Western Allies, then the potential for movement of the Soviet Union must be contained. If the Soviet Union is extruding and intruding on the borders of neighboring countries like a liquid, then those intrusions must be contained. As the concept of containment became translated into practice during the Cold War, the United States followed the entailment that Soviet pressure must be directed "along the entire boundary of that container."[15]

As metaphor and synecdoche, containment became a vessel for a variety of anxieties and fears. And like a drumbeat, a series of events provided plenty of reason for emotionalism: the Communist takeover of Czechoslovakia, the Soviet blockade of Berlin, the detonation of the Soviet atom bomb, Communists winning the civil war in China, Truman ordering the building of the hydrogen bomb. North Korea invaded South Korea, the Chinese entered the Korean War, Alger Hiss was convicted of perjury, Klaus Fuchs confessed to spying for the Soviets, and Julius and Ethel Rosenberg were found guilty of passing America's nuclear secrets to the enemy. Joseph McCarthy charged that Communists had infiltrated the State Department, and internal security became a steady preoccupation. In response, a bevy of containment activities were launched to keep the poisons out of the bruises and the tissues healthy to ward off the parasites constantly looking for weakness. Counterespionage was undertaken, loyalty oaths administered, and the Freedom Train launched across the American landscape.

Visceral responses to the descriptions of the Communist menace were back in play. George Kennan compared Communists to a "swarm of rats." In 1952 in the Supreme Court case of *Carlson* v. *Landon,* the high court upheld the ruling of a district court judge who refused to grant bail to five aliens who were arrested and held while the question of their deportations was under review. The district court judge explained that he was not going to turn the aliens loose in case they were Communists, "any more than I would turn loose a deadly germ in the community."[16] The fictional private investigator Mike Hammer, invented by novelist Mickey Spillane, waded into the Red Scare with the ruthlessness that seemed to be required, explaining that "I lived only to kill the scum and lice." Ex-Communist Louis Budenz wrote in his memoirs that Americans had no understanding of the "alien world" of Communism, "whose leadership works secretly in the shadows." Descriptive attention was given to how Communists worked to infiltrate, injure, and maim American society. The "Commies" worked individually or in cells to permeate all avenues of American life and attempted to poison all channels of public opinion. Anywhere and everywhere, one might expect to find the agents of communism burrowing in every nook and cranny of American life, burrowing in through the bruises, sores, and diseases of the American body, and once within, they become inner enemies, boring and contaminating and spreading disease. Diseases within the body are easily transformed metaphorically into unnatural, foreign substances that have the potential to spread with a certain inevitability. The more serious the illness, the more guilt can be provoked by images of dissolute living or inherent weaknesses within one's body as probable causes.[17]

Most dreaded among the metaphorical terms employed to characterize communism was the imagery captured in a phrase used frequently by the radical Right, "the cancer of communism." Rhetorical critic Edwin Black explicates the horrible potency of this metaphorical schema as it was used by extreme right wing groups in the United States during the 1960s. Cancer, says Black, was not an invasion of the body by alien organisms, nor a malfunction of bodily organs. Rather, "Cancer is conceived as a growth of some group of the body's own cells. The cancer is a part of oneself, a sinister and homicidal extension of one's own body." The polity, in this view, is a living creature. Black elaborates this view to reveal its disastrous end:

> And what organs of this afflicted body need be spared amputation? The country is deathly ill. Its policies are cowardly; its spokesmen are treasonous; its cities are anarchical; its discipline is flaccid; its poor are arrogant, its rich are greedy; its courts are unjust; its universities are mendacious.—The patient is *in extremis*. It is in this light that risks must be calculated, and in this light the prospect of nuclear war becomes thinkable. Why not chance it, after all? What alternative is there? The patient is dying; is it not time for the ultimate surgery? What is there to lose? In such a context, an unalarmed attitude toward the use of atomic weapons is not just reasonable; it is obvious.[18]

I round off my quick survey of embodied meanings of images and cognitive schemata by arriving at the most visceral of the lot. These bodily images can be perceived in very personal ways that demand constant surveillance and harsh remedies for eradication of the dangers. The body must become a fortress, defenses up, constantly on the alert.

In the days of the Red Scare, when Americans were unaware of the embedded nature of mind in body, the Communist threats to the human mind were seen to be every bit as dangerous as those in the body. And just as Communist strategies were directed toward points of weakness in the body politic, points when openings, bruises, and sores presented themselves for penetration, so warnings about and descriptions of threats to the mind looked for tendencies, proclivities, maladjustments, and aberrations that provided opportunities for penetration of the human mind.

In 1956 a subcommittee of the U.S. Senate Judiciary Committee published a handbook for American citizens in which it explained the nature of the Communist Party in America and how it worked, in an attempt to correct "current misinformation regarding the Communist movement." In a section of the report titled "What Makes a Communist Tick," the subcommittee asserts that the claim that American Communism is a product of inequalities in the social system is trite and untrue. Rather, the report states: "In a number of cases it will be found that the party is a refuge for certain psychologically maladjusted individuals." Just a page later, the report conducts brief discussions describing the types of individuals who are likely to be attracted by the Communist Party. There are, for example, the "adventurous spirits who thrive on the conspiratorial atmosphere within the party," who like secret meetings, aliases, the paraphernalia of illegality, and so forth. Then there are the timid souls, who may have an inferiority complex but become "inspired with boldness" when they join an aggressive group. Bohemians and nonconformists "of all stripes" are attracted to the Communist Party. Persons who have become embittered by some personal or emotional experience are vulnerable. In addition to these types, the committee asserts that "by its repudiation of so-called capitalist ethics and moral standards, the party provides a welcome philosophical sanction for the lunatic fringe."[19]

The categories of those susceptible to communism range broadly across troubled and troubling personality types, according to the Senate handbook. There is little room here for cool contemplation, thoughtful weighing of alternatives, or calculation of costs. The types of individuals cited by the committee are described as mentally maladjusted to some significant degree.

The handbook reflected images of the enemy already alive in American society. In Spillane's best-selling novel *One Lonely Night*, the supreme villain, Oscar Deamer, is portrayed as a psychopathic Communist who is destined to meet his end at the hands of the crusading Mike Hammer. Just before Hammer chokes Deamer to death, he tells him, "You were a Commie, Oscar, because you were batty. It was the only philosophy that would appeal to your crazy mind." The anti-Communist crusade unleashed by Senator Joseph McCarthy was characterized by creating suspicions about individuals that went beyond the bounds of reason. Individuals who appeared to be different in devious or deviant ways could easily become suspects as traitors, who, if they were not outright Communists, could be seen to be doing things that the Commies wanted done anyway. Any behavior or action that could be seen to deviate from what were taken to be American norms could be judged perverted, and therefore suspicious, and probably Communist. Senator Kenneth Wherry of Nebraska believed cities close to the American seacoasts were logical entry points for abnormal and deviant individuals. Wherry said he wanted to secure "seaports and major cities against sabotage through conspiracy of subversives and moral perverts in government establishments." Wherry went on to explain that "you can't . . . separate homosexuals from subversives. . . . I don't say every homosexual is a subversive, and I don't say every subversive is a homosexual. But a man of low morality is a menace in the government, whatever he is, and they are tied up together."[20] In the age of the Red Scare, a variety of behaviors and messages came under scrutiny, running the gamut from comic books and movies, to juvenile delinquency and sexually liberated women. For awhile, a significant number of Americans believed the minds of their fellow citizens were, or could be, susceptible to foreign influence and persuasion. What do we make of the Un-American Activities Committee? Of the blacklisting of individuals from the world of entertainment? Of all the attempts made, large and small, to purify Americanism, to eradicate all ideas and images that might undermine that purity? What do we make of the banning of *Little Red Riding Hood* in the public schools, of the Loyalty Oath, of town ordinances requiring Communists and fellow travelers to be out of the city limits in forty-eight hours, of the renaming of the Cincinnati Reds the Cincinnati Red Stockings? Or of putting locks on all gumball machines in town because the machine dispensed a tiny card with routine information about another country along with the gumball, and a card about Russia dropped into the hands of a youngster? We make of it an inordinate fear of alien and deadly conversion of the mind—a fear of mind control, of brainwashing. The fear, in its literal sense, was heightened by stories of brainwashing coming from behind the Iron Curtain, especially from China toward the end of the Korean War. The fear prompted the U.S. government to establish a special committee to study how prisoners of war could be trained to resist brainwashing. It led Dr. William Sargent, head of the Department of Psychological Medicine at Mandsley Hospital in London, who was interested in rapid and permanent means of changing human beliefs, to write a book published in 1957 titled *Battle for the Mind*. He remarks in his introduction that his concerns necessarily became enormously important because of "whole groups of nations who wish not only to confirm certain political beliefs within their boundaries, but to proselytize the outside world."[21] Worries about brainwashing and mind control seem to get to the center of things, indeed.

The Cold War was truly an ideological war. Different views of the world came into conflict, life styles were at stake, and value systems were argued and tested in the war of ideas. The nature of the conflict was discussed and described at the highest level of the Truman administration and appeared in documents that encouraged the meanings, images, and schemata that helped establish the American climate of opinion in the Cold War years. Look, for example, at words written by George Kennan in his now famous X telegram:

> The main element of any United States policy toward the Soviet Union must be that of a long-term, patient but firm and vigilant containment of Russian expansive tendencies. . . .

Thus the decision will really fall in large measure in this country itself. The issue of Soviet-American relations is in essence a test of the overall worth of the United States as a nation among nations. To avoid destruction, the United States need only measure up to its own best traditions and prove itself worthy of preservation as a great nation. . . .

Providence by providing the American people with this implacable challenge, has made their entire security as a nation dependent on their pulling themselves together and accepting the responsibilities of moral and political leadership that history plainly intended them to bear.[22]

Notice that we are introduced early to the strategic idea of containment. This major schema in the stockpile of embodied concepts became the driving metaphor undergirding America's thinking, planning, and acting. Notice that the overall worth of the United States will largely be determined within the United States itself, which means it must measure up to its own best traditions. Note finally that the security of the American people requires them all to pull together to meet the challenge. There is a tendency in these passages, especially the second two, to beckon toward the individual, the personal, within the boundaries of the United States.

National Security Council document 68, delivered to President Harry Truman in April of 1950, was not released for many eyes to see and remained classified for years. Nonetheless, its contents became known to many. It was called by some the most widely known unread document. Its purpose was to establish objectives and programs for national security. At several places in its text, the document begins to focus on internal matters in visceral ways:

our free society finds itself mortally challenged by the Soviet system. No other value system is so wholly irreconcilable with ours, so implacable in its purpose to destroy ours, so capable of turning to its own uses the most dangerous and divisive trends in our own society, no other so skillfully and powerfully evokes the elements of irrationality in human nature everywhere, and no other has the support of a great and growing center of military power.[23]

A bit later, the problem of internal subversion is emphasized:

The [Kremlin's] preferred technique is to subvert by infiltration and intimidation. Every institution of our society is an instrument which it is sought to stultify and turn against our purposes. Those that touch most closely our material and moral strength are obviously the prime targets, labor unions, civic enterprises, schools, churches, and all media for influencing opinion. The effort is not so much to make them serve obvious Soviet ends as to prevent them from serving our ends, and thus to make them sources of confusion in our economy, our culture, and our body politic.[24]

The policy of containment sketched by George Kennan implied that all surfaces of the containment vessel were significant; the enemy was to be kept away by the outer sides of the vessel, while friendly citizens were to be safely protected inside. Great fears arose when charges were made that penetration into the container by the enemy might occur or friendly elements within the container might be turned, duped, unbalanced to perform traitorous acts. Meanings evoked by embodied metaphors and images gave evidence of such fears. Poisonous currents, germlike carries, and ratlike swarms might work from the shadows to burrow, bore, spread, permeate, and infiltrate, seeking targets among the weak, the maladjusted, the deviant, the anxious, the lunatic fringe. These embodied meanings coalesced to help form a climate of opinion in America during the Cold War that judged events, actions, and individuals in accord with its fears. It is the visceral edge of those embodied meanings that provides evidence of the depth and acuity of those fears.

Notes

1. Susan Sontag, *AIDS and Its Metaphor* (New York: Farrer, Straus and Giroux, 1998), 5.
2. Andrew Ortony, ed., *Metaphor and Thought* (Cambridge: Cambridge University Press, 1979), 3–4.
3. Mark Johnson, *The Body in the Mind* (Chicago: University of Chicago Press, 1987), xxix.
4. George Lakoff and Mark Johnson, *Philosophy in the Flesh* (New York: Basic Books, 1999), 4.
5. Antonio R. Damasio, *Descartes' Error: Emotion, Reason, and the Human Brain* (New York: G. P. Putnam and Sons, 1994), 159–60.
6. Robert J. Maddox, *The Unknown War with Russia: Wilson's Siberian Intervention* (San Rafael, Calif.: Presidio Press, 1977), 4–5.
7. Joseph Tumulty to Woodrow Wilson, 31 December 1918, Wilson, file 8A, Library of Congress.
8. Norman G. Levin, *Woodrow Wilson and World Politics* (Oxford: Oxford University Press, 1968), 133–34, 131.
9. John Kenneth White, *Still Seeing Red* (Boulder: Westview Press, 1997), 33.

10. Ibid., 30.

11. George F. Kennan, "The Sources of Soviet Conduct," *Foreign Affairs* 25 (July 1947): 566–82.

12. Ibid., 20, 21, 31.

13. Johnson, *The Body in the Mind,* 21.

14. Ibid., 22.

15. Paul A. Chilton, *Security Metaphors: Cold War Discourse from Containment to Common House* (New York: Peter Lang, 1996), 152–53.

16. *Carlson v. Landon,* 342 U.S. 524 (1952). The quotation is found in the dissenting opinion of Justice Black.

17. Louis F. Budenz, *This is My Story* (New York: McGraw-Hill, 1947); Stephen J. Whitfield, *The Culture of the Cold War* (Baltimore: Johns Hopkins University Press, 1996), 33, 34, 36.

18. Edwin Black, "The Second Persona," in *Readings in Rhetorical Criticism,* ed. Carl R. Burgchardt (State College, Penn.: Strata Publishing, 1995), 194, 195.

19. Subcommittee to Investigate the Administration of the Internal Security Act and Other Internal Security Laws of the Committee on the Judiciary, United States Senate, viii, 45, 47.

20. Whitfield, *Culture of the Cold War,* 36, 43.

21. William Sargent, *Battle for the Mind* (Baltimore: Penguin Books, 1957), xix.

22. Kennan, "Sources of Soviet Conduct," 575–76, 581–82.

23. Ernest R. May, ed., *American Cold War Strategy: Interpreting NSC 68* (New York: St. Martin's Press, 1993), 29.

24. Ibid., 52.

Democracy, War, and Decivilizing Metaphors of American Insecurity

Robert L. Ivie

Democracy, as a motivating term in U.S. political culture, is readily identified with war through the ubiquitous trope of disease and related metaphorical vehicles that participate in a wider rhetorical universe of decivilizing imagery. This convergence of the language of democracy and war translates the barbarism of a distempered domestic demos into the savagery of a threatening external Other, exacerbating perceptions of peril that sustain an improbable quest for national security through global domination. My purpose is to critique this problematic relationship of metaphor to democracy and war by drawing attention to certain conventions of discourse in the American experience, specifically to clusters of decivilizing vehicles such as disease, insanity, and depravity and to literalizing constructions such as commonsense and factual styles of representation that together transform tenuous similarities of diverse terms into culturally reified and nearly incontestable categories of threat to the body politic.

At one level this rhetorical dynamic of threat perception is relatively obvious. The United States throughout the twentieth century has featured the defense of democracy in justification of hot and cold wars against fascism, communism, terrorism, and a host of other, seemingly endless foes typically characterized, and often caricatured, as congenital enemies of freedom and civilization. Woodrow Wilson's original call to make the world safe for democracy has become the post–Cold War credo of securing a global democratic peace by eradicating the remaining forces of savagery (including but not limited to rogue states, petty dictators, religious strife, ethnic cleansing, racial hatred, international terrorism, and weapons of mass destruction), supplanting these coercive forces, in Clinton's presidential words, with "a whole world" of stable democratic regimes led by the "world's greatest democracy" and only "indispensable nation."[1]

From scholars such as Spencer Weart and Bruce Russett to political leaders such as Bill Clinton, conventional wisdom insists that democracies do not fight one another.[2] This linkage of democracy to peace is so common in U.S. political rhetoric, John Lewis Gaddis observes, that it functions as a "curious myopia" of regarding countries with different forms of government as inherently hostile to America.[3] This ideological litmus test, in his view, causes misunderstandings and gross exaggerations of international and domestic dangers by treating global democratization as the measure of U.S. security in a world fragmented by nationalism, tribalism, and economic disparity. Thus, the nation's perception of threat is constructed rhetorically and interpreted primarily as a challenge to democracy's global reach and well-being. Of course, according to this same logic, threats to democracy necessarily entail threats to free enterprise and human rights— indeed, to civilization itself.

The relationship of metaphor to war in this standard construction of national peril is also relatively straightforward. As a master trope, Kenneth Burke has argued, metaphor functions heuristically to develop perspectives or general frames of acceptance out of which tragic orientations toward perfectly evil Others emerge.[4] Tragic orientations lead readily to deadly "victimage" rituals such as war, unless the cycle is somehow arrested by what Burke refers to as comic correctives aimed at broadening overly narrow and simplistic representations of reality. In this dramatistic model of symbolic action, generative or guiding metaphors become progressively less figurative over time and are taken increasingly more literally as a given perspective or frame of reference develops into a tragic orientation. The more literally a key metaphor is taken, the less subject it is to constructive, comic critique aimed at drawing attention to overlooked complexities otherwise screened out of the prevailing point of view. Also, as constitutive metaphors increasingly become fixed in meaning and tragic in orientation, a play of similarities and differences gives way to the reification of categories and identities, as if metaphorical vehicle and tenor were no longer commenting on and interacting with each other but instead one had become a proper name and the other its clear, correct, and stable referent.

George Bush, for example, demonized Saddam Hussein (tenor) during the Gulf War of 1990–91 by equating him with Adolph Hitler (vehicle), thus supplanting the cautionary analogy to Vietnam with the moral lesson of Munich and thereby transforming a nasty dictator on the loose in the Persian Gulf into a formidable threat to civilization and world order. Saddam Hussein became the symbol of aggression whose forces "stormed" Kuwait in "blitzkrieg fashion," raping, pillaging, and plundering its people.[5] Similarly, Bill Clinton upped the stakes in Kosovo by reifying the metaphor of Hitler's aggression. In declaring "a victory for a safer world, for our democratic values, and for a stronger America" and announcing that "aggression against an innocent people has been contained and is being turned back," he recalled for Americans that he had ordered the nation's armed forces into combat to arrest "the culmination of a 10-year campaign by Slobodan Milosevic" involving "some of the most vicious atrocities in Europe since the Second World War." By its decisive action, the United States with its NATO allies had "averted the wider war this conflict might well have sparked" and made it more likely that the victims of Milosevic's repression "will choose a future of democracy, fair treatment of minorities, and peace."[6] During the bombing campaign, Clinton spoke forcefully of "Milosevic's madness" in the context of "Nazi atrocities" and as a portrait of "the face of evil."[7] "Hitler," "ethnic cleansing," and "genocide" were among the defining terms of the administration's mandate for war, a point of view reflected in the cover photo of *Newsweek*'s 19 April 1999 edition, which featured a close shot of Milosevic as "The Face of Evil" placed in front of a burning fuel depot in a village near Pristina, Kosovo.[8] Such reified images of the threatening Other are a hallmark of war rhetoric, underscoring the relationship of literalized metaphor to tragic perspective in the legitimization of armed conflict.

We should not presume these rhetorical and metaphorical operations are mere public posturing or transparent rationalizations of deeper, more profound causes of war. They are consequential acts of interpretation. Declassified records of Lyndon Johnson's deliberations with his closest advisors over Vietnam War policy, for example, reveal much the same rhetorical themes and metaphorical processes at work in the definition of threat and construction of an enemy. Behind closed doors, the administration collectively struggled to articulate a coherent policy and a compelling motive for war within the symbolic framework of a "savage" opponent intent upon denying freedom and democracy to its victims.[9] As David Campbell argues, danger is not so much an objective condition as "an effect of interpretation" in which some risks instead of others are singled out as threats.[10] The realm of symbolic action, including the rhetoric of democratic peril and tragic metaphors of evil incarnate, constitutes the attitudes that define a political culture and its predisposition toward war.

Already, by advancing this claim for the motivational force and cultural import of war rhetoric considered as more than sheer propaganda, we are moving into a second, less obvious level in the analysis of metaphor's construction of threat perception. The theme of democracy imperiled by an evil adversary strikes most observers as a fair representation of a typical call to arms by a twentieth-century American president. Moreover, taking metaphorical liberties to dramatize such a war-justifying theme conforms to a common assumption that war rhetoric is inherently hyperbolic given the nature of crisis situations. To suggest, though, that the very tragedy of the situation and much of its motivational impulse exists as a reification of a metaphorically generated interpretation of reality opens our analysis to a new set of questions about the rhetorical universe of threat construction. If we take war-justifying symbolic action seriously, that is, then we are more likely to inquire further into its makeup. Knowing specifically which metaphors are involved becomes more important when we assume they make a difference in defining the character and intensity of the perceived threat. Additionally, more precise knowledge of these vehicles and their literalizing constructions for identifying the external enemy raises the unexpected issue of democracy itself as a corresponding internal enemy. I turn first to the question of which metaphorical vehicles and literalizing constructions are involved in order to address next how they implicate democracy.

Decivilizing Vehicles and Literalizing Constructions

Within the rhetorical universe of threat construction, certain metaphorical vehicles are especially prominent in the depiction of evil as an image of the threatening Other's savagery. Savagery is a multidimensional image of the enemy that contrasts the civilized victim's rationality, morality, and peaceful purposes with the irrational and immoral behavior of the uncivilized aggressor. In structural terms, it opposes force to freedom, irrationality to rationality, and aggression to defense, dimensions of contrast that encompass myriad oppositions such as those between violence and negotiation, ideology and open-mindedness, conformity and individuality, lawlessness and lawfulness, deceit and honesty, and ruthlessness versus principled conduct.[11] Enemies are dehumanized, that is, by rhetorically stripping them of their identity as civilized Others. Decivilizing vehicles are among the war rhetor's most important symbolic resources for this purpose; they articulate the key contrastive features distinguishing civilized from savage agents while synthesizing several dimensions of meaning into an integrated image of threat.

Ronald Reagan's Cold War rhetoric, as I have argued elsewhere, illustrates common types of decivilizing vehicles that are notably operative within U.S. political culture and, as Sam Keen has demonstrated, routinely manifested in other cultures as well.[12] Reagan's particular use of these vehicles was aimed at establishing a threat to the civilized world's peace and freedom from a barbarous enemy single-mindedly bent on stockpiling instruments of destruction while the United States was naively disarming for détente—Reagan's infamous "window of vulnerability." America's proper response, according to the logic of this image of Soviet savagery, was to deal with the barbarian from a position of strength, because such a foe understands and respects only raw force. Thus, a refurbished conventional and nuclear arsenal would provide an immediate margin of safety, giving the United States the edge it needed to contain and hold the Soviets at bay while establishing the "conditions of freedom and democracy as rapidly as possible in all countries," including the Soviet Union. This was Reagan's "crusade for freedom," promising "a cathedral of peace" through universal democratization backed by military strength. His rhetorical legacy rooted in a metaphor of savagery continues to guide the logic of post–Cold War American foreign policy.[13]

Reagan's dependency on the metaphor of savagery involved a wide range of decivilizing vehicles that can be placed on a rough continuum from inanimate and physical forces of nature to satanic and profane acts of men. Eight clusters of vehicles are discernable along this continuum. The enemy represented as a *natural menace* is a shadow or force of darkness, a gray presence, a gale of intimidation, a killer storm, an infectious disease, and so on. Represented as *inanimate machines,* enemies become mindless instruments of destruction. As an *animal,* the untamed aggressor stalks its neighbors like a beast of prey. Subhuman antagonists take on the characteristics of *primitives* brandishing clubs to bully and barbarously assault their weaker victims. Foes who are *criminals* resort to murder, rape, deceit, theft, and cheating. *Mentally disturbed* assailants are driven by deep fears, irrational hostilities, and mad ambition. Similarly, closed-minded *ideologues* and militant *fanatics* are immune to practical reason and rational influence of any kind. *Satanic and profane* antagonists confront the righteous forces of good with the godless menace of evil.[14]

Through this kind of terminology, Reagan was able to achieve maximum presence of his perspective on the facts of Soviet misconduct, constructing political reality out of metaphors that, as Eugene Miller has observed, create rather than discover likenesses.[15] These figures of speech became self-contained interpretations of reality in the guise of independently verified and commonsense truth, forming the preferred conclusion about the Soviet Other from which literalizing proofs could then be deduced, not arriving inductively at such an inference by following the conventions of logical exposition.[16] Accordingly, historical examples, laced with decivilizing vehicles to interpret their meaning, were used to produce a self-literalizing or reifying effect through the interplay of metaphor and evidence. Reagan characterized Soviet misconduct, for example, by observing that "since World War II, the record has included Soviet violation of the Yalta agreements leading to domination of Eastern Europe, symbolized by the Berlin Wall—a grim, gray monument to repression . . . ; the takeovers of Czechoslovakia, Hungary and Afghanistan; and the ruthless repression of the proud people of Poland."[17] Here the metaphor determines the attitude taken toward a selection of verifying historical representations even as it directs attention away from other potential points of view on the historical record.

By such symbolic operations, Reagan guided the nation through an otherwise complicated world, calling attention to supportive evidence and discounting inconsistent facts. Color graphics used in his televised address to the nation in November 1982, for example, highlighted Soviet advantages in selected categories of weaponry while ignoring indicators of U.S. military advantage in other such categories as well as overall nuclear parity. The president readily dismissed the evidence advanced by his critics as a "constant drumbeat" that confused the essential facts of Soviet belligerence. Reagan's public persona also suggested the validity of his position, as he characteristically advanced his case in an easy, unhurried, and calm presentational style while looking directly into the television audience's collective eye to convey candor and to create an impression of making straightforward, commonsense observations. His sincere gaze and placid style made it easier for Americans to submit to his version of reality, especially since he had identified himself so closely with widely shared values such as securing the peace, protecting children from nuclear nightmares, and modernizing antiquated weapons of national defense. Reagan's rhetorical equation for reifying decivilizing vehicles also included affirmations of American civility. Thus, as a rational, pacific, and democratic nation, the United States under Reagan's leadership attempted to negotiate with the Soviets despite their recalcitrance and made a point of consulting with democratically elected domestic leaders in the formulation of foreign policy.

In sum, Reagan's Cold War rhetoric illustrates both a continuum of decivilizing vehicles and certain literalizing constructions that transform figures of speech into reified tragic orientations. These clusters of vehicles and patterns of reification, however, are neither definitive nor unique to one president or even to U.S. political culture. Indeed, Sam Keen observes that the tendency to dehumanize the face of a foe is universal. Drawing on war propaganda posters and other sources from societies throughout the world, he lists what he calls archetypes of the hostile imagination, which construct the enemy as a stranger, an aggressor, as faceless, a demon, an enemy of God, a barbarian, as greedy, as criminal, a torturer, a rapist, a beast, a reptile, an insect, a germ, as death, and even as a worthy opponent. Clearly, his list of universal archetypes overlaps considerably with the clusters of vehicles found specifically in Reagan's Cold War rhetoric.[18]

Moreover, Reagan's resort to reifying constructions, including historical examples laced with decivilizing vehicles, a commonsense persona supported by a sincere presentational style, close identification with widely shared values such as protecting children and modernizing obsolete weapons, and reassuring reminders of American civility despite Soviet barbarity, is typical but only illustrative of the numerous possibilities for and variations on such strategies. Harry Truman, for instance, embodied his colorful characterizations of Soviet savagery in a plainspoken, straightforward, matter-of-fact presentational style, and American war hawks in 1812, leading up to the confrontation with Great Britain, reified an image of British diabolism using syllogistic and other signs of rational demonstration while framing selected facts within a narrow point of view to verify threatening expectations.[19]

My purpose in drawing attention to decivilizing vehicles and literalizing constructions is not to offer a comprehensive list or final delineation of either but instead to bring them clearly enough into focus to disclose the relationship between internal and external threats to which U.S. political culture seems especially prone. If the types of metaphors and strategies of reification involved are somewhat generic, the way they implicate democracy as a motive for war is particularly problematic for Americans who have identified themselves so closely with achieving a democratic peace. Instead of a motive for peace, democracy has been constructed in a context of decivilizing imagery that makes it into an object of fear, a source of danger, and a motive for war. As Campbell observes, "The ability to represent things as alien, subversive, dirty, or sick, has been pivotal to the articulation of danger in the American experience."[20] The problem to which I now turn is that Americans are alienated from democracy by its historic association with disease and other decivilizing vehicles of death, destruction, and chaos.

Democracy as the Threat from Within

Even though Clinton featured democracy throughout his presidency as the centerpiece of U.S. foreign policy, he articulated a nervous and feverish attitude toward its prospects in a divisive world and even insinuated its potential for causing trouble. During his twelve-day trip to Africa in late March and early April of 1998, for instance, Clinton spoke often and regularly of democratization, globalization, peace, and sustainable development. A democratic peace was the president's vision of Africa's future; globalization, capitalism, free enterprise, and privatization were his collective measure of progress. As Clinton told Ghanaians, "Democracy is spreading. Business is growing. Trade and investment are rising." Ghanaians should be particularly proud, he stressed, that their country boasts the first African-owned company listed on the New York Stock Exchange.[21]

To an American ear, the president's message may sound about right, and African leaders attending the Entebbe Summit for Peace and Prosperity seemed to agree at the time. They joined with Clinton to speak of "building a U.S.–Africa partnership for the 21st Century," including Africa's "full integration into the global economy" in order to stabilize Africa and insure the viability of democracy. Their joint communiqué affirmed also that the "dialogue on democratization" would accept as its core principles that "there is no fixed model for democratic institutions of transformation," that there are "alternative approaches to the democratic management of cultural diversity," and that the dialogue must take into account "differences in historical experience."[22]

This language of partnership, helping, diversity, alternative approaches, and dialogue seems consistent with the democratic theme and ethos Clinton wished to project even in retrospect while representing his African trip a year later as the "new beginning" of a "partnership built on mutual respect and mutual benefit" following "centuries of colonialism and decades of Cold War."[23] Yet, despite the glowing rhetoric, hardly any funds were committed by the Clinton administration to fulfill the promise of democracy in Africa. Nor did the president's subsequent speech in San Francisco mention the concerns of Africans, even though it was billed as the foreign-policy equivalent of his State of the Union address and was otherwise flush with the claim that "the United States has the opportunity and . . . the solemn responsibility to shape a more peaceful, prosperous, democratic world in the 21st century."[24]

This disjunction between Clinton's bold theme of partnering with African countries and his actual practice of ignoring their unique and substantial needs is indicative of a rhetorical legacy of cultural ambivalence about democracy that perpetuates the theme of U.S. exceptionalism, promotes ideological homogeneity and U.S. economic dominance, and constitutes democracy as an object of fear. Clinton's rhetoric is typical of his Cold War predecessors in that it equates the quest for democracy with the aim of world capitalism.[25] With American-style liberal democratic internationalism declaring victory over its Cold War Communist adversary, Clinton made democratization the linchpin of his foreign policy aimed at insuring U.S. security through world leadership and control. That is, democracy was reduced to a legitimizing motive for seeking U.S. security through global hegemony rather than elevated to a commitment to its actual practice. How, we might ask, did this happen? By what rhetorical process was the symbol of democracy so thoroughly circumscribed as an object of desire and contained as an object of fear?

Most immediately, the process is revealed in the way Clinton intertwined his characterization of democracy's fragility with decivilizing imagery to articulate a strong overtone of national insecurity and corresponding desire to dominate others. His message was that the United States must grasp a fleeting opportunity to build on the twin victories of World War II and the Cold War in order to secure democracy and prosperity on a global scale while always remaining alert to the risk of extending freedom and democracy to the world at large. His "myriad variations on the theme of democracy's endangerment and fragility range[d] from allusions to epidemic, plague, purgation, nurturing, and renewal through suggestions of instability, engulfment, containment, storms, darkness, crime, and chaos to invocations of bold journeys, marching, frontier spirit, and civil courage."[26] From the "depth of winter," he spoke in a conflicted, paradoxical style of his hope of forcing a spring rebirth of "the world's oldest democracy" into a hostile environment of "ancient hatreds and new plagues." In a world that had become "more free but less stable," the "fearsome" challenge was to make change America's friend instead of its enemy—in his words, to "shape change, lest it engulf us."[27] Control, not change or even democratic give and take, was Clinton's measure of national security.

A month later, the president spoke of the "imperative of American leadership" as the "great challenge" of confronting "the face of global change" and breaking free of "the death grip of gridlock" now that democracy was "on the march everywhere in the world" yet "thwarted in many places, too" and even as the economy is "still recovering from the after-effects of the Cold War," suffering slow global growth and trade barriers that dimmed the nation's prospects of expanding "the frontiers of democracy."[28] To another audience he remarked on "the ennobling burdens of democracy" together with "the proliferation of demonic weapons" of mass destruction and "resurgent ethnic conflicts" that together in today's "global village" are undermining U.S. security even as they blur the distinction between domestic and foreign policy.[29] Democracy is a "trend" not an inevitability, he stressed in a midterm address to the Nixon Center, nor will it be easy to "establish or shore up fragile democracies."[30] Indeed, democracy itself and the free flow of information it permits increases the risks of terrorism throughout the world, Clinton underscored in his May 1995 speech in Russia.[31] Thus, democracy was doubly constructed in Clinton's equivocal style as simultaneously risky and at risk, unruly as well as fragile, ailing and struggling to be reborn, and dependent on economic recovery for its own health. It was too weak to stand alone, too vulnerable to the plague of ethnic conflict, and too likely to spread the disease of terrorism. For the safety of the nation, then, democracy must be controlled and contained more than practiced and promoted.

This association of democracy with disease and other decivilizing vehicles in Clinton's foreign policy rhetoric reflects the prevailing history of the mythos of the distempered demos in U.S. political culture. During the formative years of the early republic, the people as assembled citizens engaged in decision-making deliberations were reduced to the status of bystanders, constitutionally supplanted by representatives elected and appointed from the political elite. This was the "republican remedy" Madison proposed in Federalist 10 for the "diseases" of popular government because citizen self-rule could "admit of no cure for the mischiefs of faction."[32] Democracy, according to Richard Matthews, was to Madison "a fool's illusion," since cool reason could not withstand the hot passions stirred by people assembled in groups, even if every member of the group were a Socrates.[33] Thus, as Madison wrote in Federalist 63, the Constitution would safeguard against an "infection of violent passions" by *"the total exclusion of the people in their collective capacity"* from any share in government.[34] Representation was the "healing principle" that would arrest the "decay and eventual death of the republican body politic" by allowing "the natural aristocracy" to govern in the name of the people as if it were the people.[35]

Madison's diagnosis not only prevailed over time but created a peculiar kind of democracy and a distinctly American political theory that, as Gordon Wood concludes, impoverished "later American thought."[36] George Kennan, father of the Cold War containment doctrine, steeped in political "realism" and sympathetic to Madisonian remedies, underscored the unhealthy influences to which democracy might easily succumb in his influential construction of a totalitarian threat—that "which is inherently frail and feeble, as a function of unbridled emotionalism, irrational impulses, and moralistic sensibilities, needs a totally antiseptic environment free of foreign ideological germs to insure against its demise."[37] Even the present surge of interest over the last decade in what is often called deliberative or rational democracy is a continuation of the Madisonian tradition—a fearful, elitist discourse against democratic distemper that seeks to tame popular passions and thus preserve the integrity of representative democracy and the primacy of liberalism in an age marked by the corrosive influence of mass communications and the ascendancy of the rhetorical presidency.[38] In short, a diseased domestic demos threatens the survival of the liberal republic no less than the nation's foreign adversaries; indeed, domestic and foreign Others are equally decivilized in a shared rhetorical universe of interchangeable, interlinking, and literalized vehicles.

As an object simultaneously of fear and desire, then, democracy is something that must be carefully contained, both to keep it from erupting spontaneously into a distempered frenzy of popular passion and to protect it from exposure to the deadly ideological germs of foreign predators, demons, and evil forces. Typically, democracy in this sense has been ideologically clustered with god terms such as *freedom* and *liberty* from the pantheon of liberalism, which remains America's dominant mode of power talk, and together these terms have been represented throughout U.S. history as especially fragile and vulnerable to external forces, thus providing much of the rationale for a characteristically uncompromising American foreign policy.[39] *Democracy, liberty,* and *freedom* are customarily feminized terms that require protection from brute forces threatening to overwhelm and subdue them. Similarly, they are rendered vulnerable as acts of conception and birth, a cherished child struggling against the disease of subjugation, a great experiment that could well go wrong, a flickering flame in a stormy sea of totalitarianism, a defenseless quarry pursued by relentless predators, and so on.[40]

As a motive for war, democracy must be secured according to these rhetorical conventions and in the paradoxical meaning of the term that is peculiar to U.S. political culture. The world must be made safe for democracy; indeed, peace can only be envisioned as a democratic world order.[41] Such a world order, though, promises not just an environment free of foreign ideological germs and other barbarisms but also a universal container devoid of democratic distemper. It is a world not so much safe for democracy as safe from the supposedly debilitating effects of popular democracy, a world legitimized by the symbol of self-rule but sanitized of its robust practice. Any threat to this vision of U.S. hegemony, this Wilsonian "goal of a capitalist-international system of free trade and liberal order," constitutes grounds for a call to arms to win a "democratic" peace against the forces of savagery within and without.[42]

What should be recognized here is the irony of a reified metaphor of democratic disease legitimizing wars to secure a suspect democratic peace. Through the agency of decivilizing vehicles, the nation's conflicted attitude toward difference and democracy itself serves as a readily available motive for war or domination of foreign Others or both. Americans are prone to fight for a democratic ethic they have yet to practice or trust in full and thus feel compelled to contain and control instead. The enemy tenuously contained within the body politic projects a corresponding threat onto external adversaries operating outside the porous boundary of the polity. Differences with external Others, taken as signs of deviance and omens of evil more even than as evidence of error or of competing perspectives, are exaggerated instead of ameliorated, disciplined rather than addressed, and eventually annihilated out of fear and intolerance. Once recognized and understood as such, the incongruity of a people alienated from themselves may trigger a revival of Thomas Jefferson's long dormant alternative to

Madison's overly belligerent republic of fear.[43] Just as Madison's legacy is a liberal democracy founded in the pessimistic image of a sick people, Jefferson's comparatively radical commitment to democratic practice would bolster the nation's confidence in its own health and perhaps diminish somewhat its chronic insecurity in a world indelibly marked by difference.[44]

Notes

1. William J. Clinton, "Inaugural Address," 20 January 1997, White House Virtual Library, http://www.whitehouse.gov (accessed 31 December 1997). For printed copies of President Clinton's speeches, remarks, and other public statements referenced throughout this study, see *Public Papers of the Presidents of the United States 1993:* (Volume 1) William J. Clinton (Washington, D.C.: Government Printing Office, 1994); *Public Papers of the Presidents of the United States 1994:* Book 1: William J. Clinton (Washington, D.C.: Government Printing Office, 1995); *Public Papers of the Presidents of the United States 1997:* Book 1: William J. Clinton: 1 January to 30 June (Washington, D.C.: Government Printing Office, 1999); *Public Papers of the Presidents of the United States 1997:* Book 2: William J. Clinton: 1 July–December 31, 1997 (Washington, D.C.: Government Printing Office, 1999); and *Public Papers of the Presidents of the United States 1999:* Book 1: William J. Clinton: January 1 to June 30, 1999 (Washington, D.C.: Government Printing Office, 2001).

2. Spencer R. Weart, *Never at War: Why Democracies Will Not Fight One Another* (New Haven: Yale University Press, 1998); Bruce Russett, *Grasping the Democratic Peace: Principles for a Post–Cold War World* (Princeton: Princeton University Press, 1993); William J. Clinton, "State of the Union Address," 26 January 1994, Whitehouse Virtual Library, http://www.whitehouse.gov (accessed 24 December 1997).

3. John Lewis Gaddis, *The United States and the End of the Cold War: Implications, Reconsiderations, Provocations* (New York: Oxford University Press, 1992), 13–14.

4. Kenneth Burke, *A Grammar of Motives* (Berkeley and Los Angeles: University of California Press, 1969), 503–17; idem, *Attitudes toward History,* 3d ed. (Berkeley and Los Angeles: University of California Press, 1984); idem, *Permanence and Change: An Anatomy of Purpose,* 3d ed. (Berkeley and Los Angeles: University of California Press, 1984); idem, *The Rhetoric of Religion: Studies in Logology* (Berkeley and Los Angeles:

University of California Press, 1970); William H. Rueckert, *Encounters with Kenneth Burke* (Urbana: University of Illinois Press, 1994).

5. Robert L. Ivie, "Tragic Fear and the Rhetorical Presidency: Combating Evil in the Persian Gulf," in *Beyond the Rhetorical Presidency*, ed. Martin J. Medhurst (College Station: Texas A&M University Press, 1996), 153–78, 246–49; as quoted in Carol K. Winkler, "Narrative Reframing of Public Argument: George Bush's Handling of the Persian Gulf Conflict," in *Warranting Assent: Case Studies in Argument Evaluation*, ed. Edward Schiappa (Albany: SUNY Press, 1995), 33–55.

6. William J. Clinton, "Text of President Clinton's Address to the Nation," 11 June 1999, *New York Times*, http://nytimes.com/ (accessed 11 June 1999).

7. William J. Clinton, "1999–06–02 Remarks by the President at United States Air Force Academy Commencement Ceremony," 4 June 1999, public distribution list, the White House, Office of the Press Secretary.

8. Timothy Garton Ash, "The New Adolf Hitler?" *Time.com*, 1 April 1999, http://cgi.pathfinder.com/time/magazine/articles/0,3266,22232,00.html (accessed 5 April 1999); Neil A. Lewis, "A Word Bolsters Case for Allied Intervention," *New York Times on the Web*, 4 April 1999, http://www.nytimes.com/library/world/europe/040499kosovo-legal.html (accessed 4 April 1999).

9. Robert L. Ivie, "Metaphor and Motive in the Johnson Administration's Vietnam War Rhetoric," in *Texts in Context: Critical Dialogues on Significant Episodes in American Political Rhetoric*, ed. Michael C. Leff and Fred J. Kauffeld (Davis, Calif.: Hermagoras Press, 1989), 121–41.

10. David Campbell, *Writing Security: United States Foreign Policy and the Politics of Identity* (Minneapolis: University of Minnesota Press, 1992), 1–2.

11. Robert L. Ivie, "Images of Savagery in American Justifications for War," *Communication Monographs* 47 (1980): 279–94.

12. Robert L Ivie, "Speaking 'Common Sense' about the Soviet Threat: Reagan's Rhetorical Stance," *Western Journal of Speech Communication* 48 (1984): 39–50; Sam Keen, *Faces of the Enemy: Reflections of the Hostile Imagination* (San Francisco: Harper and Row, 1986).

13. Quoted in Ivie, "Speaking 'Common Sense,'" 39–50.

14. Discussed in ibid.

15. Eugene Miller, "Metaphor and Political Knowledge," *American Political Science Review* 73 (1979): 160–62.

16. Burke, *Permanence and Change*, 98.

17. Quoted in Ivie, "Speaking 'Common Sense,'" 43.

18. Keen, *Faces of the Enemy*, 16–88.

19. Robert L. Ivie, "Literalizing the Metaphor of Soviet Savagery: President Truman's Plain Style," *Southern Speech Communication Journal* 51 (1986): 91–105; idem, "The Metaphor of Force in Prowar Discourse: The Case of 1812," *Quarterly Journal of Speech* 68 (1982): 240–53.

20. Campbell, *Writing Security,* 2.

21. William J. Clinton, "Remarks by the President to the People of Ghana," 4 March 1998, the White House, Office of the Press Secretary, http://www.pub.whitehouse.gov/uri-res/12 . . . pdi://oma.cop .gov.us/1998/3/25/20.text.2 (accessed 23 March 1999).

22. "Communique: Entebbe Summit for Peace and Prosperity," 4 March 1998, the White House, Office of the Press Secretary, http://www.pub .whitehouse.gov/uri-res/12 . . . pdi://oma.cop.gov.us/1998/3/26 /10.text.1 (accessed 25 March 1999).

23. William J. Clinton, "Remarks by President Clinton and President Rawlings of Ghana at Welcoming Ceremony," 24 February 1999, the White House, Office of the Press Secretary, http://www.pub.white-house.gov/uri-res/12 . . . pdi://oma.cop.gov.us/1999/2/24/15.text.1 (accessed 4 March 1999).

24. William J. Clinton, "Remarks by the President on Foreign Policy," 26 February 1999, the White House, Office of the Press Secretary, http://www.pub.whitehouse.gov/uri-res/12 . . . n:pdi//oma.cop .gov.us/19999/3/1/3.text.1 (accessed 4 March 1999).

25. Robert L. Ivie, "A New Democratic World Order?" in *Critical Reflections on the Cold War: Linking Rhetoric and History,* ed. Martin J. Medhurst and H. W. Brands (College Station: Texas A&M University Press, 2000), 247–65.

26. Ibid., 252.

27. William J. Clinton, "Inaugural Speech," 24 December 1993, White House Virtual Library, http://www.whitehouse.gov (accessed 20 January 1997).

28. William J. Clinton, "Remarks by the President at American University Centennial Celebration," 24 December 1993, White House Virtual Library, http://www.whitehouse.gov (accessed 26 February 1997).

29. William J. Clinton, "A Strategic Alliance with Russian Reform," 1 April 1993, White House Virtual Library, http://www.whitehouse.gov (accessed 24 December 1997).

30. William J. Clinton, "President William Jefferson Clinton Address to the Nixon Center for Peace and Freedom Policy Conference," 1 March 1995, White House Virtual Library, http://www.whitehouse.gov (accessed 31 December 1997).

31 William J. Clinton, "Remarks by the President to Students of Moscow State University," 10 May 1995, White House Virtual Library, http://www.whitehouse.gov (accessed 31 December 1997).

32. Quoted in Robert L. Ivie, "Distempered Demos: Myth, Metaphor, and U.S. Political Culture," in *Myth: A New Symposium*, ed. Gregory A. Schrempp and William F. Hansen (Bloomington: Indiana University Press, 2002), 165–79.

33 Richard K. Matthews, *If Men Were Angels: James Madison and the Heartless Empire of Reason* (Lawrence: University Press of Kansas, 1995), 51, 55.

34. Madison's emphasis. Quoted in Ivie, "Distempered Demos."

35. Gordon S. Wood, *The Creation of the American Republic, 1776–1787* (New York: W. W. Norton, 1969), 599, 606.

36. Matthews, *If Men Were Angels*, 25; Wood, *The Creation of the American Republic*, 562.

37. Robert L. Ivie, "Realism Masking Fear: George F. Kennan's Political Rhetoric," in *Post-realism: The Rhetorical Turn in International Relations*, ed. Francis A. Beer and Robert Hariman (East Lansing: Michigan State University Press, 1996), 67.

38. Joseph M. Bessett, *The Mild Voice of Reason: Deliberative Democracy and American National Government* (Chicago: University of Chicago Press, 1994); Simone Chambers, *Reasonable Democracy: Jürgen Habermas and the Politics of Discourse* (Ithaca, N.Y.: Cornell University Press, 1996); James S. Fishkin, *Democracy and Deliberation: New Directions for Democratic Reform* (New Haven: Yale University Press, 1991); Amy Gutmann and Dennis Thompson, *Democracy and Disagreement* (Cambridge, Mass.: Belknap Press, 1996); Jeffrey K. Tulis, *The Rhetorical Presidency* (Princeton: Princeton University Press, 1987).

39. Russell L. Hanson, *The Democratic Imagination in America: Conversations with Our Past* (Princeton: Princeton University Press, 1985), 13–14.

40. Robert L. Ivie, "The Ideology of Freedom's 'Fragility' in American Foreign Policy Argument," *Journal of the American Forensic Association* 24 (1986): 91–105.

41. Amos Perlmutter, *Making the World Safe for Democracy: A Century of Wilsonianism and Its Totalitarian Challengers* (Chapel Hill: University of North Carolina Press, 1997).

42. Ibid., 62.

43. Richard K. Matthews, *The Radical Politics of Thomas Jefferson: A Revisionist View* (Lawrence: University Press of Kansas, 1984).

44. James Chace and Caleb Carr, *America Invulnerable: The Quest for Absolute Security from 1812 to Star Wars* (New York: Summit Books, 1988).

The Causal Power of Metaphor

Cueing Democratic Identities in Russia and Beyond

Richard D. Anderson, Jr.

When metaphors are said to *cause* political phenomena, political scientists often object. Their objections are rarely specific. Rather than offering reasoned arguments why metaphors must be causally impotent, they often respond with bewilderment, even outrage, to sentences that start with "metaphor" as the subject and continue with "causes" appearing as the verb followed by a noun phrase mentioning any political phenomenon. The tangled underbrush of confusion may be cleared by setting forth how metaphor can cause political phenomena. The explanation begins with a brief discussion of the definition of cause and of the potential of metaphor to qualify by this definition, proceeds to reviewing a case showing an association between change in metaphor and change in politics, and then analyzes how metaphors and other linguistic phenomena can cause politics. Of course, because metaphor is only one of the devices by which discourse affects politics, the causal variable is discourse in general rather than metaphor in particular, but because discourse always uses the device of metaphor as well as other linguistic tools, metaphors are also causes.

Cause and Metaphors

In their standard textbook on methodology, the distinguished political scientists Gary King, Robert O. Keohane, and Sidney Verba argue for this definition of "cause": "the causal effect is the difference between the systematic component of observations made when the explanatory variable takes one value and the systematic component of comparable observations made when the explanatory variable takes on another value [emphasis in original deleted]."[1] Unpacked, this definition reduces to the proposition that some x causes y if three conditions are satisfied. First, x and y must be variables, that is, capable of taking more than one value and susceptible to observation. King, Keohane, and Verba claim that variables in the sciences are composed of a systematic component and a component of random fluctuation, with the latter component varying the estimate of the causal effect rather than changing its definition. Second, when x changes, a difference must appear in the value of y. Third, x must be "explanatory." The change in x must somehow "explain" y. Of course this third condition is quite vague: what does it mean "to explain"? While vague, explanation has two elements, one easily specifiable, the other not. The easily specifiable element is antecedence: the explanatory variable is the one whose value changes first. The other element is a reason why change in the explanatory variable should be expected to produce a difference in the other variable. It is this need for a reason that makes the condition vague, for the reason why one cause produces one effect may, of course, be entirely different from the reason why some other cause produces some other effect. Being peculiar to the given combination of cause and effect, the meaning of "explanation" is not specifiable in advance.

By this definition of cause, metaphors may be capable of causation. Metaphors clearly qualify by the first condition. They vary, and particularly the frequency of occurrence of a given metaphor is capable of varying. The variation displays a systematic component. In their now standard work on metaphor, George Lakoff and Mark Johnson show that metaphor consists not merely of isolated instances of original figurative language but of repetitive and pervasive patterns of language that may even seem literal to the persons engaged in communication. The semantics of every natural language consists of a large, diverse set of families of metaphors, famously exemplified by "argument is war." Thus English speakers in an argument "attack" each other's "positions" and "defend" against debaters'"thrusts" and "sallies." Communicators' choice of metaphors from this set determines the meaning that they exchange.[2]

The ability of metaphor to satisfy the second condition in relation to politics is an empirical question. If it can be shown that change in communicators' choice of metaphors (especially change in the frequency of their appearance) varies systematically with changes in politics, then metaphor satisfies the second condition for cause. The third condition is partly empirical and partly theoretical. Discovery of an empirical association between change in metaphors and change in politics leaves open the question of which is a candidate for causality, but observation that the metaphorical change precedes the political change closes that question. The real issue is theoretical: how can metaphors change politics? And particularly, why should it be supposed that both the change in metaphors and the change in politics are not attributable to some other deeper, underlying cause such as economic progress, social differentiation, or attitudinal transformation?

Metaphors and Political Change: A Case Study of Democratization

Exploration of how metaphors can change politics might usefully proceed by considering a case. Of course, no single case can demonstrate that metaphors are causal. But investigation of any single case begins the process of accumulating cases that over time can sum into an empirical test of causality. The case presented here concerns the transformation of Soviet authoritarianism into Russian electoral politics. The presentation begins with the association between political change and change in metaphors and the antecedence of the latter and segues into the reason why metaphorical change should alter politics.

Between 1985 and 1991, Soviet authoritarianism collapsed and, within the boundaries of the largest Soviet republic, Russia, politics turned electoral. While there remained controversy about whether the changes qualified Russia as "democratic," the means of selecting Russia's rulers changed dramatically. In the Soviet period Russia was ruled by a group of, normally, ten to fifteen men who composed the Politburo of the Central Committee of the Communist Party. Empowered to decide any matter that they chose to consider, the members of the Politburo were elected by the Central Committee, which at its largest size numbered about three hundred persons. Even in this election, however, the Politburo ran as a single slate nominated by its own members, and the Politburo itself had previously decided who would be chosen for the Central Committee. By contrast, since 1990 Russia has been governed by an elected legislature chosen in contested elections in which all adults may vote, and since 1991 the legislature has shared power with a president elected in the same manner. While the legislature elected in 1990 was chosen in circumstances that severely biased the results in favor of Communist candidates, a constitutional crisis in 1993 resulted in the adoption of a new Constitution. While the new Constitution may have unduly reduced the powers of the legislature relative to those of the executive and may thereby have biased presidential elections in favor of the incumbent, the legislature itself is chosen by rules that give unfair advantage to no party. Parties opposing the incumbent president have repeatedly won legislative elections.

Table 1 shows the association between these changes in Russian politics and the frequency of appearance of certain metaphors in public addresses by the Soviet Union's rulers. The table reports the frequency, per thousand words of text, of two kinds of metaphors—those that express relative size and those that express personal superiority or subordination. The size metaphors consist of five basic terms: *bolshoi* (big), *krupnyi* (large), *shirokii* (wide), *vysokii* (high), and *velikii* (great). If more abstruse terms, such as *titanic* or *gigantic,* were included, the authoritarian frequencies would increase slightly relative to the transitional and electoral frequencies. The metaphors of personal superiority or subordination include a metaphor that compares authoritarian rule to parenting, *vospitanie,* or "upbringing"; a metaphor that compares political officials to persons of superior intellect, *rabotnik,* or "person doing intellectual work"; a metaphor that compares

Table 1. Metaphors of Size and Personal Superiority and Subordination in Authoritarian, Transitional, and Electoral Russian Political Discourse

Politics	Five Size Metaphors	Four Metaphors of Personal Superiority or Subordination
Authoritarian	11.5	6.8
Transitional	6.0	3.1
Electoral	3.8	1.6
Vernacular 1977	5.3	1.6
Vernacular 1993	3.8	1.6

Occurrences per thousand words, by type of politics and measure of vernacular usage political activity to an assignment set by an authority such as a teacher, *zadacha*, or "task"; and a metaphor that compares the regime to a military formation, *stroi*, or "order" or "array," and its variants (but not including instances of *perestroika*, which means "transformation" or "reordering" and does not imply subordination). Although words formed from the root *stroi* also mean "building" or "construction" (including *perestroika*, "rebuilding") and are usually translated into English with those terms, in Russian this meaning is metaphorical: to a Russian the activity of "building" is putting something into order.[3]

The authoritarian, transitional, and electoral counts are derived from three sets of fifty political texts. For the authoritarian period, the fifty texts were originally uttered by members of the ruling Politburo. They consist of printed versions of forty-nine speeches and one "interview" (an exchange of written questions and answers) delivered between 1966 and February 1985. For the transitional period, the fifty texts were also originally uttered by members of the ruling Politburo. They also consist of speeches or interviews (originally conducted as oral exchanges and then revised and printed in newspapers) dating from 1989, the year in which Mikhail Gorbachev's reforms first eventuated in formation of a legislative body partly chosen in contested elections. For the electoral period, the fifty texts were originally uttered by prominent politicians. They consist of speeches, newspaper reports of journalists' oral interviews, or newspaper or journal articles by contestants for political power. The politicians are drawn from across the political spectrum and include a few extremists as well as persons central to the political spectrum. These texts originally appeared between October 1991, when Russian president Boris Yeltsin was already exercising effective political power after the failure of the August 1991 coup against Soviet president Gorbachev, and December 1993, when the Russian legislature was first elected under the new Constitution.

The table also presents two measures labeled "Vernacular 1977" and "Vernacular 1993." These counts report the frequency of the same lexemes as counted in two large samples (approximately a million words each) of a wide range of diverse Russian texts. A Soviet team published the first count in 1977, while a Swedish team published the second count in 1993. The two counts are interpreted as the frequency of these lexemes in the Russian vernacular. Because the resulting frequency dictionaries do not distinguish metaphorical from literal uses of the lexemes in question, the counts exaggerate the frequency with which the metaphors occur in ordinary language. By contrast, in political texts there appear to be few if any literal usages, with the exception of references to construction, which have been removed from the count. Moreover, compiled from texts published under Soviet censorship, the 1977 measure contains a heavy component of politicized texts that bias the measure toward the authoritarian norm. While the 1993 measure incorporates literary texts dating as early as 1960, no journalistic texts are included with dates earlier than 1985. Thus the corpus counted as measuring the 1993 vernacular excludes political texts from the period before the advent of Gorbachev.[4]

As table 1 reveals, as politics became more electoral, political elites used many fewer metaphors of size and of personal superiority or subordination. If the metaphors of size lent authoritarian discourse its quality that one Soviet linguist designated "the monumentality of the forms and resonance of speech," this monumentality diminished in the transitional period and disappeared in the electoral period. While the rate of decline varies by metaphor, all the metaphors are least frequent in the electoral texts. Indeed the only metaphor of subordination that persists into the electoral period is *zadacha*, "task," while the scattered instances of the others become either negative commentaries on the authoritarian past or turn into metaphors about something other than politics. *Zadacha* itself declines in frequency and, unlike metaphors of military subordination, parenthood, or intellectual superiority, is fully consistent with electoral politics. Even in an electoral polity, politicians present themselves as authorities who can guide social activities, and just as the English counterpart and translation, "problem," appears both in schoolteachers' discourse and in political discourse (as "policy problem," "social problem"), so does *zadacha* appear in both educational and political Russian. It is striking that for both types of metaphor, the frequency in electoral usage is identical to one or both measures of frequency in vernacular usage. Not too much should be made of this striking identity, since the inclusion of literal uses in the two measures of the vernacular means that the metaphorical uses must be somewhat less frequent than they are in the electoral texts, but one may safely conclude that the decreasing frequency in the three kinds of political texts converges toward the average frequency for the vernacular.

Examination of a specific example in context reveals that these metaphors are not serving only semantic purposes and may not be adding semantic meaning at all. A characteristic example from authoritarian discourse is sentence (1), originally uttered by the Politburo member overseeing propaganda work, Mikhail Suslov, in a 1979 speech:

(1) *Peredoviki . . . pokazyvaiut vysokie obraztsy otnosheniia k svoim obiazannostiam pered obshchestvom.*

The foremost workers . . . display high models of an attitude toward their obligations to society.

Since Russian *obrazets* and its English translation, "model," bear similar connotations of an ideal quality that others should emulate, the adjective "high" is superfluous to any semantic meaning. Except possibly that "high" adds emphasis, Suslov's sentence bears the same semantic meaning with or without the metaphor "high." While adding little or no semantic meaning, however, the metaphor does serve a pragmatic function. Pragmatics concerns "what [speakers] hope to achieve by talking, the relation between the form they choose and the effect they want it to have (and the effect it does have)."[5] Every utterance bears both a constative and a performative meaning, what the utterance says and what the utterance does. Both meanings depend on what knowledge people use to interpret the utterance. Across cultures people understand references to height as a scale with a metric, and they position the normal, ordinary, or everyday as occupying the middle of that scale.[6] Thus a reference to something as "high," as in sentence (1), moves whatever is called "high" out of the ordinary or normal.

Suslov's metaphor thus told his audiences that what the Communist Party wanted—in this case, conscientious labor—exceeded what people normally do, and the metaphor ranks the Communist Party's goals above theirs. Descriptions of Communist officials as engaging in the parenting activity *vospitanie*, "upbringing," over everyone else and labeling of Communist officials as *rabotniki*, "workers in intellectual activities," as opposed to *trudiashchiesia*, "laborers," the term used for everyone else, accomplished a parallel pragmatic objective of elevating Communist officials relative to everyone else. Metaphors characterizing everyone else as accepting assignments from the party or as standing in a military-style formation relative to the party pursued the same objective in reverse, informing everyone that they stood under the Communists. Talmy Givon notes:

> in paired antonymous adjectives, most typically of size, extension, elevation, texture, loudness, brightness, speed, weight etc., the positive member of the pair stands for both the possession of the property (i.e., the *positive* extreme) and the generic designation of the property (i.e., the *unmarked*). This is because the positive extreme has greater *perceptual saliency* [emphasis in original].[7]

Increasing their perceptual salience, the Communist speakers' metaphors made them seem more important and designated them as positive relative to the general population. Their metaphors also attributed to themselves a generic quality that the population under their rule was implied to lack. It was because of these pragmatic messages that the nine metaphors counted in table 1 comprised nearly 2 percent of all words used in authoritarian speeches.

During the transition year 1989, affirmations of the superiority of the Communist Party's goals and of its officials and of social subordination decreased in frequency even in the discourse of the Communist Party's own leaders, the Politburo, even though nothing had happened to the institutional or political means by which they were chosen. While they had introduced a new political institution, the Congress of People's Deputies, some of whose members were chosen in elections sufficiently fair that a few prominent Communist officials lost, the Politburo members themselves did not stand for election to the Congress except by their handpicked Central Committee. At the same time as metaphors of size and of superiority and subordination decreased, a new kind of metaphor began to increase in the Politburo's speeches and interviews, as reported in table 2. This new kind of metaphor drew on Latinate terms, most of which have precise semantic equivalents with Slavic etymology. In Communist discourse these Latinate terms had been used only in the context of international diplomacy.[8] As the 1977 frequency indicates, they had previously been extraordinarily rare in Russian, with some not occurring in the 1977 corpus at all. By intruding Latinate metaphors into discussions of domestic politics, particularly the word *dialog*, the Communist rulers implicitly compared the relationships between party and society to a negotiation between equal sovereignties. Analyzing a corpus drawn heavily from journalism from the Gorbachev era, the 1993 examination of the vernacular finds even more frequent occurrences of these metaphors—a clear sign of the well established fact that dialogue with society was more popular among journalists and intellectuals than among Politburo members.

Reluctantly calling for negotiations, Communist Party leaders required an interlocutor. As a result, the metaphor of "society" became far more frequent during 1989, and as sentence (2) exemplifies, society itself acquired new discursive properties. In sentence (2), taken from a speech by Gorbachev, "society" acquired a capacity for independent action that had been wholly denied to it in authoritarian discourse. Attribution of this capacity enabled the Communist Party to find a partner for the negotiations to

Table 2. Metaphors of Community and of Negotiation

Politics	Negotiation	Society
Authoritarian	0.3	1.2
Transitional	2.2	3.7
Electoral	1.9	1.2
Vernacular 1977	(0.04)	0.8
Vernacular 1993	3.7	0.8

Occurrences per thousand words, by type of politics and measure of vernacular usage

which the discourse of its leaders now summoned. With the emergence of electoral politics after 1991, usages of "society" moved back toward the vernacular norm, whether measured in 1977 or 1993.

(2) *Partiia tol'ko ukrepit svoi pozitsii, esli ona budet vzaimodeistvovat' . . . so vsem obshchestvom.*

The party will only strengthen its positions if it will interact with . . . the whole society.

While the 1989 discourse of the Politburo displayed noticeable change relative to that of the authoritarian era, the institutions by which its members were chosen remained, as of 1989, entirely unchanged. The Politburo was still the ruling executive of the Soviet Union, although during 1989 its powers steadily waned as Russian and other Soviet societies answered the Politburo's summons to political activism. When the Politburo disappeared, the new political powers in the emerging Russian democracy abandoned the metaphor of a negotiation between political authority and society. References to society and to negotiations diminished, and in sentence (3), taken from a speech by Russian president Yeltsin, a new metaphor now subordinated political authority to society:

(3) *Nuzhno, chtoby s pomoshch'iu Konstitutsii obshchestvo postavilo gosudarstvo sebe na sluzhbu.*

It is necessary that with the help of the Constitution the society should place the state at its service.

Of the metaphors associated with international negotiation, only references to "stabilization" and "stability" increase in the electoral corpus, and they begin to refer to society and the economy rather than to politics.

In electoral discourse references to "dialogue" also acquire new contexts. Rather than a top-down dialogue between party and society, as in transitional discourse, there emerges a horizontal dialogue among alternative contenders for political power, as in sentence (4), taken from an interview with a leader of the political party PRES:

(4) *Konstitutsionnoe soveshchanie pokazalo vozmozhnost' dialoga vsekh politicheskikh sil Rossii.*

The constitutional convention showed the possibility of a dialogue among all the political forces of Russia.

To move from vertical relationships of superiority and subordination to horizontal relationships of negotiation, electoral politicians also invoke the metaphor of sides characteristic of political discourse in established democracies, as shown in table 3. The metaphors *storonnik* and *protivnik* bear the literal meanings, respectively, of "one who is on a side" and "one who is against" and translate in their metaphorical meanings as "partisan" and "opponent." While these metaphors occur in Communist authoritarian discourse, they are used only in reference to international politics, and the Soviet Union is invariably a *storonnik,* while *protivnik* invariably refers to foreigners or to persons within the Communist world labeled as subversives allied with foreigners. In the electoral discourse they begin to refer to political groupings. They are also associated with the emergence of a political *spektr,* "spectrum," composed of parties or choices bearing color labels such as "reds," "browns," and "whites." Again, while "red" of course appears in authoritarian discourse, rather surprisingly not even the Communist Party of the Soviet Union, as opposed to its historical predecessors, is referred to as "red." "Sides" are also metaphors for choices, with both Russian and English possessing the idiom, "on one side . . . on the other side" to describe a choice. By labeling politics as an act of taking sides, the new metaphors implied to Russians the presence of choices in politics.

Table 3. Metaphors of Sides

	Politics	Sides
	Authoritarian	0.2
	Transitional	0.2
	Electoral	1.2
	Vernacular 1977	2.1
	Vernacular 1993	1.7

Occurrences per thousand words, by type of politics

Again the electoral frequency is much closer to both measures of the vernacular frequency, although this similarity should be viewed with reservation because the overwhelming majority of the vernacular occurrences are color terms used literally rather than metaphorically. It may well be the frequency of metaphorical uses in electoral discourse slightly exceeds the corresponding frequency in vernacular discourse.

In sum, as Soviet authoritarianism gave way to Russian democracy, the metaphors used to describe political relationships changed. Metaphors positioning the Communist rulers above society diminished, displaced first by metaphors comparing the relationship between the rulers and society to a dialogue between equals, superseded in turn by metaphors subordinating political authority to society and comparing politics to a choice between opposing sides. Political discourse in the authoritarian period was noticeably different from the Russian vernacular, became more similar to it in the transitional period, and then became quantitatively indistinguishable from the vernacular in the electoral period. The important point for a causal argument, of course, is that each of these changes in Russian discourse *preceded* the corresponding change in political institutions.

Political Metaphors and Democratization: Effects of Some "Deeper" Cause?

While the association between change in metaphors and democratization, and the antecedence of the former, has been shown only for Russia, it would be wholly unsurprising to find similar patterns, possibly involving somewhat different particular metaphors, across the range of other cases. One metaphor of sides, the distinction between "left" and "right," is of course ubiquitous in democratic politics. So is the metaphor of dialogue or negotiation among these sides. Conversely, the "monumentality" found in Soviet authoritarian discourse is ubiquitous in the discourse of monarchic and dictatorial rule. So is a parenting metaphor, the paternalism of the monarch or dictator over his subjects. The empirical research on many cases remains to be done, particularly the documentation that change in metaphors precedes change in political institutions, but there is every reason to expect that the Russian pattern will prove to be typical.

There remains the question of why something as seemingly weak and transient as metaphor should be capable of transforming something as durable and powerful as the fundamental institutions of politics, and particularly whether the change in metaphors cannot be attributed to some deeper, more underlying cause. The fact is, however, that political scientists have failed, despite numerous attempts over many years, to develop any coherent theory of democracy. Having carefully and thoroughly reviewed two decades of research on democratic transition, the able comparativist Barbara Geddes concludes: "It seems as though there should be a parsimonious and compelling explanation of the transitions, but the explanations proposed thus far have been confusingly complicated, careless about basic methodological details, often more useful as description than explanation, and surprisingly inconsistent with each other." She then observes that "after 20 years of observation and analysis during the third wave of academic interest in democratization, we can be reasonably certain that a positive relationship between [economic] development and democracy exists, though we do not know why." And even this relationship turns out to be quite weak. All but one of the most developed countries are democratic (the exception is Singapore), all but a few of the least developed are undemocratic (with exceptions such as Mongolia and Benin), but at intermediate levels, such as that of Russia, variation in economic development appears to exercise no influence on the probability of finding democracy in a given society.[9]

In fact even Geddes's suitably qualified and circumspect assertion exaggerates the relationship between economic development and democracy. While synchronic analysis finds that the most highly developed states are democratic, diachronic analysis would show that democratization began in those states when their economic development also had attained only the intermediate levels at which economic development and democracy are uncorrelated. In most of the states that are now democracies, democratization began in the nineteenth century, when economic development was beginning but had not progressed very far. In a few contemporary democracies, the World War II losers Japan, Germany, and Italy, where democratization occurred under Allied occupation after 1945, it began when per capita gross domestic product was very low. And of course if the measure is completion of democracy, which may be defined as extension of the right to vote to all adult citizens, the United States is an example of a state with a very high level of economic development that did not qualify as fully democratic until after 1965. It goes without saying that highly developed prewar Germany was not democratic at all.

In short, despite decades of effort, political scientists have discovered no deeper or underlying cause that accounts for both democratization and any associated change in metaphors that one would expect to discover if the research was conducted on all the cases. Of course if democratization is associated with a transformation of political metaphors, no such deeper or underlying cause could be found—and that explains why political scientists have looked in vain. By definition a metaphor represents its topic by referring to something else, implied to be similar but retaining difference. If authoritarian rulers metaphorically enlarge themselves and their activities relative to the population under their rule, or if they metaphorically compare themselves to authoritative superiors and the population to a military rank and file, these metaphors are meaningful precisely because of the realities that the rulers are *not* larger than the population and that the population is *not* standing at attention. In other words, production of metaphor is an autonomous creative act *not* derivative from any other social or physical reality except itself. Consequently, when one observes a changing pattern of metaphors in association with change in some political phenomenon, the metaphors cannot be attributable to any other cause except themselves. And of course the notion that causality is "deep" or "underlying" is itself one of the families of spatial metaphors, together with "proximate" and "ultimate," by which humans conceive causation, not any actual property of a cause. Thus something as superficial or transient as metaphor is entirely eligible as a cause.

How Metaphors Cause Democratization: Overcoming the Illogic of Collective Action

Although democratization is both an institutional change and a behavioral change, theorists have gone astray in part because they have concentrated on institutions to the neglect of behavior. While democratization means the introduction of contested elections, establishment of the institution is meaningless unless numerous people (not necessarily, or ever, everyone) shift from the political passivity characteristic of undemocratic regimes to the political activity characteristic of democracy. Formerly barred from entering the contest for power, people must begin taking sides. Initially their activism may take the forms of rebellion, riots, or protests; in established democracies, these behaviors erupt sporadically but tend to be displaced by the much less costly activity of voting. A compelling theory of democracy is lacking in part because, despite decades of empirical research and substantial accumulation of knowledge, political scientists still lack any theory of voting. Empirical correlates of voting—age, education, income, partisanship, political engagement—are well established but do not constitute a theory. The one coherent theory of voting, rational choice analysis, unfortunately offers an unambiguous and robust prediction that almost everyone will abstain from voting.[10]

The task of explaining why people vote in very large numbers requires discovery of a reason for people to pay the cost of voting despite receiving no extrinsic benefit equal to the cost. The same question is central to the study of other forms of collective political action such as protest, riots, or rebellions. Like voting, these behaviors are costly to the individual in time, effort, and risk, and they succeed without the individual's participation if enough others engage in them while failing despite the individual's participation if enough others remain unengaged. While the paradoxical quality of these activities is widely recognized under the label "the logic of collective action" (which should be called, of course, the *illogic* of collective action), less familiar are the implications of individualistic cost-benefit analysis for the repression that is a defining quality of undemocratic regimes. If everyone proceeds from contemplating the costs and benefits of action to the personal self, repression is both unnecessary and impossible to organize. It is unnecessary because repression seeks to deter behaviors— taking sides in politics—that are already deterred by the illogic of collective action. It is impossible to organize because repression itself is a form of mass collective action. It requires costly contributions by numerous police or soldiers or nobles or officials, none of whom can maintain political order by personal effort and any of whom can safely shirk his contribution while continuing to receive selective remuneration.

Although it sometimes happens that authoritarian rulers, anticipating popular upheavals, prevent the occurrence of protests by conceding the institution of elections in advance, democratization is generally a shift from one form of collective action, high-cost repression by agents of the regime, through another form of collective action—rebellion, riots, or protest by those by willing to pay high costs of participation—to, ultimately, voting by those willing to pay lower costs. When one examines collective action, it turns out to be closely connected to *identity*. Decades of empirical inquiry have revealed that voting is most strongly correlated with partisan identification, that is, the voter's affirmation that he or she identifies with a political party. Partisan identification is in turn a specific political form of the more general process that is formation of social identity. Laboratory studies by social psychologists have uncovered three facts about social identity that explain its known connection to voting and the likelihood that it is also connected to political repression and its counterparts, rebellion, rioting, and protesting. The first fact involves acceptance of costs. In laboratory experiments, when people are cued to recognize sharing of social identity with others, they will voluntarily pay costs to themselves and impose those costs on other members of their social identity *if* acceptance of costs to their own group imposes larger costs on members of some opposing group—that is, *discriminates* against the opposing group. The second fact involves perceptions. People cued to recognize shared social identity perceive larger differences between individuals within their own group and smaller differences between individuals in an opposing group—that is, they *stereotype* opposing groups. The third fact concerns the capacity of discourse to cue people that they share social identity. To produce both costly discrimination and stereotyping, it suffices to *tell* experimental subjects that they are members of one group facing an opposing group. Neither group need even exist in reality. These three facts about social identity—costly discrimination, stereotyping, and discursive cuing—enable metaphors to explain democratization.[11]

The metaphors of Soviet authoritarianism established a peculiar pattern of social identification typical of undemocratic rule. When Soviet rulers described themselves and their activities as high or large, they implied that the ruled were low or small. The rulers reinforced this message by describing themselves as superior, as giving assignments, and as parenting, while implying inferiority and submissiveness of the ruled. These cues bifurcated the Soviet populace into the opposing social identities of rulers and ruled. But the key point is that only the agents of rule received metaphorical cues to any positive social identity. The rulers called themselves "high," but they never mentioned the "lows." As Stalin, who defined the distinctive institutions of Soviet authoritarianism, said, "Either you are nothing in the eyes of the party or you are a party member with full rights."[12] The standard Soviet terminology reprised his definition by distinguishing between the positive identity *kommunist* and the residual identity *bespartiinyi*—"nonparty person"—the negative quality of which was signaled, both in English and Russian, by the negative prefix. Receiving cues to a positive political identity, officials of the regime were motivated to discriminate against the mass of "nonparty persons"; deprived of such cues, the population under rule remained collectively unresisting even if some individuals overtly objected and many engaged in the covert opposition of pilferage and vandalism. Discrimination against the population took the form of identifying and isolating, through imprisonment, deportation, or confinement to psychiatric institutions, anyone who might provide the population with positive cues to an alternative political identity that would motivate collective action against the regime.

When the Gorbachev Politburo decreased emission of cues to the shared regime identity while beginning to cue a positive identity for the populace with the metaphor of "society," official repression became disjointed, while daring individuals in the populace began to supply cues to a positive identity that would enable collective participation in the dialogue to which the Gorbachev Politburo was summoning. Because the Politburo's continuing juxtaposition of party to society preserved a separation of social identities, popular action toward political authorities was largely oppositional. The new social movements that emerged during 1985–91 sought to dislodge the existing authorities from power. When still weak and when still afraid of repression that they did not know was ending, the leaders of these movements might initially disguise their motives under slogans of support for Gorbachev and for his *perestroika*, but as repression became increasingly disorganized, the movements emerged as street protests demanding an end to authoritarianism and the installation of full democracy.

As electoral politics prevailed during 1991–93, with the disappearance of the former metaphorical cues to a horizontal cleavage separating rulers above from ruled below, people increasingly ceased to view political elites as bearers of a separate social identity. People who had formerly stereotyped the Politburo and its members now began to encounter cues from politicians that converged on the people's own customary speech. Cues to shared social identity linking politicians and public enabled people to perceive differences among rivals for political power. Recognizing differences, they began to align themselves with the politician whom they found most similar to themselves. The new politicians encouraged this differentiation by introducing the metaphor of sides. It established vertical cleavages in society separating one cluster of politicians with their respective supporters from clusters led by rival politicians. These new metaphors of sides and of colors appeared far more sporadically than the concentrated metaphors of size and superiority characteristic of authoritarian rule. Accordingly the new partisan identities in democratic Russia were far more tenuous than the concentrated, all-or-nothing identity of Communist authoritarianism. Rather than motivating their bearers to pay the high costs of repressing political opponents, the new partisan identities sufficed only to motivate payment of the low costs of voting. Even street demonstrations and other forms of protest declined substantially in attendance and frequency despite the final disappearance of the repression that had continued in weakened forms nearly to the end of the Gorbachev era. It is true that at the end of the initial electoral period there was a brief, violent outbreak of rebellion and repression in Moscow between 21 September and 4 October 1993, but even this upheaval involved very small numbers of persons, a few thousand on either side, and was quickly and easily suppressed.

Metaphors are able to explain democratization through their capacity to cue recognition of social identity. Metaphors of the undemocratic type cue division of society into high and low, superior and inferior, parent and child, giver and recipient of assignments. These metaphors distinguish between an active group that receives positive cues to its identity and a passive group that is denied cues to an identity, with the result that the former group discriminates in the form of repression, while the latter group abstains from collective opposition. Abandonment of these metaphors ends repression by withdrawing the cues to the rulers' distinctive social identity and transforms the behavior of the population. As people begin to differentiate among contestants for power, they begin to take the sides that the politicians tell them have suddenly sprung into existence. Not cued at too high an intensity, people engage only in low-cost activities, particularly voting.

Conclusion

While a shift in metaphors during democratization has been demonstrated only for the Russian case, there is every reason to believe that a comparable change can be found in other cases. If so, then all three criteria for ascribing political causality to metaphors will be met. First, both metaphors and politics are capable of systematic variation. Second, change in metaphors will occur in association with change in politics. Third, if the metaphors change first, they will be identifiable as the explanatory variable, because their capacity to cue sharing of political identity explains the shift from repression through protest to voting that is democratization. Of course a theory that locates the cause of democracy in shifting discourse, including systematic change in metaphors, is easy to disprove. One way to disprove the theory is to find a case of democratization not preceded by change in political metaphors. A second way is to show that some other factor systematically antecedes both the shift in metaphors and the democratization. Despite five or more decades of strenuous effort, social scientists have failed to identify any such factor. The autonomy from extralinguistic conditions that is inherent in the definition of metaphor explains why such a factor must be impossible to find.

Notes

1. Gary King, Robert O. Keohane, and Sidney Verba, *Designing Social Inquiry: Scientific Inference in Qualitative Research* (Princeton: Princeton University Press, 1994), 81–82.
2. George Lakoff and Mark Johnson, *Metaphors We Live By* (Chicago: University of Chicago Press, 1980).
3. For a detailed discussion of these terms' meanings, see Richard D. Anderson, Jr., "Metaphors of Dictatorship and Democracy," *Slavic Review* 60 (2002): 318–25.
4. L. N. Zasorina, ed., *Chastotnyi slovar' russkogo iazyka* (Moscow: Izdatel'stvo "Russkii Iazyk," 1977); Lennart Loenngren, ed., *Chastotnyi slovar' sovremennogo russkogo iazyka*, Acta Universitatis Upsaliensis, *Studia Slavica Upsaliensa* 32 (1993).
5. Robin Tolmach Lakoff, *Talking Power: The Politics of Language in Our Lives* (New York : Basic Books, 1990), 28.
6. Elinor Rosch, "Principles of Categorization," in *Cognition and Categorization*, ed. Elinor Rosch and Barbara B. Lloyd (Hillsdale, N.J.: Lawrence Erlbaum, 1978), 37.
7. Talmy Givon, *Mind, Code, and Context: Essays in Pragmatics* (Hillsdale, N.J.: Lawrence Erlbaum Associates, 1989), 161.
8. Included are instances of the terms *dialog, kontseptsiia, radikal'nyi, konstruktivnyi, destruktivnyi, konsolidatsiia, negativnyi, stabilizatsiia, stabil'nost,'* and *pozitivnyi.*
9. Barbara Geddes, "What Do We Know about Democratization after Twenty Years?" *Annual Review of Political Science* 2 (1999): 117–19.
10. Thomas Palfrey and Howard Rosenthal, "Voter Participation and Strategic Uncertainty," *American Political Science Review* 79 (1985): 62–78.
11. John C. Turner et al., *Rediscovering the Social Group: A Self-categorization Theory* (New York: Basil Blackwell, 1987).
12. Quoted in J. Arch Getty and Oleg V. Naumov, *The Road to Terror: Stalin and the Self-destruction of the Bolsheviks, 1932–1939,* with translations by Benjamin Sher (New Haven: Yale University Press, 1999), 233.

◆ Section II

Metaphorical War and Peace

Metaphorical War and Peace

Francis A. Beer and Christ'l De Landtsheer

Metaphors of war and peace inhabit the world of politics. Wars are, first, an important metaphorical source for different dimensions of political life. For example, a "war of all against all" is Thomas Hobbes's metaphor for the wild state of nature, the mythical origin of domestic politics; it also is used to describe the supposed actual anarchic state of international politics. The metaphor of the war thus moves smoothly from predomestic life to current international society, where it becomes the dominant paradigm of international political realism.[1]

War is also a significant source for political slogans that identify particular domestic policies, for example, President Johnson's war on poverty, President Ford's war on inflation, and President Reagan's war on drugs. Within domestic societies different groups conduct wars for their rights. Within and beyond their own borders, there are "analogies at war," "minds at war," and "wars of words."[2]

External metaphorical sources are also extensively used for targets of war and peace. The Cold War was conceived in metaphor and continued to rely on it.[3] Each nation has its own cluster of metaphors, many of which are associated with past wars.[4] American presidents have used metaphor extensively in justifying war policies. Not only military generals but also political leaders seem to fight previous wars. Franklin Roosevelt's "holy war" and Dwight Eisenhower's "crusade in Europe" drew on the religious wars of the Middle Ages. The Munich metaphor was important as Harry Truman went into Korea. Presidents Kennedy, Nixon, and Johnson invoked prior American experiences in World War II and Korea, but relied less on French metaphors from Indochina as the United States fought in Vietnam. Metaphors from prior American military engagements were employed to mobilize support and opposition during the political debates about contemporary U.S. wars in the Balkans, the Persian Gulf, and Central Asia. In the "metaphor wars" surrounding current wars, the World War I Balkan powderkeg or tinderbox, the World War II appeasement at Munich and the Holocaust, and the Vietnam quagmire were all metaphors from the past whose applicability and implications were advanced and contested by partisans on different sides of the political debate.[5]

Louis XIV's famous statement that he was the state recalls the important connection between the person of the sovereign and the sovereign personality of the state.[6] It is, therefore, not surprising that the sovereign "state-as-person," particularly as a warrior-person, has been particularly important in justifying and motivating war. It has been extensively analyzed in the context of the Gulf War, as have been other metaphors.[7]

Metaphors are also prominent in the subareas of war and peace. For example, Philip Green's early study of deterrence theory sketched important metaphorical sources for dimensions of nuclear war:

> in his discussion of limited strategic war, Schelling asserts our need for a "richer menu" of strategic possibilities. Kahn, who is a master of this kind of vocabulary, acknowledges that destruction is "likely to be greatly intensified at the upper end of the escalation ladder," which is a restrained way of saying that if a limited war gets out hand it may lead to the deaths of millions and catastrophe for whole societies. However, Kahn is more interested in the "lower end" of the "escalation ladder," and here he refers to "sanitary" campaigns in which an occasional missile base may be "taken out." This last phrase, suggesting as it does the relative good humor of a clean body-block in a football game, is one of which deterrence theorists have become particularly fond (along with "cracking up" launching pads, presumably with a pneumatic drill).[8]

Metaphor combines with irony when the movie *Dr. Strangelove* is the source for the nuclear target.[9]

Troops and tropes go together. The military is a polysemic signifier. The sailing of the great white fleet at the beginning of the twentieth century was a metaphor for America's emergence as a global power. Prominent international relations scholar Glenn Snyder refers to the "widespread belief that peace in Europe and Northeast Asia is maintained by the 'American pacifier,' the physical presence of U.S. troops." Military and quasi-military operations and weapons have their own metaphorical code names: Operations Just Cause in Panama; Urgent Fury in Grenada; Desert Shield, Desert Storm, and Enduring Freedom in the Persian Gulf; Nike, Patriot, and Zeus missiles; Apache and Blackhawk aircraft; Apollo space missions.[10]

Gender metaphors pervade war and peace discourse. The metaphorical sources for international targets would seem to be primarily masculine. Power could be, suggestively, hard or soft. States have boundaries subject to political, military, and economic intervention and penetration. States have to use it or lose it, fake it or make it, risk the impotence of being a "pitiful helpless, giant." Women represent the "underside" of this history, embedded in a military culture of "bananas, beaches, and bases."[11]

This metaphorical background of war and peace forms the context for the chapters in this section; they begin from it and add to it. Dale Herbeck's chapter, "Sports Metaphors and Public Policy: The Football Theme in Desert Storm Discourse," returns to the physicality of bodies, this time in structured collision, as football merges with war. Drawing on the literature of spectator sport warfare, Herbeck's study of Gulf War rhetoric supports his argument that sports metaphors can constitute a powerful form of political argument legitimating warlike activity, building patriotic fervor, silencing critics, and masking war's tragic human consequences.

Metaphorical embodiment also appears in the chapter by Francis A. Beer and G. Robert Boynton, "Paths through the Minefields of Foreign Policy Space: Practical Reasoning in U.S. Senate Discourse about Cambodia." "Path" is a conventional metaphor of horizontal orientation that extrapolates from physical to virtual space. The chapter draws on traditions of deliberative rhetoric and artificial intelligence. It supplements our earlier discussion of metaphorical reasoning and is based upon speeches before a U.S. Senate foreign relations subcommittee. It suggests that a "path" metaphor provides a concrete instantiation of model-based reasoning in a war and peace situation. The narrative paths suggested by the path metaphor structure rhetorical and cognitive space for ordering discussions about negotiating and fighting. The path metaphor neatly arranges actors, situations, goals, sequences, strategies, relevant precedents, alternative paths, possible endpoints, interactions, and unexpected events that appear along the way to collective problem resolution in war and peace situations.

The first two chapters in this section, as in the previous one, are generally interpretive, while the last one is again more behavioral. Christ'l De Landtsheer and Ilse De Vrij discuss how the metaphorical flow changes during international crisis, using as an example the Dutch experience at Srebrenica in former Yugoslavia. They suggest that, during international crisis periods, "politicians feel the need to address the audience with more ('impressive') rhetoric, more 'pathos,' and as a consequence they use more metaphor power" in their public speech. During the Srebrenica crisis, they found that Dutch political leaders used metaphors more obviously than during noncrisis periods. Further, the metaphors that they used were of types that the authors believed were more innovative and intense, "referring to sports, games and drama . . . , or to death and disease." Finally, De Landtsheer and De Vrij found that metaphorical usage was part of a larger pattern of more "condensed, simplifying . . . discourse" with lower levels of complexity. This pattern was significantly different from one of more "elaborate, complex, and cognitive discourse" present in more routine, peaceful periods.

De Landtsheer and De Vrij invert Anderson's earlier causal argument. Anderson found that metaphors move politics. Anderson's focus was on domestic politics, but there is also evidence from cognitive linguistics and experimental psychological research that metaphor can have analogous international consequences. "The routine anthropomorphization of nations," suggests one article, "lends them greater entitativity," or objectification. "If these nations are seen as enemies," it continues, "such diction can increase threat perception, paving the way for misperception and conflict."[12] De Landtsheer and De Vrij suggest that political crisis offers a context that enhances metaphorical frequency, innovation, intensity, and simplification—and in which such hardening is more likely to happen.

Notes

1. See Thomas Hobbes, *Leviathan*, ed. J. C. A. Gaskin (Oxford: Oxford University Press, 1998); Quentin Skinner, *Reason and Rhetoric in the Philosophy of Hobbes* (Cambridge: Cambridge University Press, 1996); Hedley Bull, *The Anarchical Society: A Study of World Order in Politics* (New York: Columbia University Press, 1995); Hans Morgenthau, *Politics among Nations: The Struggle for Power and Peace,* revised by Kenneth W. Thompson, brief ed. (New York: McGraw Hill, 1993); Kenneth Waltz, *Theory of International Politics* (Reading, Mass.: Addison-Wesley, 1983); Barry Buzan, Charles Jones, and Richard Little, *The Logic of*

Anarchy—Neorealism to Structural Realism (New York: Columbia University Press, 1993); David Johnston, *The Rhetoric of "Leviathan": Thomas Hobbes and the Politics of Cultural Transformation* (Princeton: Princeton University Press, 1986).

2. Veronika Koller, "A Shotgun Wedding: Co-occurrence of War and Marriage Metaphors in Mergers and Acquisitions Discourse," *Metaphor and Symbol* 17, no. 3 (2002): 179–203; Philip Eubanks, *A War of Words in the Discourse of Trade: The Rhetorical Constitution of Metaphor* (Carbondale: Southern Illinois University Press, 2000); Ralph R. Smith and Russel R. Windes, *Progay/Antigay: The Rhetorical War over Sexuality* (Thousand Oaks, Calif.: Sage, 2000); Rickie Solinger, ed., "Abortion Wars: A Half Century of Struggle, 1950–2000," *Rhetoric & Public Affairs* 2, no. 2 (1999): 342–44; Cheryl R. Jorgensen-Earp, *"The Transfiguring Sword": The Just War of the Women's Social and Political Union* (Tuscaloosa: University of Alabama Press, 1997); Mary Ryan, *Civic Wars: Democracy and Public Life in the American City during the Nineteenth Century* (Berkeley and Los Angeles: University of California Press, 1997); William N. Elwood, "Declaring War on the Home Front: Metaphor, Presidents, and the War on Drugs," *Metaphor and Symbolic Activity* 10, no. 2 (1995): 93–114; Barry James Balleck, "Talking War and Peace: Realist and Idealist Rhetoric in the Persian Gulf Debate" (Ph.D. diss., University of Colorado, Boulder, 1994); Martin J. Medhurst, ed., *Eisenhower's War of Words* (East Lansing: Michigan State University Press, 1994); Yuen Foong Khong, *Analogies at War: Korea, Munich, Dien Bien Phu, and the Vietnam Decisions of 1965* (Princeton: Princeton University Press, 1992), 20, 35; Dickinson McGaw, "Governing Metaphors: The War on Drugs," *American Journal of Semiotics* 8, no. 3 (1991): 57–74; Steven Kull, *Minds at War: Nuclear Reality and the Inner Conflicts of Defense Policymakers* (New York: Basic Books, 1988); David Zarefsky, *President Johnson's War on Poverty: Rhetoric and History* (Tuscaloosa: University of Alabama Press, 1986); Leah Rissman, *Love as War: Hometric Allusion in the Poetry of Sappho* (Königstein: Hain, 1983); Hermann Stelzner, "Ford's 'War on Inflation': A Metaphor That Did Not Cross," *Communication Monographs* 44 (1977): 284–97. See also Introduction, n. 87, above.

3. See, for example, Ron Robin, *The Making of the Cold War Enemy: Culture and Politics in the Military-Intellectual Complex* (Princeton: Princeton University Press, 2001); Suzanne Clark, *Cold Warriors: Manliness on Trial in the Rhetoric of the West* (Carbondale: Southern Illinois University Press, 2000); Michael J. Hostetler, "The Enigmatic Ends of Rhetoric:

Churchill's Fulton Address as Great Art and Failed Persuasion," *Quarterly Journal of Speech* 83, no. 4 (1997): 416–28; Robert L. Ivie, "Cold War Motives and the Rhetorical Metaphor: A Framework for Criticism," in *Cold War Rhetoric: Strategy, Metaphor, and Ideology,* by Martin J. Medhurst et al. (East Lansing: Michigan State University Press, 1997), 71–79; John K. White, *Still Seeing Red: How the Cold War Shapes the New American Politics* (Boulder: Westview, 1997).

4. See, for example, Valerie Holman and Debra Kelly, eds., *France at War in the Twentieth Century: Propaganda, Myth, and Metaphor* (New York: Berghahn Books, 2000).

5. Denise M. Bostdorff, "George W. Bush's Post September 11 Rhetoric of Covenant Renewal: Upholding the Faith of the Greatest Generation," Quarterly Journal of Speech 89, no. 4 (2003): 293–319; Cf. John Collins and Ross Glover, eds., *Collateral Language: A User's Guide to America's New War* (New York: New York University Press, 2002); Riikka Kuusisto, "Heroic Tale, Game, and Business Deal? Western Metaphors in Action in Kosovo," *Quarterly Journal of Speech* 88, no. 1 (2002): 50–68; Roland Paris, "Kosovo and the Metaphor War," *Political Science Quarterly* 117, no. 3 (2002): 423–50; Jeffrey Record, *Making War: Thinking History: Munich, Vietnam, and Presidential Uses of Force from Korea to Kosovo* (Annapolis, Md.: Naval Institute Press, 2002); Moya Ann Ball, "Political Language in the Search for an Honorable Peace: Presidents Kennedy and Johnson, Their Advisers, and Vietnam Decision Making," in *Beyond Public Speech and Symbols: Explorations in the Rhetoric of Politicians and the Media,* ed. Christ'l De Landtsheer and Ofer Feldman (Westport, Conn.: Praeger, 2000), 35–51; Christopher Hemmer, *Which Lessons Matter?: American Foreign Policy Decision Making in the Middle East, 1979–1987* (Albany: SUNY Press, 2000); Victor Kennedy, "Intended Tropes and Unintended Metatropes in Reporting on the War in Kosovo," *Metaphor and Symbol* 15, no. 4 (2000): 253–65; Timothy M. Cole, "Avoiding the Quagmire: Alternative Rhetorical Constructs for Post–Cold War American Foreign Policy," *Rhetoric & Public Affairs* 2, no. 3 (1999): 367–93; Christopher Hemmer, "Historical Analogies and the Definition of Interests: The Iranian Hostage Crisis and Ronald Reagan's Policy toward the Hostages in Lebanon," *Political Psychology* 20, no. 2 (1999): 267–89; Timothy M. Cole, "When Intentions Go Awry: The Bush Administration's Foreign Policy Rhetoric," *Political Communication* 13 (1996): 93–113; Suzanne M. Daughton, "Metaphoric Transcendence: Images of the Holy War in Franklin Roosevelt's First Inaugural," *Quarterly Journal of Speech* 79 (1993): 427–46;

Khong, *Analogies at War*, 20, 35; Mary E. Stuckey, "Remembering the Future: Rhetorical Echoes of World War and Vietnam in George Bush's Public Speech on the Gulf War," *Communication Studies* 43 (winter 1992): 246–56; Richard E. Neustadt and Ernest R. May, *Thinking in Time: The Uses of History for Decision Makers* (New York: Free Press, 1986).

6: Discussions of sovereignty and its limits include Stephen Krasner, *Sovereignty: Organized Hypocrisy* (Princeton: Princeton University Press, 1999); Thomas J. Biersteker and Cynthia Weber, eds., *State Sovereignty as Social Construct* (Cambridge: Cambridge University Press, 1996). See also Kurt Burch, *"Property" and the Making of the International System* (Boulder: Lynne Rienner, 1998).

7. See, for example, Francis A. Beer and Barry J. Balleck, "Body, Mind, and Soul in the Gulf War Debate," in *The Theory and Practice of Political Communication Research*, ed. Mary E. Stuckey (Binghamton: SUNY Press, 1996), 159–76; George Lakoff, "Metaphor and War: The Metaphor System Used to Justify War in the Gulf." *Peace Research* 23 (1991): 25–32 (http://lists.village.virginia.edu/sixties/HTML_docs/Texts/Scholarly/Lakoff_Gulf_Metaphor_1.html), (accessed February 21, 2004). For further discussion of war metaphors and metaphors in war, see Erna Paris, *Long Shadows: Truth, Lies, and History* (London: Bloomsbury, 2000); Robert L. Ivie, "Fire, Flood, and Red Fever: Motivating Metaphors of Global Emergency in the Truman Doctrine Speech," *Presidential Studies Quarterly* 29 (September 1999): 570–91; Francis A. Beer and Robert Hariman, "Post-realism, Just War, and the Gulf War Debate," in *Politically Speaking: A Worldwide Examination of Language Use in the Public Sphere*, ed. Ofer Feldman and Christ'l De Landtsheer (Westport, Conn.: Praeger, 1998); cf. Ruth Linn and Ilan Gur-Ze'ev, "Holocaust as Metaphor: Arab and Israeli Use of the Same Symbol," *Metaphor and Symbolic Activity* 11 (1996): 195–206; Charles C. Bebber, "Thematic Images Linking American Military Strikes of the 1980's and Rising U.S. Civil Violence," *Metaphor and Symbolic Activity* 10 (1995): 139–54; Laura S. Carney, "Not Telling Us What to Think: The Vietnam Veterans Memorial," *Metaphor and Symbolic Activity* 8 (1993): 211–19; Ann S. Pancake, "Taken by Storm: The Exploitation of Metaphor in the Persian Gulf War," *Metaphor and Symbolic Activity* 8 (1993): 281–95; James F. Voss et al., "Experts at Debate: The Use of Metaphor in the U.S. Senate Debate on the Gulf Crisis," *Metaphor and Symbolic Activity* 7 (1992): 197–214; Ruth Linn, "Holocaust Metaphors and Symbols in the Moral Dilemmas of Contemporary Israeli

Soldiers," *Metaphor and Symbolic Activity* 6 (1991): 61–86; Robert L. Ivie, "Metaphor and Motive in the Johnson Administration's Vietnam War Rhetoric," in *Texts in Context: Critical Dialogues on Significant Episodes in American Political Rhetoric*, ed. Michael C. Leff and Fred J. Kauffeld (Davis, Calif.: Hermagoras Press, 1989), 121–41; Robert L. Ivie, "Metaphor and the Rhetorical Invention of Cold War 'Idealists,'" *Communication Monographs* 54 (1987): 165–82; Robert L. Ivie, "Literalizing the Metaphor of Soviet Savagery: President Truman's Plain Style," *Southern Speech Communication Journal* 51 (1986): 91–105; Robert L. Ivie, "Speaking 'Common Sense' about the Soviet Threat: Reagan's Rhetorical Stance," *Western Journal of Speech Communication* 48 (1984): 39–50; Ronald L. Hatzenbuehler and Robert L. Ivie, *Congress Declares War: Rhetoric, Leadership, and Partisanship in the Early Republic* (Kent, Ohio: Kent State University Press, 1983); Robert L. Ivie, "The Metaphor of Force in Prowar Discourse: The Case of 1812," *Quarterly Journal of Speech* 68 (1982): 240–53. See also Robert Kagan, *Of Paradise and Power: America vs. Europe in the New World Order* (New York: Knopf, 2003); Carl H. Builder, *The Masks of War* (Baltimore: Johns Hopkins University Press, 1989); John Keegan, *The Mask of Command* (New York: Penguin Books, 1988).

8. Philip Green, *Deadly Logic: The Theory of Nuclear Deterrence* (New York: Schocken, 1968), 222–23. See also Alan Nadel, *Containment Culture: American Narratives, Postmodernism, and the Atomic Age* (Durham, N.C.: Duke University Press, 1995); Edward Schiappa, "The Rhetoric of Nukespeak," *Communication Monographs* 56 (1989): 253–72; Kull, *Minds at War;* Carol Cohn, "Sex and Death in the Rational World of Defense Intellectuals," *Signs* 12 (1987): 687–718; Stephen Hilgartner, Richard C. Bell, and Rory O'Connor, *Nukespeak: The Selling of Nuclear Technology in America* (Harmondsworth, U.K., and New York: Penguin, 1982); Herman Kahn, *On Escalation: Metaphors and Scenarios* (Baltimore: Penguin, 1968); Thomas Schelling, *The Strategy of Conflict* (New York: Oxford University Press, 1963).

9. See, for example, Margot Henriksen, *Dr. Strangelove's America: Society and Culture in the Atomic Age* (Berkeley and Los Angeles: University of California Press, 1997); Ira Chernus, *Dr. Strangegod: On the Symbolic Meaning of Nuclear Weapons* (Columbia: University of South Carolina Press, 1986). See also Herbert L. Colston and Raymond W. Gibbs, Jr., "Are Irony and Metaphor Understood Differently?" *Metaphor and Symbol* 17, no. 1 (2002): 57–80.

10. Glenn H. Snyder, "Mearsheimer's World: Offensive Realism and the Struggle for Security," *International Security* 27, no. 1 (2002): 168; Leroy G. Dorsey, "Sailing into the 'Wondrous Now': The Myth of the American Navy's World Cruise," *Quarterly Journal of Speech* 83, no. 4 (1997): 447–65; Kathy E. Ferguson, *Oh Say Can You See?: The Semiotics of the Military in Hawai'i* (Minneapolis: University of Minnesota Press, 1998).

11. Cynthia Enloe, *Bananas, Beaches and Bases: Making Feminist Sense of International Politics* (Berkeley and Los Angeles: University of California Press, 1990). See also Joseph S. Nye, *The Paradox of American Power* (Oxford: Oxford University Press, 2002); Clark, *Cold Warriors;* Karen Vasby Anderson, " 'Rhymes with Rich': 'Bitch' as a Tool of Containment in Contemporary American Politics," *Rhetoric & Public Affairs* 2, no. 4 (1999): 599–623; Roxanne L. Doty, *Imperial Encounters: The Politics of Representation in North-South Relations* (Minneapolis: University of Minnesota Press, 1996); Cynthia Weber, *Faking It: U.S. Hegemony in the "Post-phallic" Era* (Minneapolis: University of Minnesota Press, 1999); Claudia Camp and Carole Fontaine, *Semeia 61: Women, War, and Metaphor* (Atlanta: Scholars Press, 1993); Cynthia Enloe, *The Morning after: Sexual Politics at the End of the Cold War* (Berkeley and Los Angeles: University of California Press, 1993); Christine Sylvester, *Feminist Theory and International Relations in a Postmodern Era* (Cambridge: Cambridge University Press, 1993); J. Ann Tickner, *Gender in International Relations: Feminist Perspectives on Achieving Global Security* (New York: Columbia University Press, 1992); Rebecca Grant and Kathleen Newland, eds., *Gender and International Relations* (Bloomington: Indiana University Press, 1991); Joseph S. Nye, *Bound to Lead: The Changing Nature of American Power* (New York: Basic Books, 1990), 188, 260, 302; Jean Bethke Elshtain and Sheila Tobias, eds., *Women, Militarism, and War: Essays in History, Politics, and Social Theory* (Savage, Md.: Rowman and Littlefield, 1990); Susan Jeffords, *The Remasculinization of America: Gender and the Vietnam War* (Bloomington: Indiana University Press, 1989); Elise Boulding, *The Underside of History: A View of Women through Time,* original line drawings by Helen Redman (Newbury Park, Calif.: Sage, 1992).

12. Emanuele Castano, Simona Sacchi, and Peter Harry Gries, "The Perception of the 'Other' in International Relations: Evidence for the Polarizing Effect of Entitativity," *Political Psychology* (forthcoming). See also Willard van Orman Quine, "On Mental Entities," in *The Ways of Paradox and Other Essays,* rev. and enlarged ed., ed. Willard van Orman

Quine (Cambridge: Harvard University Press, 1976), 221–27. International conflict thus implies a hardening of the "state-as-person" metaphor elaborated by George Lakoff, "Metaphor and War: The Metaphor System Used to Justify War in the Gulf," *Peace Research* 23 (1991): 25–32 (http://lists.village.virginia.edu/sixties/HTML_docs /Texts/Scholarly/Lakoff_Gulf_Metaphor_1.html). Consistent with this dynamic, hardliners in the former Soviet Union had more unitary and less complex views of other international actors. See Richard D. Anderson, Jr., "Why Competitive Politics Inhibits Learning in Soviet Foreign Policy," in *Learning in U.S. and Soviet Foreign Policy*, ed. George W. Breslauer and Philip E. Tetlock (Boulder: Westview Press, 1991), 120; Glenn H. Snyder and Paul Diesing, *Conflict among Nations: Bargaining, Decision Making, and System Structure in International Crises* (Princeton: Princeton University Press, 1977), 303–4. See also Jim A. Kuypers, *Presidential Crisis Rhetoric and the Press in the Post–Cold War World* (Westport, Conn.: Praeger, 1997); Karlyn K. Campbell and Kathleen H. Jamieson, *Deeds Done in Words* (Chicago: University of Chicago Press, 1990), chap. 6.

Sports Metaphors and Public Policy

The Football Theme in Desert Storm Discourse

Dale A. Herbeck

The United States has emerged as the dominant military superpower in the post–Cold War world. Even as America's military capabilities grow, however, public support for military intervention in foreign countries is clearly waning. Absent direct threats to national security, the American public has grown weary of becoming involved in the internal affairs of distant countries. Commenting on this curious paradox, Gordon Mitchell has observed that domestic political support "erodes steadily as U.S. military engagements increasingly take on the character of police actions, where military intervention is undertaken more to enforce norms of behavior rather than to protect against direct threats to the American homeland."[1]

Recognizing that the lack of political support is a major constraint on foreign policy, there is a growing awareness that military intervention must be packaged and sold to the public. As part of this effort to market warfare, James Der Derian has identified a new phenomenon called the "MIME-NET," or the Military-Industrial-Media-Entertainment Network.[2] By transforming war into a form of entertainment, Der Derian explains how policymakers are able to justify using military force. Such efforts reflect the fact that public opinion, more than the strength of enemy forces, is often the greatest constraint on American military options. At the same time, "virtuous war presents a paradox," Der Derian continues, "the more we resort to virtual means to resolve political problems, the more we undermine the very ground upon which our political virtues rest."[3]

A growing body of scholarship is developing around spectator sport warfare.[4] Less attention has been devoted, however, to studying the language used by politicians and commentators during international conflicts. Recognizing this fact, Mitchell has suggested that an "analysis of how the spectator sport framework shapes the spatio-temporal dimensions for public deliberation can shed light on this phenomenon."[5] This chapter attempts to address this need by focusing on the unique role that sports metaphors play in our political discourse.

Since it would be impossible to do justice to all sports metaphors in a single work, this essay focuses on a cluster of metaphors used in public arguments regarding American military intervention in Iraq during the early 1990s. While a review of the controversy over American intervention, hereafter referred to as Desert Storm, suggests a wide range of competing metaphors, one common set of metaphors used by politicians, military leaders, and journalists was drawn from the American game of football.[6] By analogizing military intervention in the Mideast to football, it was possible for both advocates and commentators to situate the game, identify the competing teams and their players, comment on the respective strategies, praise winners and vilify losers, and even conduct probing postgame analysis explaining the decisive coaching moves.

At first glance, it might be suggested that such metaphors are innocuous attempts to explain Desert Storm by representing one concept, sometimes called the tenor, in terms of another idea, often called the vehicle. Referring to a general as a coach, for instance, is merely a device to explain the general's role. In other words, language is a neutral conduit used to convey information or frame arguments. Viewed from this perspective, football metaphors are nothing more than a convenient set of linguistic devices for explaining a conflict. Metaphors are convenient ornaments used to adorn meaning.

This essay challenges such a simplistic conception of metaphors, arguing that repeated references to football in Desert Storm discourse functioned to authorize military intervention, minimize the consequences of intervention, and reinforce a dominant political ideology. This conclusion is not meant to damn sports, but rather to suggest that seemingly innocuous sports metaphors can, in fact, constitute a powerful form of ideological argument. In support of this thesis, the chapter begins by identifying common football metaphors, proceeds to explain how these metaphors were used in public arguments concerning Desert Storm, and concludes by suggesting some of the argumentative implications hidden within these innocent metaphors.

Identifying Football Metaphors

The language of sport permeates public discourse in the United States. Sports metaphors routinely find their way into our politics, literature, and advertising. In an impressive effort to document the prevalence of "sportspeak," Robert A. Palmatier and Harold L. Ray identified more than seventeen hundred sports metaphors found in daily discourse.[7] Commenting on the pervasiveness of such metaphors, Francine Hardaway has gone so far as to suggest, "the language of athletic competition has found its way as a metaphor into every phase of American life."[8] Jeffrey O. Segrave has extended the comparison even further, suggesting that sport metaphors have become "part of our conventional wisdom."[9]

Despite the popularity of these metaphors, Jeffery Scott Mio laments, "with a few notable exceptions, theorists in the area of political rhetoric have not devoted much more than passing mention to metaphor."[10] Even among those with an academic interest in metaphors, sports have received comparatively little attention. Recognizing the disparity between the use of sports metaphors and the scholarly attention these metaphors have received, John J. MacAloon has observed that "among no people known to us in history have sports models, discourse, and ways of thinking so thoroughly colonized politics, a fact often noticed but not yet investigated, much less understood."[11]

To find football metaphors in discourse about Desert Storm, a programmatic series of searches of the Lexis/Nexis database was conducted. This online database, a proprietary collection available in many research libraries in the United States, includes the full text of speeches by major political figures such as the president and cabinet secretaries, transcripts of legislative sessions from the *Congressional Record* and committee hearings, articles appearing in leading newspapers and magazines, and stories disseminated by national wire services. While the Lexis/Nexis database was not designed to be representative of all political perspectives, it is sufficiently inclusive to fairly represent both political parties and leading American newspapers and periodicals.

Starting with a list of fifty-nine football metaphors identified by Palmatier and Ray,[12] the database was searched using different combinations of words and phrases. This list was contemporized as necessary to include modern football metaphors, such as references to the Super Bowl, not included in Palmatier and Ray's original list. To distinguish metaphors used in Desert Storm from general uses of football metaphors and from the discussion of actual football games, various combinations of screening terms were employed. So, for example, searches were constructed to find the use of a particular football metaphor within twenty-five words of Saddam Hussein, Iraq, or Desert Storm.

Before discussing the results, several observations about this methodology are appropriate. This simplistic search strategy surely missed football metaphors that did not fit within the parameters of the search. This is excusable, as the objective of these searches was simply to identify football metaphors, not to count the number of uses or to demonstrate that football metaphors were more prevalent than other metaphors. It should also be remembered that the use of football metaphors does not preclude the use of other metaphors. Indeed, scholars such as Winkler, Ivie, and Kuusisto have already identified competing metaphors in the public discourse surrounding Desert Storm. The presence of these metaphors is not inconsistent with the thrust of this analysis; rather it affirms the broader claim that metaphors constitute a powerful form of argument. [13]

Although all the metaphors were searched, many did not appear in the Desert Storm discourse. So, for example, "chalk talk," "skull session," and "win one for the Gipper" never appeared with the limiting terms. In contrast, numerous accounts were dismissed because they described the exploits of high school "quarterbacks" or "Ivy League" graduates who had distinguished themselves in combat. Neither of these findings is especially troublesome, as the purpose of this essay was to identify the range of metaphors used and consider how these metaphors were invoked in the public argument about Desert Storm.

Desert Storm as Football Game: Team United States versus Team Iraq

Sue Curry Jansen and Don Sabo discovered that "during the Persian Gulf War, sport/war metaphors and synecdoches gained wide currency in several institutional contexts including the government, military, war journalism, and sport media."[14] Given this finding, it was not surprising to find that football metaphors were popular in Desert Storm discourse, although both the range and the complexity of the football metaphors was unanticipated. Rather than simply claiming that war can be understood as football, a complex set of football metaphors was employed to characterize all aspects of Desert Storm. Due to the sophistication of these metaphors, it seems appropriate to organize them into the larger theme of an important football game between traditional rivals. This broader theme, in turn, was reinforced by the overlapping metaphors analogizing Desert Storm to football.

A convenient place to begin unpacking the game theme is with the respective leaders. Both George Bush and Saddam Hussein were repeatedly likened to "coaches preparing for the Super Bowl."[15] Just as these political leaders were identified as coaches, so too were the leading military commanders of the competing teams. Sometimes the title was assigned by the commentators, as in a reference to a pregame pep talk by "visiting general/coach" Schwarzkopf.[16] Other times the title was claimed, as when Lieutenant General Calvin A. H. Waller, the second-ranking officer in Operation Desert Shield behind General Schwarzkopf, claimed, "I'm like a football coach. I want everything I can possibly get and have at my side of the field when I get ready to go into the Super Bowl."[17]

Indeed, those who were critical of the military and political leaders frequently denigrated their coaching skills. Senator Bob Kerrey, an early critic of the decision to deploy American forces in the Gulf, accused President Bush of being more of "a little league football coach than a commander in chief."[18] Another commentator likened Bush to "a high-school football coach on the eve of the Big Game."[19] In an even less flattering comparison, one journalist complained, "listening to the two coaches, Saddam of the Eye Pluckers and Bush of the Butt Kickers, it sounded a lot like the old mine's-bigger-than-your's contest."[20]

As every football fan knows, selecting an appropriate strategy is an integral part of coaching. Just like a football game, each of the teams in the Gulf War had a different strategy, repeatedly referred to as a game plan. Coach Bush's "game plan," according to the analysts, "if not from the beginning, certainly from very early on was to bring Iraq to its knees by flattening it with overwhelming military force."[21] According to Assistant Coach Colin Powell, chairman of the Joint Chiefs of Staff, this game plan has a "ground component. Despite protestations to the contrary, most observers assume it also envisages a short, violent war—summed up by Mr. Bush's repeated pledge that 'this will not be another Vietnam.'"[22] In sharp contrast, opposing coach "Saddam Hussein's game plan [is] to drag out the conflict long enough to split up the coalition against him and to inflict enough American casualties to make the American public demand an end to the war."[23]

Once the coach decides on the game plan, he needs to name a starting lineup. In this instance, many commentators were more impressed at who was left on the bench. Democratic congressional leaders, for example, "have largely chosen to sit on the sidelines."[24] Several other key players also languished on the bench, albeit for very different reasons. So as not to widen the conflict, American forces acted while "waving Israel to the sidelines."[25] Further, after the outcome of the game was safely in hand, it was reported that "Saudi Arabia is agreeing to take part on the sidelines because President Bush made it clear that that was the least it could do to thank Washington for saving it from Iraq."[26]

The use of football metaphors went well beyond the talk of coaches, game plans, and the starting lineup. All the battles were fought on a mythic playing field complete with "yard markers and goal posts."[27] As in football, the goal was to advance into enemy territory and gain ground. When some commentators questioned whether war could be averted, Coach Bush responded that he was "not moving the goal posts to achieve peace in the region."[28] Just as it would be unthinkable to change the length of the playing field after the game started, it was not possible to change military objectives once the war had started.

Having cast the war as a football game, it made sense to compare the beginning of hostilities to the start of the game. As game time approached, commentators warned, "in the blistering air battles that will 'kick off' war in the gulf, U.S. pilots expect Iraq will suffer overwhelming losses, even from its own missiles."[29] In another published account, a chief warrant officer proclaimed, "it's time to quit the pregame show."[30] Offering humorous commentary on the opening kickoff immediately after the game, Coach Schwarzkopf recalled announcing to his soldiers, "Iraq has won the toss and elected to receive."[31] The same message appeared on a sign outside the main American base and on the bulletin board in the press hotel in Riyadh.[32] Of course, in this case, receiving did not mean receiving the kickoff, but rather referred to receiving the American air attack.

Once the game had started, the ensuing action was often described through football metaphors. Coach Bush, for example, frequently "huddled" with his advisers.[33] The allied attack featured a vaunted "ground game" based on a range of "running plays" designed to protect the "ball carrier."[34] At the same time, the allied defense planned to hold "him [opposing star, Saddam Hussein] to the line."[35] The allied game plan also made use of excellent "special teams, such as the combat engineers who breached Iraqi minefields and the Patriot missileers, to whom the label 'Scudbusters' seems to have stuck like Velcro."[36] Commentators highlighted the success of Patriot missiles in "intercepting" Scud missiles thrown by Iraq during the war.[37]

Other metaphors from the gridiron permeate Desert Storm discourse. President Bush complained about "a total stiff-arm" from Saddam Hussein when describing the failure of diplomacy to prevent conflict.[38] When Congress took up the issue, critics charged, "the first impulse of many Members was to punt."[39] Mistakes in policy, such as the ill-fated courtship of Iraq before the invasion of Kuwait, were referred to as "fumbles."[40] Finally, after early success, one commentator warned that "scoring the first touchdown is one thing; having the ingredients to go the distance is quite another. The most difficult plays are yet to come."[41]

There was, however, one football metaphor that dominated all others. It was the characterization of the successful strategy of flanking Iraq's army as a "Hail Mary pass." To make the image work, Coach Schwarzkopf created a situation in which his team faced the most desperate of circumstances:

> Basically, the problem we were faced with was this: . . . As far as fighting troops, we were really outnumbered 2 to 1. In addition to that, they had about 4,700 tanks vs. our 3,500 when the buildup was complete, and they had a great deal more artillery than we do. I think any student of military strategy would tell you that in order to attack a position, you should have a ratio of approximately 3 to 1 in favor of the attacker. And in order to attack a position that is heavily dug in and barricaded, such as the one we had here, you should have a ratio of 5 to 1, in the way of troops, in favor of the attacker. . . . What we did, of course, was start an extensive air campaign. . . . One of the purposes of that extensive air campaign was to isolate the Kuwaiti theater of operation by taking out all the bridges and supply lines that ran between the North and the southern part of Iraq. We also conducted a very heavy bombing campaign. . . . It was necessary to reduce these forces down to a strength that . . . made them weaker, particularly on the front-line barrier that we had to go through. . . . Once we had taken out his eyes, we did what could best be described as the "Hail Mary" play in football.[42]

In a vast sweeping motion, the allied army swept around the flank of the Iraqi line. The play, explained by Coach Schwarzkopf with a reference to a "football playbook," went for a huge gain.[43] After the allied army successfully executed the "end run" or "end sweep," they found only "second-string" Iraqi players as they rolled to a convincing victory.[44]

Even after the game was completed, football metaphors were used during the ubiquitous postgame analysis. The allied victory was so decisive that it "leveled the Arab playing field."[45] Despite the margin of victory, some of the winning players complained about the dirty tactics of their opponents. Senator Albert Gore called on Republicans to stop taking "cheap shots against Democrats who have voted against the war powers resolution on Iraq."[46] Even in victory, Coach Bush found himself compelled to respond to "Monday morning quarterbacks" who blame him for "Saddam's continued aggression because the Iraqi dictator wasn't toppled in the 1991 Persian Gulf War"[47] and "hindsight quarterbacks who are insisting that allied forces should have acted more decisively in March of 1991."[48]

Football Metaphors as Argument

At first blush, this tawdry collection of football metaphors may seem more an exercise in rhetorical excess than a serious study of war rhetoric. The discerning reader might be tempted to agree with Palmatier and Ray, who explained that "when the metaphors begin to be used by people who, like Howard Cosell 'never played the game,' they become idioms. And when they have outworn their welcome, they become clichés."[49] In this instance, many of the metaphors would seem to fall into the latter category.

Under closer scrutiny, however, it becomes apparent that this odd collection of football metaphors is more than political excess or shoddy journalism. As Murray Edelman has observed, "Metaphors and myths are devices for simplifying and giving meaning to complex and bewildering sets of observations that evoke concern."[50] In this instance, the language used did more than describe Desert Storm; the language played an important role in shaping national understanding and public response to the war. Commenting specifically on the power of sports metaphors, Richard Lipsky observed, "the kinds of metaphors and vocabularies we use inevitably structure the kind of reality we perceive and act on."[51]

Starting from this perspective, three implications of these football metaphors seem worthy of more elaboration. In the paragraphs that follow, it will be argued that by invoking football metaphors, advocates managed to silence the critics of intervention, sanitize the consequences of conflict, and build patriotic fervor. Each of these results is important, for as George Lakoff and Mark Turner have suggested, "to study metaphor is to be confronted with hidden aspects of one's own mind and one's own culture."[52]

Silencing the Critics of Intervention

The strategic use of football metaphors cast Desert Storm as a conflict between two competing teams. This move, while extremely subtle, is significant on several levels. First, football metaphors reduced a complex political decision to a simple athletic contest. By casting the conflict as Team United States versus Team Iraq, those offering football metaphors deftly transformed the discussion of complicated geopolitical and military options into our team versus their team. This ritualization of the political process is dangerous, Segrave notes, as it transforms politics into a spectator sport with the "corresponding exclusion and ultimately the atrophy of popular political will; citizenship transformed into acclamation."[53]

This shift in focus is extremely significant, for it transforms an abstract discussion of competing foreign policy options to the concrete matter of how to win the war. Recognizing this possibility, Lipsky has observed that "by transposing sports symbolism into political discourse the political participant or commentator tends to transpose sports ideologically unproblematic nature into politics. It promotes an interest in 'winning' or 'losing' while obfuscating the reasons that should underlie an interest in winning political power."[54] In this instance, defining the conflict as a competition between teams reduced the debate over Desert Storm to a game of attack, counterattack, and self-defense. Thus framed, winning became the paramount consideration. The significance of this framing is concisely captured in famous words often attributed to the late Vince Lombardi, legendary coach of the great Green Bay Packers of the 1960s: "Winning isn't everything, it's the only thing."[55]

Second, football metaphors discouraged substantive discussion of alternatives by casting the American public in the subservient role of the fans.[56] Not only did football metaphors cast the controversy as Team United States versus Team Iraq, but the metaphors also assigned specific roles to coaches, players, and spectators. Coaches are selected for their expertise and empowered to plan strategy, players are chosen for their ability to execute the coach's game plan, and fans exist to cheer their team on to victory.

Understood from this perspective, military decisions are purely strategic choices, made by coaches and executed by players, without the opportunity for input by the average fan. As Ike Balbus insightfully observed, "The goal of sports activity is always unambiguous and non-controversial; participants do not come together to discuss or debate the ends for which the activity has been established, but rather take this end for granted and apply themselves in a single-minded fashion to the task of developing the most efficient means to achieve the predetermined unchanging and non-controversial end: winning."[57]

Finally, football metaphors functioned to discourage criticism. As the youngest child quickly learns, teams are not a forum for airing grievances, but rather groups organized for a specific competitive purpose. There is never any discussion among spectators about the desirability of playing the game, nor is there room for lengthy discussion between teammates during the game. Commenting on this fact, Jansen and Sabo have written, "The use of the sport/war metaphor in the discourse of government, military, war journalism sport media, and the sport industry helped to make ideological hegemony a reality by masking the ideological diversity in the American polity and curbing resistance to the war."[58] This is not to say that spectators are disinterested, but rather to suggest that this interest usually manifests itself in a simple loyalty to a favorite team. This metaphor is problematic, because there is no place for such loyalty in politics, a forum where choices should be based on an informed consideration of the alternatives.

Sanitizing the Consequences of Conflict

The recurrent use of football metaphors masked the human pain and suffering caused by Desert Storm. By explaining the conflict as an athletic contest, football metaphors obscured the fatalities caused by this grim military game. Analogizing the war to the Super Bowl obscures the suffering on the battlefield. Claiming that Iraq has won the toss and elected to receive neglects that bombs will be falling on soldiers and noncombatants. Talking about the ground game ignores that soldiers will die invading enemy territory while striving for symbolic first downs. Highlighting missiles that are intercepted conveniently forgets about the missiles that found their way to a target. Diplomatic fumbles become unfortunate errors, while the real-world consequences of these mistakes are never disclosed.

Paula Edelson has complained that "sports-language and battle eu-phemisms not only are inaccurate, tiresome, and unoriginal, but they sani-tize the atrocities of war as effectively as any government-imposed censor."[59] In the case of Desert Storm, football metaphors provided public officials and commentators with a convenient vocabulary for describing events. This lan-guage worked from the implicit assumption that the war was ultimately a game, thereby obscuring the real casualties that were occurring on the bat-tlefield. This is significant, for there was genuine concern that the American public might prove unwilling to sacrifice American lives to achieve abstract foreign policy objectives. Invoking language appropriated from football al-lowed detailed discussion of Desert Storm, without mention of military losses that might threaten public support for intervention.

No doubt, there are other factors that help explain why Desert Storm was depicted as a relatively "clean" war. The military tightly controlled ac-cess to the battlefield and, at the same time, strategically released bomb-sight films collected by the Department of Defense.[60] Not surprisingly, the only bits of footage released "sustained the illusion of a playing field (safe, bloodless, and abstract) on which American solider-athletes performed feats of matchless daring and skill."[61] At the same time, the war was largely fought with air power and field artillery. "The dearth of reporting on casu-alties in the Persian Gulf War," Daniel C. Hallin observes, "reflects both the fact that journalists were not normally there to witness them *and* the re-turn of the definition of war as a job to be done without sentiment and without moral or political qualms."[62] The football metaphors used to frame the conflict are significant, because they helped to shape the way Desert Storm was understood by the public.

Building Patriotic Fervor

While football offers a convenient vocabulary for describing different as-pects of Desert Storm, it is important to remember that these metaphors also express a particular set of values. William Safire has insightfully ob-served, "professional football is the central metaphor of our times, combin-ing strategy with power, grace with violence, sportsmanship with brinkmanship."[63] Recognizing the power implicit in such images, Hard-away has suggested "that sports metaphors become not merely ways of re-vealing our adolescent preoccupation with aggressiveness, with winning, with games, but also ways of perpetuating those concerns, of glorifying them, of passing them on unexamined to our children through our national culture."[64]

Throughout the conflict, football metaphors were strategically used to place Team United States in symbolic opposition against Team Iraq. According to pregame accounts, Team Iraq was dangerous, but its brute physical strength was offset by low morale and poor coaching. In contrast, the American team had been superbly trained, it was expertly coached, and it possessed an awesome collection of offensive threats. During those weeks that the outcome was in serious doubt, millions of Americans watched the game live from the comfort of their living room. Footage of actual attacks was played and replayed, commentary was provided by reporters standing on the sidelines, and players were interviewed after they returned from the fray. Such accounts functioned to build support for Team United States, just as fans rally around the local team when it battles competitors from foreign cities.

Even after the last play, football metaphors were used to embellish the extent of the victory. In a postgame press conference, General Norman Schwarzkopf made reference to the "Hail Mary pass" that produced the ultimate victory. The Hail Mary pass, of course, refers to a desperate play that cannot succeed without divine intervention. One of the most famous examples of the Hail Mary pass occurred in a game between the Boston College Eagles and the University of Miami Hurricanes. In late 1984, the visiting Eagles trailed the heavily favored Hurricanes with seconds remaining in the fourth quarter. Boston College quarterback Doug Flutie dropped back and launched a long pass from his own territory that traveled the length of the field into the end zone. As time expired, wide receiver Gerard Phelan caught the ball between Miami defenders while falling backwards over the goal line to score a fantastic touchdown. Because of this spectacular play, Boston College earned an improbable 47–45 upset victory, Flutie won the Heisman Trophy as the nation's outstanding college football player, and the Eagles earned a coveted invitation to play in the Cotton Bowl.

Compared to such heroics on the football field, Schwarzkopf's dubious reference to a Hail Mary pass hardly seems an appropriate way to characterize the lopsided outcome of the game between Team United States and Team Iraq. The Hail Mary pass is a desperate effort by a beaten team, but "there was no chance of defeat in this case," Douglas Kellner writes, "so Schwarzkopf's metaphor was completely misleading."[65] In fact, the reality of the situation is so dissimilar that Schwarzkopf is forced to go to great lengths to explain that the Americans were badly outnumbered, that Iraq had the advantage of an impregnable defensive position, and that the prospects for victory were exceedingly slim. Having carefully framed the situation, Schwarzkopf can then claim that against these incredible odds, Team America successfully executed an improbable touchdown pass to earn a fantastic victory. This characterization is misleading too, as a Hail Mary pass is a desperate play. In this instance, the American strategy was "a methodically planned and incremental, highly rationalized destruction of Iraqi troops and equipment."[66] Despite the flaws in the metaphor, Schwarzkopf's powerful imagery, not substantiated by any reasonable assessment of the competing forces or the order of battle, casts a heroic tint to the American victory.

Sports Metaphors and Public Argument

In his study of the role played by sport and game in American culture, Michael Oriard suggests that sports metaphors are significant as they contain "American ideas not just about sport and play themselves, but about all the things for which sport and play have become emblems—heroism, success, gender, race, class, the law, religion, salvation; the relations of Humankind, God, and Nature."[67] References to sport, either general or specific, are more than linguistic decoration. Invoking a sports metaphor can have profound implications on the discussion of competing policy alternatives.

Two conclusions seem worth noting. First, the repeated use of sports metaphors to characterize public policy, generally without explanation or qualification, clearly demonstrates that sports are an integral part of American culture. The famed sportswriter Red Smith grasps the obvious when he writes that "one measure of the stature of sports in the American scheme is the extent to which sporting terms are employed away from the playing fields."[68] The ability of advocates to invoke an extended series of football metaphors convincingly demonstrates that Americans share a collective familiarity with their sports and further justifies the claim that sports are an essential element of American culture. "By keeping pace with the use of the sports metaphor in political discourse," Stephan R. Walk suggests, "we may fully understand the collective meanings of sport in American society."[69]

Second, it is also clear from this analysis that the repeated use of sports metaphors does more than demonstrate the importance of sport in

American culture. In Desert Storm discourse, football metaphors did more than characterize military action; they legitimated a particular course of action. In this instance, football metaphors functioned to justify intervention, and at the same time, silenced criticism of that policy. To fully understand such appeals it is important to appreciate that simple metaphors can express powerful narratives.

Recognizing the perverse consequences of sports metaphors in the legal context, some have suggested avoiding sports metaphors altogether,[70] while others have gone so far as to suggest that a conscious effort should be made to substitute nonadversarial metaphors drawn from art or literature.[71] Such criticism is naive in that it underestimates the place of sports in our culture, while simultaneously overestimating the ability of academics to influence public argument. Rather than lamenting either the prominence or the power of these powerful metaphors, a more sophisticated response would be research that heightens our awareness of sports metaphors and criticism that exposes the persuasive appeal of such potent linguistic frames. In the poignant words of Michael Ignatieff, "only the most devoted attention to what is real can help us to make judgments and take actions which are both responsible and efficacious."[72]

Notes

Earlier versions of this chapter were presented at the quadrennial meeting of the International Society for the Study of Argumentation, Amsterdam, June 1998, and the annual meeting of the International Association for Political Psychology, Amsterdam, July 1999.

1. Gordon R. Mitchell, "Spectacular Warfare," in *Arguing Communication and Culture,* ed. G. Thomas Goodnight (Washington, D.C.: National Communication Association, 2002), 1:138.

2. James Der Derian, *Virtual War: Mapping the Military-Industrial-Media-Entertainment Network* (Boulder, Col.: Westview, 2001).

3. Ibid., 202.

4. For an overview to some of this work see Gordon R. Mitchell, "Public Argument-Driven Security Studies," *Argumentation and Advocacy* 39 (summer 2002): 57–71.

5. Mitchell, "Spectacular Warfare," 140.

6. "Conflation of the metaphors and specialized vocabularies of football and war are commonplace." For a brief history on this point, see

Jeffrey O. Segrave, "The Sports Metaphor in American Cultural Discourse," *Culture, Sport, Society* 3 (spring 2000): 49.

7. The phrase "sportspeak" was coined by Robert Lipsyte, *Sportsworld: An American Dreamland* (New York: Quadrangle Books, 1975), 1. Robert A. Palmatier and Harold L. Ray, *Dictionary of Sports Idioms* (Lincolnwood, Ill.: National Textbook, 1993).

8. Francine Hardaway, "Foul Play: Sports Metaphors as Public Doublespeak," in *Sport Inside Out: Readings in Literature and Philosophy,* ed. David L. Vanderwerken and Spencer K. Wertz (Fort Worth: Texas Christian University Press, 1985), 576.

9. Jeffrey O. Segrave, "The Perfect 10: 'Sportspeak' in the Language of Sexual Relations," *Sociology of Sport Journal* 11 (1994): 96.

10. Jeffery Scott Mio, "Metaphor and Politics," *Metaphor and Symbol* 12, no. 2 (1997): 114.

11. John J. MacAloon, "An Observer's View of Sport Sociology," *Sociology of Sport Journal* 4 (1987): 115.

12. Palmatier and Ray, *Dictionary of Sports Idioms,* 214–15.

13. Carol K. Winkler, "Narrative Reframing of Public Argument: George Bush's Handling of the Persian Gulf Conflict," in *Warranting Assent: Case Studies in Argument Evaluation,* ed. Edward Schiappa (Albany: SUNY Press, 1995), 33–55; Robert L. Ivie, "Tragic Fear and the Rhetorical Presidency: Combating Evil in the Persian Gulf," in *Beyond the Rhetorical Presidency,* ed. Martin J. Medhurst (College Station: Texas A&M University Press, 1996), 153–78; Riikka Kuusisto, "The Fairy Tale and the Tragedy? The Western Metaphors of War in the Persian Gulf and Bosnia," in *Argument in a Time of Change: Definitions, Frameworks, and Critiques,* ed. James F. Klumpp (Annandale, Va.: National Communication Association, 1997), 297–303.

14. Sue Curry Jansen and Don Sabo, "The Sport/War Metaphor: Hegemonic Masculinity, the Persian Gulf War, and the New World Order," *Sociology of Sport Journal* 11 (1994): 3.

15. Colman McCarthy, "The Terrible Toll of a Gulf War," *Washington Post,* 13 January 1991, F2.

16. David Evans, "Gulf War Victory Mega-parade: It's Too Much, Too Soon," *Chicago Tribune,* 7 June 1991, 25.

17. "Ready or Not? The Mideast Conflict," *Bergen Record,* 20 December 1990, A1.

18. Bob Kerrey quoted by Morton Kondracke, "Party Pooper: The Democrats and the War," *New Republic,* 25 March 1991, 10.

19. Howard Fineman and Evan Thomas, "Saddam and Bush: The Words of War," *Newsweek*, 21 January 1991, 37.

20. Rick Anderson, "An Obvious Compromise on War and NFL Games," *Seattle Times*, 21 January 1991, C1.

21. Jack R. Payton, "Bush and U.S.: World's Top Cops," *St. Petersburg Times*, 1 August 1991, 3A.

22. Colin Powell quoted by Lionel Barber, "The Gulf War; Bush Pursues Mission without Concession or Conciliation," *Financial Times*, 7 February 1991, 2.

23. H. D. S. Greenway, "Attack Hits Nerve in Jittery Alliance," *Boston Globe*, 14 February 1991, 1.

24. Tom Kenworthy, "Hill Democrats Mute Criticism of Bush Actions; Reluctance to Question President Said to Be a Result of Political, Historical Factors," *Washington Post*, 21 February 1991, A23.

25. Walter D. Sutton, Jr., "Arab-Israeli Dispute Must Be Resolved Peacefully," *St. Petersburg Times*, 9 January 1991, 2.

26. Thomas L. Friedman, "Mideast Talks: Peace Might Be an Incidental Result," *New York Times*, 24 July 1991, A8.

27. Fineman and Thomas, "Saddam and Bush," 37.

28. Stephen Kurkjian, "Bush Plays Down Potential for War; President Seeks to Clarify Bellicose Words," *Boston Globe*, 2 November 1990, 1.

29. Laurence Jolidon, "U.S. Pilots Are Confident Iraqis No Match in Air," *USA Today*, 15 January 1991, 6A.

30. Guy Gugiotta and Caryle Murphy, "Warplanes Roar Off in Darkness in 'Desert Storm,'" *Washington Post*, 17 January 1991, A1.

31. James Adams, "Norman after the Storm," *London Sunday Times*, 27 September 1992, n.p.

32. Bill McClellan, "Remembering Those Gulfs between Wars," *St. Louis Post-Dispatch*, 27 May 1991, 3A.

33. Patrick J. Sloyan, "Iraqi Guns Preserved; Still, Effect of Allied Air Raids Called 'Good Progress,'" *Newsday*, 9 February 1991, 5.

34. J. Freeman, "TV's Desert Fox Thinks Up a Storm," *San Diego Union-Tribune*, 29 March 1991, E6; Evans, "Gulf War Victory Mega-parade," 25; J. Hanchette, "Gen. Dugan Is Latest in Line of Top Brass Booted for Comments," Gannett News Service, 19 September 1990;

35. Maureen Dowd, "War in the Gulf," *New York Times*, 22 February 1991, A1.

36. Evans, "Gulf War Victory Mega-parade," 25.

37. R. W. Apple, Jr., "War in the Gulf; U.S. Says Iraq Pumps Kuwaiti Oil into Gulf; Vast Damage Feared from Growing Slick," *New York Times*, 26 January 1991, 1.

38. "The Edge of the Abyss," *Newsweek*, 21 January 1991, 20.

39. Christopher Madison, "Follow the Leader," *National Journal*, 12 January 1991, 104.

40. Kevin Phillips, "The Vietnam Syndrome; Why Is Bush Hurting if There Is No War?" *Los Angeles Times*, 25 November 1990, M1.

41. "Shielding the World from Iraq . . . and Why an Embargo Can Work," *Chicago Tribune*, 14 August 1990, 14.

42. "Excerpts from Schwarzkopf News Conference on Gulf War," *New York Times*, 24 February 1991, A3.

43. Wayne Wickham, "NFL Films out of Element in Mideast," *USA Today*, 2 April 1991, 10C.

44. Tony Chamberlain, "Are Odes to the Game Really out in Left Field?" *Boston Globe*, 5 April 1991, 76; Lee Bowman, "One Sided; The Winners Gloat, the Losers Retreat," *St. Petersburg Times*, 28 February 1991, 4A; M. Thomas Davis, "After the Friendly Fire; Remembering Sgt. Young Dillon, a Brave Life We Left in the Gulf," *Washington Post*, 30 May 1993, C5.

45. Leslie H. Gelb, "A New Mideast Balance," *New York Times*, 6 March 1991, A25.

46. Scot Shepard, "Gore Denounces GOP Cheap Shots on War; Democrat Defends Votes of Conscience," *Atlanta Journal and Constitution*, 7 March 1991, A4.

47. "Fort Hood Troops Head for Gulf; Secretary to Confer with Allies," *Fort Worth Star-Telegram*, 14 September 1991, 1.

48. James J. Kilpatrick, "Let's Separate Hawks from Chickens on Iraq," *Atlanta Journal and Constitution*, 28 August 1992, A12.

49. Palmatier and Ray, *Dictionary of Sports Idioms*, ix.

50. Murray Edelman, *Politics as Symbolic Action* (Chicago: Markham, 1971), 67.

51. Richard Lipsky, *How We Play the Game: Why Sports Dominate American Life* (Boston: Beacon, 1981), 134.

52. George Lakoff and Mark Turner, *More Than Cool Reason: A Field Guide to Poetic Metaphor* (Chicago: University of Chicago Press, 1989), 214.

53. Segrave, "The Sports Metaphor," 52.

54. Richard Lipsky, "The Athleticization of Politics: The Political Implication of Sports Metaphors," *Journal of Sport and Social Issues* 3 (1979): 36.

55. Although generally attributed to Vince Lombardi, there is reason to believe that this quotation actually predates the legendary coach and further, that it misrepresents his philosophy of winning. The origins of the quotation are discussed at more length in David Maraniss, *When Pride Still Mattered: A Life of Vince Lombardi* (New York: Simon and Schuster, 1999), 364–70.

56. The significance of the spectator sport metaphor is more fully elaborated in Michael Mann, *States, War and Capitalism: Studies in Political Sociology* (Oxford: Blackwell, 1988), 184–85.

57. Isaac Balbus, "Politics as Sports: The Political Ascendancy of the Sports Metaphor in America," *Monthly Review* 26, no. 10 (March 1975): 30.

58. Jansen and Sabo, "The Sport/War Metaphor," 13.

59. Paula Edelson, "Sports during Wartime," *Z Magazine*, May 1991, 85.

60. See Margot Norris, "Only the Guns Have Eyes: Military Censorship and the Body Count," in *Seeing through the Media: The Persian Gulf War*, ed. Susan Jeffords and Lauren Rabinovitz (New Brunswick, N.J.: Rutgers University Press, 1994), 285–300.

61. Lewis H. Lapham, "Trained Seals and Sitting Ducks," in *The Media and the Gulf War*, ed. Hedrick Smith (Washington, D.C.: Seven Locks Press, 1992), 259.

62. Daniel C. Hallin, "Images of the Vietnam and the Persian Gulf Wars in U.S. Television," in *Seeing through the Media: The Persian Gulf War*, 55.

63. William Safire, "The Longest Huddle," *New York Times*, 23 September 1982, A27.

64. Hardaway, "Foul Play," 581.

65. Douglas Kellner, *The Persian Gulf TV War* (Boulder, Col.: Westview, 1992), 371.

66. Ibid.

67. Michael Oriard, *Sporting with the Gods: The Rhetoric of Play and Game in American Culture* (Cambridge: Cambridge University Press, 1991), ix.

68. Red Smith, "Spoken Like a True Son of Old Whittier," *New York Times*, 30 April 1973, 39.

69. Stephan R. Walk, "The Footrace Metaphor in American Presidential Rhetoric," *Sociology of Sport Journal* 12, no. 1 (March 1995): 52.

70. See Chad M. Oldfather, "The Hidden Ball: A Substantive Critique of Baseball Metaphors in Judicial Opinions," *Connecticut Law Review* 27 (1994): 17–51; and Maureen Archer and Ronnie Cohen, "Sidelined on the (Judicial) Bench: Sports Metaphors in Judicial Opinions," *American Business Law Journal* 35 (1998): 225–42.

71. Elizabeth G. Thornburg, "Metaphors Matter: How Images of Battle, Sports, and Sex Shape the Adversary System," *Wisconsin Women's Law Journal* 10 (1995): 225–81.

72. Michael Ignatieff, *Virtual War: Kosovo and beyond* (New York: Picador, 2000), 214.

Paths through the Minefields of Foreign Policy Space

Practical Reasoning in U.S. Senate Discourse about Cambodia

Francis A. Beer and G. Robert Boynton

A path metaphor is appropriate for exploring practical reasoning about United States foreign policy. Political deliberation about the future is characterized as a set of paths.[1] These paths establish narrative continuity between past, present, and future. Alternative possible future paths exist in the form of past precedents. Actors travel along the paths. The actors want certain things, and they interact on the paths. Decision makers consider other actors' capabilities, primarily military ones.

"Path" is a central metaphor in political communication. Originating in common human physical experience, the path schema fits many different political contexts. Such schematic paths have multiple dimensions—temporality, spatiality, direction, texture, volume—to name only a few.

The general topic of "pathness" is fascinating and complex. An extended linguistic literature centers on the different meanings and interpretations of "path."[2] Abstract, mathematical techniques focus on path analysis, path dependence, and critical paths. More important, "path" is one of the founding metaphors of cognitive science and artificial intelligence; for example, it is central to two of the field's most important texts.[3] These authors construct cognitive activity as exploration of a space by proceeding from one point to the next. The paths lead to problem solutions, winning moves in games, proofs of theorems, or completion of other cognitive activities.[4]

We begin with this literature and seek to apply it to a specific case of foreign policy discourse, a Senate subcommittee hearing concerned with United States foreign policy toward Cambodia. As we have suggested, the hearing is not unique in characterizing its exploration of possible U.S. actions as an exploration of paths. Yet, in this discourse, the path metaphor provides a concrete model that helps us to understand practical political reasoning.[5]

Data: The Hearing

Our data appear in the form of the published record of a hearing conducted in 1990 by the Subcommittee on East Asia and Pacific Affairs of the Committee on Foreign Relations of the U.S. Senate.[6] Verbatim records of committee hearings provide a data source long available but almost totally neglected. Considered as data, hearings are much richer than the aggregate data taken from statistical sources or the events data abstracted from newspaper "stories." They are more contemporary than official government documents released decades later for historical inquiry. They provide records of the spoken word, contemporary oral histories of international relations and foreign policy in the making. They are among the best information we have on actual cognitive and communicative processes at work in making current foreign policy.

The text of a hearing divides into three parts. Witnesses prepare written statements to enter into the record. They offer brief oral summaries of the prepared statements. And then members of the (sub)committee ask questions, which often initiate brief conversations about the subject. Here we limit our analysis to the oral interaction between senators and witnesses.

The members most active in questioning witnesses were Senator Alan Cranston (D-Calif.), the chairman of the subcommittee; Senators John Kerry (D-Mass.) and Paul Sarbanes (D-Md.), who were members of the Foreign Relations Committee but not this subcommittee; and Senator Robert Kerrey (D-Neb.), who was not a member of the Foreign Relations

Committee but who has a considerable interest in Southeast Asia. Less involved in the questioning were Senators Joseph Biden, Jr. (D-Del.), Frank Murkowski (D-Alaska), and Charles Robb (D-Va.). The witnesses included former Vice President and Secretary of State Edmund Muskie; John Bolton and David Lambertson, from the State Department; and a third panel composed of Mr. Michael Horowitz, a Washington attorney and prominent political conservative, Dr. Helen Chauncey, professor of government at Georgetown University, Dr. Jeremy Stone, president of the Federation of American Scientists, and former CIA director William Colby.

Through questions and answers, the discussion skips quickly from one subject to another. Each senator asks a number of questions, often changing the topic from one question to the next; and, as the questioning passes from one senator to the next, the flow is further disrupted. For analysis here, we divided the verbatim record into conversational units; when the subject changes, a new conversational unit starts. This kind of division is a straightforward task. Two readers selected forty-five separate conversations involving discussion of the future.

Paths

"That may have looked OK then, but in retrospect I think we have to admit that it took us down the wrong path." "Path" is an important explicit metaphor in the conversations. In the sentence quoted above, Senator Kerry draws a conclusion about earlier U.S. actions in regard to Cambodia. The "it," the action, took us down the wrong *path,* he says. Senator Sarbanes invokes the same metaphor in discussing one feature of the administration's proposals: "I take it from your answer that . . . you would not want to go down that *path.*" Mr. Lambertson, from the State Department, uses the metaphor when he says, "there are indeed many obstacles remaining in the *path* toward a comprehensive settlement of this kind." Throughout the hearing, the talk shifts easily among past, present, and future tenses, reflecting the continuity of past-present-future as one path.[7]

The participants use additional metaphors to characterize their exploration of possible actions, but "path" is particularly apt. It implies a terrain to be traversed. A path is a sequence of steps leading from the current location to another point in the space. At any step along the way, the path may turn. And if there are several paths, one may take up where you want to go, while another might be the "wrong path." Thus the conversants explore possible paths to discover the bottlenecks, the circularities, the dead ends that lead away from the position they want to reach.

Starting Points: Situations

The conversation places the actors at different starting positions. In foreign policy discourse, we can consider these starting points as locations where the discussants initialize the actors and their actions; they are where the paths begin. They describe these situations as follows.

1. The *Hun Sen government* controls Cambodia but with less support from Vietnam and the Soviet Union than in the past. It is fighting increased guerrilla activity by the Khmer Rouge, which seeks a settlement that would include elections, recognition from Western nations, and trade with the West.

2. The *Khmer Rouge* has the strongest fighting force (thirty-five thousand) of the three antigovernment factions, and they are stepping up attacks on the Hun Sen government. Their military aid from China continues. In the negotiations they supported the Sihanouk proposal.

3. *Prince Sihanouk* continues to receive support from China and the United States. China and the Bush administration view him as central to any overall restructuring of relations. He has proposed a plan to involve the Hun Sen government and its three opponents in a temporary quadripartite national council, followed by elections supervised by the UN.

4. The hearing mentions the *Son Sann faction* only three times, making it the ignored party, though it continues to receive support from the U.S.

5. *Vietnam* has withdrawn its troops from Cambodia but still supports the Hun Sen government, support that extends to the international negotiations. Vietnam, too, wants recognition and trade from the West.

6. *China* continues to support the Khmer Rouge and Sihanouk through military aid and international negotiations. No one can say what would lead China to withdraw military support from the Khmer Rouge.

7. The *Soviet Union* seems to be doing very little in Southeast Asia. It participates in negotiations of the five permanent members of the UN Security Council, but it has not been energetic there.

8. The *Bush administration* continues to support the non-Communist factions. It does not recognize and will not communicate with the Hun Sen government or Vietnam, except in the Security Council negotiations. It wants Sihanouk to be central to any settlement,

supporting his plan for a quadripartite government and an election supervised by the United Nations.

Even though many questions and answers in the hearing concern the current situation in Cambodia, there is little disagreement among senators and witnesses about these starting points. Some participants disagree with the administration's position, for example, but none disagree about what the administration position is. There are mysteries—what it should take to get China to change its position—but no disagreement about the current position of China. This sense of the present situation is the starting point for all paths into the future.

Ending Points: Goals

For the discussants, the starting points are elaborate, but the desired ending point, the goal, is simple—fair and free elections. Lambertson summarizes the administration's plan in the following way: "We are working very hard to achieve a solution built around a United Nations presence in Cambodia which would not give administrative power or governmental power to any of these factions as factions and that would, we hope, serve to get Cambodia through this transitional process safety and securely to a *fair and free election.*"[8] The administration's complicated plan projects a "fair and free election." But the administration is not alone in seeing elections as the desired outcome. Colby is a critic of the administration plan but his "end state" is the same: "I say the sooner the better on those. We are engaged in a long complicated negotiation to try to achieve a comprehensive settlement among the four parties. . . . The first order of business needs to be to achieve a legitimation of somebody representing the Cambodian people. That can only come through *elections.*"[9] "Fair and free elections" is like a mantra repeated over and over. "Elections" in Cambodia appears approximately 160 times in the conversations, modified about half the time by either "free" or "fair." Moreover, the recent elections in Nicaragua and Namibia become precedents for holding elections in Cambodia under one condition or another. "Elections" is the focal ending point of the subcommittee conversations.

Paths between: Sequences and Strategies

The participants in the hearing agree completely on the actual starting points and their desired ending point, but they agree much less on the paths between them—on how to get from here to there. These paths involve alternative sequences of action and strategic calculations.

Various paths are proposed to the subcommittee, but they reject one agreed path: continuing the status quo would lead to victory by the "genocidal" Khmer Rouge. The strong Khmer Rouge military force means to the conversants that the threatened Cambodian government cannot withstand Khmer Rouge attacks for long without outside assistance. No senator and no witness want this "wrong path" to lead to this antigoal. Many participants in the hearing cite its very possibility as a spur to action. All want action designed to prevent a Khmer Rouge victory.

Witnesses recommend three paths to elections in Cambodia: one comes from Muskie, a second is the administration's policy, and a four-person panel of outside experts offers a third. All advise the U.S. government—the first Bush administration—viewing Cambodia's future from the perspective of U.S. action. How U.S. acts will or will not lead to fair and free elections depends on what other actors do, as we discuss in the next section, but the hearing focuses on what the United States could and should do.

Inevitably we simplify the five hours of conversation, presenting only the major claims in terms of three paths. We cannot picture the complete space, with all the possible combinations of acts. Even the simplest of assumptions would require hundreds of points in the full combinatorial space. But we have two further reasons for featuring only these paths. First, the senators and witnesses do not discuss all possible combinations: they focus their discussion. And second, research by cognitive scientists on problem solving finds that experts, with chess experts the favorite example, do not reason through the entire space; rather they "see" the best possibilities and concentrate on those. Like chess experts, the senators and witnesses focus on the "best" paths.

Alternative Paths

Muskie's Path

Muskie had visited Cambodia and prepared a report for the Center for National Policy. What he learned became the basis of his testimony as the leadoff witness. Muskie's questions and answers cover a wide range of topics reaching back into the history of the Vietnam War. They elicit his impressions of all the actors in the situation and his criticisms of elements in the Bush administration's policy. Like the other witnesses, Muskie worries that the status quo would lead to a victory by the Khmer Rouge, and he argues that an election in Cambodia to legitimize the government and subsequent Western support is the best way to keep the Khmer Rouge from returning to power. Muskie makes at least six proposals.

1. The United States should begin negotiations on elections with the Hun Sen government.
2. The United States should cut off aid to the non-Communist factions, reducing their ability to attack the government and encouraging them to participate in elections.
3. The Hun Sen government should remain in office until after the elections.
4. The UN should organize the elections.
5. The United States should work with the other permanent members of the Security Council to arrange for UN–organized elections.
6. The United States should support the duly elected Cambodian government if the Khmer Rouge attempts to attack it after the elections.[10]

Muskie says that this sequence of steps, this path, would correct the explosive situation that threatens to return the Khmer Rouge to power.

The Administration's Path

A return of the Khmer Rouge is the worst possible outcome, say the administration witnesses. On this point, they agree with the other witnesses. But the administration differs in its path to preclude that possibility. It rejects direct negotiation with the Hun Sen government, preferring international talks to reach a comprehensive settlement agreeable to all actors.[11] The alternative, it says, is continued military conflict.[12] The comprehensive settlement would contain six elements:

1. a national council to include the Hun Sen government and the three opposing factions in the transition to elections,
2. an interim transfer of executive power from the Hun Sen government to the UN,
3. a UN peacekeeping force to round up arms from all sides and to police the cantonment of factions in Cambodia until after the elections,
4. a set of elections organized and supervised by the UN and a disposition of the Cambodian seat in the UN, to be worked out as part of the total package, and
5. a U.S. diplomatic recognition of Vietnam, also as part of the settlement.[13]

The result would be the election of a Cambodian government by a procedure accepted by all parties, including China and the Khmer Rouge;

therefore the election outcome would be acceptable to all parties. An important assumption is that the Khmer Rouge would not win the elections;[14] otherwise the agreement would not succeed in keeping the Khmer Rouge from power.

Outside Experts' Paths

A comprehensive settlement, such as the one proposed by the administration, would come together only after long, tedious negotiations, and that seemed the likely fate of these negotiations. In the interim, everyone agreed, the Khmer Rouge was increasing its strength on the battlefield. By permitting Khmer Rouge participation in the national council and in the elections, moreover, the administration's policy actually might ease a Khmer Rouge return to political influence. These were the major criticisms from a panel of expert witnesses, criticisms that received a very sympathetic hearing from the subcommittee members. The expert panel included Chauncey, Colby, Horowitz, and Stone. It proposed to minimize the number of agreements to be negotiated, thus speeding elections, and to keep the Khmer Rouge out of the political process. In particular, the panel suggested that

1. the United States begin direct negotiations with the Hun Sen government,
2. the United States support elections organized by the Hun Sen government,
3. the Hun Sen government stay in power until a new government is elected,
4. international observers be called in to supervise the fairness of the elections,
5. the United States use its support for the non-Communist factions fighting the Hun Sen government to encourage their participation in the elections, and
6. the United States, Vietnam, and other nations then support the duly elected government.[15]

Organization of the elections by the Hun Sen government and supervision by international observers are the major differences between this proposal and Muskie's.

If we ask how committee members and witnesses move easily between assertions about the past and the future, part of the answer is their construction of a framework for assessment. The hearing's framework parallels the frameworks for cognitive dynamics investigated by cognitive scientists:

a space of possible actions, a well-defined starting and ending point, and an exploration of sequences of action. Witnesses identify the most plausible sequences and then join the subcommittee members in assessing them.

Consistent with the principle of bounded rationality, the senators and witnesses do not explore the complete space of possibilities. Instead the witnesses, as experts, specify the best sequences to explore. Here a path framework is readily identifiable, but other frameworks for reasoning appear in other committees and subcommittees;[16] and this is consistent with the claim that people adapt their practical reasoning to their subjects, as understood by the individuals involved.

Other Desired Endpoints: Stories about What X Wants

Without exception, the hearing talks about the actors as goal directed; they do not act because of outside forces but in order to achieve their aims. "What X wants" is the key to understanding what X will do in the future.

Sihanouk's Goals

An exchange between Kerry and Lambertson illustrates these points. The question parallels one posed of Muskie. For more than a decade, with support from the United States and China, Sihanouk had led opposition to the Vietnamese-supported government of Hun Sen. Senators explore the possibility of elections to include the Hun Sen government and the non-Communist opposition, leaving out the Khmer Rouge. What would it take to get Sihanouk to join in such an arrangement?

> Senator Kerry: And you think that Sihanouk, given his history, having watched him maneuver his way through the greatest survival course in history, that this individual would not move fairly rapidly to negotiations if he saw the Khmer Rouge drying up—with the *support* for them drying? You do not think he would shift very rapidly into a posture of participating in an election?

> Mr. Lambertson: I think Sihanouk is serious when he says that he wants to see a substantial dismantling of the PRK regime, an election held under circumstances in which *Hun Sen does not have an advantage*. He goes very far in this direction. He regards the PRK as a puppet government installed by Vietnamese invasion. He is very outspoken. I think he means it.[17]

Senator Kerry finds a clue in Sihanouk's history to explain why he would be likely to participate in elections without the Khmer Rouge. Sihanouk survives by going where the support is. If support for the Khmer Rouge were to dry up, he would move again. At least, that is how Senator Kerry explains Sihanouk's actions. Lambertson disagrees, offering an alternate explanation: Sihanouk will participate only in elections where Hun Sen has no advantage; and the only way to bring that about is "a substantial dismantling of the PRK regime," to be achieved with the national council and the UN taking over the executive reins of the Cambodian government. Both explanations are goal oriented, but they differ in the goal attributed to Sihanouk. Each is brief, but each lays out a pattern of actions consistent with moving toward the goal.

What would it take to get Sihanouk to join in such an arrangement? Muskie cannot find a pattern in Sihanouk's actions to explain what he wants; Senator Kerry does find a pattern, which becomes what Sihanouk wants in this situation; and Lambertson explains what Sihanouk wants in different terms. All the explanations assume that there is something Sihanouk wants in the situation and that it will be required to get him to participate in elections.

Vietnamese Goals

When asked about the Vietnamese, Muskie likewise offers an account of what they want:

> Mr. Muskie: It was the first subject they raised, really. Both Do Muoi, who is the Chairman of the Council of Ministers, or the Prime Minister, and the Foreign Minister, Thack, that is the first subject they raised.
>
> They just do not understand. They said they understood that their cooperation on MIA/POW was a condition. Then we added to that, withdrawal from Cambodia. Then we would not go for verification of that withdrawal, so they are left hanging on that one.
>
> And then finally, the third condition we added is that they have to approve the quadripartite solution, notwithstanding their doubts about the security of Cambodia and the Khmer Rouge.
>
> They ticked it off.
>
> Senator Murkowski: Well, they are just throwing their hands up.
>
> Mr. Muskie: They threw their hands up. But they are still interested. They want to *normalize* with us. They want to *normalize* with China. They want to move toward economic development and growth. They

emphasized that over and over again. There is nothing belligerent in anything that I encountered. They would like to sell shrimp in the United States.[18]

Vietnam wants normalization of relations and expanded trade with the United States. How do we know? When the United States says that Vietnam must cooperate on identifying Americans missing in action and returning American prisoners of war before the United States recognizes Vietnam, it does that. Then when the United States says that Vietnam must withdraw from Cambodia before the United States recognizes Vietnam, it does so. When the United States then demands that Vietnam approve the quadripartite solution before gaining recognition, Vietnam just throws up its hands, but it remains interested. Muskie finds a pattern in these actions that makes plausible his answer to the question of what Vietnam wants: normalized relations with the United States.

The hearing discusses most of the actors in these terms: the Hun Sen government, Sihanouk, and the Vietnamese all want normalized relations and trade with the West. Everyone knows what the Khmer Rouge want: to take over Cambodia again. But the Chinese get special attention—almost half of the conversations about what would X want are about China. As a permanent member of the Security Council, China can facilitate or block UN action. As supplier of arms to the Khmer Rouge, China can end or sustain that challenge. What China wants is also important to all three proposals.

What X wants is important because it will lead to action consistent or inconsistent with each path into the future proposed to the subcommittee. What X wants and the explanation for it appears in the stories told about X.

Unexpected Events on the Path

A number of different types of unexpected events can happen along paths in policy space. The committee explores some of these by asking, "what would happen if?"

What Would Happen if?

"What would happen if?" is a question that seeks to discover land mines buried on the paths. Senators argue about minefields that appear along the way, making a path impassable. And in one case, as Senator Sarbones

contends, they argue that a path goes in the wrong direction. The forty-
five conversations about these paths into the future are the database for
analysis in this section.

Simple assertions—"this is what will happen"—occur infrequently. Instead the path ahead is explored, as we have already seen, by discussing
the goals of individuals or nations. In addition, the conversation explores
how multiple streams of action intersect to produce an outcome and the
ways in which different actions should lead us to change expectations
about what actors will do.

The following quotation from the hearing illustrates the "what if" question found throughout its conversations.[19]

> Senator Cranston: Could the Hun Sen government proceed to hold an
> election?
>
> Mr. Horowitz: May I comment, Mr. Chairman, because I raised this di-
> rectly with Hun Sen . . . He has opposed it shrewdly because he knows
> that if the Cambodians ran an election on their own it would not gain
> any international credibility for the government. It would be written off
> as a phony staged election; therefore, he has sought against all these in-
> ternal pressures to hold off elections . . . hoping to come up with a for-
> mula which would give his government some international recognition
> and ending the isolation of his country particularly and by international
> community of his government.

The chairman asks *why Hun Sen could not hold elections without all the inter-*
national negotiations being conducted at the time. Notice that this is the simplest possible path between the current situation and elections, the end
state espoused by everyone in the hearing. The witness answers with an
explanation. Yes, Hun Sen is under pressure to hold elections from within
Cambodia as well as from the international community of nations, he says
But such elections would subject Hun Sen to the criticism that the elections
were not free and fair, so they would not produce the international legitimacy needed for diplomacy and trade with the West. First, the witness
gives two reasons why Hun Sen might call an election. Then he invokes
what everyone in the hearing knows about Western views of elections
conducted by Communist governments: they are not likely to be free and
fair. Merely to hold elections would not work, because an important audience would dismiss them. The plausibility of the answer—why a path is
not taken—lies within the explanation. It brings together information that

senators know about international politics with information that they do not know about Cambodia.

What would happen if the United States attempts to get the *UN to organize elections and the Khmer Rouge loses?* The answer depends in part on what China, the principle supporter of the Khmer Rouge, would do. Senator Cranston asks Lambertson from the State Department about this.

> Mr. Lambertson: Based on our own conversations within the permanent five with China, based on China's evolving position over the past year—and it has changed—I remain of the view that *China wants to help* to bring about a comprehensive settlement of the kind we are talking about. That would mean that it would cooperate with the international community in addressing the problem of the Khmer Rouge and in helping to control it.
>
> Senator Cranston: That sounds pretty optimistic to me.[20]

One way to answer is with an assertion. Thus Lambertson suggests that China says it will cooperate. One can imagine times when this would be an acceptable answer, but Senator Cranston suggests that this is not one of them. In this hearing, assertions are not as convincing as explanations.

Asked if there is *any way to end Sihanouk's dependence on China,* former Secretary of State Muskie answers, "I think he has not given us a very clear view of what it is that he wants"[21]—but it takes Muskie 320 words to get to this nonanswer. He recounts the past importance of Sihanouk's connection with China; he notes that Sihanouk resigned as head of the coalition against the Hun Sen government before the Jakarta meeting, moving back to Cambodia for the first time in ten years; he reflects on the substantial decrease in "comfort" involved; he recalls that Sihanouk proposed the quadripartite national council that had become the major barrier to further progress in the negotiations; and he notes that Sihanouk could, if he wanted, play an important role in the new government even if Hun Sen won the elections. Muskie seems to be searching through Sihanouk's recent actions for clues about his "wants," for something that would explain what he knows about Sihanouk, but Muskie does not succeed in finding a successful explanation. Hence Muskie remains unable to answer the question.

Interactions within Sequences of Events

This discussion makes clear the difficulty of isolating the likely policy effects of individual actions taken by themselves. It is necessary to consider the pattern of sequencing as well as interactions within the sequences of actions that make up possible paths into the future. This kind of analysis accounts for what will happen by relating pieces of the paths that need to work together. Ten of the conversations use sequence to explain why some stretch of path is or is not viable. Four explain the likely impact of extended negotiations on the military balance in the region. Two address roles for the UN and four concern other features of the situation.

Negotiating and Fighting

Interaction appears in a pair of events of so much concern to the subcommittee that it occupies all three panels. Negotiations among all the parties are ongoing, but so is fighting. Questioned about the effects of delay, the administration agrees that the military threat from the Khmer Rouge is increasing: "It is our view that sustained fighting is likely to benefit the Khmer Rouge more than any other party."[22] And a witness on the third panel pushes the interaction even further.

> Dr. Stone: the spirit of what Mr. Colby and I have said today is that this international *negotiating* game could go on for a very long time. During that time the Khmer Rouge could get so *strong* that they could not be stopped. Some time limit, therefore, has to be put on this negotiation. . . .
>
> What we have to get away from, though, is an effort unlimited in time to get a comprehensive proposal.[23]

Negotiating and fighting are occurring in parallel, and the negotiating could become so protracted as to be moot: the Khmer Rouge might win on the battlefield what it could not get at the negotiating table, explains Stone. For him, this expressly criticizes administration policy. If the administration cannot achieve its comprehensive settlement soon, it would do better to proceed with elections under international (not U.S.) supervision rather than chancing that the Khmer Rouge might return to power by military means.

UN Conflict Resolution

Negotiations and fighting combine in one kind of interaction found in the conversations. Two others are that some events must by their very nature occur in a specific sequence and that some events must occur in a specific sequence in order to sustain a bargaining relationship.

Sequence is important in the two proposals for using the UN to resolve the conflicts. Muskie suggests that the UN supervise elections in Cambodia without waiting for a comprehensive settlement. On the expert panel, however, Jeremy Stone explains a problem with that step on the path recommended by Muskie: "the U.N. lawyers cannot figure out how to deal with the problem that the *U.N. cannot administer a country over the dead body of the Khmer Rouge* because they hold the *U.N. credentials* for the country. That is very much against the U.N.'s legalistic approach. Once you give the credentials to the country, you cannot do something over their dead body."[24]

The Khmer Rouge and the two non-Communist factions hold the Cambodian seat at the United Nations. A "legalistic approach" precludes the UN from entering a country unless invited by the party holding its seat. Before the UN could supervise elections in Cambodia, the holder of its UN seat would need to change, and that could happen only if China (and possibly the Khmer Rouge) were to agree. Since the Muskie proposal hopes to succeed by sidestepping agreements with China and the Khmer Rouge, it requires sequencing that could not work.

A different sequencing problem is explained by Michael Horowitz, also a member of the expert panel. One proposal for dismantling the Hun Sen government would have UN personnel take over its three hundred top jobs, but the UN does not have three hundred people who can speak the language, and Cambodia does not have three hundred translators. Without needed speakers or translators, explains Horowitz, the proposal cannot work. Here is another minefield right in the middle of the administration path.

A third set of explanations based on event sequences involves the comprehensive settlement pursued by the administration through negotiations tied to the UN Security Council. Under this plan, remember, all parties would agree to cease fighting, withdraw the opposing forces, have the UN head the government while a four-party national council prepared for elections, and let the UN administer the elections. According to the administration, the conflict could be resolved only if this set of actions comes together "as a package." In eight conversations, members of the subcommittee ask administration witnesses about particular actions that the United States might take, and every time the answer is that each action must be part of the total package. Five of these conversations address what X wants and how to bring it into the package. Thus Senator Cranston asks whether the UN could not proceed to install the Hun Sen government in the

Cambodian seat, but Lambertson answers, "The disposition of the Cambodian seat is going to be and should be one of the issues decided in the context of the negotiation. It is an important issue to the Cambodians. It is important politically, and it will be addressed in the settlement process." The "package" is a set of actions, with some inducing an individual or a nation to take other actions that it otherwise would prefer not to take. To say that the seat in the UN is important to the Cambodians is to suggest that a change now in seating would give the Hun Sen government less reason to go along with other parts of the package. The administration path is a specific sequencing of actions, meant to avoid mines and reach the goal; other sequences of the same actions would set off the mines, keeping the parties from their goal.[25]

The hearing treats history as the interaction of events that joins past, present, and future. This is a narrative conception of history, finding repetition or pattern only in the details. Thus the history of Cambodia is a frequent subject in the conversations, but it does not appear in comparisons to other histories, for there is no generalization across histories. Any path that tries to extend the history of Cambodia into the future sought depends on the interaction—and thus the sequencing—of events. Consequently the conversations about interactions among events articulate this conception of history in direct and vivid terms, with witnesses and subcommittee members explaining how diverse sequences configure events to interact with one another, producing futures that discussants want to achieve or avoid.

Precedents

Precedents are crucial for critics of the administration policy. Muskie, members of the third panel, and members of the subcommittee want elections in Cambodia as soon as possible: the sooner the elections, the less time for the Khmer Rouge to achieve military superiority. But there has been a major impediment to their proposals. Cranston and Horowitz discuss how that impediment has been exploded.

> Senator Cranston: I guess one thing new that we have going for us is that the traditional wisdom that a Communist regime would never willingly relinquish power with an election and instead would resort to bloodshed has now been exploded so that we have a new opportunity to convince people.

> Mr. Horowitz: This is what *Nicaragua* does. I am not sure that the Ortega government would have consented to the election had they not thought that by stacking it and making it unfair they could not fail to win it. We

have exposed that now. That is why Nicaragua is so important. Mr. Chairman, if Ortega had won in Nicaragua, I think Dr. Lambertson's policy would have been safe for the next three years—he could stand against elections on the theory that it would be stacked, and while we could try to make distinctions between U.N.–run elections and Ortega-run elections, but it wouldn't help. Ortega not only lost, but lost in a landslide, and that being the case, I think the confidence by which we all can trust moving to free elections on a rapid basis is enormously enhanced.

Critics of the administration say that they do not have to explain how a Communist nation would leave office after losing an election: "The traditional wisdom . . . has now been exploded." Nicaragua is important because the government stayed in place, as the critics propose for Cambodia, yet the Sandinistas lost. In their characterization of the Nicaraguan election, Cranston and Horowitz simplify, generalize, and match it to the Cambodian election they propose.

Four of the conversations about "what would happen if" follow this pattern closely, invoking Namibia as a further precedent to make the point. Two other conversations mention the Nicaraguan and Namibian elections to make slightly different points about how the election in Cambodia could be conducted. Likewise Kerry uses the massacre at Tiananmen Square as a precedent, saying that he cannot understand how the administration could talk to China after Tiananmen Square but could not talk to the Hun Sen government now.

Military Assessments

The military situation is another important element in thinking about "what would happen if" in Cambodia. What is the relative military capability of the Khmer Rouge and the Hun Sen government? What if China continues to supply the Khmer Rouge? What if China stops? What if Vietnam becomes involved again? The implications of these questions thread throughout the hearing.

Despite the importance of such questions, only five conversations address them directly. Senator Sarbanes specializes in them, initiating four of the five conversations. He runs through all the permutations of support for the newly elected government in Cambodia, asking who would win. Muskie answers the Hun Sen government. Lambertson says that the Khmer Rouge would probably continue to be a viable guerrilla force. And former CIA director Colby, on the third panel, replies that the Cambodian government, with assistance from Vietnam, could hold off the Khmer Rouge.[26]

The most extraordinary feature of these conversations is the lack of elaboration. There is no comparison of troops, no comparison of weaponry. The questions are elaborate, but the answers are simple assertions. The only hint of elaboration is in Colby's reply: "I think with the promise of the Vietnamese backing Phnom Penh, yes, they could [control the Khmer Rouge]. That is what has happened the last few years."[27] "That is what has happened the last few years" is the closest these witnesses get to explaining their military assessments. The only conversations that challenge the accepted view of the Khmer Rouge's military capability involve Horowitz and Stone. Horowitz tells stories, the standard practice for other subjects, and Stone cites a secret CIA briefing for another congressional committee in reply to the Horowitz stories.

We cannot be sure why these conversations take such different turns. One possible answer may lie in the practice of discussing military secrets in closed hearings; the conversants even allude to that practice at one point.[28] Whatever the reason, the military assessments are the only conversations in this hearing that address "what would happen if?" through assertions rather than explanations.

Conversations that concern the military balance are not limited to the comparisons just described. Similar conclusions appear in many other conversations, but where they form the core, explanations are scarce. In the four conversations about how the lengthy negotiations and the increasing military strength of the Khmer Rouge will intersect, for example, the assessment of the Khmer Rouge military capability serves only as a fact, even if an important one.

Conclusion

Our discussion has focused on the way in which the path metaphor frames foreign policy conversation. Hearings in the U.S. Senate Foreign Relations Subcommittee on East Asia and Pacific Affairs suggest what the path metaphor can mean in policy space. The actors and their situations are defined with clear starting positions. U.S. policymakers have clear goals in mind, and other major actors are also seen as having desired ending points. "What does X want?" is a question that explores multiple motivations. The paths between the beginning and the end appear as alternative sequences and strategies involving actions and events. Unexpected events are developed by asking, "what would happen if?" Among the unexpected landmines in the paths are sequence anomalies and event interactions. Negotiating and fighting occur in parallel, often working at cross-purposes. The United Nations is needed for conflict resolution but is composed of warring states. Historical precedents in other contexts provide unexpected answers. Military assessments are crucial but not well developed.

This pattern of practical reasoning about international relations is characterized by concepts that begin so generally as to be almost empty—but then gain substance through instantiation in the intricate relationships of a specific history. Learning proceeds by fashioning the paths of that history and extending them into the future. This is reasoning that begins with something like a construction set. The hearing takes concepts from the set as they seem relevant, and it orders them into elaborate sequences of individuals and nations acting out their wants. In this narrative, constructed jointly by the participants, the hearing constructs what the actors want, how sequences of actions interact, what precedents are relevant and how, and the consequences of military capabilities to produce confident talk about the future.

In this hearing, talk about the future is a particular form of practical reasoning. It is characterized by narrative paths into the future and assessments of those paths. Bounded rationality is evident at every point. The path metaphor helps to shape and define both the bounds and the reasoning.

Notes

1. Political deliberation about the future includes persuasion and dissuasion based on advantages and disadvantages of different courses of action. For discussion of the Aristotelian foundations of deliberative rhetoric, see Gerard A. Hauser, *Introduction to Rhetorical Theory*, 2d ed. (Prospect Heights, Ill.: Waveland, 2002); Roderick P. Hart and Courtney L. Dillard, "Deliberative Genre," in *Encyclopedia of Rhetoric*, ed. Thomas O. Sloane (Oxford: Oxford University Press, 2001), 209–17; James F. Golden, Goodwin F. Berquist, and William E. Coleman, *The Rhetoric of Western Thought*, 7th ed. (Dubuque, Iowa: Kendall/Hunt, 2000), 37. See also William Keith, ed., "Deliberative Democracy," special issue, *Quarterly Journal of Speech* 5, no. 2 (2002).

2. For example, see Paul A. Chilton, *Security Metaphors: Cold War Discourse from Containment to Common House* (New York: Peter Lang,

1996), 466; Mark Johnson, *The Body in the Mind: The Bodily Basis of Meaning, Imagination and Reason* (Chicago: University of Chicago Press, 1990), 28, 113–17; George Lakoff, *Woman, Fire and Dangerous Things* (Chicago: Chicago University Press, 1987), 609.

3. Allen Newell and Herbert A. Simon, *Human Problem Solving* (Englewood Cliffs, N.J.: Prentice-Hall, 1972); Nils J. Nilsson, *Principles of Artificial Intelligence* (Palo Alto, Calif.: Tioga Publishing, 1980).

4. Cf. Bill Gates, *The Road Ahead* (New York: Penguin, 1996); Peter B. Andersen, Berit Holmqvist, and Jens F. Jensen, *The Computer as Medium* (Cambridge: Cambridge University Press, 1993), 481–82; Ray Jackendoff, *Languages of the Mind: Essays on Mental Representation* (Cambridge, Mass.: MIT Press, 1993), 34–35, 41–42, 116; Valerie M. Hudson, *Artificial Intelligence and International Politics* (Boulder, Col.: Westview, 1991), 19, 57, 80–82; Terry Winograd, *Language as a Cognitive Process*, vol. 1, *Syntax* (Reading, Mass.: Addison-Wesley, 1983), 360.

5. Method here begins with a theoretical insight that "path" is an appropriate metaphor. It then searches for supporting evidence in the text. Some of this evidence is explicit, the appearance of the word "path" in the text. Other evidence is implicit in the text of the argument. Similar work is presented in Francis A. Beer, "Words of Reason," *Political Communication* 11 (summer 1994): 185–201; Francis A. Beer and Barry J. Balleck, "Body, Mind, and Soul in the Gulf War Debate," in *The Theory and Practice of Political Communication Research*, ed. Mary E. Stuckey (Binghamton: SUNY Press, 1996), 159–76; Francis A. Beer and G. Robert Boynton, "Realistic Rhetoric but Not Realism: A Senatorial Conversation on Cambodia," in *Post-realism: The Rhetorical Turn in International Relations*, ed. Francis A. Beer and Robert Hariman (East Lansing: Michigan State University Press, 1996), 369–83; Francis A. Beer and G. Robert Boynton, "Speaking about Dying," in *Argumentation and Values: Proceedings of the Ninth SCA/AFA Conference on Argumentation*, ed. Sally Jackson (Annandale, Va.: Speech Communication Association, 1995), 550–56; G. Robert Boynton, "Ideas and Action: A Cognitive Model of the Senate Agriculture Committee," *Political Behavior* 12 (1990): 181–213; G. Robert Boynton, "The Senate Agriculture Committee Produces a Homeostat," *Policy Sciences* 2 (1989): 51–80.

6. *Prospects for Peace in Cambodia: 1990 Hearing before the Subcommittee on East Asia and Pacific Affairs of the Committee on Foreign Relations*, United States Senate, One Hundred First Congress, Second Session,

February 28, 1990. Washington D.C.: US Government Printing Office, 1990. Italics added in the text here for emphasis.

7. Ibid., 4, 39.
8. Ibid., 39.
9. Ibid., 112.
10. Ibid., 17–23.
11. Ibid., 36–37, 45.
12. Ibid., 39, 44.
13. Ibid., 38–47.
14. Ibid., 44.
15. Ibid., 96–98.
16. Boynton, *Ideas and Action.*
17. *Prospects for Peace in Cambodia,* 46.
18. Ibid., 26.
19. Ibid., 95–96.
20. Ibid., 37.
21. Ibid., 24.
22. Ibid., 37.
23. Ibid., 98.
24. Ibid., 103.
25. Ibid., 44–47.
26. Ibid., 22–23, 40, 101.
27. Ibid., 101.
28. Ibid., 17.

Talking about Srebrenica

Dutch Elites and Dutchbat.
How Metaphors Change during Crisis

Christ'l De Landtsheer and Ilse De Vrij

This chapter tests a theory and model by De Landtsheer regarding how political metaphors (metaphors used by politicians and journalists in their "elite" discourse) change during crisis.[1] Features of economic crisis discourse and discourse by extremist political groups identified in case studies and applied in this model include increased use of metaphors, more "original" and "intense" metaphors, and metaphors of particular content.[2] The current study investigates changes of metaphor due to political or military crisis and tests this "metaphor power" model for a political crisis. It consists of a metaphor content analysis of Dutch government and newspaper texts before, during, and after the 1995 crisis in Srebrenica. We similarly tested the "integrative complexity" theory of Suedfeld et al.[3] This theory states that low levels of complexity in public speech represent black-and-white thinking, intermediate levels represent increasing differentiation between points of view, and high levels point to integrative thinking, or the ability to synthesize and to react flexibly. In several case studies a connection was made between low complexity levels and situations of military or political crisis—it was shown that complexity decreases prior to surprise attacks. Complexity theory is yet another content analytic method among those that are frequently used for archival studies of political rhetoric.[4] Applying these two methods—the metaphor power model and integrative complexity—to one particular set of texts allows us to see how they interrelate and also how the combination improves prediction and understanding of phenomena.[5] The current study demonstrates predicted "crisis" changes in the components of the metaphor power model and in integrative complexity scores. The results first indicate that the metaphor power theory could be considered as a broadening of integrative complexity theory because metaphor power corresponds with lower integrative complexity. Results, second, allow conclusions about the role of Dutch governmental officials in the Srebrenica crisis—conclusions that deepen and confirm insights from recent inquiries on the subject that were initiated by the Dutch government. The results of this study, third, testify to the predictive value of our "crisis" variables—as demonstrated by subsequent events such as the fall of the Dutch cabinet Kok II.

Dutchbat in Srebrenica

In 1993 a combination of humanitarian motivations and political ambitions led the Dutch cabinet (on its own initiative and without prior conditions) to make an air mobile battalion available for the United Nations Protection Force (UNPROFOR) in Bosnia.[6] This Dutch component of UNPROFOR, Dutchbat, was located in Srebrenica, one of the safe areas in the former Yugoslavia, and its mission was to protect the Bosnian citizens of Srebrenica. In July 1995, however, Bosnian Serbs killed thousands of Muslims in Srebrenica, which they took over without any resistance on the 11th of that month. Dutchbat had observed men and women being separated, had chased refugees away from the camp, and had filled the fuel tanks of the buses with which the ethnic purification would be carried out.[7] After "the fall of Srebrenica" on 11 July 1995 the public was horrified, the image of the Dutch army was seriously damaged, and the Dutch government lost a great deal of credibility. In the Netherlands and throughout the rest of the world, the events in and around Srebrenica attracted considerable media attention. People asked how it was possible for things to have gone so far; various inquiries and investigations were launched.[8] By November 1996, the Dutch government instructed the Netherlands Institute for War Documentation (NIOD) to carry out a study of "the events prior to, during and after the fall of Srebrenica."[9] The report concludes that the "peace mission" took place without a proper analysis of the far-reaching consequences beforehand (the mission had been turned down by other countries with arguments to back up their refusal).[10] Only weeks before the May elections in the Netherlands, the publication of this report in April 2002 caused the demission of the Purple governmental coalition Kok II. And questions since than about the unsuccessful Dutch "peace" mission in Srebrenica have not stopped. A number of Dutch politicians still have to deal with the Srebrenica crisis—yet another parliamentary inquiry commission has been installed.

The current case study on Srebrenica tests the occurrence of the "crisis pattern" of metaphors and the "crisis pattern" of integrative complexity in two series of samples. One series comprises letters from the head of the Dutch War Department (Secretary of State Voorhoeve) to the Dutch government, the other series deals with news and editorials from a prominent Dutch newspaper (*De Volkskrant*). The "crisis pattern" is assumed to dominate the speeches by Dutch political elites (mainly politicians and political journalists) during and after the Srebrenica crisis. The Dutch elite's discourse before the crisis is assumed to exhibit the "noncrisis pattern." These hypotheses are based on the assumption that Dutch political elites (and Dutch mass media) have not prepared the Dutch for the sacrifices that may accompany risky military operations—a "preparation process" that usually takes place in democratic societies. These hypotheses are in line with the recent NIOD report.[11] This report concludes that the responsible officials had been playing down the possible risks of the behavior of the warring parties too much. The consequence is that "a large circle of those involved in this policy, and in particular its advocates, took on a large responsibility for an ill-conceived and virtually impossible mission."[12]

Why Metaphors Change during Crisis

Metaphor power in political speech increases as a result of crisis. This is what can be concluded from our former case studies where a metaphor power theory and model was used and from a number of other writings.[13] This section describes the theoretical frame of this study and addresses some critical issues; it thereby draws upon three lines of thought that include political psychology, cognitive psychology, and rhetoric.

We will start this section with the line of political psychology, as we first need to describe how we conceive *crisis* in order to be able to explain its impact on the change of metaphor, which has to do with emotions. Then we draw upon a second line of thought that concerns current metaphor theory from cognitive psychology and cognitive linguistics. We will clarify the nature of metaphor, the role of the audience, and the nature of emotions. It will be argued that metaphors are not just linguistic entities, but that they are powerful agents of cognitive framing. It is because of this quality that metaphors are conceptual entities that change during crisis and are central driving factors in everyday life discourse and linguistic change. It will be furthermore argued that metaphors may be studied as products of the sender of the discourse, in this case the political elites. Metaphors used in public discourse, however, always provide us with some indications regarding the audience. We also make explicit our view of the role emotions play in the process: we do not see emotions as antipathetic to cognition. After having clarified our position on the nature of metaphor, the role of the audience, and the nature of emotion, we will draw upon rhetorical theory as a third domain. Rhetoric allows us to integrate the earlier discussed notions in order to explain the discursive changes due to crisis. Since Aristotle's *On Rhetoric* (ca. 336 BCE) metaphors are traditionally seen as crucial elements of rhetoric in their appeal to emotion (pathos). During crisis, politicians feel the need to address the audience with more ("impressive") rhetoric, more "pathos," and as a consequence they use more metaphor power.[14] Metaphor power theory itself is further detailed in the section that explains the "metaphor power" model.

Crisis

Crisis is the situation in which a society is affected by a situation that is severe enough to increase the levels of anxiety in the audience and to transform these into fear.[15] Crisis may have various origins that may equally be interrelated: economic recession and the structure of economy (economic factor), oppression and war (political factor), religion and tradition (cultural factor), ethnicity, gender, age, and nationality (sociodemographic factor). Social stress could arise because reality has become intolerable; the environment accordingly encourages citizens to escape.[16] As a consequence of this, citizens think and act according to primary processes described by Freud in which irrationality dominates. Processes are launched that encourage non-literal, metaphorical thinking. Reality prevents citizens from thinking and acting according to processes labeled by Freud as secondary. In these other processes, rationality and literal language dominate. One of the first definitions of crisis is by Lasswell, who meanly deals with political crisis when he defines *crisis* as "a situation in which severe deprivations, such as violence, are inflicted or threatened. Hence, the structure of expectation is the dominant feature of crisis."[17]

Lasswell also provided us with the "crisis style" theory, the first theory that suggests the change of metaphor due to crisis.[18] In his propaganda studies *Language of Politics* and *The Comparative Study of Symbols*,[19] Lasswell put forward the constitutive power of rhetoric in general and metaphor in particular for the formation of public opinion, especially during severe crisis situations such as war and totalitarian regimes. His definition of a "political crisis style" inspires some misunderstanding, however, as it uses the term *ornament*. Lasswell describes crisis style as "ornamental, effect-contrasted, emotive, repetitious and accessory."[20] The author contrasts this ornamental and emotive style to the "effect-modeled, varied, and cognitive style, with pure signs." This noncrisis style resembles the language of everyday life. A closer reading of the definitions—Lasswell labels crisis style as "emotive"—in combination with Lasswell's other writings[21] leads to the conclusion that Lasswell did acknowledge "the importance of figurative language and especially metaphor for the construction of knowledge and meaning."[22] It would have avoided some misunderstanding if Lasswell had used the terms *figurative* or *narrative* instead of *ornamental* in his "crisis style" definition. Political rhetoric indeed constitutes an important component of political culture, which it reflects and shapes.[23] We can conclude from the Lasswell definition that during crisis politicians tend to trigger the emotions of an audience by using figurative language or narratives, of which metaphors are seen as the most important feature.

Metaphors

According to Lakoff,[24] metaphors are more than just "ornaments"; they are not just "a property of language per se," but they are "a property of our conceptual system." The focus of metaphor lies in thought; metaphors take their place in language in view of their communicative force that entirely depends upon their conceptual qualities. Because metaphors are at the heart of cognitive framing and the communication that goes with it, metaphors change during crisis. Metaphors indeed are not just "ornaments" added to everyday literal language. Metaphors change during crisis because of "the central role that metaphor plays in reflecting and shaping how people think in a broad range of domains,"[25] as Cacciari wrote. The view from cognitive linguistics (and cognitive psychology) that is based upon the conceptual model by Lakoff and Johnson[26] has contributed to our assumption that the use of metaphors depends upon and changes according to the social context. Even though this view is seen today as having radically changed the approach to metaphor, already circa 336 B.C.E. Aristotle[27] wrote that metaphor is the best way to get hold of new ideas; therefore Aristotle cannot be interpreted as if he would have restricted metaphor to an ornament.[28] This view magnifies the role that metaphor plays even more when it is related to recent insights from communication theory regarding the "agenda-setting" and "framing" function of mass media. Mass media agendas determine the public agenda, and mass media affect the frames according to which the audience thinks about the issues that were put on these agendas.[29] Policymakers, besides, are seen as important sources for mass media agendas.[30] Metaphors are powerful framing devices in mass communication. According to Aristotle, indeed, very powerful persons are those who succeed in getting their metaphors through in the public sphere.

The way metaphors work as conceptual tools can best be illustrated by examining what metaphor consists of.[31] Metaphors firstly consist of a content that is called a *vehicle* (Richards),[32] a *focus* (Feder Kittay),[33] a *ground* (Cacciari),[34] or a *subsidiary subject* (Black).[35] This content points at the literary device from one semantic domain that is applied to another completely different semantic domain, the *subject* that is discussed. Metaphors thus secondly consist of a subject, which is entitled the *tenor* (Richards), the *frame* (Feder Kittay), the *topic* (Cacciari), or the *principal subject* (Black) of the metaphor. Thirdly, there exists a "tension" between this subject and the content of the metaphor (Cacciari, Feder Kittay, Richards). This tension consists at the same time as a bridge between various different domains. A metaphor need not be a full sentence; it may be a phrase. On the other hand, a sentence is not always sufficient to distinguish a metaphorical from a literal use of a term. Metaphor is not a unit of discourse but a use of discourse. Expressions and words do have a first-order (semantic) meaning, such as the word "butter." But they can obtain a second-order (pragmatical) meaning, when context indicates to the reader that the first-order meaning of the expression is inappropriate, as is the case when we use "butter" as follows: "the secretary of state has butter on his head." In our example from an article on the Srebrenica crisis, we could call "butter" the *subsidiary subject* and the Dutch secretary of state the *principal subject,* while the *tension* provides for the interpretation that the secretary of state is accused of ineffective behavior in the Srebrenica crisis. The *frame* belongs to a different *semantic field* (politics) than the *focus* (food). It is the *contrast* between these semantic fields that creates the metaphor and its power. The metaphor

"Dutchbat is paralyzed" refers to the principal subject, "Dutchbat," in terms of the "health" domain (the subsidiary subject of the metaphor). The content of the metaphor from the "health" domain provides for the attribution of specific properties to the metaphor topic. The subject is framed in a way that evokes the need for a "doctor" or a "powerful actor."

Political Elites and Their Publics

Our study on political crisis metaphors focuses upon the senders of the discourse, the political elites (the administrators and the press), and the crisis situation that they eventually express through the metaphor power in their communication with the citizen. The misconception of the crisis situation by the responsible officials and/or their inadequate reaction to it will appear in their rhetoric. Communication theory teaches that we will also find this misconception back in the media, the media that frame the agenda of the audience.[36] Messages, therefore, also provide information about the audience, not only about the communicator or the message topic.[37] Message, besides, are intentional acts. Political elites do not simply encode information and transmit it to a destination. They choose how to formulate their message by taking the characteristics of the audience and the audience's situation into account.[38] In order to influence audience inferences, political elites—often unconsciously—strategically use in their rhetoric implicit properties of language that influence the audience without their knowledge.[39] Not only politicians and journalists but all communicators generally consider the information they share with the addressee, and in order to produce specific interpretations they evaluate the potential interpretation.[40] Metaphors especially provide for this common ground between political elites and the citizen, because of their achievement of intimacy; as Cohen describes it: "There is a unique way in which the maker and the appreciator of a metaphor are drawn closer to one another. Three aspects are involved: the speaker issues a kind of concealed invitation; the hearer expends a special effort to accept the invitation; and this transaction constitutes the acknowledgment of a community."[41] When Dutch political officials and the media do not see the necessity of preparing Dutch citizens for a situation in which Dutch soldiers will be killed and Dutch society will suffer, Dutch citizens will probably not be aware of such a situation.

Emotions

The view of emotions from cognitive psychology corresponds with the view of metaphor from cognitive linguistics and cognitive psychology.

Metaphors may be in the first place emotive components of rhetoric; they also lead cognition in particular directions. In using metaphors one categorizes, one emphasizes the choice of category in which one places objects; one chooses a perspective, a perspective that is governed by distinct interests and conventions.[42]

According to the view of emotions that has prevailed in modern cognitive psychology and that derives from Aristotle, emotions are essential guides of cognition. Emotions and cognition can be distinguished for purposes of analysis, but they are seldom separate in practice.[43] Cognition was for a long time considered the impartial representation and use of knowledge. But emotions are, as Aristotle argued, evaluations that mediate between concerns and the events that impinge on knowledge.[44] Emotions are guides of cognition; they select among beliefs, arrange priorities, direct attention, and bias access to remembered materials. They accordingly provide heuristics that influence reasoning, judgment, and planning.[45]

More Rhetoric and Pathos

Emotion was considered by Aristotle as one of the only three (artistic) means of persuasion and rhetoric (rhetoric is the ability to see in each case the available means of persuasion).[46] These artistic means (nonartistic means include witnesses or documents) include *ethos* (the presentation of the character of the speaker as trustworthy), *pathos* (the emotions by the audience as aroused by the speaker), and *logos* (rational argument). Changes in rhetoric (rhetoric that consists of ethos, pathos, and logos) due to crisis can be explained by the theory by Windt and Ingold[47] on "impressive" and "expressive" rhetoric. According to Weinberger[48] rhetoric is pragmatic argumentation that—contrary to logical or objective argumentation (which deals only with the relation of arguments to the probandum)—aims at connecting with the audience. When crisis forces politicians into "more" rhetoric, political speech will become more metaphorical, that is, more powerful or intense metaphors will be used. When communicators take their audience into account in formulating their message, they are constructing a representation of the topic of the message that is shaped by their audience.[49] This type of style is entitled by Windt and Ingold[50] as audience-oriented, "impressive" rhetoric. The rhetoric is impressive in the sense that politicians adjust their language to meet the norms, values, and traditions of their audience. Demagogues do so to the highest possible degree because they have little concern for the ideas they are voicing and are interested only in their audience. Doctrinaires care about the purity of thought or of language, because they do not care about their audience. They try to clarify their position, and their rhetoric is "expressive." Rhetoric in democratic society usually balances between expressiveness and impressiveness. Effective political rhetoric during a crisis in a democratic society could, however, be expected to move in the direction of demagogic or predominantly "impressive" rhetoric, or rhetoric that has more pathos, ethos, and logos.[51]

How metaphors change due to crisis should be revealed both by speeches of responsible politicians and by the press. That is why we will use both of these channels in order to test our metaphor power model and theory that implies that during crisis (the Srebrenica case) political elites will undertake more rhetorical efforts (use more emotive discourse, more metaphor power). We will apply integrative complexity as a test variable for simplification of political discourse during crisis. Simplifying of reality may not be the most prominent function of metaphor; it is certainly one of its cognitive functions, because metaphor, similar to symbols and simple arguments, is a type of "mental mapping."[52] "Through resemblance, metaphor makes things clearer," wrote Aristotle in his *Poetics*.[53] It is the use of metaphor in itself that is considered to have a simplification power. While the metaphor power model we use is a multilevel model with various categories of metaphors that are conceived according to metaphor power, the metaphor model in itself does not distinguish between simple and complex metaphors. That the political discourse grows more simple or standardized during crisis was the outcome of one 1956 article by Ithiel De Sola Pool.[54] Pool concluded that variety and repetition in the use of political symbols decreases during war and for totalitarian regimes. Among recent studies that testify to the simplification of political discourse during crisis are those that employ the integrative or cognitive complexity approach.[55] We assume that high complexity—and moderate metaphor power—correspond to Lasswell's[56] "cognitive, pure sign style." We also assume that low complexity—and high metaphor power—correspond to his "effect-contrasted, emotive style." Especially democratic regimes such as the Dutch one require high levels of support from their citizens. According to Hunt[57] democracies in particular make use of the domestic mass media prior to attack; they may exhibit extraordinary persuasive efforts in order to prepare public opinion for war. That is why the crisis pattern (for metaphors and for integrative complexity) should show up both in speeches by responsible politicians and in the leading newspapers as the

Dutch population is prepared for sacrifices (which we do not expect has happened in the case of Srebrenica).

How Metaphors Change during Crisis: *The Metaphor Power Model*

The following paragraphs detail the "metaphor power" model[58] that conceptualizes a quantitative metaphor content analysis. Its theory therefore draws on quantitative semantics, the propaganda studies that Lasswell and his disciples[59] conceived using content analysis techniques. The model is an example of a political semantic analysis that aims at revealing latent dispositions rather than manifest inclinations. The model, in fact, operationalizes the "crisis style" hypotheses by Lasswell and therefore uses current psychological theory and theory in political psychology. The theory applies a metaphor power measure—or "metaphor coefficient" (symbolized by C)—to gauge the level of anxiety in a society.

Frequency of Metaphor

Metaphors are emotive components of language and are highly reassuring because they simplify reality and relax the audience. They also add specific, desired subjective connotations to the subject under discussion and can therefore also have a mobilizing effect, which can vary from rather innocent to dangerous. Aristotle already noticed that some metaphors are clearly more striking than others. According to Grant, one of the debates that surrounds metaphor concerns the types of metaphor.[60] Metaphors can be liberating and positive or the reverse but the extent to which metaphors achieve this is influenced by type. The model first takes into account the *frequency of metaphors* (F is calculated as the frequency of metaphors for 100 words). Metaphors are identified according to the often-mentioned criterion "strangeness or surprisingness in view of the context"[61] that provides for a clear and practical means of identification. How to identify metaphor was detailed in the former paragraphs. Listings of metaphors selected this way make it possible to calculate F.

Intensity of Metaphor

The model further takes into account the originality, incongruity, or referential intensity of metaphors, which is represented by the *intensity score* (or originality score), I. According to metaphor theory, innovative and original metaphors are more intense than commonly used ones. Black[62] presents a hierarchical typology of metaphors in which metaphors are either "strong" or "weak." Strong metaphors use effective words that cannot be substituted because of their particular expressiveness. Once the metaphor is understood it lends itself to further elaboration. Weak metaphors do not have these qualities and can be compared to an unfunny joke. As Tsoukas explains, all live metaphors, however, necessitate creativity on the part of those applying them; they require interpretation and need to be thought through in order to work.[63] Dormant metaphors can be distinguished from dead metaphors in that the metaphorical ground is not obvious but becomes quickly apparent, so that they still play some role. Dead metaphors, in contrast, are used as literal terms; they have become so familiar that we have ceased to be aware of their metaphorical nature.[64] Our "intensity variable" (I) was conceived as an "originality" score. I is based on a combination of Koeller's[65] distinction between conventional and original metaphors and Mooy's[66] conception of three dimensions of metaphors, one of which is strength of reference to the literary meaning of the metaphor, or as we call it here the first-order meaning of the word or expression, that forms the "subsidiary subject"[67] of the metaphor. In the case of original metaphors, the first-order meaning is still strongly present, and the contrast or incongruity between the semantic field of the subsidiary subject and the semantic field of the principal subject is considerable, so that the metaphor will be very striking. We give metaphors (contrast, incongruity, and originality) with values ranging from (1) for "weak" (w), over (2) for "normal" (n), to (3) for "original" metaphors. I stands for the sum of the weighed values of metaphor intensity (3-point scale) divided by the number of metaphor (t):

$$I = \frac{1w + 2n + 3s}{Y}$$

Content of Metaphor

The model also takes into account the content of the metaphors, the semantic field to which they belong, which is represented by the *content score* (D). A semantic field is a content domain that as Feder Kittay[68] wrote is identifiable by a lexical field. Metaphors that belong to particular semantic fields (e.g., disease or sports) are more powerful than those with such content as nature or family. Through the use of particular metaphors, anxiety can be mobilized for destructive purposes. This happens when groups of people are systematically labeled as animals, dirt, or disease—labels that encourage ethnic, religious, ideological, or nationalistic "purification" or "cleansing." The model uses descriptors for semantic fields that are relatively universal: everyday life (p), nature (n), politics, intellect, technology (po), violence and disaster (d), sports, games, and drama (sp), and death, body, and illness (m). Metaphors that fit the descriptors of the semantic fields are given values ranging from 1 (p) to 6 (m). Descriptors were awarded values on a scale according to significance given in psycholinguistic literature[69] and social-psychological theory, including the crisis behavior model by Gaus[70] that relates the need for mental escape to economic crisis. Low content scores include everyday life material reality (1) and nature (2) metaphors; intermediate scores include political, intellectual, and technology metaphors (3) and disaster and violence metaphors (4); high scores represent metaphors referring to sports, games, and drama (5) or to death and disease (6). Optimistic, material, and popular metaphors (p) are less appropriate for escape; they receive the lowest score (1), while medical metaphors (m) are seen as utterances and inductors of anxiety and receive the highest score (6). Medical metaphors denominate processes in society as biological and therefore suggest that a doctor (an authoritarian leader) could solve problems through medical treatment rather than by democratic negotiation. Medical metaphors were in literature often associated with totalitarian regimes such as the Third Reich. Nature metaphors (n) that get the score (2) are similar to popular ones (p) but are assumed to have an ambivalent function (optimistic versus pessimistic), so that they are not very reassuring; people under stress need to be reassured. Political, intellectual, and technology metaphors (po) that refer to everyday life and that are not that appropriate for escape receive the value (3). Disaster metaphors (d) express despair, depression, and aggression; they are often used in an apocalyptic sense and receive the value (4). Sports, games, and drama metaphors (sp) appeal to many people; they are highly manipulative and get the score (5). The "crisis content variable" D is calculated according to the following formula, in which t represents the total number of metaphors:

$$D = \frac{1p + 2n + 3po + 4d + 5sp + 6m}{t}$$

The Metaphor Power Coefficient

The metaphor power coefficient C is calculated by multiplying the frequency score of metaphors (F) with the originality score (I) and with the crisis content score (D). I and D respectively stand for the weighed values of metaphor intensity (3-point scale) and content (6-point scale), divided by the number of metaphors. A conclusion from earlier case studies is that political elites tend to produce speech with higher C values during a crisis. The current case study will test the metaphor model for different kind of crisis conditions that are severe political difficulties. We assume this political crisis discourse to be extremely "audience-oriented" (impressive) with high doses of pathos, including considerable metaphor power (which we symbolize by C+), while we assume the nonpolitical crisis discourse to have less pathos and less metaphor power (which we symbolize by C-).

Complexity Scores as a Test Variable

We expect crisis political discourse to be audience-oriented by its low (cognitive) complexity (symbol CC+) while the noncrisis discourse is expected to show high levels of (cognitive) complexity (symbol CC-). We assume low complexity levels to more or less correspond with the logos component of rhetoric. According to Aristotle, rhetoric should appear logical to the audience: it should consist of argumentation that is easy to follow and not too complex. Integrative complexity is measured on an ordinary 7-point scale according to the procedure detailed by Baker-Brown et al.[71] Basic scoring units were selected according to Suedfeld's procedure. The basic scoring unit refers to a section of material that focuses on an idea. Usually, this scorable unit consists of a single paragraph. Occasionally, a larger paragraph in the original material may be broken down into two or more scorable units, each having a single idea. On the other hand, several paragraphs in the original material may be combined to form one scorable unit. The sample should consist of at least forty randomly selected paragraphs, with at least five paragraphs for each time period. Furthermore, before and after the crucial time period (in this case, the fall of Srebrenica), two or three whole documents were analyzed. Prior to selecting the final sample, unscorable statements were identified and deleted. Unscorable statements and paragraphs are those text units that consist of clichés, satire, sarcasm, quotations, descriptions, breakdowns in understanding, and scorer uncertainty.

The Crisis Pattern

We expect that the features of condensed, simplifying, and emotive discourse as described above include high metaphor power (C+) and a low level of integrative complexity (CC-), and that the metaphor power coefficient (C) and integrative complexity (CC) variables follow similar—but reversed—patterns of use; this also holds for their counterpart features of elaborate, complex, and cognitive discourse, such as low metaphor power (C-) and a high level of integrative complexity (CC+).

We tested the theory by calculating the metaphor power coefficient (C) and the cognitive complexity level (CC) for samples of political discourse before, during, and after a crisis. We followed the coding instructions that were detailed by De Landtsheer and by Suedfeld and Bluck. In order to test the hypotheses, we compared quantitatively comparable samples from the Dutch political discourse according to the date of the fall of Srebrenica (11 July 1995).

The Samples

Crisis variables were calculated over the periods before (t1) and after (t2) this date. One 12,825-word sample was taken from letters written between 1992 and 1997 by Dutch secretary of state for defense Voorhoeve to the Dutch government. G symbolizes these letters, which deal with Srebrenica.

Another 13,794-word sample was composed from "news" articles (7,060 words)—symbolized by N—and public opinion articles or comments (6,734 words), symbolized by P. All these articles were taken from *De Volkskrant* during the week that the speeches were written.

The theory relies on methods conceived in the English language. Foreign language samples, however, generate no problems for testing the variables used by the theory, because all variables focus on formal style characteristics and/or general semantic concepts.[72] Metaphor is a universal style figure; cognitive complexity is about the structure of texts. The samples are entirely in Dutch. Letters and articles were included in the sample if they contained the word "Dutchbat" or "Srebrenica." The sample was appropriate for carrying out both an analysis of the metaphors and of integrative complexity.

The total sample consisted of thirty-one documents dated between 1992 and 1997. We randomly selected five paragraphs for each period of two to three months, which resulted in a final sample of fifty-five paragraphs, after removing the unscorable text units. Two whole documents before and after the fall of Srebrenica were also used. The sample with governmental letters contained many unscorable units, for example, questionnaires, quotations, and introductory statements. Spread over thirteen time periods, the total governmental sample consisted of fifty-five paragraphs from thirty-one documents.

The total press sample consisted of thirteen news-reporting articles and thirteen editorials from twenty-six documents. In contrast to governmental letters, journal articles contained only a few unscorable paragraphs. Because of their shorter length, we most often used the entire article instead of paragraphs. Except for the news articles, all the samples were appropriate for examining the metaphor coefficient (C) and integrative complexity (CC). We did not measure integrative complexity for the news articles because the journalists did not express a personal opinion, which made the measurement less productive. In order to calculate the crisis variables also for these news articles, we gave them the constant value (1).

The following hypotheses were tested:

Negative correlation between CC and C

$$C \ t1 < C \ t2$$
$$CC \ t1 > CC \ t2$$

Results

The fall of Srebrenica seriously damaged the image of the Dutch government, and it is hardly surprising that the government wanted to restore its image by persuading the audience of its credibility. The test of the "crisis" variables on the public letters sent by Secretary of State for Defense Voorhoeve to the Dutch government shows that the responsible politician Voorhoeve indeed chose to use the variables, which we assume to represent intensification of political speech after the fall of Srebrenica (t2). The letters by the secretary of state exhibit on average less cognitive complexity (CC t2= 1.91) and more intensive use of metaphors (C t2= 9.78). Before the fall (t1), the letters have on average less metaphor power (C t1= 5.01) and higher cognitive complexity (CC t1= 4.1). As can be read from table 1 and from figure 1, the finding that the crisis discourse pattern emerged in the Dutch governmental documents only after the fall of Srebrenica confirms our hypotheses.

The hypothesis that the press follows shifts in public opinion as orchestrated by the government seems to be confirmed by *De Volkskrant*'s news reporting and editorial comments. There is obviously a shared discourse: the trends are the same when we compare the speeches and the newspaper articles. The frequency, the intensity, and the strength of metaphors,

Table 1 Metaphor Coefficient (C) and Integrative Complexity (CC) in Dutch Governmental Letters before (T1) and after (T2) the Fall of Srebrenica (1992–97)

Dates (T)	Words	C	CC
3 March 1992	282	10.64	4.40
1 April 1992	1743	4.52	4.80
5 July 1994	577	1.56	3.60
2 Jan. 1995	411	0.00	4.70
23 June 1995	1163	2.43	5.00
27 July 1995	2013	10.94	2.10
3 Aug. 1995	1588	11.50	1.80
30 October 1995	844	13.12	1.80
27 Nov. 1995	610	6.40	1.80
11 Dec. 1995	953	9.76	2.20
25 April 1996	844	6.64	1.60
14 June 1996	766	12.79	2.00
20 Jan. 1997	1031	7.13	2.00
Average	12825	7.49	2.91
T1	4176	5.01	4.10
T2	8649	9.78	1.91
Corr.		CC/C	
			-0.6486

which are represented in the metaphor power coefficient, apparently increase immediately after the fall in July 1995.

Before and after the fall of Srebrenica the metaphor power coefficient C reads as follows:

For governmental speeches: 5.01 (G C t1) and 9.78 (G C t2)
For news articles: 4.798 (N C t1) and 6.447 (N C t2)
For public opinion articles: 8.293 (C t1) and 21.682 (C t2)

As can be read from tables 2 and 3, both the politician and news samples show a strong parallel decrease of C before July 1995 and the same parallel increase after July 1995. These results support the hypotheses from communication theory[73] that news routines and political journalists' affiliation with politicians in charge are serious obstacles to democracy.

The metaphor coefficients are relatively higher in the public opinion articles than in the other sources; this is due to the format. Editorial comments are more condensed and use more rhetoric than news and

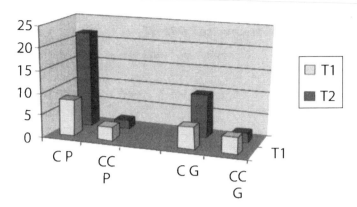

FIGURE 1. Average Metaphor Coefficient (C) and Integrative Complexity (CC) before (T1) and after (T2) the Fall of Srebrenica in Dutch Governmental Letters (G) and Dutch Newspaper Editorials (P), 1992–1997.

Table 2 Metaphor Coefficient (C) and Integrative Complexity (CC) in Editorials of *De Volkskrant* before (T1) and after (T2) the Fall of Srebrenica (1992–97)

Dates (T)	Words	C	CC
18 April 1992	667	8.49	1.2
12 May 1992	493	9.937	1.8
8 July 1994	407	2.457	5
29 July 1994	752	1.878	5.4
7 June 1995	451	18.702	2.4
12 July 1995	416	20.604	1.8
29 Aug. 1995	483	22.21	1.6
7 Sept. 1995	421	19.053	2.6
23 Oct. 1995	788	17.584	2.2
20 Dec. 1995	175	31.364	1.75
10 July 1996	426	17.358	3.2
19 July 1996	825	10.984	2
30 Jan. 1997	430	34.306	2
T1	2770	8.293	3.16
T2	3964	21.68288	2.14375
Correl.		C/CC	
			−0.5803

Table 3 Metaphor Coefficient (C) in News in *De Volkskrant* before (T1) and after (T2) the fall of Srebrenica (1992–97)

Dates (T)	Words	C
18 April 1992	424	10.691
12 May 1992	334	9.161
8 July 1994	1880	2.499
29 July 1994	555	0
7 June 1995	549	1.638
12 July 1995	1019	9.798
29 Aug. 1995	444	2.245
7 Sept. 1995	922	6.284
23 Oct. 1995	736	4.401
20 Dec. 1995	392	0.765
10 June 1996	179	1.674
19 July 1996	689	23.41
30 Jan. 1997	637	3.762
T	8760	
T1	3742	4.798
T2	5018	6.447

governmental speeches. Politicians and political commentators made more and better use of the crisis variables than reporters did.

The integrative complexity levels are also lower in editorials than in the other genres. The cognitive complexity levels before and after the fall of Srebrenica are, respectively:

For political speeches: 4.1 (G CC t1) and 1.91 (G CC t2)
For public opinion articles: 3.16 (P CC t1) and 2.143 (P CC t2)
Cognitive complexity could not be measured for news

Conclusion

The correlations between the metaphor coefficient and the integrative complexity score during the sample period (1992–97) appear to confirm our hypotheses about the existence of a crisis pattern in political speech. The test of our hypotheses on samples of governmental and press speech—including news and political comments—reveals that during a crisis, intensification of political speech takes place through the more intense use of rhetorical instruments such as metaphors and simple argumentation. This intensification was indeed expressed by the crisis variables we chose, the metaphor power coefficient (C), and integrative complexity (CC). The

Srebrenica case suggests that the variables interact in a crisis pattern of political speech the way we expected. The metaphor power coefficient (C) correlates in a negative way with cognitive complexity (CC) for governmental letters (-0.648) and for editorials (-0.580).

We also divided the three 1992–97 samples according to the date of the fall of Srebrenica into quantitatively balanced samples. The results demonstrate the following pattern for the crisis variables in governmental letters (G), news (N), and political editorials (P) before (t1) and after (t2) the fall of Srebrenica. They thereby confirm our hypothesis about a crisis pattern of political speech for the Srebrenica crisis.

$$C \ G \ t1 = 5.01 < C \ G \ t2 = 9.78$$
$$CC \ G \ t1 = 4.10 > CC \ G \ t2 = 1.91$$

$$C \ N \ t1 = 4.798 < C \ N \ t2 = 6.447$$
$$CC \ N \ t1 \ (= 1) \ / \ CC \ N \ t2 \ (= 1)$$

$$C \ P \ t1 = 8.293 < C \ P \ t2 = 21.682$$
$$CC \ P \ t1 = 3.16 > CC \ P \ t2 = 2.143$$

The qualitative research in the extensive Dutch NIOD report[74] contributes to a better understanding of the meaning of our quantitative data regarding the Srebrenica case. Our study suggests that the Dutch officials who were responsible and the Dutch press did not prepare the Dutch population for sacrifices. These results are compatible with the conclusion by the later NIOD report that Dutch officials underestimated the risks of the Dutchbat mission and started it without sufficient thought. The conclusions to be drawn from the governmental letters and from the news reports and public opinion articles in *De Volkskrant* confirm that the Dutch government operated inadequately. The government insufficiently took into account the consequences of its decision to locate Dutchbat in Srebrenica as a safe area. The government should have realized that if Dutchbat were to protect the Muslim population from the Serbs, Dutchbat would be subjected to the risk of violence. The rhetoric by the government would have anticipated a crisis, if the government had anticipated such a crisis. The rhetoric by the state secretary for defense—in this case—would have mobilized public opinion for the (possible) suffering involved in its decision to protect the Muslim population. The governmental discourse in this case would have shown the crisis communication (propaganda) pattern long before the fall of Srebrenica. Our (restricted) governmental data show that the governmental letters did not (as usually occurs preceding severe conflicts) prepare the population for sacrifices. The public opinion leaders of the press either did not do so or did so insufficiently. It can be concluded in general that the crisis variables seem to be present earlier in editorials than in news and governmental speeches. This could indicate that the political commentators' estimations of crisis were more adequate than those of the administrators. The trends in the editorials may be seen as a confirmation of this possibility. It was only after the fall of Srebrenica that Secretary of State for Defense Voorhoeve felt the need to persuade the public not of what should have been done, but why it had not been done. The current analysis makes clear that the Dutch politicians who were responsible had no intention at all of taking risks in order to protect the Muslim population in Srebrenica (a task that they deliberately asked for and that they were supposed to fulfill). It is also clear that the media followed the trace set out by their news sources, the politicians in charge—the media played the role they usually perform (especially in crisis situations). The Dutch political elites only started their "crisis talk" in July 1995, when they had to cope with feelings of guilt and accusations both at the national and at the international level and when harm was already done to the Bosnian citizens. The Dutch government finally took its responsibility in April 2002—far too late.

Discussion

The importance of the current study is threefold. The study may appear incomplete in its attempt to clarify the Srebrenica case. The timing of the changes of the discourse pattern by the Dutch political and press elites could be further investigated. More press sources and political sources should be examined for this purpose. The current study, nevertheless, indicates that the recently published political analyses ordered by the Dutch government on the Srebrenica case may be correct in their conclusions; our study adds a new dimension to these conclusions. This case is furthermore of theoretical importance, because it convincingly demonstrates that the metaphor power concept by De Landtsheer[75] can be considered as a broadening of the integrative complexity theory by Suedfeld et al.[76] As a consequence, former findings regarding the two concepts (including the finding that both public speech by political extremists and public speech during economic crisis have high metaphor power) should be reconsidered and new research can be initiated. The current study suggests that both political talk by extremists and talk during economic recession may indeed be equally affected (infected?) by lower integrative complexity. This study is finally also important in its predictive power. Based on the current crisis variables, including the metaphor power theory and the integrative complexity theory, it was possible to depict the intentions and the inadequacy of the Dutch political elites' Srebrenica policy long before the publication of the NIOD report and the subsequent demission of the Cabinet Kok II.

Notes

1. On crisis discourse in general, see Keith Spencer Felton, *Warriors' Words: A Consideration of Language and Leadership* (Westport, Conn.: Praeger, 1995); John Gastil, "Undemocratic Discourse: A Review of Theory and Research on Political Discourse," *Discourse and Society* 3, no. 4 (1992): 469–500;

2. The following case study for the Belgian press that confirmed that the political language during an economic crisis has more metaphor power than economic prosperity speech. Christ'l De Landtsheer, "The Language of Prosperity and Crisis. A Case Study in Political Semantics" *Politics and The Individual* 4, 2 (1994): 63–85. The following study of metaphors used in the European Parliament showed that the rhetoric by "extremist" political groups had more metaphor power than the speech by "democratic" politicians. Christ'l De Landtsheer. "The Political Rhetoric of a Unified Europe," *Politically Speaking: A Worldwide Examination of Language Used in the Public Sphere,* ed. Ofer Feldman and Christ'l De Landtsheer (Westport, Conn.: Praeger, 1998), 129–46.

3. The variable is derived from the conceptual complexity dimension of personality described by Oscar Jewel Harvey et al. and later modified by Harold M. Schroder and colleagues. Oscar Jewel Harvey, David E. Hunt, and Harold M. Schroder, *Conceptual Systems and Personality Organization* (New York: Wiley, 1961); Harold M. Schroder, Michael J. Driver, and Siegfried Streufert, *Human Information Processing: Individuals and Groups Functioning in Complex Social Situations* (New York: Holt, Rinehart and Winston, 1967). Complexity theory by Suedfeld et al. ("integrative complexity") differs from other types of complexity theory ("conceptual complexity") in that it does not investigate differentiation and integration as personality variables but rather as aspects of information processing. Peter Suedfeld and Susan Bluck, "Changes in Integrative Complexity Prior to Surprise Attacks," *Journal of Conflict Resolution* 32, no. 4 (1988): 626–35. Peter Suedfeld, Philip E. Tetlock, and Carmenza Ramirez, "War, Peace and Integrative Complexity," *Journal of Conflict Resolution* 21, no. 3 (1977): 427–42. Michael D.

Wallace, Peter Suedfeld, and Kimberley Thachuk, "Political Rhetoric of Leaders under Stress in the Gulf Crisis," *Journal of Conflict Resolution* 37, no. 1 (1993): 94–107.

4. Motivational analysis, which was developed by David Winter, is considered to be another important method for archival research on political discourse. David Winter, "Content Analysis of Archival Data, Personal Documents and Everyday Verbal Productions," in *Motivation and Personality: Handbook of Thematic Content Analysis,* ed. C. P. Smith (New York: Cambridge University Press, 1992), 110–25; David Winter, "Power, Affiliation and War: Three Tests of a Motivational Model," *Journal of Personality and Social Psychology* 65 (1993): 532–45.

5. In the original data collection to the current study, we used a third variable to combine with the metaphor power model and integrative complexity as a crisis communication combination. This variable consists of pragmatic ambiguous modal verbs. It is based upon the pragmatic ambiguity concept developed by Richard D. Anderson and by Eve E. Sweetser. The results of this research are described in the following paper: Christ'l De Landtsheer and Ilse De Vrij, eds., "Talking Srebrenica: Dutch Elites and Dutchbat" (paper presented at the 22d Annual Scientific Meeting of the International Society of Political Psychology Amsterdam, July 1999), 18–21. The paper also includes an empirical part that tests the cognitive and persuasive effects of the variables, separately and as a crisis communication combination. On the effects of metaphor see Joseph Opfer and Peter Anderson, "Explaining the Sound Bite: A Test of a Theory of Metaphor and Assonance" (paper presented at the Western Speech Communication Association Convention, Boise, Idaho, 1992). On pragmatic ambiguity see Richard D. Anderson, "Pragmatic Ambiguity and Partisanship in Russia's Emerging Democracy," in *Politically Speaking,* "64–78; Eve Sweetser, "Metaphor, Mythology, and Everyday Language," *Journal of Pragmatics* 24 (1995): 585–93.

6. Nederlands Instituut voor Oorlogsdocumentatie (NIOD) (Dutch Institute for War Documentation [NIOD]). Srebrenica, een "veilig" gebied. Reconstructie, achtergronden, gevolgen en analyses van de val van een Safe Area (Srebrenica, a "safe" area. Reconstruction, backgrounds, consequences, and analyses of the downfall of a safe area). (Amsterdam: NIOD, 2002), http://www.srebrenica.nl.

7. Fred Westerman and Bart Rijs, *Srebrenica: Het Zwartste Scenario* (Amsterdam: Atlas, 1997). Jan Willem Honig and Norbert Both, *Srebrenica: Record of a War Crime* (London: Penguin Books, 1996), 37–54.

8. Significant international publications include the United Nations report and that of the French parliament. In the Netherlands, various books and articles have been written, and parliamentary inquiry commissions presided over by influential politicians (Van Kemenade, Bakker) were launched.

9. Nederlands Instituut voor Oorlogsdocumentatie (NIOD) (Dutch Institute for War Documentation [NIOD]). Srebrenica, een "veilig" gebied. Reconstructie, achtergronden, gevolgen en analyses van de val van een Safe Area (Srebrenica, a "safe" area. Reconstruction, backgrounds, consequences, and analyses of the downfall of a safe area). (Amsterdam: NIOD, 2002), http://www.srebrenica.nl.

10. Ibid.

11. Ibid.

12. Ibid.

13. Christ'l De Landtsheer, "The Language of Prosperity and Crisis: A Case Study in Political Semantics," *Politics and the Individual* 4, no. 2 (1994): 63–85; De Landtsheer, "The Political Rhetoric of a Unified Europe," "129–46.

14. Theodore Windt and Beth Ingold, *Essays in Presidential Rhetoric* (Dubuque, Iowa: Kendall/Hunt Publishing, 1987).

15. This is a political psychological definition of crisis by De Landtsheer that is based on Kos and Fritzsche. Political psychology is a multidisciplinary approach that studies the major relationships between political and psychological processes. Research topics range from the public effects of media, their ethical aspects, political language and image building, major dimensions of voting behavior and political socialization, political personality, and leadership styles. *Political Psychology: Journal of the International Society of Political Psychology* (Boston: Blackwell, YEAR). Ivan Kos, "Fearful Leadership: A Comparison of Communist and Post-Communist Leadership in the former Yugoslavia" (paper presented at the eighth conference of the Dutch Society for Political Psychology in Amsterdam, 1984). Peter Fritzsche, "Social Stress: A New Approach to Explain Xenophobia" (paper presented at the eighth conference of the Dutch Society for Political Psychology in Amsterdam, 1984).

16. Helmut Gaus, *Menselijk gedrag in perioden van langdurige economische recessie: Een schets [Human Behavior in Times of Long-Term Economic Recession]* (Malle, Belgium: De Sikkel, 1981).

17. Harold D. Lasswell, "Style and the Language of Politics," in *Language of Politics: Studies in Quantitative Semantics,* ed. Harold D. Lasswell et al. (New York: George W. Stewart, 1949), 23.
18. Ibid., 28.
19. Lasswell et al., *Language of Politics;* Harold D. Lasswell, Daniel Lerner, and Ithiel De Sola Pool, eds., *The Comparative Study of Symbols: An Introduction* (Stanford, Calif.: Stanford University Press, 1952).
20. Lasswell, "Style and the Language of Politics,"28.
21. Ibid.
22. Jochen Gerstenmaier and Heinz Mandl, "Constructivism in Cognitive Psychology," in *International Encyclopedia of the Social and Behavioral Sciences,* ed. Neil J. Smelser and Paul B. Baltes (Amsterdam: Elsevier, 2001), 4:2654–59, 2655.
23. Myron Joel Aronoff, "Political Culture," in *International Encyclopedia,* 17:11641.
24. George Lakoff, "The Contemporary Theory of Metaphor," in *Metaphor and Thought,* 2d ed., ed. Andrew Ortony (Cambridge: Cambridge University Press, 1993), 202–51; George Lakoff and Mark Johnson, *Metaphors We Live By* (Chicago: University of Chicago Press, 1980).
25. Catarina Cacciari, "Cognitive Psychology of Figurative Thought and Figurative Language," in *International Encyclopedia,* 8:5632.
26. Lakoff and Johnson, *Metaphors We Live By.*
27. Aristotle, *The Complete Works of Aristotle: The Revised Oxford Translation* (Princeton: Princeton University Press, 1984).
28. David Lambourn, "Metaphor and Its Role in Social Thought: History of the Concept," in *Encyclopedia of the Social and Behavioral Sciences,* 14:9738.
29. Shanto Iyengar and Donald R. Kinder, *News That Matters: Television and American Opinion* (Chicago: University of Chicago Press, 1987); Shanto Iyengar, *Is Anyone Responsible? How Television Frames Political Issues* (Chicago: University of Chicago Press, 1991); Maxwell E. McCombs and Donald L. Shaw, "The Agenda-Setting Function of the Press," *Public Opinion Quarterly* 36 (1972): 176–87.
30. Jerry Palmer, *Spinning into Control: News Values and Source Strategies* (London: Leicester University Press/Continuum, 2000).
31. On how metaphors work, see Sam Glucksburg and Keysar Boaz, "How Metaphor Works," in *Metaphor and Thought,* 401–24; Robert E. Haskell, ed., *Cognition and Symbolic Structures: The Psychology of Metaphoric Transformation* (Norwood, N.J.: Ablex Publishing Corporation, 1987).

32. I. A. Richards, *A Philosophy of Rhetoric* (Oxford: Oxford University Press, 1936).

33. Eva Feder Kittay, *Metaphor: Its Cognitive Force and Linguistic Structure* (Oxford: Clarendon Press, 1987), 22.

34. Cacciari, "Cognitive Psychology of Figurative Thought," 8:5632–37.

35. Max Black, "More about Metaphor," in *Metaphor and Thought* (Cambridge: Cambridge University Press, 1979), 19–43; Max Black, "More about Metaphor," in *Metaphor and Thought*, 2d ed.

36. McCombs and Shaw, "The Agenda-Setting Function of the Press," 176–87; Palmer, *Spinning into Control.*

37. Edward Tony Higgins and G. R. Semin, "Communication and Social Psychology," in *International Encyclopedia*, 3:2296–99.

38. Ibid., 3:2297.

39. Ibid., 3:2298.

40. Cacciari, "Cognitive Psychology of Figurative Thought," 8:5636.

41. T. Cohen, "Metaphor and the Cultivation of Intimacy," in *On Metaphor*, ed. S. Sachs (Chicago: University of Chicago Press, 1979), quoted in Lambourn, "Metaphor and Its Role in Social Thought," 14:9742.

42. Kittay, *Metaphor*, 22.

43. Keith Oatley, "Emotion in Cognition," in *International Encyclopedia*, 7:4440.

44. Ibid., 7:4443.

45. Ibid., 7:4443.

46. George A. Kennan, "Rhetoric," in *International Encyclopedia*, 20:13318.

47. Windt and Ingold, *Essays in Presidential Rhetoric*, xix.

48. Ota Weinberger, "Argumentation in Law and Politics," *Communication and Cognition* 28, no. 1 (1995).

49. Higgins and Semin, "Communication and Social Psychology," 3:2297.

50. Windt and Ingold, *Essays in Presidential Rhetoric*, xix.

51. Ibid., xvii.

52. Peter Larsen, "Rhetorical Analysis," in *International Encyclopedia*, 20:13325.

53. Kittay, *Metaphor*, 2.

54. Ithiel De Sola Pool, "Variety and Repetition in Political Language," in *Political Behavior: A Reader in Theory and Research*, ed. Eulau, Heinz et al. (Glencoe, Ill., The Free Press, 1956), 217–31.

55. Suedfeld and Bluck, "Changes in Integrative Complexity Prior to Surprise Attacks," 626–35; Suedfeld, Tetlock, and Ramirez, "War,

Peace and Integrative Complexity," 427–42; Wallace, Suedfeld, and Thachuk, "Political Rhetoric of Leaders under Stress in the Gulf Crisis," 94–107.

56. Lasswell, "Style and The Language of Politics," 20–39.

57. Ben W. Hunt, *Getting to War: Predicting International Conflict with Mass Media Indicators* (Ann Arbor: University of Michigan Press, 1997).

58. Christ'l De Landtsheer, "The Language of Prosperity and Crisis: A Case Study in Political Semantics," *Politics and the Individual* 4, no. 2 (1994): 63–85; De Landtsheer, "The Political Rhetoric of a Unified Europe," 129–46.

59. Lasswell et al., *Language of Politics.*

60. David Grant, "Metaphors and Paradigms in Organizations," in *International Encyclopedia,* 16:10960–65.

61. Kittay, *Metaphor,* 41–42.

62. Black, "More about Metaphor," in *Metaphor and Thought,* 2d ed., 26.

63. Haridimos Tsoukas, "The Missing Link: A Transformational View of Metaphors in Organizational Science," *Academy of Management Review* 16, no. 3 (1991): 568.

64. Ibid.

65. Wilhelm Koeller, *Semiotik und Metapher: Untersuchungen zur grammatischen Struktur und der kommunikativen Funktion vorn Metaphern* (Stuttgart: Metzlersche Verlagsbuchhandlung, 1975), 233–41.

66. Jan J. Mooy, *A Study of Metaphor: On the Nature of Metaphorical Expressions with Special Reference to Their Reference* (Amsterdam: North Holland, 1976), 121.

67. Kittay, *Metaphor,* 24.

68. Ibid., 225, 229.

69. Koeller, *Semiotik und Metapher,* [*Semiotics and Metaphor*] 233–41; Elisabeth Leinfellner, *Der Euphemismus in der politischen Sprache* [*Euphemism in Political Language*](Berlin: Duncker and Humblot, 1971), quoted in De Landtsheer, "The Language of Prosperity and Crisis," 63–85.

70. Helmut Gaus, *Menselijk gedrag in perioden van langdurige economische recessie.*

71. G. Baker-Brown et al., "The Conceptual/Integrative Complexity Scoring Manual," in *Motivation and Personality: Handbook of Thematic Content Analysis,* ed. C. P. Smith (Cambridge: Cambridge University Press, 1983), 400–18, quoted in Wallace, Suedfeld and Thachuk, "Political Rhetoric of Leaders under Stress in the Gulf Crisis," 96–97.

72. On the issue of translating metaphors, one can consult Teresa Dobrzynska, "Translating Metaphor: Problems of Meaning," *Journal of Pragmatics* 24 (1995): 595–604.

73. Palmer, *Spinning into Control;* Hunt, *Getting to War.*

74. Nederlands Instituut voor Oorlogsdocumentatie (NIOD) (Dutch Institute for War Documentation [NIOD]). Srebrenica, een "veilig" gebied. Reconstructie, achtergronden, gevolgen en analyses van de val van een Safe Area (Srebrenica, a "safe" area. Reconstruction, backgrounds, consequences, and analyses of the downfall of a safe area). (Amsterdam: NIOD, 2002), http://www.srebrenica.nl.

75. De Landtsheer, "The Language of Prosperity and Crisis," 63–85; De Landtsheer, "The Political Rhetoric of a Unified Europe," 129–46.

76. Suedfeld and Bluck, "Changes in Integrative Complexity Prior to Surprise Attacks," 626–35.

◆ Section III

Metaphorical Globalization

Metaphorical Globalization

Francis A. Beer and Christ'l De Landtsheer

G lobalization is a topic that has received substantial attention in recent years. In a sense, the study and practice of international relations has been global for centuries, though the definition of global has changed. The Treaty of Tordesillas, signed in 1494, divided the newly discovered areas of the world between Spain and Portugal. More contemporary agreements at Vienna, Versailles, Yalta, and Potsdam could also be said to have divided the world after great wars.

The current meaning of "globalization" expands these understandings. There is an implicit metaphor in the first astronauts' view from space of the "small blue planet" and its companion, "spaceship earth." Robert Rubin, secretary of the treasury under President Clinton, was fond of talking about global financial architecture, which would be built from the best financial practices. Other metaphors have appeared in the titles of books such as *The Lexus and the Olive Tree* and *Jihad vs. McWorld* and are ubiquitous in the globalization literature.[1]

World politics is the target for a plenitude of metaphorical sources in such titles as *Games Advisors Play, The Grand Chessboard,* and *Hawks, Owls, and Doves.* Further, there are "hard" and "soft" international law and power. "Bandwagons," "buckpassing," "chain gangs," and "entanglement" describe alliance processes. There are "power shifts" and "problem shifts";

"black boxes" and "Pandora's boxes"; "birds of a feather" and "the Phoenix factor." There are pleas to "come home America" and to go "back to the future."[2]

The previous topics of democracy and war and peace in this book have obvious global implications as the United States reaches outward at the beginning of the twenty-first century and America seeks to become the hero of and the engine for globalization. Americanization supplies the missing content of globalization. American hegemony and the unipolar moment are an implicit metaphorical source for planetary free politics, free markets, and free speech, though it remains unclear whether America is to be Athens or Sparta.[3]

The chapters in this section start from this point and further explore metaphors of globalization. Previous chapters have discussed the power of metaphors. Shimko joins that concern with one for "metaphors of power." This is an essay about the role of metaphors in foreign policy, particularly those metaphors that have helped shape the United States' conception of the world and itself during the Cold War and into the twenty-first century, from the war on communism to the war on terrorism. The focus is on so-called metaphors of power—that is, those metaphors which frame the world and the United States' role in it in such a manner as to explain, justify, and lead to the exercise of American power. Shimko distinguishes between process and relational metaphors. "Process, or dynamic metaphors" include "power vacuums, falling dominoes, contagious disease, and spreading fires." Such metaphors "suggest a certain sequence of events will happen, how developments are likely to unfold. Furthermore, they do so in ways that virtually invite the exercise of American power." Relational metaphors specify an association "between objects/actors." "Families" and "neighbors" are examples. Shimko asks whether such metaphors "systematically 'frame' or 'structure' international relations (the 'problem' in this case) in ways that lead almost inevitably to a policy of expansion and intervention." He calls these "metaphors of power because they provide a cognitive/intellectual/discursive foundation for the exercise of power. Taken individually, some of the metaphors seem powerful enough; taken together, they combine to create an understanding of the world and the United States' role in it that makes any other policies difficult to imagine."[4]

Rosati and Campbell begin from the same ground as Shimko and move in a different direction. They focus on two major competing metaphors of American foreign policy. The first of these is the "arc of crisis." This metaphor is related to Shimko's "metaphors of power" in its strong focus on American national identity and external threats to the American body politic. It is also connected to the analysis by De Landtsheer and De Vrij of the metaphorical dynamics of crisis. The other metaphor is that of the "global community," which suggests a wider possible political identity. Rosati and Campbell use these two master metaphors to describe the evolving metaphorical thinking of President Carter, National Security Adviser Brzezinski, and Secretary of State Vance from 1977 to 1980. The Carter administration began with the broader, more optimistic metaphorical imagery associated with global community during the initial years, but it proved politically unsustainable. It then returned to the more nationalistic, pessimistic arc of crisis imagery in the latter years. Viewing metaphor through the lens of cognitive psychology, Rosati and Campbell suggest that metaphors, "which reflected the content of beliefs and goals of policymakers, served as cognitive guides through the foreign policy terrain." Echoing Anderson's findings of metaphorical political cueing, they also believe that metaphors "facilitated communication among policymakers—and between policymakers and the public—of distant political realities, thereby furthering understanding of such phenomena. Finally," they conclude, metaphors "were used by the Carter administration to justify policy stances and actions in attempts to achieve legitimization and garner political support among the public."

Timothy Luke's chapter concludes the volume. He focuses on the ways that "megametaphors" such as "globalization" and "virtualization" interact with the "politics of world definition." He suggests that "megametaphorics serve as key resources in the mythographies of modernization today as they conjure up popular doxologies with fables of alikeness and difference. Metaphors," he believes, "anchor myths, and myths create belief. And, in being believed, myths become reality in the ongoing tussles of social forces."

Notes

1. Thomas L. Friedman, *The Lexus and the Olive Tree* (New York: Anchor Books, 2000); Benjamin R. Barber, *Jihad vs. McWorld* (New York: Times Books, 1995). See also Kenneth S. Zagacki, "Spatial and Temporal Images in the Biodiversity Dispute," *Quarterly Journal of Speech* 85 (1999): 425; Suzanne Romaine, "War and Peace in the Global Greenhouse: Metaphors We Die By," *Metaphor and Symbolic Activity* 11 (1996): 175–94; Tim Rohrer, "The Metaphorical Logic of (Political) Rape: The New Wor(l)d Order," *Metaphor and Symbolic Activity* 10 (1995): 115–37; Jeffrey S. Mio, Suzanne C. Thompson, and Geoffrey

H. Givens, "The Commons Dilemma as Metaphor: Memory, Influence, and Implications for Environmental Conservation," *Metaphor and Symbolic Activity* 8 (1993): 23–42.

2. Joseph S. Nye, *The Paradox of American Power* (Oxford: Oxford University Press, 2002); Bernard I. Finel, "Black Box or Pandora's Box: State Level Variables and Progressivity in Realist Research Programs," *Security Studies* 11, no. 2 (2001): 187–227; Kenneth W. Abbott and Duncan Snidal, "Hard and Soft Law in International Governance," *International Organization* 54, no. 3 (2000): 421–56; Jean A. Garrison, *Games Advisors Play: Foreign Policy in the Nixon and Carter Administrations* (College Station: Texas A&M University Press, 1999); Zbigniew Brzezinski, *The Grand Chessboard: American Primacy and Its Geostrategic Imperatives* (New York: Basic Books, 1997); Graham T. Allison, Albert Carnesale, and Joseph S. Nye, Jr., *Hawks, Doves, and Owls: An Agenda for Avoiding Nuclear War* (New York: W. W. Norton, 1985); Eugene Gholz, Daryl G. Press, and Harvey M. Sapolsky, "Come Home America—The Strategy of Restraint in the Face of Temptation," *International Security* 21, no. 4 (1997): 5–48; Jennifer Sterling-Folker, "Competing Paradigms or Birds of a Feather? Constructivism and Neoliberal Institutionalism Compared," *International Studies Quarterly* 44, no. 1 (2000): 97–119; Jonathan M. DiCicco, "Power Shifts and Problem Shifts," *Journal of Conflict Resolution* 43, no. 6 (1999): 675–704; Randall L. Schweller, "Bandwagoning for Profit: Bringing the Revisionist State Back in," *International Security* 19 (summer 1994): 72–107; Karin M. Fierke, "Dialogues of Manoeuvre and Entanglement: NATO, Russia, and the CEEC," *Millennium: Journal of International Studies* 28 (1999): 27–52; Thomas J. Christensen and Jack Snyder, "Chain Gangs and Passed Bucks: Predicting Alliance Patterns in Multipolarity," *International Organization* 44 (spring 1990): 137–68; John J. Mearsheimer, "Back to the Future: Instability in Europe after the Cold War," *International Security* 15, no. 1 (1990): 5–57; A. F. K. Organski and Jacek Kugler, "The Costs of Major Wars: The Phoenix Factor," *American Political Science Review* 71, no. 4 (1977): 1347–66. We are indebted to Murat Ozkaleli for many of these examples.

3. Cf. Martin Walker, "Bush's Choice: Athens or Sparta," *World Policy Journal* 18, no. 2 (2001): 1–9; Fareed Zakaria, "Our Way: The Trouble with Being the World's Only Superpower," *The New Yorker,* 14 and 21 October 2002, 81; Michael Mandelbaum, *The Ideas That Conquered the World: Peace, Democracy, and Free Markets in the Twenty-first Century* (New York: Public Affairs, 2002); Lea Brilmayer, *American Hegemony:*

Political Morality in a One-Superpower World (New Haven: Yale University Press, 1994); Stephen Ambrose and Douglas G. Brinkley, *Rise to Globalism: American Foreign Policy since 1938,* 8th rev. ed. (New York: Penguin, 1997).

4. See also Robert N. Entman, *Projections of Power: Framing News, Public Opinion, and U.S. Foreign Policy* (Chicago: University of Chicago Press, 2004); Jennifer Milliken, "Metaphors of Prestige and Reputation in American Foreign Policy and International Realism," in *Post-realism: The Rhetorical Turn in International Relations,* ed. Francis A. Beer and Robert Hariman (East Lansing: Michigan State University Press, 1996), 217–38; Keith L. Shimko, "Metaphors and Foreign Policy Decision Making," *Political Psychology* 15, no. 4 (1994): 655–71.

The Power of Metaphors and the Metaphors of Power

The United States in the Cold War and After

Keith L. Shimko

Metaphors are an inescapable facet of everyday thought and speech. Cognitively, metaphorical thinking involves trying to comprehend and understand something in terms of something else. Any brief perusal of discussions of international relations reveals the pervasiveness of metaphors—arms "races," power "vacuums," falling "dominoes," and so on. This is an essay about the role of metaphors in foreign policy, particularly those metaphors that have helped shape the United States' conception of the world and itself during the Cold War and after. The focus is on so-called metaphors of power—that is, those metaphors which frame the world and the United States' role in it in such a manner as to explain, justify, and lead to the exercise of American power. It is about the power of metaphors and the metaphors of the powerful.

Introduction

The language of international relations and foreign policy is replete with metaphors, though they are often so implicitly accepted and commonly used that people fail to recognize the metaphorical roots of their expressions. This is true for both academics and policymakers alike. Great powers are characterized as "poles," smaller nations sometimes as "bandwagon"; conflicts are described as "cold wars"; deterrence requires that nations "stand firm" in order to convey resolve. We worry about who will fill power "vacuums"; in war we speak of dealing a "knockout blow"; nations are "prisoners" of insecurity and "play games" of "chicken"; agreements between nations are "houses of cards"; and so on. Indeed, at times it seems impossible to write or talk about international relations at any length without occasionally lapsing into metaphorical imagery and allusion. Despite the prevalence of metaphors in the discourse of international relations, little has changed since Deborah Larson observed more than a decade ago that "the role played by metaphors in foreign policymaking is still unexplored."[1] This lack of research is even more surprising when compared to the voluminous literature on the related issue of historical analogies.[2]

We have long recognized that the invocation of certain historical analogies incline decision makers toward some types of policies as opposed to others—for example, the Munich analogy would not lead someone to favor accommodation and concessions in order to head off a crisis. Similarly, different metaphors of international politics are conducive to various policies. How we behave in the world depends on how we think the world works and how we envisage our role in it. To the extent that different metaphors embody contrasting images of how the world works they will be consistent with different policies. This essay is interested in what I refer to as the metaphors of power—that is, those metaphors which involve conceptions of international politics that are conducive to the exercise of power. Since the United States has been the world's dominate power since the end of World War II, it is particularly useful to focus on those metaphors which have portrayed the world and the United States itself in such a way as to promote, explain, and justify the exercise of American power during the Cold War and after.

Metaphors and Problem Framing

According to Susan Sontag, drawing on a definition originally provided by Aristotle, the use of a metaphor involves "saying a thing is or is like something-it-is-not."[3] Similarly, Lakoff and Johnson tell us that the "essence of metaphor is understanding and experiencing one kind of thing in terms of another."[4] We all know some popular metaphors: he is as solid as a rock, time is money, the battle of the sexes, and the war on poverty. But why is it important for us to study metaphors? Are they not simply colorful linguistic artifacts that people use to bring a little drama to their speech? Sometimes that may be all there is to it: after all, when someone says, "John is as steady as a rock," no one really thinks he is a rock and people are not going to start treating him as if he were one. Other times, however, the use of a powerful metaphor may be instrumental—for example, to "sell" a policy to a potentially skeptical audience and frame policy debates in ways that favor one's perspective. This is partly what Schweller has in mind when he notes that "the Truman administration employed the contagion metaphor to justify intervention in Greece in 1947."[5] But was that all the contagion metaphor did—help "justify" a policy? Do metaphors ever influence, shape, or determine policy? Elsewhere Schweller suggests that metaphors might have a more profound impact. Examining the academic literature on alliances and coalition formation, he explains that "the question of how states respond to threats has been associated with the familiar 'b' words: balancing, bandwagoning, and buckpassing." He worries that "these metaphors, while descriptively colorful, have become more of a barrier than an aid to thoughtful analysis."[6] While Schweller is referring to academics in this particular case, the same can be asked of policymakers and their metaphors. But in order for something to be a barrier to thoughtful analysis, it must be part of that analysis: the metaphors themselves must be influencing how people think. With regard to policymakers, Fred Iklé looks at the metaphors used in times of war. During WWI, Iklé argues, metaphors often played critical roles in policy analysis—metaphorical arguments that one more escalation might "break the opponents back" often substituted for serious analysis. He points to "metaphorical language" as "a common source of error in political analyses."[7] Again, he really means metaphorical thinking, not merely metaphorical language, since something cannot be a source of policy error unless it were part of the analysis.

It seems reasonable to assume that sometimes metaphors are "merely" colorful language or instrumental speech intended to sell, rationalize, or justify policies. There are undoubtedly times, however, when metaphors play a more significant role (or, perhaps most commonly, metaphors will be doing many things simultaneously). To view metaphors as either "mere" rhetoric and language or as guiding cognitive constructs is a simplistic distinction, since these functions are in no way mutually exclusive. Even if the author or speaker intends his use of a metaphor to, for example, increase support for the policy being advocated, the metaphor can still be, and probably is, indicative of how they are thinking. This is because, as Lakoff and Johnson explain, *"linguistic expressions are containers for meanings."*[8] Put another way, "metaphors as linguistic expressions are possible precisely because there are metaphors in a person's conceptual system."[9] Furthermore, metaphors that might initially be "just" rhetoric may become more, as Vertzberger explains: "metaphorical expressions that are used only for literal articulation become, inadvertently and unbeknownst to the user, an input into the channeling and allocation of attention."[10] In essence the argument being made is that thought and language cannot be separated because in the final analysis people cannot think without language and cannot use language without thinking.

This was precisely the argument made by Sontag: metaphorical constructions and thinking are "mental operation[s] as old as philosophy and poetry, and the spawning ground of most kinds of understanding."[11] I am interested in metaphors because they often represent and reveal how people are thinking and how they are trying to make sense of the actors and situations that surround them. And how people think about the world influences how they behave. With regard to cancer and AIDS, Sontag was convinced that "the metaphorical trappings that deform the experience of having cancer have very real consequences: they inhibit people from seeking treatment early enough, or from making a greater effort to get competent treatment. The metaphors and myths, I was convinced, kill."[12] In a similar vein, Londa Schiebinger warns that "Metaphors are not innocent literary devices used to spice up texts. Analogies and metaphors . . . function to construct as well as describe—they have both a hypothesis-creating and proof-making function."[13] If the metaphors of illness form/deform the experience of those who suffer from the illness, it is reasonable to ask whether and how the metaphors of geopolitics form/deform the experience of those making policies in ways that have "very real consequences."

To understand how and why metaphors may have consequences, one needs to begin with the work of cognitive psychologists, which focuses on how people deal with the complexities and ambiguities of the world that surrounds them. Among the tools that people use to make sense of their world are analogical and metaphorical reasoning. When people need to understand one aspect of their environment that might be abstract or unfamiliar to them, they frequently draw comparisons to things that are more familiar to them and more concrete in nature. They search their memories for something they know about that might give them (or create for them) some understanding of something that is unfamiliar. Once the comparison is drawn, people then try to understand one thing in terms of another. This is what historical analogies do. Confronted with one crisis in which the opposition's goals might be unclear and development of the crisis unpredictable, parallels are often drawn to a previous crisis, the knowledge of which is then used to "fill in the blanks" of ignorance in the current crisis. This is a transfer of "knowledge." The Munich analogy is the most famous case in point—the crises with the Soviet Union during the Cold War, with Saddam Hussein, and with Slobodan Milosevic have all been framed as modern replays of the Munich, like the script of a play being restaged after several decades. It is a script: if I do X, then the opposite side will do Y; if I do not do X, he will do Z instead.

In the sense they are based on comparisons, metaphors are similar to analogies. Lakoff and Johnson explain that "metaphor is principally a way of conceiving one thing in terms of another, and its primary function is understanding."[14] There is, however, a critical difference between analogies and metaphors. Using the terminology adopted by cognitive psychologists, analogies are "within-domain" comparisons—for example, one person to another, one city to another, or one international crisis to another. Analogies are parallels between similar or very similar things. Metaphors, on the other hand, are "cross-domain" comparisons."[15] To say John is like Erik is analogical because a person is being compared to another person; to say John is like a shark is metaphorical because a person is being compared to a different animal. To say that Cambodia is like Vietnam is analogical; to say that Cambodia is like a falling domino is metaphorical. To compare the Cuban missile crisis to the Munich crisis is to be analogical; to compare it to a high stakes poker game of bluffs and gambles is to be metaphorical. Certainly there will be instances where the boundaries of the domains are debatable and the question of whether we are dealing with an analogy or metaphor remains open. But in most cases (such as those highlighted in this essay) it is relatively easy to differentiate.

The fact that analogies and metaphors are both similar and different suggests that their impact will also be similar in some ways and different in others. In short, while analogies are likely to provide more concrete and more specific guidance on exactly how to behave and what policies to follow, metaphors are likely to focus on what has been called "problem framing" or "problem representation." Take, for example, Khong's discussion of analogies and their significance:

> First and foremost, analogies help define the nature of the problem or situation . . . by comparing the new situation to previous situations . . . the second the third diagnostic tasks follow; analogies give the policymaker a sense of the political stakes involved and they also imply or suggest possible solutions . . . the fourth, fifth and sixth diagnostic tasks all pertain to evaluating the implicit polic[ies] prescribed.[16]

Metaphors are going to be more important in terms of defining the nature of the problem, the actors, and the sorts of dynamics involved—the earlier "diagnostic tasks" Khong lays out. Metaphors, unlike analogies, are unlikely to be sources of specific policies. For example, comparing the Soviet Union to Hitlerite Germany and a crisis with the Soviet Union to Munich can lead to real, concrete policies—for example, make no territorial concessions. But comparing the spread of communism to an infectious disease or falling dominoes really frames the nature of the problem in a broad sense more than it suggests specific policies.

Metaphors frame problems and situations by drawing attention to some aspects while discounting others: "the very systematicity that allows us to comprehend one aspect of a concept in terms of another will necessarily hide other aspects of the concept . . . a metaphorical concept can keep us from focusing on other aspects of the concept that are inconsistent with that metaphor."[17] Vertzberger makes a similar point: "metaphors add vividness to a data-set, and nondiagnostic data thereby gain a diagnostic impact they do not deserve. Diagnostic data that do not lend themselves to effective metaphorical representation may be ignored or undervalued."[18] This is what Sontag has in mind when she talks about the ability of metaphors to "deform" experience. The metaphors of geopolitics can influence policy in the same manner—they highlight certain facets of international relations while downplaying others; in imagining certain dynamics the metaphors hide the possibility that things might actually work in a different way.

Metaphors of Power in the Cold War and After

From the very beginning the Cold War was awash in metaphorical imagery. Indeed the term *Cold War*, coined by Walter Lippmann to characterize the increasing conflicts between the United States and the Soviet Union in the absence of outright war, is itself a double metaphor, with both "cold" and "war" being used metaphorically. Winston Churchill made another enduring contribution to the metaphorical Cold War when he warned of the "iron curtain" that had descended across the center of Europe, implying the existence of some sort of impermeable boundary between East and West. The nations of Eastern Europe were run by "puppets" of the Soviet Union. The metaphors kept coming: decades later, in the early 1980s, the Reagan administration's strategic and arms control policies were driven by the perception that some "window" of vulnerability had "opened" that needed to be "closed." In fact, it was in the area of nuclear arms that metaphors seemed to be a virtual cottage industry. The "meta-metaphor" of the nuclear arms "race" and the obsession with who was "ahead," "falling behind," "winning," and "losing" lasted for decades. The metaphor of arms "races" is perhaps one of the oldest and most pervasive of all geopolitical metaphors. The prevalence of this imagery is such that most of us would find it nearly impossible to think about the acquisition of arms without resorting to the metaphorical language of a "race." In the era of nuclear weapons, the impact of this metaphor may have been particularly pernicious, given the rather vacuous meaning of concepts such as "winning" and "losing" in an era of overkill and mutually assured destruction.

Yet another tried and true geopolitical metaphor is the concept of the "power vacuum." This would also be mobilized at various junctures during the Cold War. President Eisenhower (who appears to have had a particular fondness for geopolitical metaphors) observed after the 1956 Suez crisis that "the existing vacuum in the Middle East must be filled by the United States before it is filled by Russia."[19] The metaphor of the power vacuum is a prime example of what I call a metaphor of power: it embodies a conception of how the world works that is conducive to the exercise of great power. Like many influential geopolitical metaphors, this one is drawn from the natural, physical, and biological sciences. Such metaphors imply that the social world of international relations operates according to certain laws, such as the laws of physics. Perhaps such analogies are so common because they provide a comforting vision of predictability for an unpredictable world. It is a world in which nations and decision makers are oddly robbed of volition and agency (and, thus, moral responsibility?). Nature abhors a vacuum. Vacuums will be filled; they will draw things in. This is inevitable and inexorable. As Eisenhower insists, the vacuum "must" be filled. If it is not filled by the United States, it will be filled by the Soviet Union: these are the only two options. And since it is a vacuum of power, who else can fill it except those who possess power—for example, the United States. The notion that there exists these things called power vacuums that must be filled is a metaphor of power because it presents an understanding of how the world works that almost inevitably leads to the conclusion that those with power must expand to fill the vacuums. In filling power vacuums we are only doing what must inevitably be done—in fact, it is the vacuum itself that is to blame because it "draws" in power (and, thus, the powerful). The metaphor, of course, hides the obvious objection to the analysis and conclusion: perhaps no one has to "fill" the "vacuum" because it is not in fact a "vacuum" at all.

Other than the general metaphor of an arms "race" applied to nuclear weapons, perhaps the most central metaphors of the Cold War were those used to portray and understand the nature of Soviet or Communist expansion. These different metaphors all convey some notion that Soviet or Communist expansion was an almost natural or inevitable force or process that could only be halted by some significant external resistance. The two most frequently employed metaphors along these lines were the "communism as a contagious disease" and "Communist expansion as falling dominoes" metaphors. The comparison of communism to a disease can be traced to the earliest days of the Cold War (though probably even earlier to the Red Scare of the 1920s) when Secretary of State Dean Acheson warned in 1947 that "like apples in a barrel *infected* by one rotten one, the corruption of Greece would *infect* Iran and all to the East. It would carry *infection* to Africa through Asia minor."[20] Robert Ivie provides an exhaustive analysis of the dominance of disease imagery in early thinking about the Soviet threat and U.S. containment policy.[21] George Kennan argued that the Soviet Union and its agents would try to locate "diseased tissue" and would proceed to exploit vulnerable nations like a "malignant parasite."[22] With regard to its own hemisphere the goal of American policy was defined in 1952 as "an orderly political and economic growth that would make Latin American nations *resistant* to the internal *growth* of communism."[23] This metaphor continued to hold sway well into the 1980s when President Reagan predicted that if the United States "ignores the *malignancy* in Managua . . . [it will] *spread* and become a mortal threat to the entire world."[24] Reagan's assistant secretary of defense worried that "many institutions of government in the United States and among our North Atlantic allies are inadequately *inoculated* against the *disease* of appeasement."[25]

Perhaps the most famous of all Cold War metaphors is the related imagery of falling dominoes. It was President Eisenhower who provided the seminal statement of the domino theory. Discussing how the "fall" of

South Vietnam might endanger all of Southeast Asia he argued: "You have a row of dominoes set up, you knock over the first one, and what will happen to the last one is the certainty that it will go over very quickly. So you could have a beginning of a disintegration that would have the most profound influences."[26] Almost twenty-five years later the metaphor remained a part of Cold War discourse as evidenced by President Reagan's claim in 1980 that "the Soviet Union underlies all the unrest that is going on [in Latin America]. If they weren't in this game of dominoes, there wouldn't be any hot spots in the world."[27] And in this "game" of dominoes, Reagan warned, "we are the last domino."[28]

There is a potential misconception about the domino metaphor and the Cold War (and the use of metaphors generally) that must be cleared up. Throughout most of the Cold War the domino metaphor was rarely expressed as explicitly as Eisenhower did in 1956—the word "domino" itself was seldom used by subsequent policymakers. One will search in vain through piles of official documents for a few measly appearances of the word "domino," which is why the same two or three quotations always appear in discussions of the domino theory. As a result, it might be tempting to conclude that the domino metaphor was only an occasionally used rhetorical device. One does not need to find the word "domino," however, in order to conclude that the metaphor is playing a crucial role. The central metaphorical expression need not be present. Indeed, part of the power of certain metaphors lies not in their explicit repetition but in their reliance on the familiar and that which goes without being said. Lakoff and Johnson explain how metaphors often reveal themselves through "speech formulas" rather than explicit invocation of the metaphor itself. Even when the domino metaphor was not invoked explicitly, the speech formulas of falling dominoes were pervasive—for example, nations "fall" or are "toppled," governments are "supported" or "propped up," and "chain reactions" are set off. Just as one does not have to use the word "Munich" in order to be engaging in a Munich analogy, one does not have to use the word "domino" in order to be engaging in a domino analogy. Even with policymakers who were too sophisticated to accept the simplistic versions of the domino theory (e.g., Henry Kissinger), the language of the metaphor was still omnipresent. We can say that the metaphor becomes almost "naturalized" in the sense that it becomes such a deep or basic part of one's thinking and analysis so as to be unrecognized as a metaphor at any conscious level.

The possibility that the most important and powerful metaphors are those that need not be explicitly invoked creates some obvious problems for systematic empirical research. A formal content analysis might miss a pervasive metaphor if the coding rules require specific references to the central metaphorical concept. This should not confused with the problematic position that the "absence of evidence is proof." There is evidence that what people say is a reflection of what and how they are thinking, but we must be on the lookout for the more-subtle speech formulas and phrases that derive from the underlying metaphorical construct.

In what ways do these metaphorical constructions help "frame" the problem of Soviet expansionism? To some degree both the disease and domino metaphors share much in common, as Slater observes: "whether the metaphor is falling dominos, rotten apples, spreading disease, or the weakest link in the chain, the structure of the argument is the same."[29] The similarities, for example, include a conception of tight, even absolute interdependence—that is, the idea that once something happens in one place it will inevitably have ramifications for the areas around it. Strategically, this meant that even if the threat was not to an area or country deemed to be vital on its own merits, the "fall" of that country or the "spread" of Communism would eventually have an impact on areas and countries that were vital. The domino metaphor was also one that "hid" differences in nations (after all, all dominoes are the same except for the number of dots): the first domino is the same as the last. The problem, as many have pointed out, is that nations are not as identical as dominoes: Laos is not the same as Thailand.

Interestingly, these metaphors also frame the problem in a way that encourages the use of American power—that is, they are what I call metaphors of power. Both the disease and domino metaphors imply that the spread of Communism or Soviet influence is a nearly inevitable process, whether it is because of the physical and mechanical principles of falling dominoes or the epidemiological processes of contagion. People envision the falling of dominoes as something that will naturally proceed until the last one is toppled unless some external force intervenes in the process in order to prevent what would otherwise happen. Similarly, people envision the contagion of disease as something that will inevitably happen unless actions are taken to prevent it—one might inoculate people against a virus or isolate and quarantine them to prevent further contagion. That is, the metaphors suggest a certain process or dynamics; they conjure up mechanical and biological images that are then used to make sense of (or anticipate) the dynamics of international politics. These are processes or dynamics that can only be halted by intervention. And who better to intervene than those who have the power to intervene? In the case of Vietnam, Karnow uses interesting terminology in talking about the "American crusade, *propelled* as it was by the 'domino theory.'"[30] In what sense was the United States "propelled" by the imagery of falling dominoes? In the sense that the metaphor suggests that dominoes would have continued to fall without outside intervention to hold up the dominoes—the dominoes were not going to stop falling on their own. In the case of the power "vacuum" metaphor the United States was internal to the metaphor—it was subject to the forces that inevitably pull in powers. In the case of the disease and domino metaphors, the United States was external to the metaphors—not part of the process, but an external force necessary to stop the process.

The disease metaphor, it should be noted, has some connotations that the domino metaphor does not. Another aspect of diseases and viruses is that they are often stealthy—one cannot always tell who is infected and "carrying" the disease. Dominoes are visible to the naked eye, whereas viruses and germs are not. The fear of spreading disease produces a certain amount of anxiety and uncertainty at a visceral level that visions of falling dominoes really do not: people understand how dominoes fall, but they do not really fear them. This highlights an interesting aspect of metaphors: some are merely explanatory or cognitive, while others may also have an emotive and affective element, influencing how people "feel" as well as how they think. A virus exists alongside healthy cells, spreading in the body while outwardly a person appears healthy. President Truman's attorney general, foreshadowing the McCarthy era, argued that each Communist "carries in himself the *germs* of death for society."[31] In the domino metaphor the "enemy"—the cause of the "fall"—is external. Dominoes are knocked down by other dominoes. The disease metaphor adds another dimension somewhat at odds with the domino metaphor—that is, the cause of death (falling to Communism) may be internal. Ultimately, however, the internal virus had external origins and entered the host through "penetration," "subversion," or "infection." Nonetheless, the notion of Communism as a spreading disease provides the metaphorical grounding for a search for internal enemies and infected cells amidst the healthy ones. This is not something suggested by a domino metaphor. Thus, even if the underlying structures of metaphors are the same, they usually carry some unique connotations.

In the post–Cold War world the United States is no longer concerned with the spread of the disease of communism or the fall of countries into the Soviet sphere of influence. But, of course, there are still dangers. And, of course, there is a need for American power to combat these new dangers. What are these dangers and what metaphors are being used to frame them? As an example, let us look at the recent crisis in the former Yugoslavia, which highlights one of the new dangers—ethnic conflict and its spread. Here again, the metaphorical construction of the conflict is interesting and shares some things in common with the metaphors of power of the Cold War. Some of the metaphors convey a level of gravity and importance—for example, we are told that unlike some other ethnic conflicts throughout the world the conflict in Yugoslavia deserves American attention because it is in the "heart" of Europe. If this is meant to imply that Yugoslavia is geographically in the center of Europe, it is simply wrong, of course. What does it imply? Well, everyone knows that the heart is essential. A person can live without one of their limbs, but death would certainly follow were the heart to stop functioning. Thus, placing the conflict at the metaphorical heart of Europe immediately frames the issue as one of paramount importance.

But the critical metaphor of power at play in the Yugoslavian crisis is one whose underlying structure is similar to the domino and disease metaphors. Just as the United States was concerned about the "spread" of communism during the Cold War, it is worried about the spread of ethnic conflict beyond the boundaries of the former Yugoslavia (though if Yugoslavia were really in the "heart" of Europe, the conflict there should be of sufficient concern even if it did not spread). The dynamics of how ethnic conflict spreads (and, thus, how it might be stopped) has been compared by Clinton administration officials not to the falling of dominoes or the contagion of disease but to the spread of a fire. In his 24 March 1999 speech to the nation President Clinton drew upon the imagery of spreading fire to explain the need for United States intervention. "Let a fire burn in this area and the flames will spread," Clinton predicted.[32] There are interesting parallels here with fire imagery during the early years of the Cold War.[33] The vision of a spreading fire was also conveyed by Secretary of State Albright in her warning that "spreading conflict could *re-ignite* fighting in neighboring Albania and destabilize fragile Macedonia." Furthermore, and this is a particularly significant phrasing, "We must never forget that there is no natural boundary to violence in southern Europe."[34] If there is no "natural" obstacle, barrier, or boundary, and if one wants to halt the spread of the "fire" of ethnic violence, then an "unnatural" obstacle, barrier, or boundary must be created. Here the similarity to domino and disease metaphors becomes apparent. The imagery of falling dominoes and spreading disease conveyed a process without any "natural" stopping point or force. If the dominoes were to be supported or the disease contained, an external force or power would have to intervene in the otherwise inevitable process. Similarly, if the spread of the fire is to be stopped, something or someone will have to stop it: it will not stop on its own. There is no "natural" fire wall.

The metaphors of power vacuums, falling dominoes, contagious disease, and spreading fires are what we might call process or dynamic metaphors—that is, their contribution to the analysis is that they suggest a certain sequence of events that will happen, how developments are likely to unfold. Furthermore, they do so in ways that virtually invite the exercise of American power. There are, however, other types of metaphors. A relational metaphor, for example, is one that embodies a certain relationship between objects or actors. The metaphor of the "family" of nations or the "family" of democratic states is a case in point. Such metaphors can imply equality among the actors or inequality and privilege. The family metaphor is complicated in this respect because some relations within the family may be equal (e.g., between siblings of the same approximate age), whereas others may be decidedly unequal (e.g., between parents and children). When the metaphorical imagery reflects inequality and privilege it can become a metaphor of power.

The United States' relations with the nations of Central and South American has been a treasure trove of metaphorical constructions throughout history. Some of these metaphors, particularly that of the "neighborhood," with the United States as the "good neighbor," connote some measure of equality. Other metaphors clearly implied that the residents of the neighborhood were not equal. Kenworthy has shown how the unequal aspects of the family metaphor have dominated the United States' representations of the "American family."[35] Another classic example of this type of metaphor from the Cold War (though it may predate the Cold War) is the "backyard" metaphor frequently used in discussions of United States relations with Central and South America. This is a fascinating metaphor, one that might have a particular resonance for Americans, given the emphasis on home ownership in our culture. The references to "our backyard" are numerous. In 1967, to provide one example from the Cold War, Ronald Reagan, reacting to Soviet support for Castro's Cuba, argued that "we are always reacting [to the Soviet

Union]. . . . Next time we might have a few spots of our own in their backyard picked out."[36] Almost two decades later Reagan claimed that lack of support for the contras in Nicaragua would send "an unmistakable signal that the greatest power in the world is unwilling and incapable of stopping communist aggression in our own backyard."[37] Using a somewhat related metaphor, Reagan was also fond of referring to Central America as being at or on "our doorstep."[38] This is also one metaphor that seems to have lost none of its power in the post–Cold War world. Members of the Clinton administration were quick to fall back on the imagery of the backyard when it undertook the invasion of Haiti in 1994. Discussing developments in Haiti with foreign reporters in September 1994, for example, President Clinton argued that "the United States has an interest, it seems to me, in the post–Cold War world in not letting dictators break their word to the United States and to the United Nations, especially in our own backyard."[39] Elsewhere in the same interview the metaphor appears again: "here is a case where the entire world community has spoken on a matter in our backyard."[40] Secretary of State Warren Christopher also could not resist the metaphor: "I want to emphasize that that kind of regime within our own hemisphere, in our own backyard, is a very destabilizing factor."[41] It is interesting that these uses of the backyard metaphor were not part of prepared statements but were made in the context of unscripted give-and-take with reporters. This indicates that the metaphor is so internalized that it is not planted in speeches merely for instrumental purposes: it is readily and routinely accessed.

The metaphor of the backyard is obviously a metaphor of power because it suggests ownership. People are not allowed to enter your backyard without an invitation; otherwise they would be considered trespassing. People are allowed to do as they please in their own backyards because it is their property. But the imagery of the backyard is powerful in some less obvious ways. Families looking for new houses often place great emphasis on finding one with a nice backyard so that the kids will have someplace to play while being supervised by the adults. Real estate agents do not push houses with large backyards on childless single people. The backyard is primarily a space for children, not adults. In this sense the metaphor has unmistakable elements of paternalism. If one looks at some old editorial cartoons, the United States (portrayed as Uncle Sam) is often seen supervising the children of Latin America, frequently becoming annoyed when they fail to behave themselves. As is usually the case, the backyard metaphor does several things simultaneously. First, it frames the relationship between the Americas and the rest of the world—the other nations of the world are excluded from having any legitimate interest in what goes on in our backyard. Second, it frames the relationship between the United States and the nations to its south. And when all this converges with the "family" metaphor we have a coming together of the two to create a merged metaphor of power.

Conclusion

Some research on the cognitive elements of foreign-policy decision making reveals strong judgmental tendencies: oh, how stupid could the decision makers be to think that this crisis resembles Munich or that nations fall like dominoes? There is an emphasis on *mis*perception, *mis*understanding, and the inappropriate use of analogies (though explicit thought is rarely devoted to the question of how we differentiate a perception from a *mis*perception). This essay has probably not avoided this tendency altogether, but this was not my intention. There is a place for such critiques of prevailing constructs. As Susan Sontag pointed out, even if metaphorical thinking is inevitable, this does not mean that there aren't certain metaphors we shouldn't "retire." In the final analysis, however, we are not going to be able avoid to the use of metaphors. As Garrett Hardin explains, "since metaphorical thinking is inescapable it is pointless to weep about our human limitations. We must learn to live with them, to understand them, and to control them."[42]

In this essay I have tried to understand metaphors in foreign policy decision making. In doing this I have drawn on the common cognitive psychological notion of problem framing as the most useful place to begin to understand the role of metaphors. Taking the insight that metaphors frame problems, I have asked whether certain types of metaphors systematically "frame" or "structure" international relations (the "problem" in this case) in ways that lead almost inevitably to a policy of expansion and intervention. I have called these metaphors of power because they provide a cognitive, intellectual, and discursive foundation for the exercise of power. Taken individually, some of the metaphors seem powerful enough; taken together, they combine to create an understanding of the world and the United States' role in it that makes any other policies difficult to imagine. These metaphors have not disappeared with the demise of the Soviet Union and the Cold War. Some might want to debate how much power the metaphors wield, but it is hard to deny that the powerful certainly do wield their metaphors.

Notes

1. Deborah Larson, *The Origins of Containment: A Psychological Explanation* (Princeton: Princeton University Press, 1985), 55.

2. For example see Alex Hybel, *How Leaders Reason* (New York: Basil Blackwell, 1990); Yuen Foong Khong, *Analogies at War: Korea, Munich, Dien Bien Phu, and the Vietnam Decisions of 1965* (Princeton: Princeton University Press, 1992); Ernest May, *Lessons of the Past* (New York: Oxford University Press, 1973); Richard Neustadt and Ernest May, *Thinking in Time: The Uses of History for Decision Makers* (New York: Free Press, 1986); Howard Schuman and Carol Reiger, "Historical Analogies, Generational Change, and Attitudes toward War," *American Sociological Review* 57 (1982): 315–26.

3. Sontag, *Illness as a Metaphor*, 93.

4. George Lakoff and Mark Johnson, *Metaphors We Live By* (Chicago: University of Chicago Press, 1980), 5.

5. Randall L. Schweller, *Deadly Imbalances: Tripolarity and Hitler's Strategy of Global Conquest* (New York: Columbia University Press, 1998), 81.

6. Ibid., 65.

7. Fred C. Iklé, *Every War Must End* (New York: Columbia University Press, 1971), 47.

8. Lakoff and Johnson, *Metaphors We Live By*, 11, emphasis in original.

9. Ibid., 6.

10. Yaacov Vertzberger, *The World in Their Minds: Information Processing, Cognition, and Perception in Foreign Policy Decisionmaking* (Stanford, Calif.: Stanford University Press, 1990), 330.

11. Sontag, *Illness as a Metaphor*, 93.

12. Ibid., 102.

13. Londa Schiebinger, *Has Feminism Changed Science?* (Cambridge: Harvard University Press, 1999), 147.

14. Lakoff and Johnson, *Metaphors We Live By*, 36.

15. Stella Vosniadou and Andrew Ortony, "Similarity and Analogical Reasoning: A Synthesis," in *Similarity and Analogical Reasoning*, ed. Stella Vosniadou and Andrew Ortony (New York: Cambridge University Press, 1989), 7.

16. Khong, *Analogies at War*, 20–21.

17. Lakoff and Johnson, *Metaphors We Live By*, 10.

18. Vertzberger, *The World in Their Minds*, 330.

19. Stephen Walt, *The Origins of Alliances* (Chicago: University of Chicago Press, 1987), 67.

20. Dean Acheson, *Present at the Creation* (New York: Norton, 1969), 219.(emphasis added).
21. Robert L. Ivie, "Fire, Flood, and Red Fever: Motivating Metaphors of Global Emergency in the Truman Doctrine Speech," *Presidential Studies Quarterly* 29 (September 1999): 570–91.
22. Michael Hunt, *Ideology and U.S. Foreign Policy* (New Haven: Yale University Press, 1987), 154.
23. Ibid., 66.
24. Schweller, *Deadly Imbalances,* 81 (emphasis added).
25. Keith Shimko, *Images and Arms Control: Perceptions of the Soviet Union in the Reagan Administration* (Ann Arbor: University of Michigan Press, 1991), 64, emphasis added.
26. As quoted in Jerome Slater, "Dominos in Central America: Will They Fall? Does It Matter?" *International Security* 12 (1987): 105.
27. As quoted in Lars Schoultz, *Beneath the United States: A History of U.S. Policy toward Latin America* (Cambridge: Harvard University Press, 1998), 364.
28. Slater, "Dominos in Central America," 107.
29. Ibid.
30. Stanley Karnow, *Vietnam: A History* (New York: Viking Press, 1983), 43 (emphasis added).
31. Hunt, *Ideology and U.S. Foreign Policy,* 156, emphasis added.
32. White House press release, 24 March 1999, 3.
33. See Ivie, "Fire, Flood, and Red Fever."
34. Department of State press release, 4 February 1999, 2 (emphasis added).
35. Eldon Kenworthy, *America/Americas: Myth in the Making of U.S. Policy toward Latin America* (University Park: Penn State University Press, 1995), 30–32.
36. Robert Pastor, *Condemned to Repitition: The United States and Nicaragua* (Princeton: Princeton University Press, 1987), 230.
37. Eldon Kenworthy, "Selling the Policy," in *Reagan versus the Sandinistas,* ed. Thomas Walker (Boulder: Westview, 1987), 162.
38. Emil Arca and Gregory Pamel, *The Triumph of the American Spirit: The Speeches of Ronald Reagan* (Detroit: National Reproductions, 1984), 290.
39. White House Press Release, 14 September 1994.
40. Ibid.
41. White House Press Release, 10 July 1994.
42. Garrett Hardin, "Living on a Lifeboat," in *Managing the Commons,* ed. Garrett Hardin and John Baden (New York: Freeman, 1977), 261.

Metaphors of U.S. Global Leadership

The Psychological Dynamics of Metaphorical Thinking during the Carter Years

Jerel A. Rosati and Steven J. Campbell

Political leadership and foreign policy appear to be fruitful areas in which to examine the power and meaning of metaphors. Metaphorical imagery has been especially prominent and significant in terms of U.S. global leadership since World War II. One such metaphor that served as a virtual cornerstone for U.S. global leadership throughout much of the Cold War was the domino theory. This metaphor of "falling dominoes," representing the potential spread of communism if it was not contained, served as a powerful cognitive and rhetorical framework for the development and expression of U.S. foreign policy and global leadership.

The domino metaphor is but one illustration of the significance of metaphors in U.S. global leadership since World War II, indicating a need for further study in this area. Therefore, this chapter attempts to assess to what extent a metaphorical approach contributes to the study and understanding of foreign policy by examining U.S. global leadership during the Carter years. This is done, first, by describing the change in metaphorical thinking of President Carter, National Security Adviser Brzezinski, and

Secretary of State Vance from 1977 to 1980, and, second, by explaining the dynamics of policymaker cognitive stability and change over time. The implications of this analysis for future research on political leadership and foreign policy are examined, and the usefulness of a metaphorical approach for the study of foreign policy and the future of U.S. global leadership is explored.

The Use of Metaphors in the Study of Foreign Policy and International Relations

The use of the metaphorical approach in the study of foreign policy has been rather limited.[1] Much research has examined metaphors as rhetorical and/or legitimating devices used by officials as opposed to metaphors serving as cognitive "guides" for officials (cognitive metaphors).[2] However, the distinction between these two general types of metaphors is not always black and white. As Nicholas Howe notes, metaphors used by political officials can reveal how those speakers conceive of politics.[3] The repeated and systemic use of certain metaphors, according to Howe, reveals the fundamental attitudes and the logical frameworks of these political professionals.

Keith Shimko writes that metaphors are comparisons drawn from completely different realms of experience.[4] In addition, he contends that metaphors do not provide specific policy guidance but rather general guidance or a conceptual lens. Shimko states that metaphors may serve to guide officials, but in doing so metaphors can oversimplify situations and blind officials to other considerations and creative thinking. Thus, Shimko argues that metaphorical reasoning is used for problem framing (representation) but not for problem solving (as with analogies).[5] Metaphors help to frame a problem; however, Shimko contends that the framing ranges from a more specific framing to a very general framing of the problem. Furthermore, the meanings and associations that are conjured up by metaphors differ, in that some metaphors conjure up a whole host of associations—for example, "war"—while other metaphors are more limited—for example, "dominoes."

Betty Glad and Charles Taber, who examine how the domino theory was misapplied to Vietnam (due partly to "wrong" lessons learned from Munich), state that the domino theory was problematic due to its oversimplicity and invalid assumptions.[6] In addition, they note that metaphors contain generalizations—often tacit—about the characteristics of empirical objects and the relationships between them.[7] Thus, Glad and Taber contend that U.S. officials are influenced by their metaphorical thinking due to the central role and position of the United States in the world. They conclude that metaphors of the nature of the world order and the position of one's own nation in that order play a central role in how decision makers define their interests, the nature of the threats to those interests, and possible policy responses.

Bertram Spector defines metaphors as "figures of speech that compare one thing to another, but go beyond mere comparison to suggest that one thing *is* the other." In his article on the potential utility of metaphorical thinking for dealing with the complexities and difficulties of international negotiation, Spector writes that "Metaphorical reasoning enables a 'mental excursion' away from the hard facts to other realms of thought and other disciplines that are somehow related." Such a digression appears to allow one to contemplate new perspectives from other experiences. In addition, Spector notes psychological studies that examined the impact of metaphorical thinking under various problem-solving situations. The findings, according to Spector, "attest to the greater insight into problems offered by metaphors and the resultant effectiveness of metaphorical approaches in aiding the solution process in comparison with other problem solving heuristics."[8]

Overall, then, the purpose and role of metaphors in foreign policy are basically threefold. First, they reflect the content of beliefs and goals of policymakers, thus serving as cognitive frames and guides through the foreign policy terrain. Second, metaphors facilitate communication among policymakers—and between policymakers and the public—of distant political realities, thereby promoting some understanding of such phenomena. Finally, metaphors are used by policymakers to justify policy stances and actions in attempts to achieve legitimization and garner political support among the public.[9]

The above literature provides a foundation and springboard from which we can now utilize a metaphorical approach in examining U.S. global leadership during the Carter years (1977–80). In the next section, both individual and collective metaphorical thinking by President Jimmy Carter, National Security Adviser (NSA) Zbigniew Brzezinski, and Secretary of State Cyrus Vance will be examined. In addition, the metaphorical thinking held by these officials over time will be assessed, as well as its implications for U.S. global leadership.

Early Optimistic Metaphorical Thinking in 1977: The Quest for Global Community

Global change and an increasingly complex international system were the major themes of the new administration in its first year. The Carter administration's initial philosophy abided by an overarching, optimistic metaphorical vision of "global community." This metaphorical view rejected America's Cold War view of an essentially bipolar world in which U.S. foreign policy was driven primarily by the objective of "containing" Soviet expansionism and replaced it with a multipolar view. Thus, the dramatic global changes that were occurring ushered in a new international system containing a "new worldwide mosaic of global, regional, and bilateral relations."[10] Carter administration officials perceived a very complex world, one in which interdependence and pluralism were facts of life that could not be ignored. The world was so complex that neither the United States nor the Soviet Union could control the destiny of the planet.[11]

In this new world the United States could lead, but it could no longer command or control. "However wealthy and powerful the United States may be—however capable the leadership," stated President Carter, "this power is increasingly only relative, the leadership increasingly is in need of being shared. No nation has a monopoly of vision, of creativity, or of ideas. Bringing these together from many nations is our common responsibility and our common challenge."[12]

The complexity of the international system made mutual cooperation a prerequisite to building a global community. President Carter expressed this belief in a speech before the United Nations:

> We have already become a global community—but only in the sense that we face common problems and we share, for good or evil, a common future. In this community, power to solve the world's problems—particularly economic and political power—no longer lies in the hands of a few nations. Power is now widely shared among many nations with different cultures and different histories and different aspirations.[13]

Therefore, the Carter administration, guided by an overarching metaphorical view of global community, replaced anticommunism with the promotion of human rights and preventive diplomacy as part of a larger goal to promote a new system of world order—a quest for global community. The principal architect of this quest was Brzezinski, as represented by his 1970 book, *Between Two Ages: America's Role in the Technetronic Era*, and his directorship of the Trilateral Commission. Brzezinski described his vision of what he meant by a global community before the Trilateral Commission on 30 October 1977:

> A secure and economically cooperative community of the advanced industrial democracies is the necessary source of stability for a broad system of international cooperation. We are aware of the pitfalls . . . that leaves out the majority of mankind who live in the developing countries. . . . At the same time, a wider and more cooperative world system has to include also that part of the world which is ruled by communist governments.[14]

The Carter administration sought to improve the world, attempting to promote a new system of world order based upon international stability, peace, and justice. Members of the administration recognized that the effort to promote a more stable, peaceful, and just international system would be difficult. President Carter realized that "we can only improve this world if we are realistic about its complexities. The disagreements that we face are deeply rooted, and they often raise difficult philosophical as well as territorial issues. They will not be solved easily. They will not be solved quickly."[15] This was why the Carter administration felt it was so important to work with others in resolving problems and building a global community. Mutual cooperation and preventive diplomacy were believed to be the basis for addressing important global issues and actors.

Raymond Moore contends that fundamental to the Carter administration's pursuit of a global community was its perception of the Soviet Union, which was at first "viewed optimistically as a country with limited capabilities, occasionally opportunistic but basically cooperative and peaceful in its intentions."[16] Carter himself was especially sanguine about "the Soviets' peaceful intentions; as a result, East-West and Soviet-American relations could be regarded in context with other world problems." In addition to enhancing East-West relations, an improvement in North-South relations was very crucial for the Carter goal of promoting a global community: "We will cooperate more closely with the newly influential countries in Latin America, Africa, and Asia. We need their friendship in a common effort as the structure of world power changes."[17]

Images of the Soviet Union

Normalizing and generally improving global relations were considered vital for dealing with change in a complex world. In this vein, the administration's metaphor of "global community" represented an approach to foreign policy that embodied a "regionalist" explanation of conflict in the Third World. Disputes were not to be seen through a Cold War lens (which was the problem in Vietnam). Legitimate nationalist aspiration was not to be equated with communism, even if nationalist or separatist movements had Soviet backing. Carter held that, since Vietnam, "we've learned that this world . . . is too large and too varied to come under the sway of either one of two superpowers."[18] As a responsible superpower, the United States had an interest in and a duty to seek resolution of regional conflict. However, in a complex world of limits, the United States must seek the assistance of allies and "regional influentials"—"leadership is increasingly in need of being shared."[19] By the end of 1977 a combination of "global community" and "regionalist" statements appeared to presage a new era of "cooperative multilateralism" in U.S.–Third World relations. In this context, the global community metaphor served to facilitate communication and understanding of distant political realities.

According to Moore, while Carter, Vance, and Brzezinski all shared an optimistic view of the Soviet Union at the outset, there were subtle differences between them.[20] Carter and Vance were basically highly optimistic about a cooperative relationship with the Soviet Union, while Brzezinski was merely "hopeful": "I think we're [United States and Soviet Union] reasonably vigilant to the fact that the competition goes on and therefore we have to compete. But we are also very much aware of the fact that in this shrinking world the imperative of cooperation has become more urgent."[21] Brzezinski wanted to promote a cooperative relationship with the Soviet Union, yet he was more skeptical than President Carter and Secretary Vance concerning the sincerity of Soviet peaceful intentions. He believed that "just as the United States has gone through an imperialist cycle, and then waned, so it is my hope that the Russians will increasingly move into the world in a more cooperative, less imperially assertive fashion and begin participating in what is gradually, truly emerging: namely, a global community."[22] Thus, Brzezinski was both hopeful yet skeptical that the Soviet Union would play a cooperative role.

Changes in 1978

Moore states that these subtle differences in thought were outweighed by the degree of consensus among the three policy makers as the second year of the administration unfolded. However, Moore, Hargrove, and

Rosati note that this consensus began to show strain in early 1978 over the question of the appropriate U.S. response to Soviet logistical support given to Cuban and Ethiopian troops fighting against Somali guerillas in the Ogaden region of Ethiopia (the Horn of Africa crisis).[23] Brzezinski wanted the United States to make a show of force by sending an aircraft carrier task force into the area. Vance and his advisers agreed that the Soviets were seeking to exploit a local situation but did not interpret the issue as one of U.S.–Soviet rivalry. Carter sided with Vance.

The Carter administration's optimism concerning a complex international system and global change continued into its second year, although differences in individual metaphorical thinking clearly emerged. While President Carter and Secretary of State Vance adhered to the metaphor of global community, Brzezinski's metaphorical thought began to change, placing greater emphasis on political-military issues and the need to contain the Soviet Union's foreign interventionism. In spite of growing concern about Soviet behavior, Carter and Vance remained committed to their original view of the Soviet Union and saw the Soviets as opportunistic but ultimately failing. Brzezinski, on the other hand, became increasingly pessimistic concerning Soviet cooperation and the positive benefits of a complex international system.

Competing Metaphorical Representations in 1979

In 1979 the differences in individual metaphorical thinking of the Carter administration regarding the international system sharpened. Although Vance continued to adhere to the view of a complex international system and remained optimistic concerning a new world order (the global community metaphor), Brzezinski perceived an increasingly fragmented and unstable international system open to Soviet interventionism (the "arc of crisis" metaphor). Carter at times shared Vance's optimism but also displayed pessimism more in line with Brzezinski's metaphorical thinking. Consequently, two competing metaphors existed in 1979.

An analysis of the speeches of Carter, Vance, and Brzezinski in 1979 reveals these differing metaphorical representations of the world. Carter generally shared Vance's optimism about the stability of the international system, with Soviet actions causing occasional eruptions of pessimism. Much of Carter's uncertainty was a function of his metaphorical thinking about the Soviet Union—he appeared to be increasingly torn between the cooperative and competitive aspects of the U.S.–Soviet relationship.

Brzezinski, in contrast to Vance, described the Soviet Union as the cause of increasing global instability. Rosati notes, "One still heard about the importance of promoting international cooperation and pursuing a global community, but those themes were overshadowed by Brzezinski's perception."[24]

For Brzezinski, the principal concern became the growing "arc of crisis," constituting a change in his metaphorical view from that of "global community." He believed the international system was not only becoming increasingly fragile and unstable, but that the Soviet Union was growing in power and willing to project that power globally. In his view, these two trends produced the "arc of crisis." He contended that the Soviet Union was at the root of the problem of global instability, emphasizing, metaphorically, that an "arc of crisis" existed in the Persian Gulf in Iran and along a line extending into southern Africa.[25] Chaos and instability would result if the Soviet Union was able to successfully exploit the situation.

Calling the region of "vital importance" to the United States, the NSC adviser warned that its fragile social and political structures had already led to power vacuums that "could well be filled by elements hostile to our values and sympathetic to our adversaries."[26] As Brzezinski's comment suggested, the regional turmoil was part of a broad clash of interests between Moscow and Washington and a general deterioration in Soviet-American relations.

Key to Brezezinski's altered metaphorical thought was American troubles in Iran and in other parts of the Muslim world, which seemed only to multiply in the first few months after the overthrow of the shah in early 1979. Brzezinski later stated that: "The Iranian disaster shattered the strategic pivot of a protected tier shielding the crucial oil-rich region of the Persian Gulf from possible Soviet intrusion. The northeast frontier of Turkey, the northern frontiers of Iran and Pakistan, and the neutral buffer of Afghanistan created a formidable barrier, which was pierced once Iran ceased to be America's outpost."[27]

Thus, throughout 1979 two divergent metaphorical views, represented by Vance and Brzezinski, competed for ascendance within the Carter administration. With Carter unable to adhere fully to either of the two competing metaphors, nor able to reconcile the differences between them, it was an incoherent metaphor that survived as a divided administration entered its final year.

Pessimistic Thinking Prevails in 1980 around the "Arc of Crisis"

The fourth year (1980) witnessed the termination of the Carter administration's metaphorical vision of a global community, though Vance continued to fight for the "global community" metaphor up to his resignation. Global change was no longer seen to be positive. The predominant focus became the containment of Soviet expansionism and maintenance of the West's security in Europe, the Far East, and, of immediate concern, Southwest Asia. Carter and Brzezinski were the major proponents of this new metaphorical picture of an "arc of crisis" in the international system.

Unlike the earlier years, when the emphasis was on positive change and an effort to create a new world order, the international system was now seen as turbulent and unstable. The "arc of crisis" metaphor was now perceived to be dominant in terms of an increasingly fragmented international system. Two events in particular overwhelmed the thinking of administration officials, especially Carter: the taking of American hostages in revolutionary Iran and the Soviet military intervention in Afghanistan. No longer was the world viewed as being increasingly pluralistic. Rather the Soviet Union was now the dominant international actor, and U.S. foreign policy concentrated overwhelmingly on the Soviet Union.

The Soviet Union was considered the major destabilizing force in the world and a direct threat to the West. Brzezinski specifically argued that the Persian Gulf represented the "third central strategic zone"—after, first, Western Europe and, second, the Far East—vital to the United States and the West after World War II, that was under challenge by Soviet expansionism.[28] Carter's response to Soviet expansionism and its future threat was to reinstate the containment strategy to the forefront of U.S. foreign policy. Following the invasion of Afghanistan, the *Carter Doctrine* was enunciated.

In sum, although a number of diverse issues were perceived to be important during 1977 (reflecting a more optimistic metaphorical view), by 1980 the administration concentrated overwhelmingly on a much smaller set of issues, primarily of a political-military nature (reflecting a more pessimistic metaphorical view). In addition, the movement from actor diversity to concentration on fewer actors, especially the role of the Soviet Union, reinforces the description of the Carter administration's change in its metaphorical thinking from global community (pluralism and hope for greater international cooperation) to the "arc of crisis" (threatened global stability).

Explaining the Evolution of
Metaphorical Thinking among Policymakers

The key to understanding the change in the Carter administration's metaphorical thought from "global community" to the "arc of crisis" is to examine the image of the three policymakers who comprised the collectivity. As the individual metaphorical views evolved, the administration's metaphorical thinking also evolved. Whereas Brzezinski and especially Carter experienced a great deal of change in their metaphorical thinking of the international system, Vance's metaphorical view was relatively stable over time. Because determining why one person's metaphorical thought was stable and another person's metaphorical thought changed is extremely difficult, what follows is a brief explanation of the evolution of the three individual metaphorical views based on three interrelated factors: the individual personalities, the occurrence of major events, and the impact of domestic forces.

Change in Carter's Metaphorical Thinking

Over time, President Carter experienced the most profound metaphor change. The key factors that interacted to change his metaphorical thinking were his personal lack of knowledge in global affairs and open-minded personality, the crucial events involving the hostages in Iran and the Soviet invasion of Afghanistan, and the presidential election of 1980 during a time when the domestic climate was becoming more nationalistic.[29]

Indeed, Gaddis Smith echoes most of the above factors as leading to Carter's transformation (and ultimate failure):

> Carter failed because he asked the American people to think as citizens of the world with an obligation toward future generations. He offered a morally responsible and farsighted vision. But the clamor of political critics, the behavior of the Soviet Union, the discordant voices of his advisers, and the impossibility of seeing clearly what needed to be done—all combined to make Carter's vision appear naïve. In 1980, he fell back on an appeal to the combative nationalistic instincts of the American people.[30]

Carter had not developed many central beliefs concerning the nature of the international system when he assumed the presidency. Carter's lack of knowledge was combined with a receptivity to new ideas—he had an intense desire to know more about the world. However, Carter's experience level was still such that his central belief in human nature provided the guideposts by which he evaluated the world around him.

According to Brzezinski, Carter's personal philosophy was the point of departure for his foreign policy, and the central theme was a religious impulse to make the world more humane.[31] Another adviser recalled, "It's part of the President's background, his evangelism, that he did believe when he came to office that he could make the lions lie down with the lamb, that you could sit down and reason with people and get them to do what they ought to do."[32]

Thus, Carter entered office with a genuine conviction in the boundless possibilities for relations among human beings.[33] Quite naturally, this led him to harbor optimistic metaphorical thinking of many of the world's actors, most notably the Soviet Union. "My intention," he later explained, "was to cooperate with the Soviets wherever possible."[34] Therefore, whenever the Soviets acted opportunistically abroad and violated these behavior standards, Carter experienced periods of dissonance. Initially, he responded with surprise and confusion. As the pattern of Soviet behavior contrary to his expectations persisted, surprise and confusion turned to frustration and disenchantment.[35]

Two events—the hostage seizure in Iran and the Soviet invasion of Afghanistan—compelled Carter to reassess his notions of the Soviet Union and the world. By the time he left office, Carter's metaphorical imagery of the Soviets had been transformed from "global community" to the "arc of crisis." The watershed was Afghanistan, the first combat use of Soviet troops outside of the Warsaw Pact area in Eastern Europe since World War II.[36] In an interview with Frank Reynolds on ABC-TV's *World News Tonight*, Carter confessed how the Soviet invasion affected him:

> My opinion of the Russians has changed most drastically in the last week than even the previous two and a half years before that. It's only now dawning on the world the magnitude of the action that the Soviets undertook in invading Afghanistan . . . to repeat myself, this action of the Soviets has made a more dramatic change in my own opinion of what the Soviets' ultimate goals are than anything they've done in the previous time I've been in office.[37]

The Soviet invasion of Afghanistan in late 1979 had a more profound effect on Carter than any other unanticipated event in his administration. He felt personally betrayed in his efforts to win ratification of SALT II. The invasion "changed Carter as a person," one of his closest aides thought. "It steeled and toughened him and made him more forceful, as seen in his re-taliatory actions of suspending high technology sales to the Soviets, the grain embargo and the boycott of the summer Olympics."[38] "I was sobered . . . by our strained relations with the Soviets," Carter later acknowledged, "but I was determined to make them pay for their unwarranted aggression."[39]

The domestic environment acted to spur and reinforce Carter's commit-ment to more pessimistic metaphorical thinking of the international sys-tem. The public became more concerned with the Soviet Union and America's military capability. This trend was further promoted by the rise of the "new Right" and neoconservatism. Numerous individuals and groups who argued for a stronger U.S. foreign policy based upon fear of Soviet communism received considerable attention and gained legitimacy within the political system.[40] Nineteen eighty was also an election year, and the public agenda was basically defined by the political Right. Presi-dent Carter had to campaign for reelection in a domestic environment that was increasingly inhospitable to his earlier metaphorical view of the inter-national system. Thus, the "arc of crisis" metaphor served to legitimize the administration's tougher policies and its responsiveness to public opinion.

President Carter's new pessimistic metaphorical picture of the Soviet Union was consistent with the mood of the country. However, in the minds of most Americans the international prominence of the United States was considered to be at a low, and Carter was perceived to be a weak leader. Thus, the nationalistic environment surrounding the election not only promoted a change in Carter's metaphorical thinking but also con-tributed to his lack of support for reelection.

Change in Brzezinski's Metaphorical Thinking

Zbigniew Brzezinski's metaphorical view of the international system also changed during the course of the administration. However, Brzezinski's change is particularly difficult to explain due to previous modifications in his thinking and the integral role his personality played in forming his metaphorical thought.

Prior to 1978, Brzezinski's metaphorical thinking of the international system had undergone two other major transitions. A Polish immigrant and a prominent Sovietologist, Brzezinski developed a very pessimistic view during the 1950s and early 1960s of the Soviet Union. He saw communism as the major threat in a bipolar international system and the need for containment—consistent with the metaphor of falling dominoes.[41] Then in the late 1960s and early 1970s, his thinking changed, and he joined those promoting the metaphorical view of a global community—best represented by his book *Between Two Ages: America's Role in the Technetronic Era* and his directorship of the Trilateral Commission.[42] This represented the metaphorical thinking with which he entered the White House.

As noted above, Brzezinski was the least optimistic about Soviet activities from the beginning of the Carter administration. Nevertheless, many people argue that he never shared a similar optimistic metaphor of the international system as did Carter and Vance—that he entered office with a pessimistic metaphorical view but initially was forced to assume a more optimistic one in line with the president's preferences.[43] Whether Brzezinski "privately" believed in promoting cooperation based on the metaphor of global community in 1977 is an open question. What is important is that he acted in "public" and as a "decision maker" within the Carter administration as if he adhered to such a philosophy.[44] In other words, Brzezinski articulated optimistic metaphorical thought along with Carter and Vance, even though he was more skeptical about the Soviets' role within the international system. He continued to behave in this manner until the Somali-Ethiopia conflict triggered a change in 1978. Richard Melanson's study of U.S. foreign policy during the Carter years arrived at the same conclusion, although based on a different method—interviews of Carter administration National Security Council and State Department Policy Planning staff officials.[45]

The interaction of Brzezinski's personality and external events seems critical in explaining his loss of optimism. Brzezinski was noted for being extremely ambitious and for having coveted a high-level foreign policy position within the U.S. government.[46] Very attuned to elite opinion, he was often in the forefront of the most popular trends of thought in U.S. foreign policy, which may explain his abandonment of his early pessimistic metaphorical thinking and his commitment to the metaphorical view of global community in a complex world. However, Brzezinski was considered to have a large ego and to be terribly insecure. Once he reached the pinnacle of power in U.S. foreign policy, Brzezinski found he no longer needed to conform to external opinion. In this sense, Alexander and Juliette George's personality study of Woodrow Wilson may prove helpful in understanding Brzezinski's evolution in his metaphorical thinking: as a "power-seeker" he was much more receptive to other people's preferences than as a "power-holder."[47]

Brzezinski's intense personality made his primitive beliefs of a growing and expansionist Soviet Union particularly susceptible to arousal.[48] When challenged by events in the Horn of Africa, memories of the past over-whelmed and shattered his optimism for the future—and the optimistic metaphorical image of a quest for global community was replaced by a much more pessimistic metaphorical image of the Soviet threat to the "arc of crisis" throughout the world.

Continuity in Vance's Metaphorical Thinking

Unlike Carter and Brzezinski, Vance's metaphorical thought was relatively stable throughout his three and a half years in office. According to Destler, Gelb, and Lake, "it was an irony that Vance was to help usher in the new era. He was by birth, style, temperament, character, and career, an exemplar of the old Establishment."[49] A common characteristic of an individual raised within the foreign policy establishment is to avoid theatrics and operate at a distance from the public spotlight. Therefore, Vance's metaphoric stability is difficult to assess because, although he was long on government experience, little is known about the man.

Vance's experience with the Vietnam War appears to have been central to his thinking. While serving as deputy secretary of defense under President Johnson between 1964 and 1967, he became increasingly pessimistic about the war.[50] Yet it was not until he officially left Washington that he realized how far the American public had turned against the war.[51] The tragic consequences of America's intervention in Indochina dramatically altered and solidified his metaphorical thinking in a more optimistic direction—of the importance of resolving conflict and promoting a global community of greater stability, cooperation, and peace. This was consistent with his background as a lawyer and special presidential envoy to settle important conflicts in Panama, the Dominican Republic, Detroit (following racial violence), Cyprus, and Korea throughout the 1960s. Vance believed that negotiation and diplomacy were the key means of promoting conflict resolution.

External events such as foreign interventionism in Africa, the Iran hostage crisis, and the Soviet invasion of Afghanistan only reinforced Vance's belief in the need to exercise restraint and respond to the causes, not the symptoms, of the conflicts. The restoration of containment and militarization to the forefront of American foreign policy in the 1980s and the specific decision to rescue the hostages against Vance's advice left him with little choice. Three days before the military rescue attempt he submitted his resignation, becoming the first secretary of state to voluntarily resign on a matter of principle in over sixty years.

Conclusion

The overarching and optimistic metaphorical thinking of "global community" in Carter's presidency represented an imaginative and intelligent attempt to restore consensus and purpose after Vietnam, resulting in what some have termed the first post–Cold War presidency.[52] Carter's new foreign policy was a sensitive and politically sophisticated attempt to respond to the erosion of American hegemony and to the rise of interdependence, although it naturally had contradictory outcomes, such as problems in arms control with the Soviet Union and achievements with the Middle East Peace Accords. By 1980, another metaphorical train of thought—the "arc of crisis"—had effectively replaced "global community." The CIA was engaged in covert operations in Iran, Central America, Afghanistan, and Africa, and the "Second Cold War" had begun.[53]

As evident in the above analysis, the change in metaphorical thinking made clear the changes in the Carter administration's policies. Metaphorical thinking, which reflected the content of beliefs and goals of policymakers, served as cognitive guides through the foreign policy terrain. In addition, the metaphors facilitated communication among policymakers—and between policymakers and the public—of distant political realities, thereby furthering understanding of such phenomena. Finally, the metaphorical views were used by the Carter administration to justify policy stances and actions in attempts to achieve legitimization and garner political support among the public.

Several implications arise from this study for future research on political leadership and foreign policy. First, attention to metaphor usage by political leaders in foreign policy is important in order to grasp the leader's intention(s) and purposes. This contributes to a fuller understanding of the political process in foreign policy. Second, metaphors may serve different—even overlapping—roles depending on the mix of international, governmental, domestic, and individual policymaker sources of foreign policy. Thus, multiple sources should be kept in mind when determining the role and meaning of a metaphor to avoid distortion. Finally, the power of metaphors in foreign policy should not be discounted or ignored. The above analysis attests to this, and further research is needed to more fully explore this phenomenon.

In sum, the usefulness of a metaphorical approach for the study of foreign policy and the future of U.S. global leadership is considerable. Since little research has been done in this area, many fruitful avenues of investigation remain open, which can shed crucial light on the meaning and power of metaphors in U.S. foreign policy—particularly as America embarks into the next millennium as a global leader.

Notes

1. See, e.g., Jerel A. Rosati, "The Power of Human Cognition in the Study of World Politics," *International Studies Review* 43 (fall 2000): 45–75.

2. See Dickinson McGaw, "Governing Metaphors: The War on Drugs," *American Journal of Semiotics* 8, no. 3 (1991): 53–74; William N. Elwood, "Declaring War on the Home Front: Metaphor, Presidents, and the War on Drugs," *Metaphor and Symbolic Activity* 10, no. 2 (1995): 93–114; George Lakoff, "Metaphor and War: The Metaphor System Used to Justify War in the Gulf," *Peace Research* 23 (1991): 25–32; Jeffery Scott Mio, "Metaphor and Politics," *Metaphor and Symbol* 12, no. 2 (1997): 113–33; Murray Edelman, *Politics as Symbolic Action: Mass Arousal and Quiescence* (Chicago: Markham, 1971); Henry Jamieson and G. H. Jamieson, *Communication and Persuasion* (London: Croom Helm, 1985).

3. Nicholas Howe, "Metaphor in Contemporary American Political Discourse," *Metaphor and Symbolic Activity* 3 (1988): 87–104.

4. Keith Shimko, "Metaphors and Foreign Policy Decision Making," *Political Psychology* 15, no. 4 (December 1994): 655–71. On the other hand, analogies "involve parallels/comparisons drawn from the same general realm of experience" (ibid., 659). Linda T. Krug, *Presidential Perspectives on Space Exploration: Guiding Metaphors from Eisenhower to Bush* (New York: Praeger, 1991), xviii, states that "metaphor, by its very nature, is the only phenomenon capable of bringing together two disparate experiences (such as pioneers of the West and space exploration) and, in the process, creating a third, unified perspective (space pioneers). Metaphors, then, can open up new ways of thinking about situations and events."

5. Keith Shimko, "Foreign Policy Metaphors: Falling 'Dominoes' and Drug 'Wars,'" in *Foreign Policy Analysis: Continuity and Change in Its Second Generation*, ed. Laura Neack, Jeanne A. K. Hey, and Patrick J. Haney (Englewood Cliffs, N.J.: Prentice Hall, 1995), 71–84.

6. Betty Glad and Charles S. Taber, "Images, Learning, and the Decision to Use Force: The Domino Theory of the United States," in *Psychological*

Dimensions of War, ed. Betty Glad (Beverly Hills, Calif.: Sage Press, 1990), 150–75.

7. Krug, *Presidential Perspectives,* also contends that metaphors are not neutral, but contain assumptions that lead to particular kinds of actions.

8. Bertram I. Spector, "Metaphors of International Negotiation," *International Negotiation* 1, no. 1 (1996): 2–3. See, e.g., Tom Bouchard, "Comparison of Two Group Brainstorming Procedures," *Journal of Applied Psychology* 56 (1972): 418–21; Ronald Dreistadt, "The Use of Analogies and Incubation in Obtaining Insights in Creative Problem Solving," *Journal of Psychology* 71 (1969): 159–75; William Gordon, *The Metaphorical Way* (Cambridge: Porpoise Books, 1971); George Prince, *The Practice of Creativity* (New York: Harper, 1970).

9. The research strategy for determining metaphorical images is based on a qualitative content analysis of multiple sources, including government documents, speeches, interviews, memoirs, and secondary sources.

10. Jimmy Carter, "A Foreign Policy Based on America's Essential Character" (address made at the commencement exercises of Notre Dame University, South Bend, Ind., 22 May 1977), *Department of State Bulletin* (13 June 1977): 622.

11. See Jerel A. Rosati, *The Carter Administration's Quest for Global Community: Beliefs and Their Impact on Behavior* (Columbia: University of South Carolina Press, 1987).

12. Jimmy Carter, "U.S. Role in a Peaceful Global Community" (address made before the 32d U.N. General Assembly, 4 October 1977), *State Department Bulletin* (24 October 1977): 522.

13. Ibid., 547.

14. Zbigniew Brzezinski, "American Policy and Global Change" (address made before before the Trilateral Commission, Bonn, Germany, 25 October 1997), *Congressional Record* (1 November 1997): H12000.

15. Jimmy Carter, "Peace, Arms Control, World Economic Progress, Human Rights: Basic Priorities of U.S. Foreign Policy" (address made to representatives to the United Nations, U.N. General Assembly Hall, 17 March 1977), *State Department Bulletin* (11 April 1977): 329.

16. Raymond A. Moore, "The Carter Presidency and Foreign Policy," in *The Carter Years: The President and Policy Making,* ed. M. Glenn Abernathy, Kilys M. Hill, and Phil Williams (New York: St. Martin's Press, 1984), 458.

17. Carter, "A Foreign Policy," 624.

18. Jerel A. Rosati, "Jimmy Carter: A Man before His Time? The Emergence and Collapse of the First Post–Cold War Presidency," *Presidential Studies Quarterly* 23 (1993): 463.

19. Carter, "U.S. Role," 452.

20. Moore, "The Carter Presidency."

21. Zbigniew Brzezinski, Interview, *US News and World Report,* 30 May 1977, *DOD Selected Statements,* 1 June 1977, 4.

22. Zbigniew Brzezinski, Interview, *Washington Post,* 9 October 1977, *DOD Selected Statements,* 1 November 1977, 29.

23. Moore, "The Carter Presidency"; Erwin C. Hargrove, *Jimmy Carter as President: Leadership and the Politics of the Public Good* (Baton Rouge: Louisiana State University Press, 1988); Rosati, *The Carter Administration's Quest.*

24. Jerel A. Rosati, "The Impact of Beliefs on Behavior: The Foreign Policy of the Carter Administration," in *Foreign Policy Decision Making: Perception, Cognition, and Artificial Intelligence,* ed. Donald A. Sylvan and Steve Chan (New York: Praeger, 1984), 181.

25. Zbigniew Brzezinski, interview by James Reston, *New York Times,* 31 December 1978, *DOD Selected Documents,* 1 January 1979.

26. Zbigniew Brzezinski, Interview, *Newsweek,* 8 January 1979, 14.

27. Zbigniew Brzezinski, *Power and Principle: Memoirs of the National Security Adviser, 1977–1981* (New York: Farrar, Straus and Giroux, 1983), 356.

28. Zbigniew Brzezinski, "The Quest for Global Security: The Third Phase" (remarks before the Council on Foreign Relations in Denver, Colorado, on 25 October 1980), White House Press Release (25 October 1980).

29. See Jerel A. Rosati, "Continuity and Change in the Foreign Policy Beliefs of Political Leaders: Addressing the Controversy over the Carter Administration," *Political Psychology* 9, no. 3 (1998): 471–505.

30. Gaddis Smith, *Morality, Reason, and Power: American Diplomacy in the Carter Years* (New York: Hill and Wang, 1986), 247.

31. Brzezinski, *Power and Principle,* 48–49.

32. Jody Powell, "Oral History on Carter Administration," White Burkett Miller Center of Public Affairs, University of Virginia, *Project on the Carter Presidency,* transcripts, vols. 18, 20.

33. See, e.g., Jimmy Carter, *Why Not the Best?* (New York: Bantam, 1975); Betty Glad, *Jimmy Carter: In Search of the Great White House* (New York: W. W. Norton, 1980); Seyom Brown, *The Faces of Power: Constancy and*

Change in United States Foreign Policy from Truman to Clinton, 2d ed. (New York: Columbia University Press, 1994).

34. Jimmy Carter, *Keeping Faith: Memoirs of a President* (Toronto: Bantam Books, 1982), 218.

35. Not everybody subscribes to this interpretation. In "Jimmy Carter and the Soviet Invasion of Afghanistan: A Psychological Perspective," in *Politics and Psychology: Contemporary Psychodynamic Perspectives*, ed. Joan Offerman-Zucherberg (New York: Plenum Press, 1991), 117–42, Betty Glad and Brian Whitmore contend that Carter's personality, with its grandiose and narcissistic elements, as well as his inability to understand the value trade-offs necessary to achieve his goals as president, were instrumental in his response to the Soviet invasion of Afghanistan, as well as his dealings with Moscow throughout his administration.

36. Richard Ned Lebow and Janice Gross Stein, "Afghanistan, Carter, and Foreign Policy Change: The Limits of Cognitive Models," in *Order, Diplomacy, Force, and Leadership: Essays in Honor of Alexander George*, ed. Dan Caldwell and Timothy J. McKeown (Boulder: Westview, 1993), 110.

37. Jimmy Carter, interview by Frank Reynolds, *World NewsTonight*, ABC, 19 January 1980, as reported in the *New York Times*, 20 January 1980, 4.

38. Stuart Eizenstat, "The Presidency in Trouble," paper, White Burkett Miller Center of Public Affairs, University of Virginia, *Project on the Carter Presidency*, 1983.

39. Carter, *Keeping Faith*, 476.

40. See James W. Sanders, *Peddlers of Crisis: The Committee on the Present Danger and the Politics of Containment* (Boston: South End Press, 1983).

41. See, e.g., Zbigniew Brzezinski and Samuel P. Huntington, *Political Power: USA/USSR* (New York: Viking, 1963); Zbigniew Brzezinski and Carl J. Friedrich, *Totalitarian Dictatorship and Autocracy* (New York: Praeger, 1956).

42. Zbigniew Brzezinski, *Between Two Ages: America's Role in the Technetronic Era* (New York: Penguin, 1970).

43. See, e.g., Sanders, *Peddlers of Crisis;* Smith, *Morality, Reason, and Power.*

44. For a distinction between "private," "public," and "operational" or "decision-maker" beliefs, see Rosati, *The Carter Administration's Quest*, 190–92.

45. Richard A. Melanson, *Writing History and Making Policy: The Cold War, Vietnam, and Revisionism* (Lanham, Md.: University Press of America, 1983).

46. Elizabeth Drew, "Brzezinski," *New Yorker,* 1 May 1978, 95–118, 121–30.

47. Alexander L. George and Juliette L. George, *Woodrow Wilson and Colonel House* (New York: Dover Publications, 1956), distinguish between "power-seeker" and "power-holder," contending that in Wilson's efforts to gain power in order to overcome his low self-esteem, he conformed to the dominant beliefs of individuals who could significantly influence his rise. However, once Wilson successfully gained a position of power, he would demonstrate incredible rigidity and closed-mindedness after he took a stand.

48. See Michael Rokeach, *Beliefs, Attitudes, and Values* (San Francisco: Josey-Bass, 1968).

49. I. M. Destler, Leslie H. Gelb, and Anthony Lake, *Our Own Worst Enemy: The Unmaking of American Foreign Policy* (New York: Simon and Schuster, 1984), 95.

50. Timothy Hoopes, *The Limits of Intervention: An Inside Account of How the Johnson Policy of Escalation in Vietnam Was Reversed* (New York: McKay, 1969); Derek S. McLellan, *Cyrus Vance* (Totowa, N.J.: Rowman and Allenheld, 1985).

51. Don Oberdorfer, *Tet!* (New York: Doubleday, 1971).

52. Rosati, "Jimmy Carter."

53. John Dumbrell, *American Foreign Policy: Carter to Clinton,* 2d ed. (New York: St. Martin's Press, 1996), 52–53.

Megametaphorics

Rereading Globalization and Virtualization as Rhetorics of World Politics

Timothy W. Luke

What is "world politics?" For some, the answers to this question are easy: it involves anything "political" about the current world system of states, economies, and nations. For others, this question is much more difficult: it is the politics of world definition, world construction, world action. And, for still others, the question mixes a measure of response from each of the previous approaches. This essay turns at the third path, imagining the politics of world definition as part of the nitty-gritty power dynamics of our world, because this questioning never occurs in a vacuum.[1] To answer what is "world politics," one must dive into metaphorics, images, and representations. Only then can one see how the questioners and their answers spin up various rhetorics of world politics to shape political institutions and movements around the world.

This chapter compares two common rhetorical formations circulating in the United States and around the world—"globalization" in economic discourses and "virtualization" in studies of informational society—to examine how these terms are being used and perhaps abused. Real changes are

taking place in the world, but it is their metaphoric work-ups, which construct or mediate these changes, that stand out. Without the metaphoric
processing of globalization and virtualization talk, these new formations
would not be as fully understood. Such rhetorical skeins of questions and
answers typically recast national community, economic prosperity, and cultural identity with a metaphoric about megasystemic changes that cannot
be escaped.[2] As a result, these notions often become essential terms for explaining many of the world's contemporary political threats, economic
crises, and cultural splits. The circulation of such terms in both mass media
and social science during the 1990s in the United States also gives one
some instructive examples of how megametaphorics shape political
discourse.

Metaphors and Politics

Metaphors draw likenesses between objects, ideas, or events. From the
Greek *metapherein*, the metaphorical "comes from beyond" and "over,"
meta, and "makes comparisons" or "brings analogies," *pherein*. Metaphors
serve as metaphrases for thought, translating the nonidentical into the un-
different through artful allusions. Their "as ifs" and "not unlikes" often
prove to be critical moments of mental metamorphosis, which transform
human action and cognition simply by suggesting that what seems dissimilar might be alike, causing those who once acted differently and reasoned
oppositely to come together. Megametaphors are great, extended, mighty,
or powerful metaphorics that often circulate as ready-made, easy-to-use,
knockoff modes of reasoning. Great, extended forms of mighty alikeness or
great difference are the narrative nuclei that sustain politics, enabling those
who would rule to define friend and foe, same and other, here and there in
the rhetorical ontologues that anchor their statecraft.

For those who share Lyotard's incredulity in metanarrative at this moment in world history, megametaphorics also can serve as satisfying or sug-
gestive navigational bearings with their own polysemic qualities.[3] Not
quite paralogies and plainly not confirmed truths, megametaphors, like
globalization, sustainability, and virtualization, slip into politics, as figura-
tions for basic foreground or deep background, for many accounts of the
world's collective action. For those who are less anxious about modernity
in its present forms, the lexical powers of megametaphors are even more
useful for creating a common language out of uncommon experiences and
extraordinary changes. Such myths get circulated so widely, rapidly, and

deeply that they soon become commonplaces, which then begin to position everyone in the same conceptual and practical commons.

Megametaphorics articulate an array of images to account for events, and these accounts, once set forth as iconic expressions, also stand for individual and collective experiences. In megametaphors, one uncovers the *cultus,* or the impulse to find meaning, in culture, and the acculturalizing mechanisms for propagating meaningful impulses of interpretation. Beyond the physics of worldwide markets or digital technics, megametaphors simultaneously project and capture new metaphysics of meaning to suggest why so many inchoate events "are like" globalization, sustainability, or virtualization. As Burke claims, metaphors must not be easily dismissed. Actually, they are not far removed from the rigor of scientific reasoning. Indeed, "whole works of scientific research, even entire *schools,* are hardly more than the patient repetition, in all of is ramifications, of a fertile metaphor."[4]

By exploring how some megametaphors flow in certain discourses, this chapter examines the manner in which discursive terms produce codirection, coevaluation, and cooperation in political activity by pulling many together through the extended reach of powerful allusions. Everything is always discursively mediated, but discursive mediations are not everything.[5] Consequently, one can use megametaphors to understand how discourse produces disciplinary outcomes and why people and things keep to the mediated interactions shaped by such discourses.

Megametaphors also serve as ontopolitical scripts to anchor conventional assumptions about who are political agents, where are they based, what is political, and what behaviors are appropriate for such political actors.[6] They continuously rejigger notions of what is nature, what is society, what is politics, and what is valuable. Their matrices of likeness and difference however are often, as Walker observes, highly overdetermined.[7] And this overdetermination provides the source code for their cultural impact. Globalization is difficult to conceptualize except as the loss of sovereignty, and virtualization is tough to imagine without suppressing materiality. These two world-transforming events seem to be happening, and megametaphor suggests what aspects among them are "like" and "unlike." As maps of the world made out of words, metametaphors orient new ontopolitical actions as world map readings.[8] Thus, the world is remade, in part, out of words as the territory of the world begins to match the practicable coordinates captured by words.[9]

The Doxic Effects of Metaphor

Those who resolutely cling to a naive instrumental understanding of language in which words always have definite meanings, clear uses, and neutral loadings will be disappointed with this approach to megametaphors. Yet other approaches to language are all too often unsophisticated, presumptuous, and confused. This investigation instead follows Bourdieu, who suggests that "when dealing with the social world, the ordinary use of ordinary language makes metaphysicians of us."[10] Megametaphorics are about using words in quite artful performances precisely because of their metaphysical scope. Language is action, and the word-making moves of megametaphorics have world-making outcomes. They can be fixed in highly "rooted" formations, but they tend instead to flow more loosely and rapidly in a "rhizomatic" fashion.

In this respect, Bourdieu is correct: "The social world is the locus of struggles over words which owe their seriousness—and sometimes their violence—to the fact that words to a great extent make things, and that changing words, and, more generally, representations (for example, pictorial representation, like Manet), is already a way of changing things. Politics is, essentially, a matter of words."[11] This observation is true inasmuch as individuals and groups tussle, over words, with language and in deeds, for greater symbolic power. And the megametaphoric act of naming things, and thereby bringing them into being out of nothingness, is, as Bourdieu argues, "the most typical demonstration" of such power in action.[12]

Megametaphors capture, in a sense, many versal possibilities as they get caught up in the politics of actualizing their more complete universalization. All who seek to advance to greater levels of globalization or virtualization can articulate their polysemic performative discourses with such terms, which illustrate what it is "like" to be global, attain sustainable development, and become virtual. At the same time, experts will opine about these phenomena and laypersons will believe their opinions, as they are contained within these conceptual claddings, confirming the new *doxa* of these discourses.[13] By presuming to suggest what such changes should be, their exponents cause parallel events and processes to come into effect, which test what they should and should not be. Difference is not necessarily erased. It often is instead defined, defended, and distributed more widely. The hesitant multiversal qualities of such transformations, at the same time, become much more definitive and universal, because megametaphors anchor the mythic invention of their referents. Globalization could be many different things, as could virtuality, but they all require very specific forms of completion, definition, and execution because of how they are imagined by the doxosophers who discover, define, and then deploy them in social life. Such doxosophical agents may seem to be popular organic intellectuals, but in the main, they live and work in the far more artificial domains of business, industry, and the professions.[14] Hence, it is more plausible to regard them as "inorganic intellectuals."

Inorganic intellectuals appear to be the creators, and the creations, of fully mediatized and highly educated publics who accept, as Bourdieu claims, "the vague debates of a political philosophy without technical content, a social science reduced to journalistic commentary for election nights, and uncritical glossing of unscientific opinion polls."[15] Because they openly trade in and out of the ideology markets where ordinary opinions are dearly embraced by some simply because they have already been accepted by many, these figures become popular doxosophers. Not surprisingly, such inorganic intellectuals are " 'technicians of opinion who think themselves wise,'" and they always "pose the problems of politics in the very same terms in which they are posed by businessmen, politicians, and political journalists (in other words the very people who can afford to commission surveys)."[16] While Marx reminds us that the ruling ideas of every epoch are those of the owning class, such ideas rarely are propounded artfully by those individuals.[17] More articulate voices, however, can always be found, and the powers of persuasion mobilized by such inorganic intellects mix and match the themes and tones of megametaphoric discourse.

Megametaphors are important, because they feed into a habitus shared by major corporate, governmental, and professional authorities. Allusions to alikeness and definitions of difference in megametaphorical constructs can be expressed through actions when agents share a habitus. As Bourdieu maintains, "the habitus fulfills a function which another philosophy consigns to a transcendental conscience: it is a socialized body, a structured body, a body which has incorporated the immanent structures of a world or of a particular sector of that world—a field—and which structures the perception of that world as well as action in that world."[18] The ideas of necessity, desirability, and universality implied by megametaphors such as globalization and virtualization are imparted to institutions and other ideas through habitus, as it "retranslates the intrinsic and relational characteristics of a position" in the world with its many styles of living into "a unitary set of choices of persons, goods, practices."[19] Once the doxic effects of megametaphors such as globalizing and virtualizing begin to shape the fields of action and decision, they are integrated into the shared habitus. Inside of such doxological systems of classification, division, and valorization, megametaphors make "distinctions between what is good and what is bad, between what is right and what is wrong, between what is distinguished and what is vulgar," as the constructs of the world carried by words push and pull everyone toward world constructions that match the wording of megametaphorical discourses.[20]

As these megametaphorics become constructed discursively in contemporary technoscience and civic discourse, the art of government finds "the principles of its rationality" tied to "the specific reality of the state," where the rhetorical programs of globalization and virtualization are shaped to serve the systemic requirements of politics.[21] Government can come fully into its own when it has the welfare of populations, the improvement of their condition, the increase of their wealth, security, longevity, health, and so forth as its objects. And megametaphors can give rational firms and governments all of the planet's life to reformat as "endangered populations" needing various corporate commodities and state ministrations to transform their lives into objects of managerial control as part and parcel of "a range of absolute new tactics and techniques."[22] Coping with globality and virtuality simply crystallize the latest consolidation of instrumental rationality's "three movements: government, population, political economy, which constitute . . . a solid series, one which even today has assuredly not been dissolved"[23] in the buzz of megametaphorics.

Finding the world's communities and individuals focused on their protection in terms of "safety" or "security" turns into a key theme of many political operations, economic interventions, and ideological campaigns to raise public standards of collective morality, personal responsibility, and collective vigor. The world politics being given new definitions in these megametaphorics, therefore, operates as "a whole series of different tactics that combined in varying proportions the objective of disciplining the body and that of regulating populations."[24] Megametaphors bolster the symbolic order of society to the extent that they are, first, systematic and coherent as discursive frameworks, and, second, consistent and agreeable with objective conditions in the institutional structures of society. In these dispositions, megametaphorics, in turn, ensure popular belief broadly in the established order as well as coordinate effectively the actions and thoughts of the ruling, owning, controlling elites by finding the right relations of "*doxic submission* which attaches us to the established order with all the ties of the unconscious."[25]

Megametaphorical interconnections become even more intriguing in the aftermath of the Cold War. On the one hand, economists, industrialists, and political leaders increasingly represent the strategic terrain of the post-1991 world system in languages in which all nations compete ruthlessly to control the future development of the world economy by developing new technologies, dominating more markets, and exploiting every national economic asset. On the other hand, the threatening phenomenon of "failed states," ranging from basket cases such as Rwanda, Somalia, or Angola to crippled entities such as Ukraine, Afghanistan, or Kazakhstan, often is attributed to the severe environmental frictions associated with rapid economic growth.[26] Consequently, a genuine world politics, whose key issues range from global stability to virtual community, is getting greater consideration in the name of creating jobs, fostering growth, or advancing technological development in the politics of the post–Cold War era.

Globalization

Globalization megametaphorics allude to a whole new world. Reich speaks plainly about "the emerging global economy," because it is likened to the loss of borders, the end of boundaries, and the disappearance of state sovereignties, "as almost every factor of production—money, technology, factories, and equipment—moves effortlessly across borders," so completely and so rapidly that "the very idea of an American economy is becoming meaningless, as are the notions of an American corporation, American capital, American products, American technology."[27] These *doxa* quickly spread without question, as many feel they can account for the shared loss of national borders in an "omnipolitan" economy and society.[28]

In the concentration of commercialized values and economic practices within worldwide exchange, globality begins to equal a *"world-city,* the city to end all cities," and "in these basically eccentric or, if you like, *omnipolitan* conditions, the various social and cultural realities that still constitute a nation's wealth will soon give way to a sort of 'political' *stereo-reality* in which the interaction of exchanges will no longer look any different from the—automatic—interconnection of financial markets today."[29] In keeping with Fredric Jameson's explorations of postmodernity, the context created by globalization "is what you have when the modernization process is complete and nature is gone for good."[30] Economy and society, culture and politics, science and technology all acquire the qualities of a second or even third nature with their own time within, over, or beyond the now-lost verities of first nature's time and space now long buried, or at least suppressed, by multiple modernizing projects.

The megametaphorics of globalization, whether they are spun by statesmen or journalists, emphasize the unlikeness of the present (1989 and after) to the recent past (prior to 1989). Reich's vision of "nationality" versus "transnationality" or Friedman's old "Cold War system" versus the emergent "globalization system" is meant to construct a world of difference and alikeness betwixt and between various qualities from the contemporary moment in history.[31] For Friedman, globalization is the trope tying together neoliberal capitalist rationalization, informational technics, mass consumption culture, and integrated world markets. Its megametaphorics are considerably different than those of the Cold War, as this doxological summation from Friedman suggests:

> If the defining perspective of the Cold War world was "division," the defining perspective of globalization is "integration." The symbol of the Cold War system was a wall, which divided everyone. The symbol of the globalization system is a World Wide Web, which unites everyone. The defining document of the Cold War system was "The Treaty." The defining document of the globalization system is "The Deal." . . . While the defining measurement of the Cold War was weight—particularly the throw weight of missiles—the defining document of the globalization system is speed—speed of commerce, travel, communication, and innovation. Globalization is about Moore's law, which states that the computing power of silicon chips will double every eighteen to twenty-four months. In the Cold War, the most frequently asked question was: "How big is your missile?" In globalization, the most frequently asked question is: "How fast is your modem?." . . . If the defining anxiety of the Cold War was fear of annihilation from an enemy you knew all too well in a world struggle that was fixed and stable, the defining anxiety in globalization is fear of rapid change from an enemy you can't see, touch, or feel—a sense that your job, community or workplace can be changed at any moment by anonymous economic and technological forces that are anything but stable.[32]

His extended explication of alikenesses and differences in globalization remediates the world's meaning in the measures of increasing speed, instability, and collaboration all tied to remaking the world into 1s and 0s.

Time and value in globalization are much more than merely getting in motion, as Friedman submits, they are "on speed." Whether one names it "McWorld," "time-space compression," or "fast capitalism," the current situation, as Virilio suggests, is increasingly one of "chrono-politics" in which the sense of temporal chronologies, spatial geographies, and moral axiologies shared by many human beings is reshaped by speed.[33] While Virilio's overall project is not without faults, his sense of the power of speed is quite useful. In globalization, speed rules over many more aspects of everyday life as it experiences "the dromocratic revolution."[34] These effects are global in their scope and impact, even though their disparate influences in any single locality are not yet entirely understood.

Consequently, globalization articulates a megametaphorical domain with its own cultural kinematics for time and value, in which conventional understandings of alikeness are being reshaped by technological, social, and economic motions in themselves. "Since movement creates the event," as Virilio argues, "the real is *kinedramatic*."[35] A world that moves faster, then, begins to circulate and valorize discourses of speed. A critical appreciation of such kinedramatics suggests that global events often flow on a global scale but at a local level. Perhaps these "kineformations," which are serving as an unstable new mode of cultural organization, are more accurately the new global and local frames of new "glocality." This is a dominant metaphorical allusion for this New World Order.[36]

Those who collaborate in the construction of actual transnationality in capitalist kineformations may not necessarily hold as dear their nominal nationality within territorial space. In moving from the perspectives of territoriality to the acceleration effects of instant communication and rapid transportation, "all of Earth's inhabitants may well wind up thinking of themselves more as *contemporaries* than as *citizens;* they may in the process slip out of the contiguous space, distributed by quota, of the old Nation-State (or City-State), which harbored the *demos,* and into the atopic community of a Planet-State" that unfolds as "a sort of *omnipolitan* periphery whose *centre will be nowhere and circumference everywhere.*"[37] The omnipolitanization of the planet is articulated in many "real time" events: the greenhouse effect, new national diasporas, holes in the ozone layer, the global demographic explosion, twenty-four hour a day currency markets, ATT World Net, narcocapitalist agrarian economies, the environmental movement, AOL everywhere, and 7x24 TV news channels.[38]

Transnationalized kineformations generate their own intracorporate economies of time and value, hollowing nation-states out to maintain adequate profitability at fairly low levels of capacity utilization by in- and out-sourcing anything from anywhere to sell to anybody. Omnipolitanization around the world advances further with every downsizing, value-adding, or restructuring maneuver by transnational capitalism. Omnipolitan time and value expand because, as Greider notes, to succeed,

> firms must become globalized, not American or German or Japanese, but flexible hydras with feet planted in many different markets, making so-called world products that are adaptable across different cultures. Multinational are already from nation to nation, continent to continent, maximizing profit by continually adjusting the sources of output to capitalize on the numerous shifting variables: demand, price, currency values, politics. To function on the global plane, managers must be prepared to sacrifice parts of the enterprise, even the home base, at least temporarily, to protect themselves against the transient tides that undermine profit margins.[39]

Sacrificing home base, however, often means forsaking its grounded values and leaving its time zones to accelerate along the "real time" lines of capital's transnational valorizing flight. This is globalizing time: the transnational rush of financial, monetary, and capital telemetry on the bottom of 7x24 TV news channels or front and center in major market intranet monitors.[40] The glocal is kinedramatic, and from within these endlessly repeating kinedramas, speed controls events as it makes time and sets value.

One sees the discursive traditions and common values of omnipolitan society becoming more kinedramatic as shared movements crystallize through televisual reality or collective interactions in telematic connectivity coalesce in common emotions, that is, shock from images out of Bosnia, repulsion at news feed from Rwanda, fear in contemplating Chernobyl, pathos from the wreck of *Exxon Valdez*, loss on the passing of Mother Teresa, grief in Princess Di's car crash, agony in Kosovo's refugees teeming into Macedonia.[41] Reich captures the kineformative qualities of capital in contradictions between "nominal nationality" and "actual transnationality" in the corporate world. Old territorialized containments of national, high-volume enterprise with the values of top-down control and centralized executive ownership are being displaced by new telemetrical webs of transnational, high-value enterprises unified by their rapid reactions to problem-solving, problem-identifying, solution-creating, solution-brokering challenges. In this mode of valorization, efficient capital becomes a new type of kineformation, whose variable informational and industrial geometries operate

> in many places around the globe other than the United States. As the world shrinks through efficiencies in telecommunications and transportation, such groups in one nation are able to combine their skills

with those of people located in other nations in order to provide the greatest value to customers located almost anywhere. The threads of the global web are computer, facsimile machines, satellites, high-resolution monitors, and modems—all of them linking designers, engineers, contractors, licensees, and dealers worldwide.[42]

Such transnational formations can completely bypass nominal nationality and territorial spatiality, centering their movements of capital, labor, technology, and goods within their own new "real time" interactions.

In 1990, for example, "more than half of America's exports and imports, by value, were simply the transfers of such goods and services *within* global corporations,"[43] which suggests much of America's, and many other nation's, GNP is simply the gross corporate product of transnational networks operating inside their increasingly irrelevant national borders. Using just-in-time outsourcing techniques, as Reich notes, goods and services "can be produced efficiently in many different locations, to be combined in all sorts of ways to serve customer needs in many places. Intellectual and financial capital can come from anywhere, and be added instantly."[44] Producers, consumers, accumulators, and exchangers are all internationalized composites, moving in shared channels of mobilization at common rates of speed in the same time frames. This world of globalization, as Friedman claims, "turns all friends and enemies into 'competitors.'"[45]

Now there are so many centers of time-urgent value generation intent upon fixing their own timely equilibriums of energy and motion in omnipolitan governmentality to find "the right disposition of things, arranged so as to lead to a convenient end," that most managers of global businesses no longer pace their sense of right disposition, convenient ends, or even useful things in narrow national terms.[46] The Gillette Corporation's chair, Alfred M. Zeien, claims, for example, that his firm does not "find foreign countries foreign," and, as a result, it plans not "to tailor products to any marketplace, but to treat all marketplaces the same."[47] This tailoring of marketplaces to products as fast as tastes change, or can be changed, is the fast-acting power of glocality.

The globalized kineformation of commodities merge as part and parcel with major shifts that no longer "isolate the economy as a specific sector of reality"[48] but rather generalize economics as the universal totality of what is real. Once there, deterritorialized fast capitalist agencies, and not territorialized nation-states, increasingly generate the disciplines and delights needed "to manage a population" not only as a "collective mass of phenomena, the level of its aggregate effects," but also "the management of population in its depths and details.[49] Individuals, in turn, judge their personal success more often by the goods and services shared by the other "successful fifth" of global co-accelerants than by the state of the "failed four-fifths," who while they might still be perhaps fellow citizens are no longer commotive contemporaries riding on the same fast capitalist tracks in global flows.[50]

Glocalities melt all that was once locally solid into air so that their displaced particles might mix and match with all of the other fluidized particularities speeding along in global flows. As one key architect of these changes asserts, the most rational form of global order might be one of complete borderlessness. Therefore, the state should do nothing to retard global flows; it should instead serve as an active accelerant, changing "so as to: allow individuals access to the best and cheapest goods and services from anywhere in the world; help corporations provide stable and rewarding jobs anywhere in the world regardless of the corporation's national identity; coordinate activities with other governments to minimize conflicts arising from narrow interest; avoid abrupt changes in economic and social fundamentals."[51]

Globalization begins as a megametaphor, but it becomes the thought and action of people caught up in kinematic social formations engaged in acts of fast-acting conflict or cooperation. Reich asks "who is 'us'?," and his answer obviously is everyone "on the go" transnationally, not anyone "stuck in place" nationally. For the globalized, "to disconnect is to disinform oneself."[52] Shared speed becomes like a shared lifeworld, and it forms new agents from these accelerated states of globalized consciousness.

Virtualization

The rapidity of change in the digital domains of the Internet is widely acknowledged in the megametaphorics of the present. To write about it or reconsider the effects of its current mix of functionalities, as the dot-com "boom" and then "bust" nicely illustrate, is a hazardous enterprise, but the digerati rise to the challenge. For them, virtualization is partly the effects of computer networks, digital discourses, and online organizations on everyday life and partly the rush of rhetoric about what many think those effects are. Their doxic effects are widespread and influential.

Because technologies have "anonymous histories" that shape space, temper time, and package performance apart from the conscious intention of their users, the figure of virtualization in computer-mediated communications over information networks might respecify how political subjectivity works in digital environments.[53] Most important, digital networks seem to create new notions of alikeness in operational domains and cultural discourses far beyond the scope and method of how territorial states work now. In this manner, the *doxa* hold that "netizenship" is potentially far more than "e-citizenship," because virtual life on the Net is much more, and far less, than simply living in any city, polis, or state.

As the post-IPO Internet address retailer, Network Solutions, once suggested in many of its cable television ads, the Net's bitscapes still serve as today's equivalent of the Wild West—a telematic *terra nullius* in which anyone potentially can grab their "dot-coms" and get rich. This commercialization of virtual life is transforming the hyperrealities of cyberspace.[54] The old interface values of disembodied subjectivity, distributed community, and cybernetic play inherited from the early days of the Net are rapidly being eclipsed by newer interface values tied to reimagining cyberspace as hyper–real estate, virtual markets, and online e-commerce. This flexible geometry of indefinite boundaries, open architectures, and unfixed locations online in the netropolis of "virtual life" constantly contradicts the fixed geometries of definite boundaries, closed communities, and inflexible locations offline in the polis still out there in "the meat world" of "real life."

Nations of citizens always have been, on the one hand, cultivated by particular media regimes and market circumstances.[55] The construction of single mother tongues, rigid territorial borders, and cohesive mass populations, as Anderson argues, evolved alongside the development of older megametaphorics circulated by a national press.[56] Print capitalism was the material foundation of those nation-states, and "nations are therefore nations of people influenced by the same newspapers."[57] Cybernetic nodes for netizens, on the other hand, are being generated out of other media regimes and market circumstances, which are tied to telematic virtualizations. Virtualization, then, evolves around flows of digital information that are influenced by the same webs of hypertextual tools, links, and codes.[58]

Among nations, one has a "home" group or ground by virtue of birth and development in an off-line place with other real subjects. Around nodes, one builds "home" pages by organizing virtual objects at specific online sites. As Turkle notes,

> On the Web, the idiom for constructing a "home" identity is to assemble a "homepage" of virtual objects that correspond to one's interests. One constructs a homepage by composing or "pasting" on it words, images, and sounds, and by making connections between it and other sites on

the Internet or the Web. Like the agents in emergent AI, one's identity emerges from whom one knows, one's associations, and connections. People link their homepage to pages about such things as music, paintings, television shows, cities, books, photographs, comic strips, and fashion models. . . . If we take the homepage as a real estate metaphor for the self, its decor is postmodern: Its different rooms with different styles are located on computers all over the world but through one's efforts, they are brought together to be of a piece.[59]

Hypertextuality constitutes virtualization's most crucial practice, unifying many disparate elements into the digital objects that now carry individual identities and articulate a new mode for reproducing identities virtually. With the pull of browsers, one builds his or her own quasi-social, ultra-selfish pastiche of fragments from the public sphere in which Lycos, AOL, Netscape, or *The Wall Street Journal* will connect you only with information that you preselect as what you want to see.[60] Virtuality's megametaphorics assume the emergence of netizens, who work as freelancers amidst social instability, beyond local ties, but they continuously are laced together just-in-time with others all over the world by networks of data. Whether they are flush with stock options in 1998 or surfing for work in 2002, the virtual creates community out of connectivities.

The *doxa* suggest that this hyperindividuation of virtualization also recasts personal and social agency. Whereas nations once mandated modes or behavior and thought, virtual networks presume an individual "as *actor, designer, juggler* and *stage director* of his own biography, identity, social networks, commitments and convictions. Put in plain terms, 'individualization' means the disintegration of the certainties of industrial society as well as the compulsion to find and invent new certainties for oneself and others without them."[61] Informationalization forces users to become electronic existentialists. The standard biographies of older industrial societies also become DIY histories out in the flows of capital, data, labor, and product. Beck observes, "to use Sartre's term, people are *condemned* to individualization. . . . whatever a man or woman was and is, whatever he or she thinks or does, constitutes the *individuality* of that particular person."[62]

Individual identity in worlds managed by PeopleSoft or sustained through e-business may become one of multiple personality (dis)order. On the one hand, a strongly centered nation-state opens up into many decentered virtual webs. The welfare state's experiments in conditioning people, as Beck claims, for "*ego-centered ways of life*" pays off in spades online as particular persons morph their way through the day as multiple personalities.[63]

Life on the screen, however, raises tremendous identity questions for netizens, because these multiple personalities can be quite disordering as well as very ordered, particularly in rough economic times. The waning stability of uniform national identities in place is captured by Turkle's endorsement of pluralized nodal identities online:

> Every era constructs its own metaphors for psychological well-being. Not so long ago, stability was socially valued and culturally reinforced. Rigid gender roles, repetitive labor, the expectation of being in one kind of job or remaining in one town over a lifetime, all of these made consistency central to definitions of health. But these stable social worlds have broken down. In our time, health is described in terms of fluidity rather than stability. What matters most now is the ability to adapt and change—to new jobs, new career directions, new gender roles, new technologies.[64]

Virtual communities anchored to telematic interaction provide Turkle with the new normative structures to enforce these normalizing expectations. They now apply in societalized online environments "not only to human mental and physical spheres, but also to the bodies of corporations, governments, and businesses. . . . in these environments, people either explicitly play roles (as in MUDs) or more subtly shape their online selves. Adults learn about being multiple and fluid—and so do children."[65] As De Kerckhove observes, all of these aesthetic traces are signs of nodality reshaping territory, identity, and power:

> There is no horizon on the Net, only expansions and contractions, and our relationship to it begins a formidable expansion of psychological size. The loss of a clear sense of boundaries, the expansion of our mental frameworks by satellite, the online redistribution of our powers of action, all of these add up to a confused body image. We can't be absolutely sure anymore where we begin and where we end.[66]

The recalibration of normalization routines around flexibility and plurality in networks moves Turkle to see virtualization "as a space for growth."[67] She recognizes, like Robert Jay Lifton, the worth of a "protean self" for avoiding either "a dogmatic insistence on unity" or a "return to systems of belief, such as religious fundamentalism, that enforce conformity."[68] Economic crashes, like boom market frenzies, only change what is collectivized, how and by whom, or for how long.[69] For Turkle, the netizen's digital being, which emerges in real life from virtual life, "is capable, like Proteus, of fluid transformations but is grounded in coherence and moral outlook. It is multiple but integrated."[70] In defiance of American First!ers, such as Pat Buchanan, France First!ers, such as Claude Le Pen, or Russia First!ers, such as Vladimir Zhirinovsky, Turkle finds the new bottom line for netizens: "You can have a sense of self without being one self."[71] More-over, online practices and theories carried by "experiences in MUDs, on the WELL, on local bulletin boards, on commercial network services, and on the World Wide Web" all are bring these netropolitan realities home.[72]

At the virtual intersections of network places and connectivity spaces, as Gergen claims, "our range of social participation is expanding exponen-tially. As we absorb the views, values, and visions of others, and live out the multiple plots in which we are enmeshed, we enter a postmodern con-sciousness."[73] Actually, the multimediations of the digital domain, as Deib-ert affirms, carry a functional bias toward decentered and fragmented identities "and away from modern conceptions of the autonomous sover-eign individual," in which cyberspace generates "a plurality of 'worlds' and multiple 'realities,' each of which is contingent on social constructions, or 'language-games' that constitute and orient the field of experience."[74]

Turkle's reflections about "life on the screen" easily support such rhi-zomic visions of multiculturalized virtuality among the netizenry of online environments. In cyberspace, identity is often a series of multiple roles in which society and community become composite materials concocted out of various codes, discourses, and games. Multiculturalized menus for virtu-ality, then, "blur the boundaries between self and game, self and rule, self and simulation" such that, as one player observes, " 'you are what you pre-tend to be . . . you are what you play.' But people don't just become who they play, they play who they are or who they want to be or who they don't want to be."[75]

Such tendencies, as Turkle suggests, add up to netizens "taking things at their interface value" in which "people are increasingly comfortable with substituting representations of reality for the real."[76] Therefore, the online emulations of territoriality, sovereignty, or community, which might be generated out of computer-mediated communications, mean that "pro-grams are treated as social actors we can do business with, provided that they work."[77] If people treat computers "in ways that blur the boundary between things and people," then all of those things and people, which once had fixed boundaries and clear distinctions, begin to blur along many of their historical borders as well.[78] Telematic networks, while not quite political entities, are increasingly taken at their interface values. Their representations of reality become more openly accepted as framing, composing, and building what is "the real" by nodes in the network, whether it is economic prosperity or market collapse.

Summary: Doxosophical Politics

This analysis suggests megametaphorics serve as key resources in the mythographies of modernization today as they conjure up popular doxologies with fables of alikeness and difference. Metaphors anchor myths, and myths create belief. And, in being believed, myths become reality in the ongoing tussles of social forces. By being believed, for those whose deeds actuate and affirm their content, megametaphors cannot be ignored. And, within many established institutional regimes, megametaphorics serve as powerful screens whose filters are manipulated by inorganic intellectuals and vested interests to further the alikenesses of globalization and virtualization.

The events that these megametaphors depict as unfolding in the economy and society do not necessarily exist as such. Rather the perception of their existence gains greater focus in the dictive frames suggested by such megametaphors. They outline more determinate visions of what can be, should be, and will be done. For many people, believing in the doxosophies derived from such megametaphors, following the programmatic designs of inorganic intellectuals who propound such beliefs, and then accepting all their doxic effects in thought and action somehow will all lead to even more of the same being done. Doxic constructs plow open fields of interpretative interaction where ideas can link up with institutions. Those institutions, in turn, remediate ideas so fully that the symbolic order actuates and affirms them in other realms of psychological and social behavior.[79]

Doxic effects quickly insinuate themselves into both official policy and critical analysis through the work of doxosophers, such as Robert Reich, Al Gore, or Sherry Turkle, as well as corporate and government executives, such as Bill Clinton, Warren Christopher, or Bill Gates. In this respect, the doxosophies of neo-liberal markets and virtual organizations are turning into a concrete neo-liberal utopia that, as Bourdieu claims, now

> generates a potent belief, "free trade faith," not only among those who
> live from it materially such as financiers, big businessmen, etc., but also
> those who derive from it their justifications for existing, such as the sen-
> ior civil servants and politicians who deify the power of markets in the
> name of economic efficiency, who demand the lifting of the administra-
> tive or political barriers that could hinder the owners of capital in their

purely individual pursuit of maximum individual profit instituted as a model of rationality, who want independent central banks, who preach the subordination of the national states to the demands of economic freedom for the masters of the economy, with the suppression of all regulations on all markets, starting with the labor market, the forbidding of deficits and inflation, generalized privatization of public services, and the reduction of public and welfare spending.[80]

The alikenesses spun up from these beliefs are continuously displayed in the spectacles of global media as they cover the common efforts of all "those high representatives of the state who abase the dignity of their position by bowing before the bosses of multinationals, Daewoo or Toyota, or competing to charm Bill Gates with their smiles and gestures of complicity."[81]

Looked at by themselves, megametaphors seem somewhat colorless. When one, however, hears such "ready-made phrases all day," as Bourdieu worries, they become a doxosophy, or "a whole philosophy and a whole worldview which engender fatalism and submission."[82] Few things are more pressing than the disposition of the world in such megametaphors, because they flow quickly and widely in political rhetorics, economic arguments, and cultural controversies. This fact alone turns them into key strategic assets for anyone who is intent upon prevailing in these struggles so they cannot be discounted.

Notes

1. James Rosenau, *Turbulence in World Politics: A Theory of Change and Continuity* (Princeton: Princeton University Press, 1990); R. B. J. Walker, *Inside/Outside: International Relations as Political Theory* (Cambridge: Cambridge University Press, 1993); Timothy W. Luke, "Discourses of Disintegration, Texts of Transformation: Re-reading Realism in the New World Order," *Alternatives* 18 (1993): 229–58.

2. Robert Reich, *The Work of Nations: Preparing Ourselves for 21st Century Capitalism* (New York: Knopf, 1991); Al Gore, Jr., *Earth in the Balance: Ecology and the Human Spirit* (Boston: Houghton Mifflin, 1992); Sherry Turkle, *Life on the Screen: Identity in the Age of the Internet* (New York: Touchstone, 1997).

3. Jean François Lyotard, *The Postmodern Condition: A Report on Knowledge* (Minneapolis: University of Minnesota Press, 1984), xiii–xxv.

4. Kenneth Burke, *Permanence and Change: An Anatomy of Purpose* (Indianapolis: Bobbs-Merrill, 1954), 95.
5. Charles Peirce, *Philosophical Writings of Peirce,* ed. J. Buchler (New York: Dover, 1955); Algirdas J. Greimas, *On Meaning: Selected Writings in Semiotic Theory* (Minneapolis: University of Minnesota Press, 1987); Eugene Halton, *Bereft of Reason: On the Decline of Social Thought and Prospects for Its Renewal* (Chicago: University of Chicago Press, 1995).
6. William Connolly, "The Irony of Interpretation," in *The Politics of Irony: Essays in Self-betrayal,* ed. Daniel W. Conway and John E. Seery (New York: Routledge, 1992).
7. R. B. J. Walker, "The Antipolitics of Clayoquot Sound" (paper presented at the Western Political Science Association annual meeting, 25–27 March 1999, 4.
8. Connolly, "The Irony of Interpretation."
9. Timothy W. Luke, "Governmentality and Contra-governmentality: Rethinking Sovereignty and Territoriality after the Cold War," *Political Geography* 15, nos. 6/7 (1996): 491–507.
10. Pierre Bourdieu, *In Other Words: Essays toward a Reflexive Sociology* (Stanford, Calif.: Stanford University Press, 1990), 54.
11. Ibid.
12. Ibid., 55.
13. Pierre Bourdieu, *Practical Reason: On the Theory of Action* (Stanford, Calif.: Stanford University Press, 1998).
14. Antonio Gramsci, *Selections of the Prison Notebooks,* ed. Quintin Hoare and Geoffrey N. Smith (New York: International Publishers, 1971), 101–33; Pierre Bourdieu, *The Field of Cultural Production: Essays on Art and Literature* (New York: Columbia University Press, 1993), 112–14; Pierre Bourdieu, *Acts of Resistance: Against the Tyranny of the Market* (New York: New Press, 1998), 29–59.
15. Bourdieu, *Acts of Resistance,* 29–59.
16. Bourdieu, *In Other Words,* 7.
17. Karl Marx and Friedrich Engels, *The German Ideology* (New York: International Publishers, 1960), 27–43.
18. Bourdieu, *Practical Reason,* 81.
19. Ibid., 8.
20. Ibid.
21. Michel Foucault, *The Foucault Effect: Studies in Governmentality,* ed. Graham Burchell, Colin Gordon, and Peter Miller (Chicago: University of Chicago Press, 1991), 97.
22. Ibid., 100.

23. Ibid., 102.

24. Michel Foucault, *The History of Sexuality,* vol. 1, *An Introduction* (New York: Vintage, 1980), 146.

25. Bourdieu, *In Other Words,* 55.

26. Robert Kaplan, *The Ends of the Earth* (New York: Random House, 1996).

27. Reich, *The Work of Nations,* 8.

28. Hans Peter Martin and Harald Schumann, *The Global Trap: Globalization and the Assault on Democracy and Prosperity* (London: Zed Press, 1998).

29. Paul Virilio, *Open Sky* (London: Verso, 1997), 75.

30. Fredric Jameson, *Postmodernism, or The Cultural Logic of Late Capitalism* (Durham, N.C.: Duke University Press, 1991), ix.

31. Reich, *The Work of Nations,* 243–315; Thomas Friedman, *The Lexus and the Olive Tree* (New York: Farrar, Straus and Giroux, 1999), ix–xix.

32. Friedman, *The Lexus and the Olive Tree,* 8–12.

33. Benjamin Barber, *Jihad vs. McWorld* (New York: Times Books, 1995); David Harvey, *The Condition of Postmodernity* (Oxford: Blackwell, 1989); Ben Agger, *Fast Capitalism* (Urbana: University of Illinois Press, 1989).

34. Paul Virilio and Sylvia Lotringer, *Pure War* (New York: Semiotext[e], 1983), 43–51.

35. Paul Virilio, *The Art of the Motor* (Minneapolis: University of Minnesota Press, 1995), 23.

36. William Greider, *One World, Ready or Not: The Manic Logic of Global Capitalism* (New York: Simon and Schuster, 1997), 11–53.

37. Virilio, *The Art of the Motor,* 36; Virilio, *Open Sky,* 74.

38. Timothy W. Luke, "At the End of Nature: Cyborgs, 'Humachines,' and Environments in Postmodernity," *Environment and Planning A* 29 (1997): 1367–80.

39. Greider, *One World, Ready or Not,* 50–51.

40. Paul Kennedy, *Preparing for the Twenty-first Century* (New York: Random House, 1993), 47–64.

41. Timothy W. Luke and Gearoid Ó Tuathail, "On Videocameralistics: The Geopolitics of Failed States, the CNN International, and (UN) Governmentality," *Review of International Political Economy* 4 (1997): 709–33.

42. Reich, *The Work of Nations,* 111.

43. Ibid., 114.

44. Ibid., 112.

45. Friedman, *The Lexus and the Olive Tree,* 11.

46. Foucault, *The Foucault Effect,* 93.

47. Louis Uchitelle, "Gillette's World View: One Blade Fits All," *New York Times,* 3 January 1994, C3.

48. Foucault, *The Foucault Effect,* 102.

49. Ibid.

50. Reich, *The Work of Nations,* 268–300.

51. Kenechi Ohmae, *The Borderless World: Power and Strategy in an Interlocked Economy* (New York: Harper and Row, 1990), appendix.

52. James Seabrook, "Rocking in Shangri-La," *New York Times,* 10 October 1994, 64–78.

53. Sigfried Giedion, *Mechanization Takes Command: A Contribution to Anonymous History* (New York: Norton, 1948).

54. Andrew L. Shapiro, *The Control Revolution: How the Internet Is Putting Individuals in Charge and Changing the World We Know* (New York: Century Foundation, 1999), 169–230.

55. Ron Deibert, *Parchment, Printing and Hypermedia: Communication in World Order Transformation* (New York: Columbia University Press, 1997).

56. Benedict Anderson, *Imagined Communities,* rev. ed. (London: Verso, 1991), 37–39.

57. Ulrich Beck, *The Reinvention of Politics* (Oxford: Polity Press, 1997), 72.

58. Kevin Kelly, *Out of Control: The Rise of Neo-biological Civilization* (Reading, Mass.: Addison-Wesley, 1994).

59. Turkle, *Life on the Screen,* 258–59.

60. Mark Slouka, *War of the Worlds: Cyberspace and the High-Tech Assault on Reality* (New York: Basic Books, 1995).

61. Beck, *The Reinvention of Politics,* 95.

62. Ibid., 96.

63. Ibid., 97.

64. Turkle, *Life on the Screen,* 255.

65. Ibid., 255–56.

66. Derrick De Kerckhove, *Connected Intelligence: The Arrival of the War Society* (Toronto: Somerville, 1998), 38.

67. Turkle, *Life on the Screen,* 263.

68. Ibid., 258.

69. Ibid.

70. Ibid.

71. Turkle, *Life on the Screen,* 258.

72. Ibid.

73. Kenneth Gergen, *The Saturated Self: Dilemmas of Identity in Contemporary Life* (New York: Basic Books, 1991), 15–16.
74. Deibert, *Parchment, Printing and Hypermedia,* 187.
75. Turkle, *Life on the Screen,* 192.
76. Ibid., 23.
77. Ibid., 104.
78. Ibid., 102.
79. Pierre Bourdieu, *Outline of a Theory of Practice* (Cambridge: Cambridge University Press, 1977), 1–30.
80. Bourdieu, *Acts of Resistance,* 100–1.
81. Ibid., 102.
82. Ibid., 57.

◆ Conclusion

Metaphorical World Politics

Metaphorical World Politics

Francis A. Beer and Christ'l De Landtsheer

This book has presented a blended space where metaphors and world politics appear together. This is an unusual juxtaposition. Metaphorical aficionados usually come from literary world. Students and practitioners of world politics tend to live within the unexamined metaphorical boundaries described by a physicalist realism. If one searches for "metaphor" in the indexes of books about international relations, one will generally look in vain. We hope that this book will stimulate those who come to it primarily interested in metaphors to think about their international applications. Others concerned mainly with world politics may consider how metaphors help to constitute and fine-tune international political thought and action.

We began very simply by laying out our understanding of the meaning of metaphor and its importance for international relations. We sketched a short list of some metaphorical sources that seemed particularly relevant for political targets. Subsequent chapters provided more detailed discussions about the political relevance of some of these source terms, with particular attention to their targets in world politics—democracy, war and peace, and globalization.

We have been concerned with the general place of metaphor on the map of politics and the location of specific metaphors on the political terrain. At the same time, we have also been interested in metaphorical power, the way in which metaphors and politics shape each other. Assuming that we could identify some frequent metaphors, we should hope to have more detailed information about their specific political implications. From a theoretical perspective, we have followed Kenneth Burke, who argued that metaphor was a master trope.[1] We have tried to show how metaphor, broadly defined, constitutes speech and inevitably shapes political thought and action. Metaphor does this first in a general way, by framing discourse. Political actors are aware of some of these constitutive effects and intend them when they speak. Other effects are unintended and unobserved consequences of the language as it is commonly used. Metaphor also works in a more local, specific way. Political leaders react to specific circumstances with new metaphors; political followers react to metaphors in new ways. The chapters in this book present further interpretation, qualitative evidence, and quantitative data suggesting how metaphor works in different world political contexts. Taken as a whole, the book presents a cluster of ideas, interpretations, evidence, and references associated with metaphorical world politics.

We have presented a metaphorical perspective on world politics and a world political perspective on metaphor. We believe that metaphor has been, is, and will continue to be an unavoidable element of the thought, talk, and action that makes up the complex network of world political agents and structures. The book contains examples, which constitute the beginning of a list, of metaphors that political leaders have used and can use in the context of world politics. Our materials have largely come from English-language sources; they should obviously be supplemented by resources in other languages. We wish we could go further, providing an exhaustive inventory of world political metaphors.

Many of the authors have argued that metaphors both reflect and constitute our political world. Metaphors come from our past experiences and help to form our future actions. At the same time, individual authors have probed further, showing how political leaders finely tune their metaphors in particular situations—political change and crisis—to lead and respond to public opinion. We hope that further research can show the intricate ways in which different metaphors interact. We should like to present models and research from a variety of perspectives that formally specify the linkages and weightings of metaphors connected with other important variables in the complex global network. These connections should be situated in the vast variety of world political contexts and evaluated in practice. We should wish to provide a template of metaphorical management, specifying which metaphors should be used by which political leaders in which situations and how these metaphors might be interpreted by different audiences. We should like to be able to project changing metaphorical trends and the way that they fit into political, economic, social, cultural, and scientific environments of the future. To take one small example, new communications technologies provide new experiences for billions of people. These experiences are the foundations on which popular metaphors rest and also increasingly use metaphors in their own design processes.[2]

Political propaganda, psychological warfare, campaign advertising, mass marketing, and organizational communication are only a few of the fields that would find this knowledge useful. Some of this work has been done, but the complete task is beyond the scope of what is reasonable for us to attempt here and will have to await future research. In a larger sense, this ambition represents the next steps beyond what we have done. At the same time, it derives from a desire based on its own metaphors of progress, goals, and certainty;[3] ultimately, it runs up against theoretical limits inherent in the expansive logic of metaphor. The metaphorical substitution model allows for infinite substitutability; the syntactical model places no limits on the copula; the combinatorial model implies the potential mathematical explosion of joining the tens of thousands of words in each language.

Human experience, memory, and language are constantly changing, and, as they do, metaphors necessarily evolve with them. New metaphors are born; old metaphors either lose their edge or pass away. If metaphor is a matter of perspective, we are simultaneously in a hall of mirrors and a hall of windows. We can look in at ourselves and out at politics through the metaphorical perspective. We can see other perspectives through the metaphorical perspective. Other perspectives can see metaphor through their own perspectives, which, from a metaphorical perspective, are metaphorical.

Politics occurs in a metaphorical world, and world politics is inevitably metaphorical. As political leaders react to international events and try to advance their own agendas, they metaphorically call upon old worlds to create new worlds of meaning.

Notes

1. See Kenneth Burke, *A Grammar of Motives* (Berkeley and Los Angeles: University of California Press, 1969), 503–5.

2. See, for example, W. Lance Bennett and David L. Paletz, eds., *Taken by Storm: The Media, Public Opinion, and U.S. Foreign Policy in the Gulf War* (Chicago: University of Chicago Press, 1994); Andrew Herman and Thomas Swiss, eds., *The World Wide Web and Contemporary Cultural Theory: Magic, Metaphor, and Power* (New York: Routledge, 2000); Richard Coyne, *Designing Information Technology in the Postmodern Age: From Method to Metaphor* (Cambridge, Mass.: MIT University Press, 1995).

3. Min Lin, *Certainty as a Social Metaphor: The Social and Historical Production of Certainty in China and the West* (Westport, Conn.: Greenwood, 2001); Mary Catherine Bateson, *Our Own Metaphor: A Personal Account of a Conference on the Effects of Conscious Purpose on Human Adaptation* (Washington, D.C.: Smithsonian Institution Press, 1991).

References

Abbott, Kenneth W., and Duncan Snidal. "Hard and Soft Law in International Governance." *International Organization* 54, no. 3 (2000): 421–56.

Abrams, Jerold J. "Philosophy *after* the Mirror of Nature: Rorty, Dewey, and Pierce on Pragmatism and Metaphor." *Metaphor and Symbol* 17, no. 3 (2002): 227–42.

Acheson, Dean. *Present at the Creation.* New York: Norton, 1969.

Adams, James. "Norman after the Storm." *London Sunday Times,* 27 September 1992.

Agger, Ben. *Fast Capitalism.* Urbana: University of Illinois Press, 1989.

Alexiou, Margaret. *After Antiquity: Greek Language, Myth, and Metaphor.* Ithaca, N.Y.: Cornell University Press, 2002.

Alker, Hayward R. "Rescuing 'Reason' from the 'Rationalists': Reading Vico, Marx and Weber as Reflective Institutionalists." *Millennium* 19, no. 2 (1990): 161–84.

Allbritton, David W. "When Metaphors Function as Schemas: Some Cognitive Effects of Conceptual Metaphors." *Metaphor and Symbolic Activity* 10 (1995): 33–46.

Allison, Graham T., Albert Carnesale, and Joseph S. Nye, Jr., eds. *Hawks, Doves, and Owls: An Agenda for Avoiding Nuclear War.* New York: W. W. Norton, 1985.

Almond, Gabriel A., and G. Bingham Powell, Jr., eds. *Comparative Politics Today: A World View.* 7th ed. New York: Longman, 2003.

Ambrose, Stephen, and Douglas G. Brinkley. *Rise to Globalism: American Foreign Policy since 1938.* 8th rev. ed. New York: Penguin, 1997.

Andersen, Peter B., Berit Holmqvist, and Jens F. Jensen. *The Computer as Medium.* Cambridge: Cambridge University Press, 1993.

Anderson, Benedict. *Imagined Communities.* Rev. ed. London: Verso, 1991.

Anderson, John R. *Learning and Memory: An Integrated Approach.* New York: Wiley, 2000.

Anderson, Karen Vasby. " 'Rhymes with Rich': 'Bitch' as a Tool of Containment in Contemporary American Politics." *Rhetoric & Public Affairs* 2, no. 4 (1999): 599–623.

Anderson, Richard D., Jr. "Metaphors of Dictatorship and Democracy." *Slavic Review* 60 (2002): 312–35.

———. "Pragmatic Ambiguity and Partisanship in Russia's Emerging Democracy." In *Politically Speaking: A Worldwide Examination of Language Used in the Public Sphere*, edited by Ofer Feldman and Christ'l De Landtsheer, 64–78. Westport, Conn.: Praeger, 1998.

Anderson, Rick. "An Obvious Compromise on War and NFL Games." *Seattle Times*, 21 January 1991, C1.

Apple, R. W., Jr. "War in the Gulf; U.S. Says Iraq Pumps Kuwaiti Oil into Gulf; Vast Damage Feared from Growing Slick." *New York Times*, 26 January 1991, 1.

Arca, Emil, and Gregory Pamel. *The Triumph of the American Spirit: The Presidential Speeches of Ronald Reagan*. Detroit: National Reproductions, 1984.

Archer, Maureen, and Ronnie Cohen. "Sidelined on the (Judicial) Bench: Sports Metaphors in Judicial Opinions." *American Business Law Journal* 35 (1998): 225–42.

Aristotle. *The Complete Works of Aristotle: The Revised Oxford Translation*, edited by Johnathan Barnes, Princeton: Princeton University Press, 1984.

Aronoff, Myron Joel. "Political Culture." pp. 11640–11644, In *International Encyclopedia of the Social and Behavioral Sciences*. edited by Neil J. Smelser and Paul B. Baltes. Amsterdam: Elsevier, 2001.

Ash, Timothy Garton. "The New Adolf Hitler?" *Time.com*, 1 April 1999, http://cgi.pathfinder.com/time/magazine/articles/0,3266,22232,00.html (accessed 5 April 1999).

Azuma, Shoji. "Linguistic Strategy of Involvement: An Emergence of New Political Speech in Japan." In *Beyond Public Speech and Symbols: Explorations in the Rhetoric of Politicians and the Media*, edited by Christ'l De Landtsheer and Ofer Feldman, 69–85. Westport, Conn.: Praeger, 2000.

Bacon, Francis. *The New Organon*. Edited by Lisa Jardine and Michael Silverthorne. New York: Cambridge University Press, 2000.

Baker-Brown, G., E. J. Ballard, Susan Bluck, B. de Vries, Peter Suedfeld, and Philip E. Tetlock. "The Conceptual/Integrative Complexity Scoring Manual." In *Motivation and Personality: Handbook of Thematic Content Analysis*, edited by C. P. Smith, 400–18. Cambridge: Cambridge University Press, 1983.

Balbus, Isaac. "Politics as Sports: The Political Ascendancy of the Sports Metaphor in America." *Monthly Review* 26, no. 10 (March 1975): 26–39.

Ball, Moya Ann. "Political Language in the Search for an Honorable Peace: Presidents Kennedy and Johnson, Their Advisers, and Vietnam Decision Making." In *Beyond Public Speech and Symbols: Explorations in the Rhetoric of*

Politicians and the Media, edited by Christ'l De Landtsheer and Ofer Feldman, 35–51. Westport, Conn.: Praeger, 2000.

Balleck, Barry James. "Talking War and Peace: Realist and Idealist Rhetoric in the Persian Gulf Debate." Ph.D. diss., University of Colorado, Boulder, 1994.

Barber, Benjamin R. *Jihad vs. McWorld*. New York: Times Books, 1995.

Barber, Lionel. "The Gulf War: Bush Pursues Mission without Concession or Conciliation." *Financial Times*, 7 February 1991, 2.

Barcelona, Antonio. *Metaphor and Metonymy at the Crossroads: A Cognitive Perspective*. New York: Mouton de Gruyter, 2000.

Barnden, John A., and Mark G. Lee, eds. "Metaphor and Artificial Intelligence." Special issue, *Metaphor and Symbol* 16, nos. 1/2 (2001): 1–142.

Barnes, Trevor J. *Logics of Dislocation: Models, Metaphors, and Meanings of Economic Space*. London: Taylor and Francis, 1996.

Barry, Herbert, III. "Popular Metaphors for Some Presidents of the United States." Paper presented at the International Society of Political Psychology, Amsterdam, 1999.

Bartels, Dennis. "Metaphor, Morality, and Marxism." *Journal of Communication Inquiry* 2 (1995): 118–31.

Barthes, Roland. *Writing Degree Zero*. Translated by Annette Lavers and Colin Smith. New York: Hill and Wang, 1968.

Bateson, Gregory. *Steps to an Ecology of Mind*. New York: Ballantine Books, 1972.

Bateson, Mary Catherine. *Our Own Metaphor: A Personal Account of a Conference on the Effects of Conscious Purpose on Human Adaptation*. Washington, D.C.: Smithsonian Institution Press, 1991.

Battalio, John T., ed. *Essays in the Study of Scientific Discourse: Methods, Practice, and Pedagogy*. Stanford, Conn.: Ablex, 1998.

Bebber, Charles C. "Thematic Images Linking American Military Strikes of the 1980's and Rising U.S. Civil Violence." *Metaphor and Symbolic Activity* 10 (1995): 139–54.

Beck, Ulrich. *The Reinvention of Politics*. Oxford: Polity Press, 1997.

Beer, Francis A. "Games and Metaphors." *Journal of Conflict Resolution* 30, no. 1 (March 1986): 171–91.

———. *Integration and Disintegration in NATO*. Columbus: Ohio State University Press, 1969.

———. *Meanings of War and Peace*. College Station: Texas A&M University Press, 2001.

———. *Peace against War*. San Francisco: W. H. Freeman, 1981.

———. "Validities: A Political Science Perspective." *Social Epistemology* 7, no. 1 (1993): 85–105.

———. "Words of Reason." *Political Communication* 11 (summer 1994): 185–201.

Beer, Francis A., and Barry J. Balleck. "Body, Mind, and Soul in the Gulf War Debate." In *The Theory and Practice of Political Communication Research,* edited by Mary E. Stuckey, 159–76. Binghamton: SUNY Press, 1996.

Beer, Francis A., and G. Robert Boynton. "Realistic Rhetoric but Not Realism: A Senatorial Conversation on Cambodia." In *Post-realism: The Rhetorical Turn in International Relations,* Francis A. Beer and Robert Hariman, 369–83. East Lansing: Michigan State University Press, 1996.

———. "Speaking about Dying." In *Argumentation and Values: Proceedings of the Ninth SCA/AFA Conference on Argumentation,* edited by Sally Jackson, 550–56. Annandale, Va.: Speech Communication Association, 1995.

Beer, Francis A., and Laura Brunell. "Women's Words: Gender and Rhetoric in the Gulf War Debate." In Francis A. Beer, *Meanings of War and Peace,* 106–14. College Station: Texas A&M University Press, 2001.

Beer, Francis A., and Christ'l De Landtsheer. "Metaphorical Politics: Mobilization or Tranquilization." In *Proceedings of the Fourth International Conference of the International Society for the Study of Argumentation,* edited by Frans H. van Eemeren, Rob Grootendorst, J. Anthony Blair, and Charles A. Willard, 42–48. Amsterdam: SIC STAT, 1999.

Beer, Francis A., and Robert Hariman, eds. "Post-realism, Just War, and the Gulf War Debate." In *Politically Speaking: A Worldwide Examination of Language Use in the Public Sphere,* edited by Ofer Feldman and Christ'l De Landtsheer. Westport, Conn.: Praeger, 1998 pp.184–193.

———. *Post-realism: The Rhetorical Turn in International Relations.* East Lansing: Michigan State University Press, 1996.

Beer, Francis A., Alice F. Healy, and Lyle E. Bourne, Jr. "Dynamic Decisions: Experimental Reactions to War, Peace, and Terrorism." In *Political Psychology as a Perspective on Politics: Advances in Political Psychology,* vol. 1, edited by Margaret G. Hermann. London: Elsevier, 2004.

Belgian National Television BRT 1. "Confrontatie" [Confrontation] 2S February, 1986.

Benjamin, Walter. "On Some Motifs in Baudelaire." In *Illuminations: Essays and Reflections,* Hannah Arendt, ed. with an introduction by Harry Zohn, 155–200. New York: Schocken, 1969.

Bennett, W. Lance, and David L. Paletz, eds. *Taken by Storm: The Media, Public Opinion, and U.S. Foreign Policy in the Gulf War.* Chicago: University of Chicago Press, 1994.

Berman, Michael, and David Brown. *The Power of Metaphor.* Carmarthen, U.K.: Crown House Publishing, 2000.

Berthoff, Ann E. *Richards on Rhetoric: I. A. Richards Selected Essays (1929–1974).* Oxford: Oxford University Press, 1994.

Bessett, Joseph M. *The Mild Voice of Reason: Deliberative Democracy and American National Government.* Chicago: University of Chicago Press, 1994.

Biersteker, Thomas J., and Cynthia Weber, eds. *State Sovereignty as Social Construct.* Cambridge: Cambridge University Press, 1996.

Billow, Richard, Jeffrey Rossman, Nona Lewis, Deborah Goldman, Susan Kraemer, and Ross Patrick. "Metaphoric Communication and Miscommunication in Schizophrenic and Borderline States." In *Cognition and Symbolic Structures: The Psychology of Metaphoric Transformation,* edited by Robert E. Haskell. Norwood, N.J.: Ablex Publishing, 1987.

Bineham, Jeffery L. "Some Ethical Implications of Team Sports Metaphors in Politics." *Communication Reports* 4 (1991): 35–42.

Bjelić, Dusan, and Obrad Savić, eds. *Balkan as Metaphor: Between Globalization and Fragmentation.* Cambridge, Mass.: MIT University Press, 2002.

Black, Edwin. "The Second Persona." In *Readings in Rhetorical Criticism,* edited by Carl R. Burckhart, 188–97. State College, Penn.: Strata Publishing, 1995.

Black, Max. *Models and Metaphors.* Ithaca, N.Y.: Cornell University Press, 1962.

———. "More about Metaphor." In *Metaphor and Thought,* 2d ed, edited by Andrew Ortony, 19–41. Cambridge: Cambridge University Press, 1996.

Blanton, Shannon L. "Images in Conflict: The Case of Ronald Reagan and El Salvador." *International Studies Quarterly* 40, no. 1 (1996): 23–44.

Borisoff, Deborah, and Dan F. Hahn. "Thinking with the Body: Sexual Metaphors." *Communication Quarterly* 41 (1993): 253–60.

Bosman, Jan. "Persuasive Effects of Political Metaphors." *Metaphor and Symbolic Activity* 2 (1987): 97–113.

Bosman, Jan, and Louk Hagendoorn. "Effects of Literal and Metaphorical Persuasive Messages." *Metaphor and Symbolic Activity* 6 (1991): 271–92.

Bostdorff, Denise M. "George W. Bush's Post September 11 Rhetoric of Covenant Renewal: Upholding the Faith of the Greatest Generation," *Quarterly Journal of Speech* 89, no. 4 (2003): 293–319

Bostdorff, Denise M. *The Presidency and the Rhetoric of Foreign Crisis.* Columbia: University of South Carolina Press, 1994.

Bouchard, Tom. "Comparison of Two Group Brainstorming Procedures." *Journal of Applied Psychology* 56 (1972): 418–21.

Boulding, Elise. *The Underside of History: A View of Women through Time.* Original line drawings by Helen Redman. Newbury Park, Calif.: Sage, 1992.

Bourdieu, Pierre. *Acts of Resistance: Against the Tyranny of the Market.* New York: New Press, 1998.

———. *The Field of Cultural Production: Essays on Art and Literature.* New York: Columbia University Press, 1993.

———. *In Other Words: Essays toward a Reflexive Sociology.* Stanford, Calif.: Stanford University Press, 1990.

———. *On Television.* Translated by Priscilla Parkhurst. New York: New Press, 1996.

———. *Outline of a Theory of Practice.* Cambridge: Cambridge University Press, 1977.

———. *Practical Reason: On the Theory of Action.* Stanford, Calif.: Stanford University Press, 1998.

Bowman, Lee. "One Sided; The Winners Gloat, the Losers Retreat." *St. Petersburg Times,* 28 February 1991, 4A.

Boynton, G. Robert. "Ideas and Action: A Cognitive Model of the Senate Agriculture Committee." *Political Behavior* 12 (1990): 181–213.

———. "The Senate Agriculture Committee Produces a Homeostat." *Policy Sciences* 2 (1989): 51–80.

Braun, Claude M. "A Note on the Effect of Semantic Anomaly on the Intensity of Emotional Impact of Metaphors." *Metaphor and Symbolic Activity* 7 (1992): 1–10.

Bredeck, Elizabeth. *Metaphors of Knowledge: Language and Thought in Mauthner's Critique.* Detroit: Wayne State University Press, 1992.

Breuning, Marijke. "The Role of Analogies and Abstrct Reasoning in Decision-Making: Evidence from the Debate over Truman's Proposal for Development Assistance." *International Studies Quarterly* 47 (2003): 229–245.

Brilmayer, Lea. *American Hegemony: Political Morality in a One-Superpower World.* New Haven: Yale University Press, 1994.

Brown, Michael P. *Closet Space: Geographies of Metaphor from the Body to the Globe.* New York: Routledge, 2000.

Brown, Seyom. *The Faces of Power: Constancy and Change in United States Foreign Policy from Truman to Clinton.* 2d ed. New York: Columbia University Press, 1994.

Bryan, Ferald J. "Vico on Metaphor: Implications for Rhetorical Criticism." *Philosophy and Rhetoric* 19 (1986): 255–65.

Brzezinski, Zbigniew. "Address before the Trilateral Commission," 31 October 1977.

———. "American Policy and Global Community." Address made before the Trilateral Commission in Bonn, Germany, on 25 October 1977, *Congressional Record*, 1 November 1977.

———. *Between Two Ages: America's Role in the Technetronic Era*. New York: Penguin, 1970.

The Grand Chessboard: American Primacy and Its Geostrategic Imperatives (New York: Basic Books, 1997)

———. Interview by James Reston, *New York Times*, 31 December 1978. *DOD Selected Documents*, 1 January 1979.

———. Interview, *Newsweek*, 8 January 1979, 4.

———. Interview, *US News and World Report*, 30 May 1977. *DOD Selected Statements*, 1 June 1977.

———. Interview, *Washington Post*, 9 October 1977. *DOD Selected Statements*, 1 November 1977.

———. *Power and Principle: Memoirs of the National Security Adviser, 1977–1981*. New York: Farrar, Straus and Giroux, 1983.

———. "The Quest for Global Security: The Third Phase." Remarks before the Council on Foreign Relations in Denver, Colorado, White House Press Release, 25 October 1980.

———. *Time*, 15 January 1979.

Brzezinski, Zbigniew, and Carl J. Friedrich. *Totalitarian Dictatorship and Autocracy*. New York: Praeger, 1956.

Brzezinski, Zbigniew, and Samuel P. Huntington. *Political Power: USA/USSR*. New York: Viking, 1963.

Büchler, Pavel, and Nikos Papastergiadis, eds. *Random Access: On Crisis and Its Metaphors*. London: River Oram Press; Concord, Mass.: Paul and Company, 1995.

Buckley, Anthony D., and Mary Catherine Kenney. *Negotiating Identity: Rhetoric, Metaphor, and Social Drama in Northern Ireland*. Smithsonian Series in Ethnographic Inquiry. Washington, D.C.: Smithsonian Institution Press, 1995.

Builder, Carl H. *The Masks of War*. Baltimore: Johns Hopkins University Press, 1989.

Bull, Hedley. *The Anarchical Society: A Study of World Order in Politics*. New York: Columbia University Press, 1995.

Burch, Kurt. *"Property" and the Making of the International System*. Boulder: Lynne Rienner, 1998.

Burke, Kenneth. *Attitudes toward History*. 3d ed. Berkeley and Los Angeles: University of California Press, 1984.

————. *A Grammar of Motives.* Berkeley and Los Angeles: University of California Press, 1969.

————. *Language as Symbolic Action.* Berkeley and Los Angeles: University of California Press, 1966.

————. *Permanence and Change: An Anatomy of Purpose.* Indianapolis: Bobbs-Merrill, 1954.

————. *Permanence and Change: An Anatomy of Purpose.* 3d ed. Berkeley and Los Angeles: University of California Press, 1984.

————. *The Rhetoric of Religion: Studies in Logology.* Berkeley and Los Angeles: University of California Press, 1970.

Butcher, Samuel H. *Aristotle's Theory of Poetry and Fine Art.* 4th ed. New York: Dover Publications, 1951.

Buzan, Barry, Charles Jones, and Richard Little. *The Logic of Anarchy—Neorealism to Structural Realism.* New York: Columbia University Press, 1993.

Cacciari, Catarina. "Cognitive Psychology of Figurative Thought and Figurative Language." In *International Encyclopedia of the Social and Behavioral Sciences,* edited by Neil J. Smelser and Paul B. Baltes, 8:5632–37. Amsterdam: Elsevier, 2001.

Cameron, Lynne. *Metaphor in Educational Discourse (Advances in Applied Linguistics).* New York: Continuum, 2002.

Cameron, Lynne, and Graham Low, eds. *Researching and Applying Metaphor.* Cambridge: Cambridge University Press, 1999.

Camp, Claudia and Carole Fontaine, *Semeia 61: Women, War, and Metaphor* (Atlanta: Scholars Press, 1993)

Campbell, David. *Writing Security: United States Foreign Policy and the Politics of Identity.* Minneapolis: University of Minnesota Press, 1992.

Campbell, Karlyn K., and Kathleen H. Jamieson. *Deeds Done in Words.* Chicago: University of Chicago Press, 1990.

Cantor, Paul. "Friedrich Nietzsche: The Use and Abuse of Metaphor." In *Metaphor, Problems and Perspectives,* edited by David S. Miall, 71–88. Atlantic Highlands, N.J.: Humanities Press, 1982.

Carney, Laura S. "Not Telling Us What to Think: The Vietnam Veterans Memorial." *Metaphor and Symbolic Activity* 8 (1993): 211–19.

Carpenter, Ronald H. "America's Tragic Metaphor: Our Twentieth-Century Combatants as Frontiersmen." *Quarterly Journal of Speech* 76 (1990): 1–22.

Carter, Jimmy. "A Foreign Policy Based on America's Essential Character." Address made at the commencement exercises of Notre Dame

University, South Bend, Ind., 22 May 1977. *Department of State Bulletin* (13 June 1977): 621–25.

_____. Interview by Frank Reynolds, *World News Tonight*, ABC, 31 December 1980.

_____. *Keeping Faith: Memoirs of a President.* Toronto: Bantam Books, 1982.

_____. *New York Times*, 1 January 1981.

_____. "Peace, Arms Control, World Economic Progress, Human Rights: Basic Priorities of U.S. Foreign Policy." Address made to representatives to the United Nations, U.N. General Assembly Hall, 17 March 1977. *State Department Bulletin* (11 April 1977): 329–34.

_____. "U.S. Role in a Peaceful Global Community." Address made before the 32d U.N. General Assembly, 4 October 1977. *State Department Bulletin* (24 October 1977).

_____. *Why Not the Best?* New York: Bantam, 1975.

Castano, Emanuele, Simona Sacchi, and Peter Hayes Gries. "The Perception of the 'Other' in International Relations: Evidence for the Polarizing Effect of Entitativity." *Political Psychology* (forthcoming).

Chace, James, and Caleb Carr. *America Invulnerable: The Quest for Absolute Security from 1812 to Star Wars.* New York: Summit Books, 1988.

Chamberlain, Tony. "Are Odes to the Game Really out in Left Field?" *Boston Globe*, 5 April 1991, 76.

Chambers, Simone. *Reasonable Democracy: Jürgen Habermas and the Politics of Discourse.* Ithaca, N.Y.: Cornell University Press, 1996.

Chandler, Stephen R. "Metaphor Comprehension: A Connectionist Approach to Implications for the Mental Lexicon." *Metaphor and Symbolic Activity* 6 (1991): 227–58.

Chernus, Ira. *Dr. Strangegod: On the Symbolic Meaning of Nuclear Weapons.* Columbia: University of South Carolina Press, 1986.

Chilton, Paul A. *Security Metaphors: Cold War Discourse from Containment to Common House.* New York: Peter Lang, 1996.

Chilton, Paul A., and Mikhail Ilyin. "Metaphor in Political Discourse: The Case of the 'Common European House.'" *Discourse and Society* 4, no. 1 (January 1993): 7–31.

Ching, Marvin K. "Games and Play: Pervasive Metaphors in American Life." *Metaphor and Symbolic Activity* 8 (1993): 43–65.

Christensen Thomas J., and Jack Snyder. "Chain Gangs and Passed Bucks: Predicting Alliance Patterns in Multipolarity." *International Organization* 44 (spring 1990): 137–68.

Christopher, Renny. *The Vietnam War/the American War: Images and Representations in Euro-American and Vietnamese Exile Narratives.* Amherst: University of Massachusetts Press, 1995.

Claiborne, Robert. *Loose Cannons and Red Herrings: A Book of Lost Metaphors.* New York: Ballantine Books, 1989.

Clark, Suzanne. *Cold Warriors: Manliness on Trial in the Rhetoric of the West.* Carbondale: Southern Illinois University Press, 2000.

Clinton, William J. "Inaugural Address," 31 December 1997. White House Virtual Library, http://www.whitehouse.gov (accessed 20 January 1997).

———. "Inaugural Speech," 20 January 1993. White House Virtual Library, http://www.whitehouse.gov (accessed 24 December 1997).

———. "1999–06–02 Remarks by the President at United States Air Force Academy Commencement Ceremony," 4 June 1999. Public distribution list, White House, Office of the Press Secretary (accessed 4 June 1999).

———. "President William Jefferson Clinton Address to the Nixon Center for Peace and Freedom Policy Conference," 1 March 1995. White House Virtual Library, http://www.whitehouse.gov (accessed 31 December 1997).

———. "Remarks by the President at American University Centennial Celebration," 26 February 1993. White House Virtual Library, http://www.whitehouse.gov (accessed 24 December 1997).

———. "Remarks by the President on Foreign Policy," 26 February 1999. White House, Office of the Press Secretary, http://www.pub.whitehouse.gov/uri-res/12 ... n:pdi//oma.cop.gov.us/19999/3/1/3.text.1 (accessed 4 March 1999).

———. "Remarks by the President to the People of Ghana," 23 March 1998. White House, Office of the Press Secretary, http://www.pub.whitehouse.gov/uri-res/12 ... pdi://oma.cop.gov.us/1998/3/25/20.text.2 (accessed 4 March 1999).

———. "Remarks by the President to Students of Moscow State University," 10 May 1995. White House Virtual Library, http://www.whitehouse.gov (accessed 31 December 1997).

———. "Remarks by President Clinton and President Rawlings of Ghana at Welcoming Ceremony," 24 February 1999. White House, Office of the Press Secretary, http://www.pub.whitehouse.gov/uri-res/12 ... pdi://oma.cop.gov.us/1999/2/24/15.text.1 (accessed 4 March 1999).

———. "State of the Union Address," 26 January 1994. White House Virtual Library, http://www.whitehouse.gov (accessed 24 December 1997).

_____. "A Strategic Alliance with Russian Reform," 1 April 1993. White House Virtual Library, http://www.whitehouse.gov (accessed 24 December 1997).

_____. "Text of President Clinton's Address to the Nation." 11 June 1999, *New York Times*, http://nytimes.com/ (accessed 11 June 1999).

Cohen, T. "Metaphor and the Cultivation of Intimacy." In *On Metaphor*, edited by S. Sachs. Chicago: University of Chicago Press, 1979.

Cohn, Carol. "Sex and Death in the Rational World of Defense Intellectuals." *Signs* 12 (1987): 687–718.

Cole, Timothy M. "Avoiding the Quagmire: Alternative Rhetorical Constructs for Post–Cold War American Foreign Policy." *Rhetoric & Public Affairs* 2, no. 3 (1999): 367–93.

_____. "When Intentions Go Awry: The Bush Administration's Foreign Policy Rhetoric." *Political Communication* 13 (1996): 93–113.

Collins, Christopher. *Authority Figures: Metaphors of Mastery from the Iliad to the Apocalypse*. Lanham, Md.: Rowman and Littlefield; University Press of America, 1996.

Collins, John, and Ross Glover, eds., *Collateral Language: A User's Guide to America's New War*. New York: New York University Press, 2002.

Colston, Herbert L., and Raymond W. Gibbs, Jr. "Are Irony and Metaphor Understood Differently?" *Metaphor and Symbol* 17, no. 1 (2002): 57–80.

Condit, Celeste M., Benjamin R. Bates, Ryan Galloway, Sonja Brown Givens, Caroline K Haynie, John W. Jordan, Gordon Stables, and Hollis Marshall West. "Recipes of Blueprints for Our Genes? How Contexts Selectively Activate the Multiple Meaning of Metaphors." *Quarterly Journal of Speech* 88, no. 3 (August 2002): 303–25.

Confino, Alon. *The Nation as a Local Metaphor: Wurttemberg, Imperial Germany, and National Memory*. Chapel Hill: University of North Carolina Press, 1997.

Connolly, William. "The Irony of Interpretation." In *The Politics of Irony: Essays in Self-betrayal*, edited by Daniel W. Conway and John E. Seery. New York: Routledge, 1992.

Coolidge, Archibald Cary. *Political Metaphors*. Mount Pleasant, S.C.: Maecenas Press, 2000.

Corcoran, Paul E. "Presidential Concession Speeches: The Rhetoric of Defeat." *Political Communication* 11, no. 2 (1994): 107–64.

Coyne, Richard. *Designing Information Technology in the Postmodern Age: From Method to Metaphor*. Cambridge, Mass.: MIT University Press, 1995.

Crawford, Allen. *Thunder on the Right*. New York: Pantheon, 1980.

Crelinstein, Ronald D. "In Their Own Words: The World of the Torturers." Paper presented at the III Pioom Symposium, *Torturers and Their Masters: The Politics of Pain,* University of Leiden, the Netherlands, 1991.

Dallmayr, Fred R. *Language and Politics: Why Does Language Matter to Political Philosophy?* Notre Dame, Ind.: University of Notre Dame Press, 1984.

Damasio, Antonio R. *Descartes' Error: Emotion, Reason, and the Human Brain.* New York: G. P. Putnam and Sons, 1994.

Dancygier, B. "How Polish Structures Space: Prepositions, Direction Nouns, Case, and Metaphor" from *Amsterdam Studies in the Theory and History of Linguistic Science. Series IV, Current Issues in Linguistic Theory.* no. 178, (2000): 27–46. Amsterdam: J. Benjamins.

Danesi, Marcel. *Vico, Metaphor, and the Origin of Language.* Bloomington: Indiana University Press, 1993.

Daughton, Suzanne M. "Metaphoric Transcendence: Images of the Holy War in Franklin Roosevelt's First Inaugural." *Quarterly Journal of Speech* 79 (1993): 427–46.

Davis, M. Thomas. "After the Friendly Fire; Remembering Sgt. Young Dillon, a Brave Life We Left in the Gulf." *Washington Post,* 30 May 1993, C5.

De Baecque, Antoine. *The Body Politic: Corporeal Metaphor in Revolutionary France, 1770–1800.* Stanford, Calif.: Stanford University Press, 1993.

De Kerckhove, Derrick. *Connected Intelligence: The Arrival of the War Society.* Toronto: Somerville, 1998.

De Landtsheer, Christ'l. "Function and the Language of Politics: A Linguistic Uses and Gratifications Approach." *Communication and Cognition* 3/4 (1991): 299–344.

———. "Introduction to the Study of Political Discourse." In *Politically Speaking: A Worldwide Examination of Language Used in the Public Sphere,* edited by Ofer Feldman and Christ'l De Landtsheer, 1–16. Westport, Conn.: Praeger, 1998.

———. "Language and Ideology: A Representation of the Function of Ideology in the Political Use of Language." In *Political Psychology in the Netherlands: Proceedings of the First Conference on Political Psychology in the Netherlands,* edited by Marten Brouwer, Japp Van Ginneken, Louk Hagendoorn and Jos Meloen, 91–97. Amsterdam: Mola Russa, 1986.

———. "The Language of Prosperity and Crisis: A Case Study in Political Semantics." *Politics and the Individual* 4, no. 2 (1994): 63–85.

———. "The Language of Unification: Specification of a Coding Process as a Basis for Observation." In *Sprache im Umbruch. Politischer Sprachwandel im zeichen von "Wende" und "Vereinigung"* (Language in transition in the

German unification process), edited by Armin Burkhardt and K. Peter Fritzsche, 287–314. Berlin: W. de Gruyter, 1992.

———. "Political Communication." In "How to Make a Politician." Special issue, *Politics, Groups and the Individual* 2 (1995): 1–20.

———. "The Political Rhetoric of a Unified Europe." In *Politically Speaking: A Worldwide Examination of Language Used in the Public Sphere,* edited by Ofer Feldman and Christ'l De Landtsheer, 129–46. Westport, Conn.: Praeger, 1998.

———. "Public Speech, Symbols, and Democratic Citizenship East West." In *Beyond Public Speech and Symbols: Explorations in the Rhetoric of Politicians and the Media,* edited by Christ'l De Landtsheer and Ofer Feldman, 401–44. Westport, Conn.: Praeger, 2000.

De Landtsheer, Christ'l, and Ilse De Vrij. "Dutch Elites and Dutchbat: Talking about Srebrenica." Paper presented at the 22d annual scientific meeting of the International Society of Political Psychology, Amsterdam, July 1999.

De Landtsheer, Christ'l, and Lise van Oortmerssen. "A Psycholinguistic Analysis of the European Union's Political Discourse regarding the Israeli-Palestinian Conflict." In *Beyond Public Speech and Symbols: Explorations in the Rhetoric of Politicians and the Media,* edited by Christ'l De Landtsheer and Ofer Feldman, 158–82. Westport, Conn.: Praeger, 2000.

De Man, Paul. *Allegories of Reading: Figural Language in Rousseau, Nietzsche, Rilke, and Proust.* New Haven: Yale University Press, 1979.

De Sola Pool, Ithiel. "Variety and Repetition in Political Language." In *Political Behavior: A Reader in Theory and Research,* edited by Heinz Eulau, Samuel Eldersfeld, and Morris Janowitz, 217–31. Glencoe, Ill.: The Free Press, 1956.

Der Derian, James. *Virtual War: Mapping the Military-Industrial-Media-Entertainment Network.* Boulder: Westview, 2001.

Derrida, Jacques. *Margins of Philosophy.* Translated by Alan Bass. Chicago: University of Chicago Press, 1982.

Destler, I. M., Leslie H. Gelb, and Anthony Lake. *Our Own Worst Enemy: The Unmaking of American Foreign Policy.* New York: Simon and Schuster, 1984.

Deutsch, Karl W. *The Nerves of Government: Models of Political Communication and Control.* New York: Basic Books, 1966.

Dews, Shelly, and Ellen Winner. "Muting the Meaning: A Social Function of Irony." *Metaphor and Symbolic Activity* 10 (1995): 3–19.

DiCicco, Jonathan M. "Power Shifts and Problem Shifts." *Journal of Conflict Resolution* 43, no. 6 (1999): 675–704

Diebert, Ron. *Parchment, Printing and Hypermedia: Communication in World Order Transformation*. New York: Columbia University Press, 1997.

Dirven, René. *Metaphor and Metonymy in Comparison and Contrast*. New York: Mouton de Gruyter, 2002.

———. *Metaphor and Nation: Metaphors Afrikaners Live By*. New York: Peter Lang, 1994.

———. "Metaphors in Politics: The Case of Apartheid." *Communication and Cognition* 22, no. 1 (1989): 22–38.

Dobrzynska, Teresa. "Translating Metaphor: Problems of Meaning." *Journal of Pragmatics* 24 (1995): 595–604.

Docking, Shay. *The Landscape as Metaphor*. Frenchs Forest, N.S.W.: Reed, 1983.

Dorsey, Leroy G. "Sailing into the 'Wondrous Now': The Myth of the American Navy's World Cruise." *Quarterly Journal of Speech* 83, no. 4 (1997): 447–65.

Doty, Roxanne L. *Imperial Encounters: The Politics of Representation in North-South Relations*. Minneapolis: University of Minnesota Press, 1996.

Douglass, David. "Research and Metaphor in Communication Studies." Paper presented at the annual meeting of the Western States Communication Association, Sacramento, Calif., February 2000.

Dowd, Maureen. "War in the Gulf." *New York Times*, 22 February 1991, A1.

Dreistadt, Ronald. "The Use of Analogies and Incubation in Obtaining Insights in Creative Problem Solving." *Journal of Psychology* 71 (1969): 159–75.

Drew, Elizabeth. "Brzezinski," *New Yorker*, 1 May 1978, 95–118, 121–30.

———. *Portrait of an Election*. New York: Simon and Schuster, 1981.

Dumbrell, John. *American Foreign Policy: Carter to Clinton*. 2d ed. New York: St. Martin's Press, 1996.

Edelman, Murray. *Constructing the Political Spectacle*. Chicago: University of Chicago Press, 1988.

———. *Politics as Symbolic Action: Mass Arousal and Quiescence*. Chicago: Markham, 1971.

———. *The Symbolic Uses of Politics*. Urbana: University of Illinois Press, 1974.

Edelson, Paula. "Sports during Wartime." *Z Magazine*, May 1991, 85–87.

"The Edge of the Abyss." *Newsweek*, 21 January 1991, 20

Eizenstat, Stuart. "The Presidency in Trouble." Paper, White Burkett Miller Center of Public Affairs, University of Virginia, *Project on the Carter Presidency*, 1983.

Ellis, Joseph J. *Founding Brothers: The Revolutionary Generation.* New York: Alfred A. Knopf, 2000.

Elshtain, Jean Bethke, and Sheila Tobias, eds. *Women, Militarism, and War: Essays in History, Politics, and Social Theory.* Savage, Md.: Rowman and Littlefield, 1990.

Elwood, William N. "Declaring War on the Home Front: Metaphor, Presidents, and the War on Drugs." *Metaphor and Symbolic Activity* 10, no. 2 (1995): 93–114.

Emerson, Michael. "1992 and after: The Bicycle Theory Rides Again." *Political Quarterly* 59, no. 3 (July–September 1988): 289–99.

Enloe, Cynthia. *Bananas, Beaches and Bases: Making Feminist Sense of International Politics.* Berkeley and Los Angeles: University of California Press, 1990.

———. *The Morning after: Sexual Politics at the End of the Cold War.* Berkeley and Los Angeles: University of California Press, 1993.

Entman, Robert N. *Projections of Power: Framing News, Public Opinion, and U.S. Foreign Policy.* Chicago: University of Chicago Press, 2004.

Etzioni, Amitai. "The Community of Communities." *Responsive Community* 7, no. 1 (1996–97): 21–32.

Eubanks, Philip. *A War of Words in the Discourse of Trade: The Rhetorical Constitution of Metaphor.* Carbondale: Southern Illinois University Press, 2000

Evans, David. "Gulf War Victory Mega-parade: It's Too Much, Too Soon." *Chicago Tribune,* 7 June 1991, 25.

"Excerpts from Schwarzkopf News Conference on Gulf War." *New York Times,* 24 February 1991, A3.

Ezrahi, Yaron. "The Theatrics and Mechanics of Action: The Theater and the Machine as Political Metaphors." *Social Research* 62, no. 2 (1995): 299–322.

Fahnestock, Jeanne. *Rhetorical Figures in Science.* New York: Oxford University Press, 1999.

Farrell, Thomas B. *Norms of Rhetorical Culture.* New Haven: Yale University Press, 1993.

Farrell, Thomas B., and G. Thomas Goodnight. "Accidental Rhetoric: The Root Metaphors of Three Mile Island." *Communication Monographs* 48 (1981): 271–300.

Fauconnier, Gilles, and Mark Turner. *The Way We Think: Conceptual Blending and the Mind's Hidden Complexities.* New York: Basic Books, 2003.

Feldman, Ofer. "Personality and Politics in Japan." *Politics and the Individual* 4, no. 2 (1994): 27–46.

Felton, Keith Spencer. *Warriors' Words: A Consideration of Language and Leadership.* Westport, Conn.: Praeger, 1995.

Ferguson, Kathy E. *Oh Say Can You See?: The Semiotics of the Military in Hawai'i.* Minneapolis: University of Minnesota Press, 1998.

Fernandez, James W., ed. *Beyond Metaphor: The Theory of Tropes in Anthropology.* Stanford, Calif.: Stanford University Press, 1991.

Ferrarotti, Franco. "Le radici tagliate [Cut roots]." *Critica Sociologica* 116 (January–March 1996): iii–iv.

Feuchtwang, Stephan. *Popular Religion in China: The Imperial Metaphor.* Richmond: Curzon Press, 2001.

Feuer, Lewis S. *Einstein and the Generations of Science.* New York: Basic Books, 1974.

Fierke, Karin. "Dialogues of Manoeuvre and Entanglement: NATO, Russia, and the CEEC." *Millennium: Journal of International Studies* 28 (1999): 27–52.

Finel, Bernard I. "Black Box or Pandora's Box: State Level Variables and Progressivity in Realist Research Programs." *Security Studies* 11, no. 2 (2001): 187–227.

Fineman, Howard, and Evan Thomas. "Saddam and Bush: The Words of War." *Newsweek,* 21 January 1991, 37.

Fischer, Frank, and John Forester, eds. *The Argumentative Turn in Policy Analysis and Planning.* Durham, N.C.: Duke University Press, 1993.

Fishkin, James S. *Democracy and Deliberation: New Directions for Democratic Reform.* New Haven: Yale University Press, 1991.

Forceville, Charles F. *Pictorial Metaphor in Advertising.* London: Routledge and Kegan Paul, 1996.

"Fort Hood Troops Head for Gulf; Secretary to Confer with Allies." *Fort Worth Star-Telegram,* 14 September 1991, 1.

Foucault, Michel. *The Foucault Effect: Studies in Governmentality.* Edited by Graham Burchell, Colin Gordon, and Peter Miller. Chicago: University of Chicago Press, 1991.

———. *The History of Sexuality.* Vol. 1, *An Introduction.* New York: Vintage, 1980.

Freeman, J. "TV's Desert Fox Thinks Up a Storm." *San Diego Union-Tribune,* 29 March 1991, E6.

Friedman, Martin, et al. *Visions of America: Landscape as Metaphor in the Late Twentieth Century.* Denver: Denver Art Museum, 1994.

Friedman, Thomas L. *The Lexus and the Olive Tree.* New York: Anchor Books, 2000.

———. *The Lexus and the Olive Tree.* New York: Farrar, Straus and Giroux, 1999.

———. "Mideast Talks: Peace Might Be an Incidental Result." *New York Times,* 24 July 1991, A8.

Fritzsche, Peter. "Social Stress: A New Approach to Explain Xenophobia." Paper presented at the eighth conference of the Dutch Society for Political Psychology, Amsterdam, 1984.

Gaddis, John Lewis. *The United States and the End of the Cold War: Implications, Reconsiderations, Provocations.* New York: Oxford University Press, 1992.

Gage, John T. "The Reasoned Thesis: The E-word and Argumentative Writing as a Process of Inquiry." In *Argument Revisited; Argument Redefined: Negotiating Meaning in the Composition Classroom,* ed. Barbara Emmel, Paula Resch, and Deborah Tenney, 3–18. Thousand Oaks, Calif.: Sage, 1996.

Gannon, Martin J., ed. *Cultural Metaphors.* Thousand Oaks, Calif.: Sage, 2001.

———. *Understanding Global Cultures: Metaphorical Journeys through 23 Nations.* Abridged. Thousand Oaks, Calif.: Sage, 2001.

Garrison, Jean A. *Games Advisors Play: Foreign Policy in the Nixon and Carter Administrations.* College Station: Texas A&M University Press, 1999.

Gastil, John. "Undemocratic Discourse: A Review of Theory and Research on Political Discourse." *Discourse and Society* 3, no. 4 (1992): 469–500.

Gates, Bill. *The Road Ahead.* New York: Penguin, 1996.

Gatherer, Derek. "Why the 'Thought Contagion' Metaphor Is Retarding the Progress of Memetics." *Journal of Memetics: Evolutionary Models of Information Transmission* 2 (1998), http://jom-emit.cfpm.org/1998/v012/gatherer_d.html, accessed 8 July 2004.

Gaus, Helmut. *Menselijk Gedrag in Perioden Van Langdurige Economische Recessie: Een Schets* (Human behavior during long-term economic recession). Malle, Belgium: De Sikkel, 1981.

Geddes, Barbara. "What Do We Know about Democratization after Twenty Years?" *Annual Review of Political Science* 2 (1999): 115–44.

Gelb, Leslie H. "A New Mideast Balance." *New York Times,* 6 March 1991, A25.

George, Alexander L., and Juliette L. George. *Woodrow Wilson and Colonel House.* New York: Dover Publications, 1956.

Gergen, Kenneth. *The Saturated Self: Dilemmas of Identity in Contemporary Life.* New York: Basic Books, 1991.

Gerhart, Mary, and Allan Russell. *Metaphoric Process: The Creation of Scientific and Religious Understanding.* Fort Worth: Texas Christian University Press, 1984.

Gerstenmaier, Jochen, and Heinz Mandl. "Constructivism in Cognitive Psychology." In *International Encyclopedia of the Social and Behavioral Sciences,* edited by Neil J. Smelser and Paul B. Baltes, 4:2654–59. Amsterdam: Elsevier, 2001.

Getty, J. Arch, and Oleg V. Naumov. *The Road to Terror: Stalin and the Self-destruction of the Bolsheviks, 1932–1939.* With translations by Benjamin Sher. New Haven: Yale University Press, 1999.

Gholz, Eugene, Daryl G. Press, and Harvey M. Sapolsky. "Come Home America—The Strategy of Restraint in the Face of Temptation." *International Security* 21, no. 4 (1997): 5–48.

Gianos, Phillip L. *Political Behavior: Metaphors and Models of American Politics.* Pacific Palisades, Calif.: Palisades Publishers, 1982.

Gibbs, Raymond W., and Gerard J. Steen, eds. *Metaphor in Cognitive Linguistics.* Amsterdam: Benjamins, 1999.

Gil, José. *Metamorphoses of the Body.* Minneapolis: University of Minnesota Press, 1998.

Gill, Jerry H. *Wittgenstein and Metaphor.* Atlantic Heights, N.J.: Humanities Press, 1996.

Gilroy, Paul. *Against Race: Imagining Political Culture beyond the Color Line.* Cambridge, Mass.: Belknap Press, 2000.

Gineste, Marie-Dominique, Bipin Indurkhya, and Veronique Scart. "Emergence of Features in Metaphor Comprehension." *Metaphor and Symbol* 15 (2000): 117–36.

Givon, Talmy. *Mind, Code, and Context: Essays in Pragmatics.* Hillsdale, N.J.: Lawrence Erlbaum Associates, 1989.

Glad, Betty. *Jimmy Carter: In Search of the Great White House.* New York: W. W. Norton, 1980.

Glad, Betty, and Charles S. Taber. "Images, Learning, and the Decision to Use Force: The Domino Theory of the United States." In *Psychological Dimensions of War,* edited by Betty Glad. Beverly Hills, Calif.: Sage, 1990.

Glad, Betty, and Brian Whitmore. "Jimmy Carter and the Soviet Invasion of Afghanistan: A Psychological Perspective." In *Politics and Psychology: Contemporary Psychodynamic Perspectives,* edited by Joan Offerman-Zuckerberg. New York: Plenum Press, 1991.

Glicksohn, Joseph, Susan Kraemer, and Osnat Yisraeli. "A Note on Metaphoric Thinking and Ideational Fluency." *Metaphor and Symbolic Activity* 8 (1993): 67–71.

Glucksburg, Sam (with a contribution by Matthew S. McGlone). *Understanding Figurative Language: From Metaphors to Idioms.* New York: Oxford University Press, 2001.

Glucksberg, Sam, and Keysar Boaz. "How Metaphor Works." In *Metaphor and Thought*, 2d ed., edited by Andrew Ortony, 401–24. Cambridge: Cambridge University Press, 1993.

Goatly, Andrew. *The Language of Metaphors*. London: Routledge, 1997.

Goldberg, Philip. *The Babinski Reflex: And 70 Other Useful and Amusing Metaphors from Science, Psychology, Business, Sports, and Everyday Life*. Los Angeles: J. P. Tarcher; New York: St. Martin's Press, 1990.

Golden, James F., Goodwin F. Berquist, and William E. Coleman. *The Rhetoric of Western Thought*. 7th ed. Dubuque, Iowa: Kendall/Hunt, 2000.

Goldhagen, Daniel. *Hitler's Willing Executioners: Ordinary Germans and the Holocaust*. New York: Knopf, 1996.

Goldstein, Judith, and Robert O. Keohane, eds. *Ideas and Foreign Policy: Beliefs, Institutions, and Political Change*. Ithaca, N.Y.: Cornell University Press, 1993.

González Manet, Enrique. *The Hidden War of Information*. Translated by Laurien Alexandre. Norwood, N.J.: Ablex, 1988.

Goodnight, G. Thomas. "The Personal, Technical, and Public Spheres of Argument: A Speculative Inquiry into the Art of Public Deliberation." In *Contemporary Rhetorical Theory: A Reader*, edited by John Louis Lucaites, Celeste Michelle Condit, and Sally Caudill, 251–64. New York: Guilford, 1999.

Gordon, William. *The Metaphorical Way*. Cambridge, UK: Porpoise Books, 1971.

Gore, Al, Jr. *Earth in the Balance: Ecology and the Human Spirit*. Boston: Houghton Mifflin, 1992.

Gozzi, Raymond, Jr. *The Power of Metaphor in the Age of Electronic Media*. Hampton Press Communication Series. Cresskill, N.J.: Hampton Press, 1999.

Graber, Doris. *Verbal Behavior and Politics*. Chicago: University of Illinois Press, 1976.

Graesser, Arthur C., Jeffrey S. Mio, and Kevin Millis. "Metaphors in Persuasive Communication." In *Models of Literary Understanding*, vol. 13, edited by Dietrich Meutsch, 131–54. Amsterdam: Elsevier, 1988.

Gramsci, Antonio. *Selections of the Prison Notebooks*. Edited by Quintin Hoare and Geoffrey N. Smith. New York: International Publishers, 1971.

Grant, A. J. "Vico and Bultmann on Myth: The Problem with Demythologizing." *Rhetoric Society Quarterly* 30, no. 4 (fall 2000): 49–82.

Grant, David. "Metaphors and Paradigms in Organizations." In *International Encyclopedia of the Social and Behavioral Sciences*, edited by Neil J. Smelser and Paul B. Baltes, Vol. 16, 10960–65. Amsterdam: Elsevier, 2001.

Grant, Rebecca, and Kathleen Newland, eds. *Gender and International Relations*. Bloomington: Indiana University Press, 1991.

Green, David. *Language and Politics in America: Shaping Political Consciousness from McKinley to Reagan*. Ithaca, N.Y.: Cornell University Press, 1987.

Green, Philip. *Deadly Logic: The Theory of Nuclear Deterrence*. New York: Schocken, 1968.

Greenfield, James. *The Real Campaign*. New York: Summit, 1982

Greenway, H. D. S. "Attack Hits Nerve in Jittery Alliance." *Boston Globe*, 14 February 1991, 1.

Greider, William. *One World, Ready or Not: The Manic Logic of Global Capitalism*. New York: Simon and Schuster, 1997.

Greimas, Algirdas J. *On Meaning: Selected Writings in Semiotic Theory*. Minneapolis: University of Minnesota Press, 1987.

Gresson, Aaron D. "Transitional Metaphors and the Political Psychology of Identity Maintenance." In *Cognition and Symbolic Structures: The Psychology of Metaphoric Transformation*, edited by Robert E. Haskell, 163–85. Norwood, N.J.: Ablex Publishing Corporation, 1987.

Groenendyk, Kathi L. "The Importance of Vision: Persuasion and the Picturesque." *Rhetoric Society Quarterly* 30, no. 1 (winter 2000): 9–28.

Gugiotta, Guy, and Caryle Murphy. "Warplanes Roar Off in Darkness in 'Desert Storm.'" *Washington Post*, 17 January 1991, A1.

Gutmann, Amy, and Dennis Thompson. *Democracy and Disagreement*. Cambridge, Mass.: Belknap Press, 1996.

Hacker, Jacob S. *The Road to Nowhere: The Genesis of President Clinton's Plan for Health Security*. Princeton: Princeton University Press, 1997.

Hacker, Kenneth L. "Political Linguistic Discourse Analysis: Analyzing the Relationships of Power and Language." In *The Theory and Practice of Political Communication Research*, edited by Mary E. Stuckey, 28–55. Albany: SUNY Press, 1996.

Hahn, Dan F. *Political Communication: Rhetoric, Government, and Citizens*. 2d ed. State College, Penn.: Strata, 2003.

Hall, Donald. "The Body Politic." In *Exiles and Marriages*. New York: Viking, 1955, 79.

Hallin, Daniel C. "Images of the Vietnam and the Persian Gulf Wars in U.S. Television." In *Seeing through the Media: The Persian Gulf War*, edited by Susan Jeffords and Lauren Rabinovitz, 45–57. New Brunswick, N.J.: Rutgers University Press, 1994.

Halton, Eugene. *Bereft of Reason: On the Decline of Social Thought and Prospects for Its Renewal*. Chicago: University of Chicago Press, 1995.

Hanchette, J. "Gen. Dugan Is Latest in Line of Top Brass Booted for Comments." Gannett News Service, 19 September 1990.

Hankins, Sarah Russell. "Archetypal Alloy: Reagan's Rhetorical Image." *Central States Speech Journal* 34 (1983): 33–43.

Hanson, Russell L. *The Democratic Imagination in America: Conversations with Our Past.* Princeton: Princeton University Press, 1985.

Hardaway, Francine. "Foul Play: Sports Metaphors as Public Doublespeak." In *Sport Inside Out: Readings in Literature and Philosophy,* edited by David L. Vanderwerken and Spencer K. Wertz, 576–82. Fort Worth: Texas Christian University Press, 1985.

Hardin, Garrett. "Living on a Lifeboat." In *Managing the Commons,* edited by Garrett Hardin and John Baden. New York: Freeman, 1977.

Hargrove, Erwin C. *Jimmy Carter as President: Leadership and the Politics of the Public Good.* Baton Rouge: Louisiana State University Press, 1988.

Hariman, Robert. "Allegory and Democratic Public Culture in the Postmodern Era." *Philosophy and Rhetoric* 35 (2002): 267–96.

_____. *Political Style.* Chicago: University of Chicago Press, 1995.

Hariman, Robert, and John Louis Lucaites. "Dissent and Emotional Management in a Liberal-Democratic Society: The Kent State Iconic Photograph." *Rhetoric Society Quarterly* 31, no. 3 (2001): 5–31.

_____. "Performing Civic Identity: The Iconic Photograph of the Flag Raising on Iwo Jima." *Quarterly Journal of Speech* 88, no. 4 (2002): 363–92.

Harold, Christine L. "The Green Virus: Purity and Contamination in Ralph Nader's 2000 Presidential Campaign." *Rhetoric & Public Affairs* 4, no. 4 (winter 2001): 581–603.

Harpine, William D. "Bryan's 'A Cross of Gold': The Rhetoric of Polarization at the 1896 Democratic Convention." *Quarterly Journal of Speech* 87, no. 3 (2001): 303–25.

Harris, Jonathan G. *Foreign Bodies and the Body Politic: Discourses of Social Pathology in Early Modern England.* Cambridge: Cambridge University Press, 1988.

Hart, Roderick P., Sharon E. Jarvis, William P. Jennings, and Deborah Smith-Howell. *Political Keywords: American Language at Work.* New York: Oxford University Press, forthcoming.

Hart, Roderick P., and Courtney L. Dillard. "Deliberative Genre." In *Encyclopedia of Rhetoric,* edited by Thomas O. Sloane, 209–17. Oxford: Oxford University Press, 2001.

Harvey, David. *The Condition of Postmodernity.* Oxford: Blackwell, 1989.

Harvey, Oscar Jewel, David E. Hunt, and Harold M. Schroder. *Conceptual Systems and Personality Organization.* New York: Wiley, 1961.

Haskell, Robert E., ed. *Cognition and Symbolic Structures: The Psychology of Metaphoric Transformation*. Norwood, N.J.: Ablex Publishing Corporation, 1987.

Hatzenbuehler, Ronald L., and Robert L. Ivie. *Congress Declares War: Rhetoric, Leadership, and Partisanship in the Early Republic*. Kent, Ohio: Kent State University Press, 1983.

Hauser, Gerard A. *Introduction to Rhetorical Theory*. 2d ed. Prospect Heights, Ill.: Waveland, 2002.

Hemmer, Christopher. "Historical Analogies and the Definition of Interests: The Iranian Hostage Crisis and Ronald Reagan's Policy toward the Hostages in Lebanon." *Political Psychology* 20, no. 2 (1999): 267–89.

———. *Which Lessons Matter?: American Foreign Policy Decision Making in the Middle East, 1979–1987*. Albany: SUNY Press, 2000.

Henriksen, Margot A. *Dr. Strangelove's America: Society and Culture in the Atomic Age*. Berkeley and Los Angeles: University of California Press, 1997.

Heradstveit, Daniel, and G. Matt Bonham. "Attribution Theory and Arab Images of the Gulf War." *Political Psychology* 17, no. 2 (1996): 271–92.

Herman, Andrew, and Thomas Swiss, eds. *The World Wide Web and Contemporary Cultural Theory: Magic, Metaphor, and Power*. New York: Routledge, 2000.

Herman, Vimala, ed. *Cognitive Linguistics and the Verbal Arts: From Metaphor to Blending*. Cambridge: Cambridge University Press, 2004.

Herrmann, Richard K., James F. Voss, Tonya Y. E. Schooler, and Joseph Ciarrochi. "Images in International Relations: An Experimental Test of Cognitive Schemata." *International Studies Quarterly* 41, no. 3 (1997): 403–35.

Higgins, Edward Tony, and G. R. Semin. "Communication and Social Psychology." In *International Encyclopedia of the Social and Behavioral Sciences*, edited by Neil J. Smelser and Paul B. Baltes, Vol. 4, 2296–99. Amsterdam: Elsevier, 2001.

Hilgartner, Stephen, Richard C. Bell, and Rory O'Connor. *Nukespeak: The Selling of Nuclear Technology in America*. Harmondsworth, U.K., and New York: Penguin, 1982.

Hinds, Lynn B., and Theodore O. Windt. *The Cold War as Rhetoric: The Beginnings, 1945–1950*. New York: Praeger, 1991.

Hobbes, Thomas. *Leviathan*. Edited by J. C. A. Gaskin. Oxford: Oxford University Press, 1998.

Hogan, J. Michael, ed. *Rhetoric and Community: Studies in Unity and Fragmentation*. Columbia: University of South Carolina Press, 1998.

Holman, Valerie, and Debra Kelly, eds. *France at War in the Twentieth Century: Propaganda, Myth, and Metaphor*. New York: Berghahn Books, 2000.

Holyoak, Keith J., and Paul Thagard. *Mental Leaps: Analogy in Creative Thought*. Cambridge, Mass.: MIT Press, 1995.

Honig, Jan Willem, and Norbert Both. *Srebrenica: Record of a War Crime*. London: Penguin Books, 1996.

Hoopes, Timothy. *The Limits of Intervention: An Inside Account of How the Johnson Policy of Escalation in Vietnam Was Reversed*. New York: McKay, 1969.

Horner, Avril. *Landscapes of Desire: Metaphors in Modern Women's Fiction*. New York: Harvester Wheatsheaf, 1990.

Hostetler, Michael J. "The Enigmatic Ends of Rhetoric: Churchill's Fulton Address as Great Art and Failed Persuasion." *Quarterly Journal of Speech* 83, no. 4 (1997): 416–28.

Howe, Nicholas. "Metaphor in Contemporary American Political Discourse." *Metaphor and Symbolic Activity* 3 (1988): 87–104.

Hudson, Valerie M. *Artificial Intelligence and International Politics*. Boulder: Westview, 1991.

Hunt, Ben W. *Getting to War: Predicting International Conflict with Mass Media Indicators*. Ann Arbor: University of Michigan Press, 1997.

Hunt, Michael. *Ideology and U.S. Foreign Policy*. New Haven: Yale University Press, 1987.

Huntington, Samuel. *The Clash of Civilizations and the Remaking of World Order*. New York: Simon and Schuster, 1996.

Huntley, Wade L. "Kant's Third Image: Systemic Sources of the Liberal Peace." *International Studies Quarterly* 40, no. 1 (1996): 45–76.

Hybel, Alex. *How Leaders Reason*. New York: Basil Blackwell, 1990.

Ignatieff, Michael. *Virtual War: Kosovo and beyond*. New York: Picador, 2000.

Iklé, Fred C. *Every War Must End*. New York: Columbia University Press, 1971.

Indurkhya, Bipin. "Modes of Metaphor." *Metaphor and Symbolic Activity* 6 (1991): 1–27.

———. "The Thesis That All Knowledge Is Metaphorical and Meanings of Metaphor." *Metaphor and Symbolic Activity* 9 (1994): 61–73.

Ivie, Robert L. "Cold War Motives and the Rhetorical Metaphor: A Framework for Criticism." In *Cold War Rhetoric: Strategy, Metaphor, and Ideology*, by Martin J. Medhurst, Robert L. Ivie, Philip Wander, and Robert L. Scott, 71–79. East Lansing: Michigan State University Press, 1997.

———. "Distempered Demos: Myth, Metaphor, and U.S. Political Culture." In *Myth: A New Symposium*, Edited by Gregory A. Schrempp and William F. Hansen, 165–79. Bloomington: Indiana University Press, 2002.

———. "Fire, Flood, and Red Fever: Motivating Metaphors of Global Emergency in the Truman Doctrine Speech." *Presidential Studies Quarterly* 29 (September 1999): 570–91.

———. "The Ideology of Freedom's 'Fragility' in American Foreign Policy Argument." *Journal of the American Forensic Association* 24 (1986): 91–105.

———. "Images of Savagery in American Justifications for War." *Communication Monographs* 47 (1980): 279–94.

———. "Literalizing the Metaphor of Soviet Savagery: President Truman's Plain Style." *Southern Speech Communication Journal* 51 (1986): 91–105.

———. "Metaphor and Motive in the Johnson Administration's Vietnam War Rhetoric." In *Texts in Context: Critical Dialogues on Significant Episodes in American Political Rhetoric.* Edited by Michael C. Leff and Fred J. Kauffeld, 121–41. Davis, Calif.: Hermagoras Press, 1989.

———. "Metaphor and the Rhetorical Invention of Cold War 'Idealists.'" *Communication Monographs* 54 (1987): 165–82.

———. "The Metaphor of Force in Prowar Discourse: The Case of 1812." *Quarterly Journal of Speech* 68 (1982): 240–53.

———. "A New Democratic World Order?" In *Critical Reflections on the Cold War: Linking Rhetoric and History.* Edited by Martin J. Medhurst and H. W. Brands. College Station: Texas A&M University Press, 2000.

———. "Realism Masking Fear: George Kennan's Political Rhetoric." In *Post-realism: The Rhetorical Turn in International Relations.* Edited by Francis A. Beer and Robert Hariman, 55–74. East Lansing: Michigan State University Press, 1996.

———. "Speaking 'Common Sense' about the Soviet Threat: Reagan's Rhetorical Stance." *Western Journal of Speech Communication* 48 (1984): 39–50.

———. "Tragic Fear and the Rhetorical Presidency: Combating Evil in the Persian Gulf." In *Beyond the Rhetorical Presidency.* Edited by Martin J. Medhurst, 153–78. College Station: Texas A&M University Press, 1996.

Iyengar, Shanto. *Is Anyone Responsible? How Television Frames Political Issues.* Chicago: University of Chicago Press, 1991.

Iyengar, Shanto, and Donald R. Kinder. *News That Matters: Television and American Opinion.* Chicago: University of Chicago Press, 1987.

Jackendoff, Ray. *Languages of the Mind: Essays on Mental Representation.* Cambridge, Mass.: MIT Press, 1993.

Jameson, Fredric. *Postmodernism, or The Cultural Logic of Late Capitalism.* Durham, N.C.: Duke University Press, 1991.

Jamieson, G. Harry. *Communication and Persuasion.* London: Croom Helm, 1985.

Jamieson, Kathleen Hall. "The Metaphoric Cluster in the Rhetoric of Pope Paul VI and Edmund G. Brown, Jr." *Quarterly Journal of Speech* 66 (1980): 51–72.

Jamieson, Kathleen Hall, and Paul Waldman. *The Press Effect: Politicians, Journalists, and the Stories That Shape the Political World.* Oxford: Oxford University Press, 2003.

Jamieson, Kim. *Communication and Persuasion.* London: Croom Helm, 1985.

Jansen, Sue Curry, and Don Sabo. "The Sport/War Metaphor: Hegemonic Masculinity, the Persian Gulf War, and the New World Order." *Sociology of Sport Journal* 11 (1994): 1–17.

Jeffords, Susan. *The Remasculinization of America: Gender and the Vietnam War.* Bloomington: Indiana University Press, 1989.

Jensen, Kenneth M., ed. *Origins of the Cold War: The Novikov, Kennan, and Roberts Long Telegrams of 1946.* Washington, D.C.: U.S. Institute of Peace, 1991.

Jervis, Robert. *The Logic of Images in International Relations.* New York: Columbia University Press, 1989.

Johnson, Joel T., and Shelley E. Taylor. "The Effect of Metaphor on Political Attitudes." *Basic and Applied Social Psychology* 2 (1981): 305–16.

Johnson, Mark. *The Body in the Mind: The Bodily Basis of Meaning, Imagination and Reason.* Chicago: University of Chicago Press, 1990.

Johnston, David. *The Rhetoric of Leviathan: Thomas Hobbes and the Politics of Cultural Transformation.* Princeton: Princeton University Press, 1986.

Jolidon, Laurence. "U.S. Pilots Are Confident Iraqis No Match in Air." *USA Today,* 15 January 1991, 6A.

Jones, Gwyneth. "The Neuroscience of Cyberspace: New Metaphors for the Self and Its Boundaries." In *The Governance of Cyberspace: Politics, Technology and Global Restructuring.* Edited by Brian D. Loader, 46–63. London: Routledge, 1997.

Jordan, Emma Coleman. *Lynching: The Dark Metaphor.* New York: Basic Books, 1999.

Jorgensen-Earp, Cheryl R. *"The Transfiguring Sword": The Just War of the Women's Social and Political Union.* Tuscaloosa: University of Alabama Press, 1997.

Kagan, Robert. *Of Paradise and Power: America vs. Europe in the New World Order.* New York: Knopf, 2003.

Kahn, Herman. *On Escalation: Metaphors and Scenarios.* Baltimore: Penguin, 1968.

Kamalipour, Yahya. *Images of the U.S. around the World: A Multicultural Perspective.* Albany: SUNY Press, 1999.

Kaplan, Robert. *The Ends of the Earth*. New York: Random House, 1996.

Karnow, Stanley. *Vietnam: A History*. New York: Viking Press, 1983.

Karvonen, Lauri. "Political Language: Do Women Make a Difference?" *Innovation* 7, no. 4 (1994): 441–52.

Keegan, John. *The Mask of Command*. New York: Penguin Books, 1988.

Keen, Sam. *Faces of the Enemy: Reflections of the Hostile Imagination*. San Francisco: Harper and Row, 1986.

Keith, William, ed. "Deliberative Democracy." Special issue, *Quarterly Journal of Speech* 5, no. 2 (2002).

Kell, Carl L., and L. Raymond Camp. *In the Name of the Father: The Rhetoric of the New Southern Baptist Convention*. Carbondale: Southern Illinois University Press, 1999.

Kellner, Douglas. *The Persian Gulf TV War*. Boulder: Westview, 1992.

Kelly, Kevin. *Out of Control: The Rise of Neo-biological Civilization*. Reading, Mass.: Addison-Wesley, 1994.

Kennan, George F. "The Sources of Soviet Conduct." *Foreign Affair* 25 (July 1947): 566–82.

Kennedy, George A. *Aristotle on Rhetoric: A Theory of Civic Discourse*. Oxford: Oxford University Press, 1991.

———. "Classical Rhetoric." In *Encyclopedia of Rhetoric*. Edited by Thomas O. Sloane, 92–115. Oxford: Oxford University Press, 2001.

———. "Rhetoric." In *International Encyclopedia of the Social and Behavioral Sciences*. Edited by Neil J. Smelser and Paul B. Baltes, 13317–23. Amsterdam: Elsevier, 2001

Kennedy, Paul. *Preparing for the Twenty-first Century*. New York: Random House, 1993.

Kennedy, Victor. "The Computational Metaphor of Mind: More Bugs in the Program." *Metaphor and Symbol* 14, no. 4 (1999): 281–92.

———. "Intended Tropes and Unintended Metatropes in Reporting on the War in Kosovo." *Metaphor and Symbol* 15, no. 4 (2000): 253–65.

———. "Metaphors in the News—Introduction." *Metaphor and Symbol* 15, no. 4 (2000): 209–11.

Kennedy, Victor, and John Kennedy. "Metaphor and Visual Rhetoric." Special issue, *Metaphor and Symbolic Activity* 8 (1993): 149–255.

Kenworthy, Eldon. *America/Americas: Myth in the Making of U.S. Policy toward Latin America*. University Park: Penn State University Press, 1995.

———. "Selling the Policy." In *Reagan versus the Sandinistas*. Edited by Thomas Walker, 159–81. Boulder: Westview, 1987.

Kenworthy, Tom. "Hill Democrats Mute Criticism of Bush Actions; Reluctance to Question President Said to Be a Result of Political, Historical Factors." *Washington Post,* 21 February 1991, A23.

Khong, Yuen Foong. *Analogies at War: Korea, Munich, Dien Bien Phu, and the Vietnam Decisions of 1965.* Princeton: Princeton University Press, 1992.

Kilpatrick, James J. "Let's Separate Hawks from Chickens on Iraq." *Atlanta Journal and Constitution,* 28 August 1992, A12.

Kinder, Donald, and Adam Berinsky. "Making Sense of Political Issues through Frames." *The Political Psychologist* 4, no. 2 (1999): 3–8.

King, Gary, Robert O. Keohane, and Sidney Verba. *Designing Social Inquiry: Scientific Inference in Qualitative Research.* Princeton: Princeton University Press, 1994.

King, James R. "Models as Metaphors." *Metaphor and Symbolic Activity* 6 (1991): 103–18.

Kinney, Katherine. *Friendly Fire: American Images of the Vietnam War.* Oxford: Oxford University Press, 2000.

Kintsch, Walter. *Comprehension: A Paradigm for Cognition.* Cambridge: Cambridge University Press, 1998.

Kintsch, Walter, and Anita R. Bowles. "Metaphor Comprehension: What Makes a Metaphor Difficult to Understand?" *Metaphor and Symbol* 17, no. 4 (2002): 249–63.

Kirkpatrick, Jeanne. "Dictatorships and Double Standards." *Commentary* 68 (November 1979).

Kissinger, Henry. *Diplomacy.* New York: Simon and Schuster, 1994.

Kittay, Eva Feder. "Metaphor as Rearranging the Furniture of the Mind: A Reply to Donald Davidson's 'What Metaphors Mean.'" In *From a Metaphorical Point of View: A Multidisciplinary Approach to the Cognitive Content of Metaphor.* Edited by Zdravko Radman, 73–116. New York: W. de Gruyter, 1995.

_____. *Metaphor: Its Cognitive Force and Linguistic Structure.* Oxford: Clarendon Press, 1987.

Koeller, Wilhelm. Semiotik und Metapher. Untersuchungen zur grammatischen Struktur und der kommunikativen Funktion von Metaphern. [Semiotics and Metaphors. Study of the Grammatical Structure and the Communication Function of Metaphors]. *Studien zur Allgemeinen Vergleich in der Literatur-wissenschaft, 10.* Fuer den Drueck ueberarbeitete Kasseler Dissertation. [*Comparative Literature Studies, 10.* Revised Doctoral Thesis from Kassel]. Sturrgart: Metzlersche Verlagsbuchhandlung, 1975.

Kofman, Sarah. *Nietzsche and Metaphor.* Translated by Duncan Large. London: Athlone, 1993.

Koller, Veronika. "A Shotgun Wedding: Co-occurrence of War and Marriage Metaphors in Mergers and Acquisitions Discourse." *Metaphor and Symbol* 17, no. 3 (2002): 179–203.

Kondracke, Morton. "Party Pooper: The Democrats and the War." *New Republic,* 25 March 1991, 10.

Kos, Ivan. "Fearful Leadership: A Comparison of Communist and Post-Communist Leadership in the former Yugoslavia." Paper presented at the Eight Conference of the Dutch Society for Political Psychology. Amsterdam, the Netherlands, 1984.

Kövecses, Zoltán. *Metaphor and Emotion: Language, Culture, and Body in Human Feeling.* Cambridge: Cambridge University Press, 2000.

———. "Tocqueville's Passionate 'Beast': A Linguistic Analysis of the Concept of American Democracy." *Metaphor and Symbolic Activity* 9 (1994): 113–33.

Krasner, Stephen. *Sovereignty: Organized Hypocrisy.* Princeton: Princeton University Press, 1999.

Kreuz, Roger J., Debra L. Long, and Mary B. Church. "On Being Ironic: Pragmatic and Mnemonic Implications." *Metaphor and Symbolic Activity* 6 (1991): 149–62.

Krug, Linda T. *Presidential Perspectives on Space Exploration: Guiding Metaphors from Eisenhower to Bush.* New York: Praeger, 1991.

Kull, Steven. *Minds at War: Nuclear Reality and the Inner Conflicts of Defense Policymakers.* New York: Basic Books, 1988.

Kurkjian, Stephen. "Bush Plays Down Potential for War; President Seeks to Clarify Bellicose Words." *Boston Globe,* 2 November 1990, 1.

Kuusisto, Riikka. "The Fairy Tale and the Tragedy? The Western Metaphors of War in the Persian Gulf and Bosnia." In *Argument in a Time of Change: Definitions, Frameworks, and Critiques,* edited by James F. Klumpp, 297–303. Annandale, Va.: National Communication Association, 1997.

———. "Heroic Tale, Game, and Business Deal? Western Metaphors in Action in Kosovo." *Quarterly Journal of Speech* 88, no. 1 (2002): 50–68.

Kuypers, Jim A. *Presidential Crisis Rhetoric and the Press in the Post–Cold War World.* Westport, Conn.: Praeger, 1997.

Lacity, Mary C., et al. *Information Outsourcing: Myths, Metaphors, and Realities.* New York: John Wiley and Sons, 1995.

Laffey, Mark, and Jutta Weldes. "Beyond Belief: Ideas and Symbolic Technologies in the Study of International Relations." *European Journal of International Relations* 3, no. 2 (1997): 193–237.

Lakoff, George. "The Contemporary Theory of Metaphor." In *Metaphor and Thought*, 2d ed., edited by Anthony Ortony, 202–51. Cambridge: Cambridge University Press, 1993.

――――. "Master Metaphor List." http://cogsci.berkeley.edu/, accessed 21 February 2004.

――――. "Metaphor and War: The Metaphor System Used to Justify War in the Gulf." *Peace Research* 23 (1991): 25–32 (http://lists.village .virginia.edu/sixties/HTML_docs/Texts/Scholarly/Lakoff_Gulf_Metaphor _1.html), accessed 21 February 2004.

――――. "Metaphor, Morality, and Politics, or Why Conservatives Have Left Liberals in the Dust." *Social Research* 62, no. 2 (summer 1995): 177–213.

――――. "Metaphors of War." *Propaganda Review* 8 (fall 1991): 18–21, 54–59.

――――. *Moral Politics: What Conservatives Know That Liberals Don't.* Chicago: University of Chicago Press, 1995.

――――. *Women, Fire and Dangerous Things.* Chicago: Chicago University Press, 1987.

Lakoff, George, and Mark Johnson. *Metaphors We Live By.* Chicago: University of Chicago Press, 1980.

――――. *Philosophy in the Flesh: The Embodied Mind and Its Challenge to Western Thought.* New York: Basic Books, 1999.

Lakoff, George, and Rafael Nuñez. *Where Mathematics Comes From: How the Embodied Mind Brings Mathematics into Being.* New York: Basic Books, 2001.

Lakoff, George, and Mark Turner. *More Than Cool Reason: A Field Guide to Poetic Metaphor.* Chicago: University of Chicago Press, 1989.

Lakoff, Robin Tolmach. *Talking Power: The Politics of Language.* New York: Basic Books, 1989.

――――. *Talking Power: The Politics of Language in Our Lives.* New York: Basic Books, 1990.

Lambourn, David. "Metaphor and Its Role in Social Thought: History of the Concept." In *Encyclopedia of the Social and Behavioral Sciences*, edited by Neil J. Smelser and Paul B. Baltes, 14:9738–43. Amsterdam: Elsevier, 2001.

Lapham, Lewis H. "Trained Seals and Sitting Ducks." In *The Media and the Gulf War*, edited by Hedrick Smith, 256–63. Washington, D.C.: Seven Locks Press, 1992.

Larsen, Peter. "Rhetorical Analysis." In *International Encyclopedia of the Social and Behavioral Sciences*, edited by Neil J. Smelser and Paul B. Baltes, 13323–27. Amsterdam: Elsevier, 2001.

Larson, Deborah. *The Origins of Containment: A Psychological Explanation.* Princeton: Princeton University Press, 1985.

Lasky, Melvin J. *Utopia and Revolution: On the Origins of a Metaphor, or Some Illustrations of the Problem of Political Temperament and Intellectual Climate and How Ideas, Ideals, and Ideologies Have Been Historically Related.* Chicago: University of Chicago Press, 1985.

Lasswell, Harold D. "Style and the Language of Politics." In *The Language of Politics: Studies in Quantitative Semantics,* edited by Harold D. Lasswell Nathan Leites and associates, 3–19. Cambridge Mass: MIT Press, 1949.

———. *World Politics and Personal Insecurity.* New York: Free Press, 1965.

Lasswell, Harold D., Nathan Leites and associates. *The Language of Politics: Studies of Quantitative Semantics.* Cambridge Mass: MIT PRess: G. W. Stewart, 1949.

Lasswell, Harold D., Daniel Lerner, and Ithiel De Sola Pool, eds. *The Comparative Study of Symbols: An Introduction.* Stanford, Calif.: Stanford University Press, 1952.

Latour, Bruno. *Pandora's Hope: Essays on the Reality of Science Studies.* Cambridge: Harvard University Press, 1999.

———. *Science in Action: How to Follow Scientists and Engineers through Society.* Cambridge: Harvard University Press, 1987.

Lay, Mary M., Laura J. Gurak, Clare Gravon, and Cynthia Myntti, eds. *Body Talk: Rhetoric, Technology, Reproduction.* Madison: University of Wisconsin Press, 2000.

Leary, David, ed. *Metaphors in the History of Psychology.* Cambridge Studies in the History of Psychology. Cambridge: Cambridge University Press, 1990.

Lebow, Richard Ned, and Janice Gross Stein. "Afghanistan, Carter, and Foreign Policy Change: The Limits of Cognitive Models." In *Order, Diplomacy, Force, and Leadership: Essays in Honor of Alexander George,* edited by Dan Caldwell and Timothy J. McKeown. Boulder: Westview, 1993.

Leff, Michael. "Topical Invention and Metaphoric Interaction." *Southern States Communication Journal* 48 (1983): 214–29.

Lessl, Thomas M. "Gnostic Scientism and the Prohibition of Questions." *Rhetoric and Public Affairs* 5, no. 1 (2002): 133–57.

Levin, Norman G. *Woodrow Wilson and World Politics.* Oxford: Oxford University Press, 1968.

Levin, Samuel R. "Vico and the Language of the 'First Poets.'" In *Metaphoric Worlds: Conceptions of a Romantic Nature,* 106–30. New Haven: Yale University Press, 1988.

Lewin, Philip. "Affective Schemas in the Appropriation of Narrative Texts." *Metaphor and Symbolic Activity* 7 (1992): 11–34.

Lewis, Neil A. "A Word Bolsters Case for Allied Intervention." *New York Times*, 4 April 1999, http://www.nytimes.com/library/world/europe/040499kosovo-legal.html (accessed 4 April 1999).

Lin, Min. *Certainty as a Social Metaphor: The Social and Historical Production of Certainty in China and the West.* Westport, Conn.: Greenwood, 2001.

Lindgren, David T. *Trust but Verify: Imagery Analysis in the Cold War.* Annapolis, Md.: U.S. Naval Institute Press, 2000.

Linn, Ruth. "Holocaust Metaphors and Symbols in the Moral Dilemmas of Contemporary Israeli Soldiers." *Metaphor and Symbolic Activity* 6 (1991): 61–86.

Linn, Ruth, and Ilan Gur-Ze'ev. "Holocaust as Metaphor: Arab and Israeli Use of the Same Symbol." *Metaphor and Symbolic Activity* 11 (1996): 195–206.

Lipsky, Richard. "The Athleticization of Politics: The Political Implication of Sports Metaphors." *Journal of Sport and Social Issues* 3 (1979): 28–37.

———. *How We Play the Game: Why Sports Dominate American Life.* Boston: Beacon, 1981.

———. *Sportsworld: An American Dreamland.* New York: Quadrangle Books, 1975.

Litfin, Karen. *Ozone Discourses: Science and Politics in Global Environmental Cooperation.* New York: Columbia University Press, 1994.

Little, Joseph. "Analogy in Science: Where Do We Go From Here?" *Rhetoric Society Quarterly* 30, no. 1 (winter 2000): 69–92.

Lobell, Steven F. "Second Image Reversed Politics: Britain's Choice of Freer Trade or Imperial Preferences, 1903–1906, 1917–1923, 1930–1932." *International Studies Quarterly* 43, no. 4 (1999): 671–93.

Loenngren, Lennart, ed. *Chastotnyi slovar' sovremennogo russkogo iazyka.* Acta Universitatis Upsaliensis. *Studia Slavica Upsaliensa* 32 (1993).

Lucaites, John Louis, Celeste Michelle Condit, and Sally Caudill, eds. *Contemporary Rhetorical Theory: A Reader.* New York: Guilford, 1999.

Luke, Timothy W. "At the End of Nature: Cyborgs, 'Humachines,' and Environments in Postmodernity." *Environment and Planning A* 29 (1997): 1367–80.

———. "Discourses of Disintegration, Texts of Transformation: Re-reading Realism in the New World Order." *Alternatives* 18 (1993): 229–58.

———. "Governmentality and Contra-governmentality: Rethinking Sovereignty and Territoriality after the Cold War." *Political Geography* 15, nos. 6/7 (1996): 491–507.

Luke, Timothy W., and Gearoid Ó Tuathail. "On Videocameralistics: The Geopolitics of Failed States, the CNN International, and (UN) Governmentality." *Review of International Political Economy* 4 (1997): 709–33.

Luthur, Catherine A. *Press Images, National Identity and Foreign Policy.* New York: Routledge, 2002.

Lyotard, Jean François. *The Postmodern Condition: A Report on Knowledge.* Minneapolis: University of Minnesota Press, 1984.

Maasen, Sabine, and Peter Weingart. *Metaphors and the Dynamics of Knowledge.* London: Routledge, 2000.

MacAloon, John J. "An Observer's View of Sport Sociology." *Sociology of Sport Journal* 4 (1987): 103–15.

MacCormac, Earl R. *A Cognitive Theory of Metaphor.* Cambridge, Mass.: MIT/Bradford, 1985.

Maddox, Robert J. *The Unknown War with Russia: Wilson's Siberian Intervention.* San Rafael, Calif.: Presidio Press, 1977.

Madison, Christopher. "Follow the Leader." *National Journal,* 12 January 1991, 104.

Mahler, Margaret S., and Manuel Furer. *On Human Symbiosis and the Vicissitudes of Individuation.* New York: International University Press, 1968.

Mailloux, Steven. *Rhetorical Power.* Ithaca, N.Y.: Cornell University Press, 1989.

Malmkjaer, Kirsten, ed. *The Linguistics Encyclopedia.* London: Routledge, 1991.

Mandelbaum, Michael. *The Ideas That Conquered the World: Peace, Democracy, and Free Markets in the Twenty-first Century.* New York: Public Affairs, 2002.

Mann, Michael. *States, War and Capitalism: Studies in Political Sociology.* Oxford: Blackwell, 1988.

Maraniss, David. *When Pride Still Mattered: A Life of Vince Lombardi.* New York: Simon and Schuster, 1999.

Markman, Peter T., and Roberta H. Markman. *Masks of the Spirit: Image and Metaphor in Mesoamerica.* Berkeley and Los Angeles: University of California Press, 1994.

Marks, Lawrence, Robin J. Hammeal, Marc H. Bornstein, and Linda B. Smith, eds. *Perceiving Similarity and Comprehending Metaphor.* Chicago: University of Chicago, 1987.

Martin, Hans Peter, and Harald Schumann. *The Global Trap: Globalization and the Assault on Democracy and Prosperity.* London: Zed Press, 1998.

Marvin, Carolyn, and David W. Ingle. *Blood Sacrifice and the Nation: Totem Rituals and the American Flag.* Cambridge: Cambridge University Press, 1999.

Marx, Karl, and Friedrich Engels. *The German Ideology.* New York: International Publishers. 1960.

Massen, Sabine. *Metaphors and the Dynamics of Knowledge.* Routledge Studies in Social and Political Thought. New York: Routledge, 2000.

Matthews, Richard K. *If Men Were Angels: James Madison and the Heartless Empire of Reason.* Lawrence: University Press of Kansas, 1995.

———. *The Radical Politics of Thomas Jefferson: A Revisionist View.* Lawrence: University Press of Kansas, 1984.

May, Ernest R., ed. *American Cold War Strategy: Interpreting NSC68.* New York: St. Martin's Press, 1993.

———. *Lessons of the Past.* New York: Oxford University Press, 1973.

Mazlish, Bruce, and Edwin Diamond. *Jimmy Carter: A Character Portrait.* New York: Simon and Schuster, 1979.

McCarthy, Colman. "The Terrible Toll of a Gulf War." *Washington Post,* 13 January 1991, F2.

McClellan, Bill. "Remembering Those Gulfs between Wars." *St. Louis Post-Dispatch,* 27 May 1991, 3A.

McCloskey, Donald N. *The Rhetoric of Economics.* Madison: University of Wisconsin Press, 1985.

McCombs, Maxwell E., and Tony Bell. "The Agenda-Setting Role of Mass Communications." In *An Integrated Approach to Communications Theory and Research,* edited by Michael B. Salwen and Don W. Stacks, 93–110. Mahwah, N.J.: Lawrence Erlbaum Associates, 1996.

McCombs, Maxwell E., and Donald L. Shaw. "The Agenda-Setting Function of the Press." *Public Opinion Quarterly* 36 (1972): 176–87.

McGaw, Dickinson. "Governing Metaphors: The War on Drugs," *American Journal of Semiotics* 8, no. 3 (1991): 53–74.

McGhee Nelson, Elizabeth M. "The Effect of Metaphor on Group Reminiscence." *Metaphor and Symbolic Activity* 8 (1993): 297–309.

McGuire, John Michael. "Pictorial Metaphors: A Reply to Sedivy." *Metaphor and Symbol* 14, no. 4 (1999): 293–302.

McLellan, Derek S. *Cyrus Vance.* Totowa, N.J.: Rowman and Allenheld, 1985.

McLuhan, Marshal. *Understanding Media.* London: Routledge and Kegan Paul, 1964.

Mearsheimer, John J. "Back to the Future: Instability in Europe after the Cold War." *International Security* 15, no. 1 (1990): 5–57.

Medhurst, Martin J., ed. *Eisenhower's War of Words.* East Lansing: Michigan State University Press, 1994.

Medhurst, Martin J., and H. W. Brands, eds. *Critical Reflections on the Cold War—Linking Rhetoric and History.* College Station: Texas A&M University Press, 2000.

Medhurst, Martin J., Robert L. Ivie, Philip Wander, and Robert L. Scott. *Cold War Rhetoric: Strategy, Metaphor, and Ideology.* East Lansing: Michigan State University Press, 1997.

Melanson, Richard A. *Writing History and Making Policy: The Cold War, Vietnam, and Revisionism.* Lanham, Md.: University Press of America, 1983.

Metzger, David. *The Lost Cause of Rhetoric: The Relation of Rhetoric and Geometry in Aristotle and Lacan.* Carbondale: Southern Illinois University Press, 1995.

Miall, David S., ed. *Metaphor: Problems and Perspectives.* Atlantic Highlands, N.J.: Humanities Press, 1982.

Miller, Donald F. *The Reason of Metaphor: A Study in Politics.* Newbury Park, N.J.: Sage, 1992.

Miller, Eugene. "Metaphor and Political Knowledge." *American Political Science Review* 73 (1979): 160–62.

Milliken, Jennifer. "Metaphors of Prestige and Reputation in American Foreign Policy and International Realism." In *Post-realism: The Rhetorical Turn in International Relations,* edited by Francis A. Beer and Robert Hariman, 217–38. East Lansing: Michigan State University Press, 1996.

Mio, Jeffrey S. "Metaphor and Politics." *Metaphor and Symbol* 12, no. 2 (1997): 113–33.

Mio, Jeffrey S., and Arthur C. Graesser. "Humor, Language, and Metaphor." *Metaphor and Symbolic Activity* 6 (1991): 87–102.

Mio, Jeffrey S., and Albert N. Katz, eds. *Metaphor: Implications and Applications.* Mahwah, N.J.: Lawrence Erlbaum Associates, 1996.

Mio, Jeffrey S., Suzanne C. Thompson, and Geoffrey H. Givens. "The Commons Dilemma as Metaphor: Memory, Influence, and Implications for Environmental Conservation." *Metaphor and Symbolic Activity* 8 (1993): 23–42.

Mireille, Andráes. *Lacan et la question du métalangage.* Paris: Point hors ligne, 1987.

Mitchell, Gordon R. "Public Argument-Driven Security Studies." *Argumentation and Advocacy* 39 (summer 2002): 57–71.

———. "Spectacular Warfare." In *Arguing Communication and Culture,* edited by G. Thomas Goodnight, 1:137–44. Washington, D.C.: National Communication Association, 2002.

Mitrany, David. *A Working Peace System.* Chicago: Quadrangle Books, 1966.

Mooij, Jan J. *A Study of Metaphor: On the Nature of Metaphorical Expressions, with Special Reference to Their Reference.* Amsterdam: North Holland, 1976.

Moore, Raymond A. "The Carter Presidency and Foreign Policy." In *The Carter Years: The President and Policy Making,* edited by M. Glenn Abernathy, Kilys M. Hill, and Phil Williams. New York: St. Martin's Press, 1984.

Mooy, Jan J. *A Study of Metaphor: On the Nature of Metaphorical Expressions with Special Reference to Their Reference.* Amsterdam: North Holland, 1976.

Morey-Gaines, Ann-Janine. *Apples and Ashes: Culture, Metaphor, and Morality in the American Dream.* American Academy of Religion Academy Series, no. 38. Chico, Calif.: Scholars Press, 1981.

Morgenthau, Hans J. *Politics among Nations: The Struggle for Power and Peace.* Revised by Kenneth W. Thompson, brief ed. New York: McGraw Hill, 1993.

Morris, Kenneth E. *Jimmy Carter: American Moralist.* Athens: University of Georgia Press, 1996.

Morris, Ray. "Visual Rhetoric in Political Cartoons: A Structuralist Approach." *Metaphor and Symbolic Activity* 8 (1993): 195–210.

Müller-Richter, Klaus. *"Kampf der Metapher!" Studien zum Widerstreit des eigentlichen und uneigentlichen Sprechens: zur Reflexion des Metaphorischen im philosophischen und poetologischen Diskurs.* Vienna: Österreichische Akademie der Wissenschaften, 1996.

Murray, Shoon K., and Jonathan. A. Cowden. "The Role of 'Enemy Images' and Ideology in Elite Belief Systems." *International Studies Quarterly* 43, no. 3 (1999): 455–81.

Nadel, Alan. *Containment Culture: American Narratives, Postmodernism, and the Atomic Age.* Durham, N.C.: Duke University Press, 1995.

Nate, Richard. "Metaphor." In *Encyclopedia of Rhetoric,* edited by Thomas O. Sloane, 493–96. Oxford: Oxford University Press, 2001.

Nederlands Instituut voor Oorlogsdocumentatie (NIOD) (Dutch Institute for War Documentation [NIOD]). *Srebrenica, een 'veilig' gebied. Reconstructie, achtergronden, gevolgen en analyses van de val van een Safe Area* (Srebrenica, a 'safe' area. Reconstruction, backgrounds, consequences, and analyses of the downfall of a safe area). Amsterdam: NIOD, 2002. http://www.srebrenica.nl.

Nelson, John S. *Tropes of Politics: Science, Theory, Rhetoric Action.* Madison: University of Wisconsin Press, 1998.

Nelson, John S., and G. R. Boynton. *Video Rhetorics.* Urbana: University of Illinois Press, 1997.

Neustadt, Richard, and Ernest May. *Thinking in Time: The Uses of History for Decision Makers.* New York: Free Press, 1986.

Newell, Allen, and Herbert A. Simon. *Human Problem Solving.* Englewood Cliffs, N.J.: Prentice-Hall, 1972.

Nietzsche, Friedrich. *On the Genealogy of Morals.* New York: Vintage Books, 1989.

Nilsson, Nils J. *Principles of Artificial Intelligence.* Palo Alto, Calif.: Tioga Publishing, 1980.

Nisbett, Richard E. *Culture of Honor: The Psychology of Violence in the South.* Boulder: Westview, 1996.

————. *The Geography of Thought: How Asians and Westerners Think Differently . . . and Why.* New York: Free Press, 2003.

Noble, David W. *The End of American History: Democracy, Capitalism, and the Metaphor of Two Worlds in Anglo-American Historical Writing, 1880–1980.* Minneapolis: University of Minnesota Press, 1985.

Nogales, Patti. *Metaphorically Speaking.* Stanford, Calif.: Center for the Study of Language and Information, 1999.

Norris, Margot. "Only the Guns Have Eyes: Military Censorship and the Body Count." In *Seeing through the Media: The Persian Gulf War,* edited by Susan Jeffords and Lauren Rabinovitz, 285–300. New Brunswick, N.J.: Rutgers University Press, 1994.

Nothstine, William L. " 'Topics' as Ontological Metaphor in Contemporary Rhetorical Theory and Criticism." *Quarterly Journal of Speech* 74 (1988): 151–63.

Nye, Joseph S., Jr. *Bound to Lead: The Changing Nature of American Power.* New York: Basic Books, 1990.

————. *The Paradox of American Power.* Oxford: Oxford University Press, 2002.

Oatley, Keith. "Emotion in Cognition." In *International Encyclopedia of the Social and Behavioral Sciences,* edited by Neil J. Smelser and Paul B. Baltes, 7:4440–44. Amsterdam: Elsevier, 2001.

Obeng, Samuel G. "Language and Politics: Indirectness in Political Discourse." *Discourse and Society* 8, no. 1 (1997): 49–83.

Oberdorfer, Don. *Tet!* New York: Doubleday, 1971.

Ogden, Charles K., and Ivor A. Richards. *The Meaning of Meaning.* New York: Harcourt, Brace, Jovanovich, 1989.

Ohmae, Kenechi. *The Borderless World: Power and Strategy in an Interlocked Economy.* New York: Harper and Row, 1990.

Oldfather, Chad M. "The Hidden Ball: A Substantive Critique of Baseball Metaphors in Judicial Opinions." *Connecticut Law Review* 27 (1994): 17–51.

Olds, Linda E. *Metaphors of Interrelatedness: Toward a Systems Theory of Psychology.* SUNY series, Alternatives in Psychology. Albany: SUNY Press, 1992.

Onuf, Nicholas Greenwood. *World of Our Making: Rules and Rule in Social Theory and International Relations.* Columbia: University of South Carolina Press, 1989.

Opfer, Joseph, and Peter Anderson. "Explaining the Sound Bite: A Test of a Theory of Metaphor and Assonance." Paper presented at the Western Speech Communication Association Convention, Boise, Idaho, 1992.

Organski, A. F. K., and Jacek Kugler. "The Costs of Major Wars: The Phoenix Factor." *American Political Science Review* 71, no. 4 (1977): 1347–66.

Oriard, Michael. *Sporting with the Gods: The Rhetoric of Play and Game in American Culture.* Cambridge: Cambridge University Press, 1991.

Ortony, Andrew, ed. *Metaphor and Thought.* Cambridge: Cambridge University Press, 1979 and 1993 editions.

Osborn, Michael. "Archetypal Metaphor in Rhetoric: The Light-Dark Family." *Quarterly Journal of Speech* 53 (April 1967): 115–26.

———. "The Evolution of the Archetypal Sea in Rhetoric and Poetic." *Quarterly Journal of Speech* 63 (1977): 347–63.

———. "Patterns of Metaphor among Early Feminist Orators." In *Rhetoric and Community: Case Studies in Unity and Fragmentation,* edited by J. Michael Hogan, 3–26. Columbia: University of South Carolina Press, 1998.

———. "Rhetorical Depiction." In *Form, Genre, and the Study of Political Discourse,* edited by Herbert W. Simons and Aram A. Aghazarian, 79–107. Columbia: University of South Carolina Press, 1986.

Osborn, Michael, and Douglas Ehninger. "The Metaphor in Public Address." *Speech Monographs* 29 (1962): 223–34.

Oxford English Dictionary II. 2d ed. CD-ROM, version 3.0. Oxford: Oxford University Press.

Palfrey, Thomas, and Howard Rosenthal. "Voter Participation and Strategic Uncertainty." *American Political Science Review* 79 (1985): 62–78.

Palmatier, Robert. A. *Speaking of Animals: A Dictionary of Animal Metaphors.* Westport, Conn: Greenwood Press, 1995.

Palmatier, Robert A. *Sports Talk: A Dictionary of Sports Metaphors.* New York: Greenwood Press, 1989.

Palmatier, Robert A., and Harold L. Ray. *Dictionary of Sports Idioms.* Lincolnwood, Ill.: National Textbook, 1993.

Palmer, Jerry. *Spinning into Control: News Values and Source Strategies.* London: Leicester University Press/Continuum, 2000.

Pancake, Ann S. "Taken by Storm: The Exploitation of Metaphor in the Persian Gulf War." *Metaphor and Symbolic Activity* 8 (1993): 281–95.

Paprotté, Wolf, and René Dirven, eds. *The Ubiquity of Metaphor: Metaphor in Language and Thought.* Amsterdam: J. Benjamins, 1985.

Paris, Erna. *Long Shadows: Truth, Lies, and History.* London: Bloomsbury, 2000.

Paris, Roland. "Kosovo and the Metaphor War." *Political Science Quarterly* 117, no. 3 (2002): 423–50.

Partridge, Eric. *Origins: A Short Etymological Dictionary of Modern English.* London: Routledge and Kegan Paul, 1982.

Payton, Jack R. "Bush and U.S.: World's Top Cops." *St. Petersburg Times,* 1 August 1991, 3A.

Peirce, Charles. *Philosophical Writings of Peirce.* Edited by J. Buchler. New York: Dover, 1955.

Perelman, Chaim. *The Realm of Rhetoric.* Translated by William Kluback. Notre Dame: University of Notre Dame Press, 1982.

Perlmutter, Amos. *Making the World Safe for Democracy: A Century of Wilsonianism and Its Totalitarian Challengers.* Chapel Hill: University of North Carolina Press, 1997.

Perry, Stephen. "Rhetorical Functions of the Infestation Metaphor in Hitler's Rhetoric." *Central States Speech Journal* 34 (winter 1983): 229–35.

Peters, John D. "Bowels of Mercy." *BYU Studies* 38 (1999): 27–41.

———. *Speaking into the Air.* Chicago: University of Chicago Press, 1999.

Phillips, Kevin. "The Vietnam Syndrome; Why Is Bush Hurting if There Is No War?" *Los Angeles Times,* 25 November 1990, M1.

Ping-Lin Liu, A. *Adaptation of Traditional Storytelling to Political Propaganda in Communist China.* Cambridge, Mass.: Center for International Studies, MIT, 1965.

Political Psychology. Journal of the International Society of Political Psychology. Boston, USA: Blackwell Publishing.

Powell, Jody. "Oral History on Carter Administration," White Burkett Miller Center of Public Affairs, University of Virginia, *Project on the Carter Presidency,* transcripts, vols. 18, 20.

Prince, George. *The Practice of Creativity.* New York: Harper, 1970.

Pugh, Sharon L., ed. *Bridging: A Teacher's Guide to Metaphorical Thinking.* Urbana, Ill.: National Council of Teachers of English; Bloomington, Ind.: ERIC Clearinghouse on Reading and Communication Skills, 1992.

Putnam, Robert D. *Bowling Alone: The Collapse and Revival of American Community.* New York: Simon and Schuster, 2000.

Quine, Willard van Orman. "On Mental Entities." In *The Ways of Paradox and Other Essays,* revised and enlarged ed., edited by Willard van Orman Quine, 221–27. Cambridge: Harvard University Press, 1976.

Quinn, Sean. "Courting the White House and Sniping at State." *Washington Post,* 20 December 1979.

Radman, Zdravko. *From a Metaphorical Point of View: A Multidisciplinary Approach to the Cognitive Content of Metaphor.* New York: W. de Gruyter, 1995.

Radman, Zdravko. *Metaphors: Figures of the Mind.* Boston: Kluwer Academic, 1997.

Ramírez, Juan Antonio. *The Beehive Metaphor: From Gaudi to Le Corbusier.* Translated by Alexander R. Tulloch. London: Reaktion, 2001.

Raschke, Carl A. *Fire and Roses: Postmodernity and the Thought of the Body.* Albany: SUNY Press, 1996.

"Ready or Not? The Mideast Conflict." *Bergen Record,* 20 December 1990, A1.

Record, Jeffrey. *Making War, Thinking History: Munich, Vietnam, and Presidential Uses of Force from Korea to Kosovo.* Annapolis, Md.: Naval Institute Press, 2002.

Reddy, Michael. "The Conduit Metaphor: A Case of Frame Conflict in Our Language about Language." In *Metaphor and Thought,* 2d ed., edited by Andrew Ortony, 164–201. Cambridge: Cambridge University Press, 1993.

Reich, Robert. *The Work of Nations: Preparing Ourselves for 21st Century Capitalism.* New York: Knopf, 1991.

Rhodes, Gillian. "Superportraits: Caricatures and Recognition." *Metaphor and Symbol* 14, no. 2 (1999): 149–57.

Richards, I. A. *A Philosophy of Rhetoric.* Oxford: Oxford University Press, 1936.

———. *Richards on Rhetoric: I. A. Richards, Selected Essays (1929–1974).* Edited by Ann E. Berthoff. New York: Oxford University Press, 1991.

Ricoeur, Paul. *La métaphore vive.* Paris: Editions du Seuil, 1975.

———. *The Rule of Metaphor: Multidisciplinary Studies of the Creation of Meaning in Language.* Translated by Robert Czerny, Kathleen McLaughlin, and John Costello. Toronto: University of Toronto Press, 1975.

Riker, William H. *The Strategy of Rhetoric: Campaigning for the American Constitution.* New Haven: Yale University Press, 1996.

Rissman, Leah. *Love as War: Hometric Allusion in the Poetry of Sappho.* Königstein: Hain, 1983.

Robin, Ron. *The Making of the Cold War Enemy: Culture and Politics in the Military-Intellectual Complex.* Princeton: Princeton University Press, 2001.

Rogotti, Francesca. *Metafore della politica.* Bologna: Il Mulino, 1989.

Rohrer, Tim. "The Metaphorical Logic of (Political) Rape: The New Wor(1)d Order." *Metaphor and Symbolic Activity* 10 (1995): 115–37.

———. "To Plow the Sea: Metaphors for Regional Peace in Latin America." *Metaphor and Symbolic Activity* 6 (1991): 163–81.

———. "Understanding through the Body? Increased fMRI and ERP Activity in the Motor and Perceptual Cortices in Response to Relevant Semantic Stimuli." Boulder: Institute of Cognitive Science, public speech, 24 January 2003.

Rokeach, Michael. *Beliefs, Attitudes, and Values.* San Francisco: Jossey-Bass, 1968.

Romaine, Suzanne. "War and Peace in the Global Greenhouse: Metaphors We Die By." *Metaphor and Symbolic Activity* 11 (1996): 175–94.

Rorty, Richard. *Philosophy and the Mirror of Nature.* Princeton: Princeton University Press, 1979.

Rosati, Jerel A. *The Carter Administration's Quest for Global Community: Beliefs and Their Impact on Behavior.* Columbia: University of South Carolina Press, 1987.

———. "Continuity and Change in the Foreign Policy Beliefs of Political Leaders: Addressing the Controversy over the Carter Administration." *Political Psychology* 9, no. 3 (1998): 471–505.

———. "The Impact of Beliefs on Behavior: The Foreign Policy of the Carter Administration." In *Foreign Policy Decision Making: Perception, Cognition, and Artificial Intelligence,* edited by Donald A. Sylvan and Steve Chan. New York: Praeger, 1984.

———. "Jimmy Carter: A Man before His Time? The Emergence and Collapse of the First Post–Cold War Presidency." *Presidential Studies Quarterly* 23 (1993): 459–76.

———. "The Power of Human Cognition in the Study of World Politics." *International Studies Review* 43 (fall 2000): 45–75.

———. "Studying Images and Their Impact on Behavior: The Case of the Carter Administration." In *Political Leadership for the New Century: Personality and Behavior among Political Leaders,* edited by Ofer Feldman and Linda O. Valenty. Westport, Conn.: Greenwood, 2002.

Rosch, Elinor. "Principles of Categorization." In *Cognition and Categorization*, edited by Elinor Rosch and Barbara B. Lloyd, 27–49. Hillsdale, N.J.: Lawrence Erlbaum, 1978.

Rosenau, James. *Turbulence in World Politics: A Theory of Change and Continuity.* Princeton: Princeton University Press, 1990.

Ross, James Collins. "Talking Immigration: A Rhetorical Analysis of U.S. Senate Debates, 1924–1965–1996." Ph.D. diss., University of Colorado, Boulder 2002.

Rueckert, William H. *Encounters with Kenneth Burke.* Urbana: University of Illinois Press, 1994.

Russett, Bruce. *Grasping the Democratic Peace: Principles for a Post–Cold War World.* Princeton: Princeton University Press, 1993.

Ryan, Marie-Laure. *Possible Worlds, Artificial Intelligence, and Narrative Theory.* Bloomington: Indiana University Press, 1991.

Ryan, Mary. *Civic Wars: Democracy and Public Life in the American City during the Nineteenth Century.* Berkeley and Los Angeles: University of California Press, 1997.

Safire, William. "The Longest Huddle." *New York Times,* 23 September 1982, A27.

Said, Edward. *Orientalism.* Harmondsworth, U.K.: Penguin, 1995.

Sanders, James W. *Peddlers of Crisis: The Committee on the Present Danger and the Politics of Containment.* Boston: South End Press, 1983.

Sapir, J. David, and J. Christopher Crocker. *The Social Use of Metaphor: Essays on the Anthropology of Rhetoric.* Philadelphia: University of Pennsylvania Press, 1977.

Sargent, William. *Battle for the Mind.* Baltimore: Penguin Books, 1957.

Schafer, Mark. "Images and Policy Preferences." *Political Psychology* 18, no. 4 (1997): 813–29.

Schäffner, Christina, and Peter Porsch. "Meeting the Challenge on the Path to Democracy: Discursive Strategies in Government Declarations in Germany and the former GDR." *Discourse and Society* 4 (1993): 33–55.

Schatzki, Theodore, and Wolfgang Natter, eds. *The Social and Political Body.* New York: Guilford, 1996.

Schelling, Thomas. *The Strategy of Conflict.* New York: Oxford University Press, 1963.

Scheuer, Jeffrey. *The Sound Bite Society: Television and the American Mind.* London: Routledge, 2001.

Schiappa, Edward. "The Rhetoric of Nukespeak." *Communication Monographs* 56 (1989): 253–72.

Schiebinger, Londa. *Has Feminism Changed Science?* Cambridge: Harvard University Press, 1999.

Schlesinger, Mark, and Richard Lau. "The Meaning and Measure of Policy Metaphors." *American Political Science Review* 94, no. 3 (September 2000): 611–26.

Schneider, William. "Conservatism, Not Interventionism: Trends in Foreign Policy Opinion, 1974–1982." In *Eagle Defiant: United States Foreign Policy in the 1980s,* edited by Key A. Oye, Richard J. Lieber, and Donald Rothchild. Boston: Little, Brown, and Co., 1983.

Schoultz, Lars. *Beneath the United States: A History of U.S. Policy toward Latin America.* Cambridge: Harvard University Press, 1998.

Schroder, Harold M., Michael J. Driver, and Siegfried Streufert. *Human Information Processing: Individuals and Groups Functioning in Complex Social Situations.* New York: Holt, Rinehart and Winston, 1967.

Schuman, Howard, and Carol Rieger. "Historical Analogies, Generational Change, and Attitudes toward War." *American Sociological Review* 57 (1982): 315–26.

Schweller, Randall L. *Deadly Imbalances: Tripolarity and Hitler's Strategy of Global Conquest.* New York: Columbia University Press, 1998.

Schweller, Randall L. "Bandwagoning for Profit: Bringing the Revisionist State Back in." *International Security* 19 (summer 1994): 72–107.

Seabrook, James. "Rocking in Shangri-La." *New York Times,* 10 October 1994.

Sedivy, Sonia. "Metaphoric Pictures, Pulsars, Platypuses." *Metaphor and Symbol* 12, no. 2 (1997): 95–112.

Segrave, Jeffrey O. "The Perfect 10: 'Sportspeak' in the Language of Sexual Relations." *Sociology of Sport Journal* 11 (1994): 995–1113.

———. "The Sports Metaphor in American Cultural Discourse." *Culture, Sport, Society* 3 (spring 2000): 48–60.

Selzer, Jack, and Sharon Crowley, eds. *Rhetorical Bodies.* Madison: University of Wisconsin Press, 1999

Semino, Elena, and Michela Masci. "Politics Is Football: Metaphor in the Discourse of Silvio Berlusconi in Italy." *Discourse and Society* 7, no. 2 (April 1996): 243–69.

Serfaty, Simon. "Brzezinski: Play It Again, Zbig." *Foreign Policy* 32 (1978): 3–21.

Shafer, D. Michael. *Deadly Paradigms: The Failure of US Counterinsurgency Policy.* Princeton: Princeton University Press, 1988.

Shapiro, Andrew L. *The Control Revolution: How the Internet Is Putting Individuals in Charge and Changing the World We Know.* New York: Century Foundation, 1999.

Shapiro, Michael J., ed. *Language and Politics.* New York: New York University Press, 1984.

Shapiro, Michael J. *Violent Cartographies: Mapping Cultures of War.* Minneapolis: University of Minnesota Press, 1997.

Shepard, Scot. "Gore Denounces GOP Cheap Shots on War; Democrat Defends Votes of Conscience." *Atlanta Journal and Constitution,* 7 March 1991, A4.

Shibles, Warren. *Metaphor: An Annotated History and Bibliography.* Whitewater, Wis.: Language Press, 1971.

"Shielding the World from Iraq . . . and Why an Embargo Can Work." *Chicago Tribune,* 14 August 1990, 14.

Shimko, Keith L. "Foreign Policy Metaphors: Falling 'Dominoes' and Drug 'Wars.'" In *Foreign Policy Analysis: Continuity and Change in Its Second Generation,* edited by Laura Neack, Jeanne A. K. Hey, and Patrick J. Haney. Englewood Cliffs, N.J.: Prentice-Hall, 1995.

_____. *Images and Arms Control: Perceptions of the Soviet Union in the Reagan Administration.* Ann Arbor: University of Michigan Press, 1991.

_____. "Metaphors and Foreign Policy Decision Making." *Political Psychology* 15, no. 4 (December 1994): 655–71.

Simons, Herbert W., and Aram A. Aghazarian, eds. *Form, Genre, and the Study of Political Discourse.* Columbia: University of South Carolina Press, 1986.

Skinner, Quentin. *Reason and Rhetoric in the Philosophy of Hobbes.* Cambridge: Cambridge University Press, 1996.

Slater, Jerome. "Dominos in Central America: Will They Fall? Does It Matter?" *International Security* 12 (1987): 105–34.

Sloane, Thomas O., ed. *Encyclopedia of Rhetoric.* Oxford: Oxford University Press, 2001.

Slouka, Mark. *War of the Worlds: Cyberspace and the High-Tech Assault on Reality.* New York: Basic Books, 1995.

Sloyan, Patrick J. "Iraqi Guns Preserved; Still, Effect of Allied Air Raids Called 'Good Progress.'" *Newsday,* 9 February 1991, 5.

Smith, Gaddis. *Morality, Reason, and Power: American Diplomacy in the Carter Years.* New York: Hill and Wang, 1986.

Smith, Ralph R., and Russel R. Windes. *Progay/Antigay: The Rhetorical War over Sexuality.* Thousand Oaks, Calif.: Sage, 2000.

Smith, Red. "Spoken Like a True Son of Old Whittier." *New York Times,* 30 April 1973, 39.

Smith, Ruth C., and Eric M. Eisenberg. "Conflict at Disneyland: A Root-Metaphor Analysis." *Communication Monographs* 54 (1987): 367–80.

Snyder, Glenn H. "Mearsheimer's World: Offensive Realism and the Struggle for Security." *International Security* 27, no. 1 (2002): 149–73.

Snyder, Glenn H., and Paul Diesing. *Conflict among Nations: Bargaining, Decision Making, and System Structure in International Crises.* Princeton: Princeton University Press, 1977.

Soames, Scott. *Beyond Rigidity: The Unfinished Semantic Agenda of Naming and Necessity.* Oxford: Oxford University Press, 2002.

Solinger, Rickie, ed. "Abortion Wars: A Half Century of Struggle, 1950–2000," *Rhetoric & Public Affairs* 2, no. 2 (1999): 342–44.

Sommer, Elyse, and Dorrie Weiss, eds. *Metaphors Dictionary.* New York: Gale Research, 1995.

Sontag, Susan. *AIDS and Its Metaphor.* New York: Farrar, Straus and Giroux, 1998.

———. *Illness as a Metaphor and AIDS and Its Metaphors.* New York: Doubleday, 1989.

Soskice, Janet. *Metaphor and Religious Language.* Oxford: Clarendon, 1985.

Spackman, Barbara. *Fascist Virilities: Rhetoric, Ideology, and Social Fantasy in Italy.* Minneapolis: University of Minnesota Press, 1996.

Spector, Bertram I. "Metaphors of International Negotiation." *International Negotiation* 1, no. 1 (1996): 1–9.

Spivey, Nancy Nelson. *The Constructivist Metaphor: Reading, Writing, and the Making of Meaning.* San Diego, Calif.: Academic Press, 1997.

Sproull, Robert L. *A Scientist's Tools for Business: Metaphors and Modes of Thought.* Rochester, N.Y.: University of Rochester Press, 1997.

Stanford, William B. *Greek Metaphor: Studies in Theory and Practice.* New York: Johnson Reprint Corporation, 1972.

Stearney, Lynn M. "Feminism, Ecofeminism, and the Maternal Archetype: Motherhood as a Feminine Universal." *Communication Quarterly* 42 (1994): 145–59.

Steen, Gerard. *Understanding Metaphor in Literature.* Harlow, U.K.: Longman, 1994.

Stein, Morris. *Stimulating Creativity.* Vols. 1 and 2. New York: Academic Press, 1974.

Stellardi, Giuseppe. *Heidegger and Derrida on Philosophy and Metaphor: Imperfect Thought.* Amherst, N.Y.: Humanity Books, 2000.

Stelzner, Hermann. "Ford's 'War on Inflation': A Metaphor That Did Not Cross." *Communication Monographs* 44 (1977): 284–97.

Sterling-Folker, Jennifer. "Competing Paradigms or Birds of a Feather? Constructivism and Neoliberal Institutionalism Compared." *International Studies Quarterly* 44, no. 1 (2000): 97–119.

Stern, Josef. *Metaphor in Context.* Cambridge, Mass.: MIT Press, 2000.

Sternberg, Robert J. *Metaphors of Mind: Conceptions of the Nature of Intelligence.* New York: Cambridge University Press, 1990.

Stockwell, Peter. Review of *Researching and Applying Metaphor,* edited by Lynne Cameron and Graham Low. *Metaphor and Symbol* 15, no. 4 (2000): 275–77.

Stone, Doris A. *Policy Paradox and Policy Reason.* Glenview, Ill.: Scott, Foresman, 1988.

Stuckey, Mary E. *The President as Interpreter-in-Chief.* Chatham, N.J.: Chatham House, 1991.

———. "Remembering the Future: Rhetorical Echoes of World War and Vietnam in George Bush's Public Speech on the Gulf War." *Communication Studies* 43 (winter 1992): 246–56.

———. *The Theory and Practice of Political Communication Research.* Albany: SUNY Press, 1996.

Subcommittee to Investigate the Administration of the Internal Security Act and Other Internal Security Laws of the Committee on the Judiciary, United States Senate (1956). *The Communist Party of the United States of America: A Handbook for Americans.* Washington, D.C.: Government Printing Office.

Suedfeld, Peter, and Susan Bluck. "Changes in Integrative Complexity Prior to Surprise Attacks." *Journal of Conflict Resolution* 32, no. 4 (1988): 626–35.

Suedfeld, Peter, Philip E. Tetlock, and Carmenza Ramirez. "War, Peace and Integrative Complexity." *Journal of Conflict Resolution* 21, no. 3 (1977): 427–42.

Sutton, Walter D., Jr. "Arab-Israeli Dispute Must Be Resolved Peacefully." *St. Petersburg Times,* 9 January 1991, 2.

Sweetser, Eve. "Metaphor, Mythology, and Everyday Language." *Journal of Pragmatics* 24 (1995): 585–93.

Sylvan, Donald A., and James F. Voss, eds. *Problem Representation in Foreign Policy Decision-Making.* Cambridge: Cambridge University Press, 1998.

Sylvester, Christine. *Feminist Theory and International Relations in a Postmodern Era.* Cambridge: Cambridge University Press, 1993.

Tano, Daisuke. "The Birth of the *Arbeiter* Body and Politics in the Third Reich." *Soshioroji* 40, no. 2 (1995): 59–78.

Taran, Sergiy. "Mythical Thinking, Aristotelian Logic, and Metaphors in the Parliament of Ukraine." In *Beyond Public Speech and Symbols: Explorations in the Rhetoric of Politicians and the Media,* edited by Christ'l De Landtsheer and Ofer Feldman, 120–43. Westport, Conn.: Praeger, 2000.

Taub, Sarah F. *Language from the Body: Iconicity and Metaphor in American Sign Language.* New York: Cambridge University Press, 2001.

Thornborrow, Joanna. "Metaphors of Security: A Comparison of Representation in Defence Discourse in Post–Cold-War France and Britain." *Discourse and Society* 4 (1993): 99–119.

Thornburg, Elizabeth G. "Metaphors Matter: How Images of Battle, Sports, and Sex Shape the Adversary System." *Wisconsin Women's Law Journal* 10 (1995): 225–81.

Tickner, J. Ann. *Gender in International Relations: Feminist Perspectives on Achieving Global Security.* New York: Columbia University Press, 1992.

Tolaas, Jon. "Notes on the Origin of Some Spatialization Metaphors." *Metaphor and Symbolic Activity* 6 (1991): 203–18.

Traugott, Elizabeth Closs. " 'Conventional' and 'Dead' Metaphors Revisited." In *The Ubiquity of Metaphor: Metaphor in Language and Thought,* edited by Wolf Paprotté and René Dirven, 17–56. Amsterdam: J. Benjamins, 1985.

Tsoukas, Haridimos. "The Missing Link: A Transformational View of Metaphors in Organizational Science." *Academy of Management Review* 16, no. 3 (1991): 566–85.

Tulis, Jeffrey K. *The Rhetorical Presidency.* Princeton: Princeton University Press, 1987.

Tumulty, Joseph. Joseph Tumulty to Woodrow Wilson, 31 December 1918. Wilson, file 8A, Library of Congress.

Turkle, Sherry. *Life on the Screen: Identity in the Age of the Internet.* New York: Touchstone, 1997.

Turner, Bryan S. *The Body and Society: Explorations in Social Theory.* Oxford: Basil Blackwell, 1984.

Turner, John C., Michael A. Hogg, Penelope J. Oakes, Stephen D. Reicher, and Margaret S. Wetherell. *Rediscovering the Social Group: A Self-categorization Theory.* New York: Basil Blackwell, 1987.

Turner, Mark, and Gilles Fauconnier. "Conceptual Integration and Formal Expression." *Metaphor and Symbolic Activity* 10, no. 3 (1995): 183–205.

Uchitelle, Louis. "Gillette's World View: One Blade Fits All." *New York Times,* 3 January 1994, C3.

U.S. Senate *Prospects for Peace in Cambodia: 1990 Hearing before the Subcommittee on East Asia and Pacific Affairs of the Committee on Foreign Relations, United States Senate, One Hundred First Congress, Second Session, February 28, 1990.* Washington D.C.: US Government Printing Office, 1990.

Vance, Cyrus. *Hard Choices: Critical Years in America's Foreign Policy.* New York: Simon and Schuster, 1983.

Van Noppen, Jean-Pierre, Sabine de Knop, and R. Jongen. *Metaphor: A Bibliography of Post-1970 Publications.* Amsterdam: J. Benjamins, 1985.

Van Noppen, Jean-Pierre, and Edith Hols. *Metaphor II: A Classified Bibliography of Publications, 1985 to 1990.* Amsterdam: J. Benjamins, 1990.

Vertzberger, Yaacov. *The World in Their Minds: Information Processing, Cognition, and Perception in Foreign Policy Decisionmaking.* Stanford, Calif.: Stanford University Press, 1990.

Vila, Pablo. *Crossing Borders, Reinforcing Borders: Social Categories, Metaphors, and Narrative Identities on the U.S.–Mexico Frontier.* Austin: University of Texas Press, 2000.

Virilio, Paul. *The Art of the Motor.* Minneapolis: University of Minnesota Press, 1995.

———. *Open Sky.* London: Verso, 1997.

Virilio, Paul, and Sylvia Lotringer. *Pure War.* New York: Semiotext(e), 1983.

Vosniadou, Stella, and Anthony Ortony. "Similarity and Analogical Reasoning: A Synthesis." In *Similarity and Analogical Reasoning,* edited by Stella Vosniadou and Anthony Ortony, 1–18. New York: Cambridge University Press, 1989.

Voss, James F., Joel. W. Kennet, Jennifer Wiley, and Tonya Schooler. "Experts at Debate: The Use of Metaphor in the U.S. Senate Debate on the Gulf Crisis." *Metaphor and Symbolic Activity* 7 (1992): 197–214.

wa Mwachofi, Ngure. "Apprehending the Power and Ideological Import of Metaphor in President de Klerk's Rhetoric." *Howard Journal of Communications* 5, no. 4 (1995): 331–52.

Waddell, Craig, ed. *And No Birds Sing: Rhetorical Analyses of Rachel Carson's Silent Spring.* Carbondale: Southern Illinois University Press, 2000.

Walk, Stephan R. "The Footrace Metaphor in American Presidential Rhetoric." *Sociology of Sport Journal* 12, no. 1 (March 1995): 36–55.

Walker, Martin. "Bush's Choice: Athens or Sparta." *World Policy Journal* 18, no. 2 (2001): 1–9.

Walker, R. B. J. "The Antipolitics of Clayoquot Sound." Paper presented at the Western Political Science Association annual meeting, 25–27 March 1999.

———. *Inside/Outside: International Relations as Political Theory.* Cambridge: Cambridge University Press, 1993.

Walker, Stephen G., ed. *Role Theory and Foreign Policy Analysis.* Durham, N.C.: Duke University Press, 1987.

Walker, Stephen G., Mark Schafer, and Michael D. Young. "Systematic Procedures for Operational Code Analysis: Measuring and Modeling Jimmy Carter's Operational Code." *International Studies Quarterly* 42, no. 1 (1998): 175–92.

Wallace, Michel D., Peter Suedfeld, and Kimberley Thachuk. "Political Rhetoric of Leaders under Stress in the Gulf Crisis." *Journal of Conflict Resolution* 37, no. 1 (1993): 94–107.

Walt, Stephen. *The Origins of Alliances.* Chicago: University of Chicago Press, 1987.

Waltz, Kenneth. *Theory of International Politics.* Reading, Mass.: Addison-Wesley, 1983.

Wander, Philip. "Critical and Classical Theory: An Introduction to Ideology Criticism." In *Cold War Rhetoric,* edited by Martin Medhurst, Robert L. Ivie, Philip Wander, and Robert L. Scott, 131–52. East Lansing: Michigan State University Press, 1997.

Wang, Jianwei. *Limited Adversaries: Post–Cold War Sino-American Mutual Images.* Oxford: Oxford University Press, 2000.

Warner, Michael. *Publics and Counterpublics.* New York: Zone Books; Cambridge, Mass.: MIT Press, 2002.

Way, Eileen C. *Knowledge, Representation, and Metaphor.* Boston: Kluwer Academic Publishers, 1991.

Weart, Spencer R. *Never at War: Why Democracies Will Not Fight One Another.* New Haven: Yale University Press, 1998.

Weber, Cynthia. *Faking It: U.S. Hegemony in the "Post-phallic" Era* (Minneapolis: University of Minnesota Press, 1999).

Weele, Cor van der. *Images of Development: Environmental Causes in Ontogeny.* Albany: SUNY Press, 1999.

Weinberger, Ota. "Argumentation in Law and Politics." *Communication and Cognition* 28, no. 1 (1995): 37–54.

Weinreich-Haste, Helen. *The Sexual Metaphor.* Cambridge: Harvard University Press, 1994.

Westerman, Fred, and Bart Rijs. *Srebrenica: Het Zwartste Scenario* (Srebrenica: A Black Scenario). Amsterdam: Atlas, 1997.

White Burkett Miller Center of Public Affairs, University of Virginia, *Project on the Carter Presidency,* transcripts, vol. 18.

White House, Office of the Press Secretary. "Communique: Entebbe Summit for Peace and Prosperity," 25 March 1998, http://www.pub.whitehouse.gov/uri-res/12 . . . pdi://oma.cop.gov.us/1998/3/26/10.text.1 (accessed 4 March 1999).

White, John K. *Still Seeing Red: How the Cold War Shapes the New American Politics.* Boulder: Westview, 1997.

Whitfield, Stephen J. *The Culture of the Cold War.* Baltimore: Johns Hopkins University Press, 1996.

Whittock, Trevor. *Metaphor and Film.* Cambridge Studies in Film. New York: Cambridge University Press, 1990.

Wickham, Wayne. "NFL Films out of Element in Mideast." *USA Today,* 2 April 1991, 10C.

Wilkinson, Peter R. *Thesaurus of Traditional English Metaphors.* 2d ed. London: Routledge, 2002.

Windt, Theodore, and Beth Ingold. *Essays in Presidential Rhetoric.* Dubuque, Iowa: Kendall/Hunt Publishing, 1987.

Winkler, Carol K. "Narrative Reframing of Public Argument: George Bush's Handling of the Persian Gulf Conflict." In *Warranting Assent: Case Studies in Argument Evaluation,* edited by Edward Schiappa, 33–55. Albany: SUNY Press, 1995.

Winograd, Terry. *Language as a Cognitive Process.* Vol. 1, *Syntax.* Reading, Mass.: Addison-Wesley, 1983.

Winter, David. "Content Analysis of Archival Data, Personal Documents and Everyday Verbal Productions." In *Motivation and Personality: Handbook of Thematic Content Analysis,* edited by C. P. Smith, 110–25. New York: Cambridge University Press, 1992.

———. "Power, Affiliation and War: Three Tests of a Motivational Model." *Journal of Personality and Social Psychology* 65 (1993): 532–45.

Wood, Gordon S. *The Creation of the American Republic, 1776–1787.* New York: W. W. Norton, 1969.

Wu, Kuang-ming. "Novelty, the Emerging Norm in Metaphor." In *On Metaphoring: A Cultural Hermeneutic,* 167–73. Boston: Brill, 2001.

Yankelovich, Daniel, and Linda Kaagen. "Assertive America." *Foreign Affairs* 59 (1980): 696–713

Young, Robert M. *Darwin's Metaphor: Nature's Place in Victorian Culture.* New York: Cambridge University Press, 1985.

Youngkin, Betty Rogers. *The Contributions of Walter J. Ong to the Study of Rhetoric: History and Metaphor.* Lewiston, N.Y.: Mellen University Press, 1995.

Zagacki, Kenneth. "Pope John Paul II and the Crusade against Communism." *Rhetoric and Public Affairs* 4 (2001): 689–710.

———. "Spatial and Temporal Images in the Biodiversity Dispute." *Quarterly Journal of Speech* 85 (1999): 417–35.

Zakaria, Fareed. "Our Way: The Trouble with Being the World's Only Superpower." *The New Yorker,* 14 and 21 October 2002, 81.

Zarefsky, David. *President Johnson's War on Poverty: Rhetoric and History.* Tuscaloosa: University of Alabama Press, 1986.

Zashin, Elliot, and Phillip C. Chapman. "The Uses of Metaphor and Analogy: Towards a Renewal of Political Language." *Journal of Politics* 36 (1974): 290–326.

Zasorina, Lidiia N., ed. Chastotnyi slovar' russkogo iazyka. Moscow: Izdatel'stvo "Russkii Iazyk," 1977.

About the Contributors

Richard D. Anderson, Jr., is Associate Professor of Political Science at UCLA. He is the author of *Public Politics in an Authoritarian State* (1993), a study of how Soviet leaders before perestroika used public declarations of their visions of socialism to compete for backing from officials known collectively as the *nomenklatura*. Since the collapse of the Soviet Union, most of his publications have concerned how change in the public discourse of Soviet and then Russian political elites has engineered the shift from dictatorship to democracy. A synopsis of this research is presented in his contribution to the co-authored volume *Post-Communism and the Theory of Democracy* (2001).

Francis A. Beer is Professor of Political Science at the University of Colorado, Boulder. His most recent book is *Meanings of War and Peace* (2001). Prior books include *Post-realism: The Rhetorical Turn in International Relations*, edited by Francis A. Beer and Robert Hariman (1996); *Peace against War: The Ecology of International Violence* (1981); and *Integration and Disintegration in NATO: Processes of Alliance Cohesion and Prospects for Atlantic Community* (1969). His present interests center on cognition, communication, and culture in international relations with a particular concern for war and peace.

G. Robert Boynton is Professor of Political Science at the University of Iowa. He is the author of *Mathematical Thinking about Politics, The Art of Campaign Advertising,* and the co-author with John S. Nelson of *Video Rhetorics.* He is currently doing research on global news broadcasting.

Steven J. Campbell is Visiting Assistant Professor in the Department of Political Science and Public Affairs at the University of Toledo. His most recent publication deals with transnational lobbying strategies, and his current research interests involve political psychology as applied to U.S. foreign policy officials and decision making.

Christ'l De Landtsheer is Professor of Communication at the University of Antwerp, Belgium. She is a co-editor, with Ofer Feldman, of *Politically Speaking: A Worldwide Examination of Language Used in the Public Sphere*

(1998) and *Beyond Public Speech and Symbols: Explorations in the Rhetoric of Politicians and the Media* (2000). Her research interests are in the area of political psychology and political communication.

Ilse De Vrij serves as a public communications advisor for the Dutch government at the local level, specializing in mergers between municipalities. Her expertise is in the field of organizations in transition and public crisis communication.

Richard B. Gregg was Professor of Speech Communication at Pennsylvania State University. He shared the 1995 Marie Hochmuth Nichols Award for Distinguished Scholarship in Rhetoric and Public Address for his contribution to the book *Eisenhower's War of Words: Rhetoric and Leadership* (1994). His book *Symbolic Inducement and Knowing: A Study in the Foundations of Rhetoric* (1984) received the James A. Winans, Herbert Wichelns Award for Distinguished Scholarship in Rhetoric and Public Address from the National Communication Association in 1984. His research and teaching interests were in the areas of rhetorical theory and criticism, with a concern for a cognitive orientation to rhetorical behavior, and contemporary American political discourse, with a focus on the Cold War.

Dale A. Herbeck is Professor and Chair of the Communication Department at Boston College. He is coauthor of *Freedom of Speech in the United States* (2001), and he has contributed chapters and scholarly articles to such journals as *Argumentation, Argumentation and Advocacy, Communication Research Reports,* and the *Free Speech Yearbook.* His scholarship has been recognized with the McGuffey Award from the Textbook and Academic Author's Association, the James Madison Award from the Southern States Communication Association, the Past President's Award from the Eastern Communication Association, and the Robert M. O'Neill Award from the Commission on Freedom of Expression. His research and teaching interests include argumentation, communication law, and freedom of expression.

Robert L. Ivie is Professor in Communication and Culture and a member of the interdisciplinary faculties in American Studies and Cultural Studies at Indiana University, Bloomington. He is founding editor of the journal *Communication and Critical/Cultural Studies* and author of *Democracy and American's War on Terror* (forthcoming). His research focuses on rhetoric as a mode of political critique and cultural production, with particular emphasis on democracy and the problem of war. He is coauthor of *Cold War Rhetoric: Strategy, Metaphor, and Ideology,* revised edition (1997), and *Congress*

Declares War: Rhetoric, Leadership, and Partisanship in the Early Republic (1983).

Timothy W. Luke is University Distinguished Professor of Political Science, Co-Director for the Center for Digital Discourse and Culture, and Associate Dean, Division of Liberal Arts, in the College of Arts and Sciences at Virginia Polytechnic Institute and State University in Blacksburg, Virginia. He has just completed a critical study of ideological politics at several major museums in the United States, which is entitled *Museum Politics: Power Plays at the Exhibition* (2002). Other recent books are *Capitalism, Democracy, and Ecology: Departing from Marx* (1999), *The Politics of Cyberspace* (1998), co-edited with Chris Toulouse, and *Ecocritique: Contesting the Politics of Nature, Economy, and Culture* (1997). He also is the author of *Shows of Force: Politics, Power, and Ideology in Art Exhibitions* (1992). His research interests include the politics of cultural conflict and interpretation, particularly with regard to the rise of information societies, globalization in international affairs, and contemporary ecological criticism.

Jerel A. Rosati is Professor of Political Science and International Studies and has been at the University of South Carolina since 1982. His area of specialization is the theory and practice of foreign policy, focusing on the United States policy-making process, decision-making theory, and the political psychological study of human cognition. He is the author and editor of five books and over forty articles and chapters. He has received numerous outstanding teaching awards. He has been Research Associate in the Foreign Affairs and National Defense Division of the Library of Congress's Congressional Research Service, Visiting Professor at Somalia National University, and Visiting Scholar at the Foreign Affairs College in Beijing, China. Recently, he was Program Director and Academic Director of a U.S. Department of State Fulbright American Studies Institute on U.S. Foreign Policy for eighteen scholar-practitioners from all over the world.

Keith L. Shimko is Associate Professor of Political Science at Purdue University. He is the author of *Images and Arms Control: Perceptions of the Soviet Union in the Reagan Administration* (1991). His most recent book is *Perspectives and Controversies* (2004).

Name Index

Abbott, Kenneth W., 196n. 2
Abernathy, M. Glenn, 233n.16
Abrams, Jerold, J., 48n. 75
Acheson, Dean, 206. References: 215n. 20
Adams, James, 136n. 31
Adams, John, 23
Agger, Ben, 256n. 33
Aghazarian, Aram A., 46n. 66
Albright, Madeleine, 210
Alexandre, Laurien, 50n. 87
Alexiou, Margaret, 40n. 36
Alker, Hayward R., 48n. 74
Allbritton, David W., 39n. 29
Allison, Graham T., 196n. 2
Almond, Gabriel A., 49n. 80
Ambrose, Stephen, 197n. 3
Andersen, Peter B., 160n. 4
Anderson, Benedict, 249. References: 257n. 56
Anderson, John R., 38n. 26
Anderson, Karen Vasby, 119n. 11
Anderson, Peter, 35n. 10, 184n. 5
Anderson, Richard D., Jr., 14, 16, 56, 114, 184n. 5, 195. References: 108n. 3, 120n. 13, 184n. 5
Anderson, Rick, 136n. 20
Apple, R. W., Jr., 137n. 37
Arca, Emil, 215n. 38
Archer, Maureen, 138n. 70
Arendt, Hannah, 41n. 43
Aristotle: "alien names" doctrine of, 13; defined the metaphor, 59; on emotions, 170; metaphorical theory of, 8, 15, 166, 167, 170, 171, 172, 200; *On Rhetoric* by, 166; *Poetics* by,

59, 171; rhetorical triad of, 24, 27, 31, 175. References: 159n. 1, 186n. 27
Aronoff, Myron Joel, 186n. 23
Ash, Timothy Garton, 88n. 8
Azuma, Shoji, 46n. 64

Bacon, Francis, 48n. 74
Baden, John, 215n. 42
Baker-Brown, G., 175. References: 188n. 71
Balbus, Isaac (Ike), 130. References: 44n. 53, 138n. 57
Ball, Moya Ann, 116n. 5
Ballard, E. J., 175
Balleck, Barry James, 43n. 52, 50n. 87, 115n. 2, 117n. 7, 160n. 5
Baltes, Paul B., 186n. 22
Barber, Benjamin R., 193. References: 195n. 1, 256n. 33
Barber, Lionel, 136n. 22
Barcelona, Antonio, 36n. 14
Barnden, John A., 49n. 79
Barnes, Trevor J., 32n. 2
Barry, Herbert, III, 23. References: 46n. 68
Bartels, Dennis, 32n. 2
Barthes, Roland, 49n. 78
Bass, Alan, 39n. 32
Bateson, Gregory, 51n. 89
Bateson, Mary Catherine, 264n. 3
Battalio, John, T., 48n. 75
Bebber, Charles C., 117n. 7
Beck, Ulrich, 250. References: 257nn. 57, 61–63

319

Segrave, Jeffrey O., 123, 129.
  References: 134n. 6, 135n. 9, 137n.
  53
Semin, G. R., 187nn. 37–39, 49
Semino, Elena, 43n. 53
Sergiy Taran, Seggiy, 40n. 38
Shapiro, Andrew L., 257n. 54
Shapiro, Michael J., 35n. 8, 52n. 96,
Shaw, Donald L., 186n. 29, 187n. 36
Shepard, Scot, 137n. 46
Sher, Benjamin, 108n. 12
Shibles, Warren, 33n. 3
Shimko, Keith L., 17, 194, 218, 232n.
  4. References: 197n. 4, 215n. 25,
  232nn. 4, 5
Sihanouk (Prince), 144, 149–50, 151,
  153
Silverthorne, Michael, 48n. 74
Simon, Herbert A., 160n. 3
Simons, Herbert W., 46n. 66
Sinclair, Upton, 64
Skinner, Quentin, 114n. 1
Slater, Jerome, 208. References: 215nn.
  26, 28–29
Sloane, Thomas O. 32n. 2, 34n. 6,
  159n. 1
Slouka, Mark, 257n. 60
Sloyan, Patrick J., 136n. 33
Smelser, Neil J., 186n. 22
Smith, C. P., 184n. 4, 188n. 71
Smith, Gaddis, 226. References: 234n.
  30
Smith, Geoffrey N., 255n. 14
Smith, Hedrick, 138n.
Smith, Linda B., 32n. 2
Smith, Ralph R., 115n. 2
Smith, Red, 133. References: 138n. 68
Smith, Ruth C., 42n. 48
Snidal, Duncan, 196n. 2
Snyder, Glenn H., 113. References:
  119n. 10, 120n. 13
Snyder, Jack, 196n. 2
Soames, Scott, 37n. 18
Solinger, Rickie, 115n. 2

Sommer, Elyse, 46n. 63
Son Sann, 144
Sontag, Susan, 59–60, 200–1, 202, 204,
  213. References: 72n. 1, 214nn. 3,
  11–12
Soskice, Janet, 33n. 3
Spackman, Barbara, 43n.51
Spector, Bertram I., 219. References:
  233n. 8
Spillane, Mickey, 67, 69
Sproull, Robert, L., 48n. 75
Stalin, Joseph, 105
Stanford, William B., 33n. 4
Stearney, Lynn M., 42n. 48, 44n. 54
Steen, Gerard J., 32n. 2, 37n. 24
Stein, Janice Gross, 235n. 36
Stelzner, Hermann, 115n. 2
Sterling-Folker, Jennifer, 196n. 2
Stern, Josef, 36n. 12, 39n. 30
Sternberg, Robert J., 33n. 3
Stockwell, Peter, 31n. 1
Stone, Jeremy, 143, 148, 154, 155, 158
Streufert, Siegfried, 183n. 3
Stuckey, Mary E., 36n. 11, 43n. 52,
  57n. 1, 117nn. 5, 7, 160n. 5
Suedfeld, Peter, 163, 175, 176, 182,
  183n. 3. References: 187n. 55, 188n.
  71, 189n. 76
Suslov, Mikhail, 96–97
Sutton, Walter D., Jr., 136n. 25
Sweetser, Eve E., 184n. 5. References:
  184n. 4
Swiss, Thomas, 264n. 2
Sylvan, Donald A., 49n. 79, 234n. 24
Sylvester, Christine, 119n. 11

Taber, Charles S., 218–19. References:
  232n. 6
Tano, Daisuke, 43n. 50
Taub, Sarah F., 42n. 49
Tenney, Deborah, 40n. 37
Tetlock, Philip E., 163, 175. References:
  120n. 13, 183n. 3, 187n. 55

Subject Index